MOON HANDBOOKS

MONTEREY & CARMEL

KRISTIN LEAL

D0170089

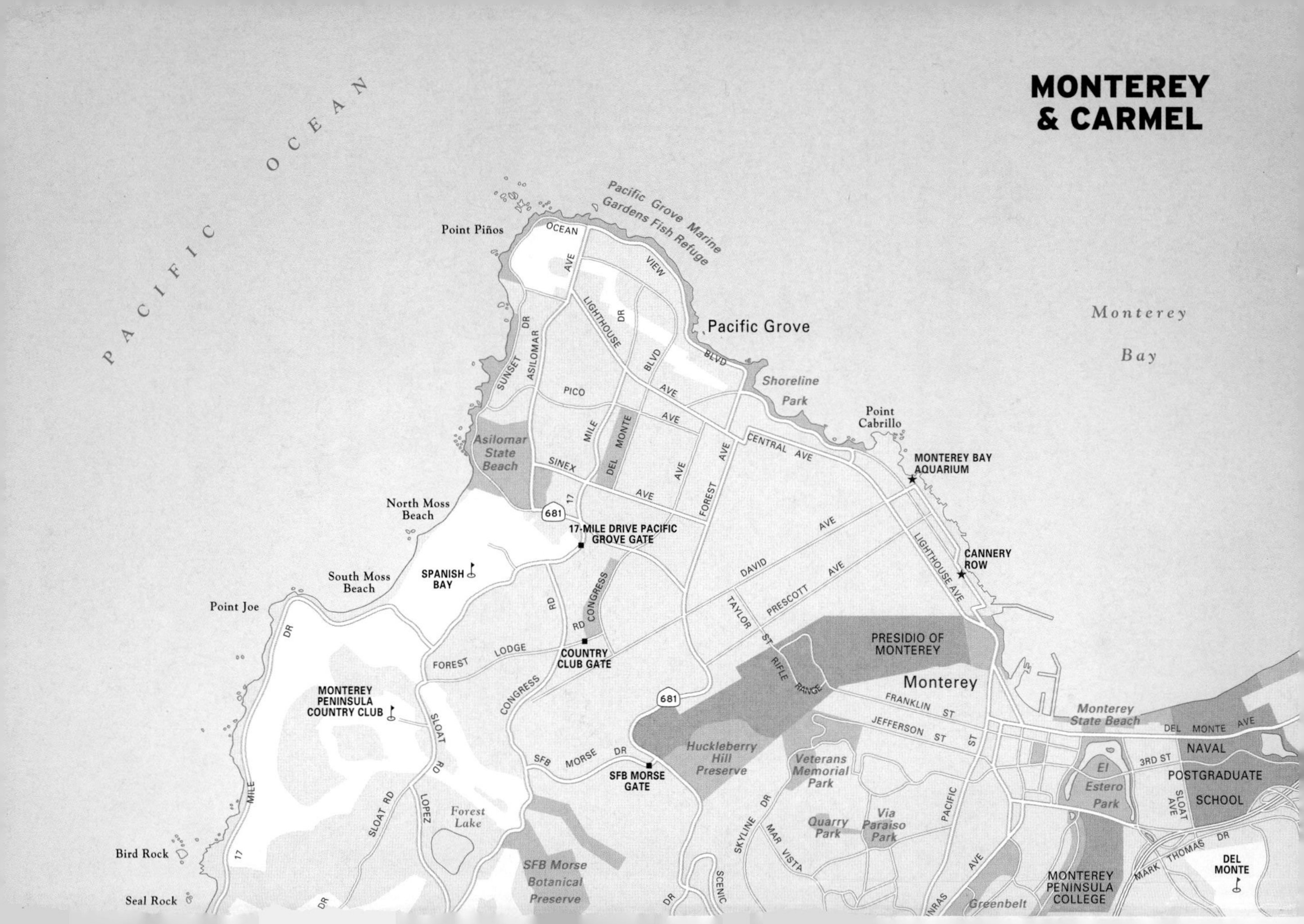

MONTEREY & CARMEL

Monterey Bay

PACIFIC OCEAN

Pacific Grove Marine Gardens Fish Refuge

Point Piños

Pacific Grove

Shoreline Park

Point Cabrillo

MONTEREY BAY AQUARIUM

CANNERY ROW

LIGHTHOUSE AVE

PRESIDIO OF MONTEREY

Monterey

Franklin ST

Jefferson ST

PACIFIC ST

Via Paraiso Park

Quarry Park

Veterans Memorial Park

Huckleberry Hill Preserve

MAR VISTA

SKYLINE DR

SCENIC

DEL MONTE AVE

NAVAL POSTGRADUATE SCHOOL

DEL MONTE

3RD ST

SLOAT AVE

MARK THOMAS DR

El Estero Park

Monterey State Beach

Greenbelt

MONTEREY PENINSULA COLLEGE

FREMONT AVE

CENTRAL AVE

FOREST AVE

DAVID AVE

PRESCOTT AVE

Taylor ST

RIFLE RANGE

17

DEL MONTE AVE

MILE AVE

PICO AVE

SINEX AVE

CONGRESS

17-MILE DRIVE PACIFIC GROVE GATE

COUNTRY CLUB GATE

SFB MORSE GATE

LIGHTHOUSE DR

VIEW DR

OCEAN AVE

ASILOMAR

SUNSET DR

Asilomar State Beach

North Moss Beach

SPANISH BAY

South Moss Beach

Point Joe

LODGE RD

FOREST RD

CONGRESS RD

SLOAT RD

SFB MORSE DR

SFB Morse Botanical Preserve

Forest Lake

LOPEZ

MONTEREY PENINSULA COUNTRY CLUB

17 MILE DR

SLOAT RD

Bird Rock

Seal Rock

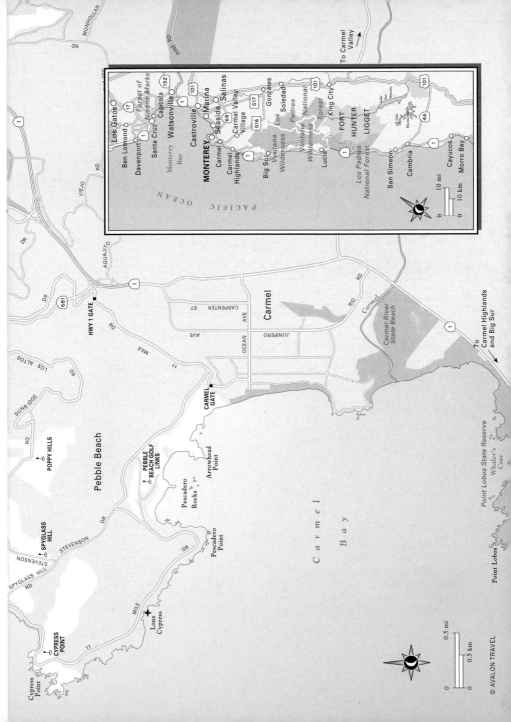

© AVALON TRAVEL

Contents

▶ **Discover Monterey & Carmel**.................... **7**
Planning Your Trip 8
Explore Monterey & Carmel....... 11
• Monterey: Maritime Escape 11
• Steinbeck Country............. 14
• Carmel: Art and Wine 15
• Santa Cruz: Coast and Mountains. . 17
• Kayaking Coastal Waters 18
• Hit the Trail................... 20
• Big Sur to Morro Bay Road Trip .. 21
• Central Coast Wine Tasting...... 23

▶ **Monterey** **25**
Sights 29
Sports and Recreation 40
Entertainment and Events 47
Shopping 52
Accommodations 54
Food 56
Information and Services......... 61
Getting There and Around 62
Pacific Grove 63
Pebble Beach................... 72
Northern Monterey County 79

▶ **Carmel**...................... **88**
Carmel-by-the-Sea 91
Carmel Valley 109

▶ **Salinas and Inland Monterey**............. **117**
Salinas 120
Inland Monterey 126

▶ **Santa Cruz** **134**
Sights......................... 137
Wineries...................... 145
Sports and Recreation 147
Entertainment and Events 156
Shopping 160
Accommodations 162
Food 166
Information and Services........ 170
Getting There and Around 170
Santa Cruz Mountains 172

▶ **Big Sur** **179**
Carmel to Lucia................ 182
Lucia to San Simeon 203
Information and Services........ 207
Getting There and Around 208

▶ **San Simeon, Cambria, and Morro Bay**.............. **209**
San Simeon 212
Cambria 218
Cayucos 227
Morro Bay 234

▶ **Background**.................. **248**
   The Land 248
   Flora and Fauna................. 250
   History........................ 254
▶ **Essentials** **256**
   Getting There and Around........ 256
   Tips for Travelers 259
   Information and Services......... 260

▶ **Resources** **262**
   Suggested Reading.............. 262
   Internet Resources.............. 263
▶ **Index**........................ **265**
▶ **List of Maps** **274**

Discover Monterey & Carmel

Soul seekers have come to the Monterey Coast for generations. The indigenous Ohlone people flourished alongside its bountiful seascape and healing waters. The Spanish built houses of worship along its cliffs. And its beauty has made it the cradle of great works of art: paintings, photographs, novels, poems, and other creative endeavors by the likes of John Steinbeck, Robert Louis Stevenson, Robinson Jeffers, and countless others.

The land that stirs this creativity is vast. It reaches from the Santa Cruz Mountains in the north to the sleepy seaside village of Morro Bay in the south. And it is dramatic. Wind-buffeted pines cover rugged coastal bluffs above curved beaches lapped by thunderous waves. Rolling hills drop suddenly and precipitously to the surf below.

This natural beauty and the art it inspires continue to draw visitors here today. In Monterey, the world-class aquarium affords an intimate look at the sea life that thrives in the Bay. Carmel offers wine-tasting, gallery hopping and boutique shopping. And miles of hiking and biking trails wind through the hills and forests, offering a direct connection to the landscape.

Whatever it is that calls you here, the power of the land is inescapable. You'll hear it in the primal cries of elephant seals along the shoreline. You'll sense it as you look out at the horizon, where the expansive Pacific Ocean merges with the sky. The Monterey Coast is sure to inspire you.

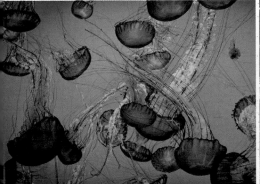

Planning Your Trip

▶ WHERE TO GO

Monterey

Home to Steinbeck's Cannery Row, The Monterey Bay Aquarium, and Old Fisherman's Wharf, the city of Monterey has several world-class sights. Monterey Bay is a marine sanctuary with a 10,000-foot submarine canyon that dwarfs the Grand Canyon and attracts vast amounts of wildlife. Nearby Pacific Grove is a winter stopover for migrating monarch butterflies, and Pebble Beach is known for its unparalleled coastal golf courses. The northern reaches of the county offer a variety of outdoor recreation at the Elkhorn Slough National Estaurine Research Reserve, and you'll find sandy beaches stretching all along the bay.

Carmel

Created as an artists' haven in the early 19th century, Carmel-by-the-Sea is a charming village with no house numbers; houses are given names instead. There are many famed locations to visit, including Clint Eastwood's Mission Ranch restaurant, Robertson Jeffers Tor House, and the Carmel Mission, the jewel of California's string of Spanish missions. The Carmel Valley offers warm afternoons filled with wine tasting and antiques shopping, and Point Lobos State Natural Reserve, a stunning piece of land abutting the sea.

Salinas and Inland Monterey

Time moves at bit more slowly here, and many of the Salinas Valley towns are straight out of the Wild West. The setting is mostly rural, with vast stretches of agricultural land, which includes a number of wineries and vineyards. This is also Steinbeck country and home to the National Steinbeck Center. Mission San

IF YOU HAVE...

the Neptune Pool at Hearst Castle

- **A LONG WEEKEND:** Visit Monterey and Carmel.
- **3-4 DAYS:** Add Santa Cruz and Big Sur.
- **A WEEK:** Make the 170-mile road trip along scenic Highway 1 from Santa Cruz to Morro Bay.

Juan Bautista is in the small historic San Juan Bautista Old Town. For outdoor recreation, the rock formations at Pinnacles National Monument make for stellar hiking and rock climbing. The Fremont Peak State Park and Observatory offers a close-up view of the night sky.

Santa Cruz

Surf City, here we come. From redwood forests in the mountains to wide sandy beaches, the Santa Cruz region celebrates diversity. The Beach Boardwalk is an amusement park with roller coasters practically right on the beach. A visit to the Santa Cruz Surfing Museum and Lighthouse will give you a feel for the history of the sport that shaped this coastal town. A visit to Natural Bridges State Park, Santa Cruz Main Beach, and Cowell Beach offers opportunities for surfing, body boarding, beach volleyball, or just plain lounging in the sun.

Big Sur

Sheer cliffs hug the shoreline and steep canyons expose lush redwood forests. Highway 1 along the 90-mile trek is known as the Big Sur Scenic Byway, and there are numerous entry points to the rugged landscape. Miles of hiking trails weave through the Los Padres National Forest's Ventana Wilderness, and Andrew Molera State Park, Pfeiffer Big Sur State Park, and Limekiln State Park. And the hot springs at the Esalen Institute overlook the ocean.

San Simeon, Cambria, and Morro Bay

South of Big Sur, small coastal towns grace the shoreline as the landscape evens out, although the views are no less breathtaking. Legendary Hearst Castle grandly overlooks the ocean from its perch above the village of

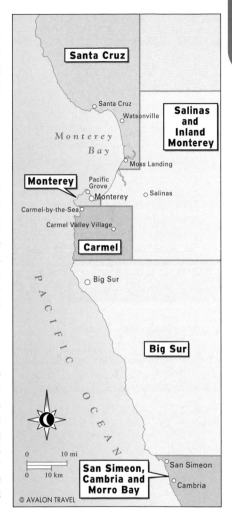

San Simeon. The quiet town of Cambria is lined with art galleries and cute shops, and wine-tasting along Highway 46 allows you to sample some of Coastal California's best vintages. The seaside town of Morro Bay is known for its beach vibe. When the fog lifts, it feels like summer never ends.

Tee time is prime time at any of the Pebble Beach golf courses.

▶ WHEN TO GO

Monterey and Carmel are year-round destinations that offer different activities in each season. The summer months (late May-Aug.) see the most visitors, and popular sights are more crowded during this time. Campgrounds fill up early, beaches become populated, and advance reservations are a must anywhere you stay. Summer weather tends to bring fog, so days can be somewhat chilly. Sunny days are not rare, however, and people hit the beach year-round. The upside of visiting during summer is that there are festivals and events nearly every weekend.

The best time to visit is during the fall (late Aug.-Oct.). The weather heats up and sunny days are nearly guaranteed. The crowds thin out and accommodations become more available. The winter months (Oct.-Feb.) tend to be wet with tumultuous storms at times, but worthwhile for the monarch butterflies making their way along the coast, along with elephant seals and migrating gray whales (Nov-Feb). Spring (Mar.-May) is the time to watch wildflowers bloom while taking advantage of the mild weather, perfect for hiking and camping before the summer hits.

Before You Go

Make lodging and camping reservations well in advance; especially in summer. If you are planning to camp at the state parks, you will not be able to find a campsite without booking ahead; visit www.reserveamerica.com to save your space.

Explore Monterey & Carmel

It is easy to spend a few weeks lingering and exploring the diverse landscapes and cultures of the Monterey and Carmel region, but most people tend to visit for long weekends or day trips, or travel coastal Highway 1 and experience this region on a road trip. The itineraries below give suggestions for planning long weekends in Monterey, Carmel, and Santa Cruz, with a day trip to the Salinas and the inland Monterey area. Big Sur and Highway 1 to Morro Bay are organized as a road trip along California's magnificent Pacific Coast Highway. Feel free to string together these itineraries to fit your schedule and interests.

▶ MONTEREY: MARITIME ESCAPE

Day 1
Begin your day early where the locals do and feast on specialty pancakes at First Awakenings in Pacific Grove within the Tin Cannery. After breakfast, breathe in the salty air and walk south along Ocean View Boulevard to Lovers Point; the trail has impressive views with ice plants that create an unreal seascape as they showcase brilliant magenta blooms in spring. If you're driving, go all the way to Asilomar State Beach and enjoy climbing around the tide pools.

The Monterey Bay Aquarium opens at 9:30 A.M. and takes at least 2-3 hours to tour, with a rotation of feeding times throughout the day. New exhibits are continually opening, including the majestic new seahorses. On your way out, make sure to get stamped just in

Watch the jellyfish drift at the Monterey Bay Aquarium.

Old Fisherman's Wharf in Monterey

case you want to go back in before they close. On summer weekends, they host Evenings by the Bay (Jun.-Sept.) and stay open until 8 P.M., with free wine tasting from local vineyards and jazz music. For lunch, hit the café or restaurant in the aquarium, the C Restaurant in the Intercontinental Clement Monterey, or Bubba Gump's next door.

You can walk along Cannery Row north toward the wharf and make a stop at the Coast Guard Pier to get a close look the local sea lions. Then it's off to Old Fisherman's Wharf where you will find the pier teeming with souvenir shops, waterfront restaurants, and fishing charters. You will have time to board a boat with one of the many whale-watching companies. Any season is good for whale and dolphin sightings, as these animals make their way into the bay year-round. After all that walking and whale watching, you should be pretty hungry, and dinner at Old Fisherman's Grotto is delightful.

Day 2

For your second day, step back in time and experience the historic side of Monterey. First, you will want to get breakfast at the Trailside Café on the north end of Cannery Row. Your history hunt begins at Custom House Plaza and then continues along the Monterey State Historic Park Path of History. Along the trail are many museums, gardens, historic landmarks, and historic buildings. The path will lead you to Downtown Monterey on Alvarado Street. Follow the round yellow markers in the sidewalks as you explore the old adobes. Drop into the Monterey Museum of Art to wander the gallery before crossing the street to check out Colton Hall and pick up lunch at one of the many eateries downtown.

After lunch head to the Elkhorn Slough National Estuarine Research Reserve. Hitch a ride on a slough safari, sailing excursion, fishing voyage, or rent a kayak to view the abundance of wildlife.

Head back to downtown Monterey for dinner

and a movie. Dine at Montrio Bistro; they feature locally sourced ingredients and sustainably caught seafood. Finish the night by catching a flick at the Osio Theater, just a few steps away.

Day 3

Start your day with breakfast in Pacific Grove at Red House Café on Lighthouse Avenue, set in an old Victorian-style home. Everything is made on-site, including the delicious baked goods. Visit Point Piños Lighthouse and Lovers Point Park. If you're visiting early November-late February, be sure to see the migrating monarch butterflies at the Monarch Sanctuary and Pacific Grove Museum of Natural History.

Next, drive to Spanish Bay in Pebble Beach. For lunch, spoil yourself at one of the resort's many restaurants. After lunch, follow the signs to 17-Mile Drive, where you will see Bird Rock, Point Joe, the Lone Cypress, and impressive mansions. Leave through the Carmel Gate and take a right on San Antonio Avenue to the stop

sign, and then a short block down and left on Scenic Road, where you can drive along the shore to Carmel River State Beach. On the way back to Monterey, stop at one of the many pullouts along Asilomar State Beach and explore the tide pools and sandy coves.

Back in Monterey, enjoy a dinner of fresh California cuisine at either Jacks or The Sardine Factory.

Optional: Day Trip to Salinas and Inland Monterey

Head inland to get a taste of California's past. A 33-mile drive from Monterey on Highway 156, San Juan Bautista and Salinas make a good day trip.

Begin your journey with a tour at Mission San Juan Bautista and gain insight into the early days of Monterey County. Take a walk around the grounds, including the gardens and the old town square at San Juan Bautista State Historic Park and Plaza.

Walk over to 3rd Street for antiques shopping at places like Bluebird Antiques and

Carmel River State Beach

Mission San Juan Baustista

STEINBECK COUNTRY

Salinas welcomes you to Steinbeck's legacy.

With novels like *East of Eden* and *Cannery Row,* Steinbeck made his mark with epic tales set in the region. Born in Salinas in 1902, he wrote many works of social fiction about rural laborers and fruit pickers on California agricultural lands, including *The Grapes of Wrath* and *Of Mice and Men.*

Begin exploring Steinbeck country in **Salinas's Old Town.** The **National Steinbeck Center** is a sizable museum with many exhibits and programs devoted to the author. A cultural museum and archive resource center contains an array of art and exhibits created to educate and inspire.

Visit the birthplace of the author at **Steinbeck House** and enjoy a gourmet lunch with fresh produce from the valley in a Queen Anne-style Victorian home. Visit the **Roosevelt School,** where Steinbeck attended 3rd-8th grades, on Central Avenue. Stop by his grave site at the **Garden of Memories Cemetery** at Abbott Street and East Romie Lane to pay your respects.

In downtown Monterey, visit the **Laura Soto Adobe,** Steinbeck's home when *Cannery Row* was published. Steinbeck was also known to spend his evenings at the restaurants and bars on the lower end of **Alvarado Street.**

Then take a walk to **Cannery Row** and wander through **Steinbeck's Spirit of Monterey Wax Museum** on the bottom floor of the **Steinbeck Plaza.**

Make your way into the **Tin Cannery,** an old canning factory now filled with shops. The walls are adorned with large photos of the cannery's history, bringing the flavor of Steinbeck's tales to life.

Collectibles, Attic Angels, and Sweet Pea Antiques. For lunch, dine at Jardines de San Juan. The menu is northern Mexican, and there is extensive outdoor seating in the garden.

After lunch, head to Fremont Peak State Park and Observatory to fill the rest of the day with hiking, a picnic dinner, and stargazing.

There are five trails to choose from, with the Peak Trail climbing to 3,169 feet. On a clear day, views expand from the ocean to the Sierra Nevada Mountain Range. Settle in for a picnic dinner at the Madrone Picnic Area. Get cozy and gaze at the stars. The observatory is open to the public April-October on moonless Saturdays starting at 8 P.M.

► CARMEL: ART AND WINE

Day 1

In the cool early morning fog, begin your day with pastries and coffee to-go from Carmel Bakery. Then follow Ocean Avenue to Carmel Beach. Take a stroll on the sand or the dirt path along the road as you watch dogs frolic and surfers brave the waves. The shops along Ocean Avenue tend to open around 10 A.M. on weekends. Visit the art galleries and browse more than 40 stores in Carmel Plaza. Head to The Barnyard for lunch at From Scratch, a local favorite. After lunch, visit the Carmel Mission.

To fill out the rest of your afternoon, head three miles south of Carmel to Point Lobos State Reserve. Cruise the park on foot or by car and stop at a few key sights: Whalers Cove Museum, the Cypress Trail, and China Cove.

Finish the day with a fresh seafood dinner at the Flying Fish Grill.

Day 2

It's time to experience the more rustic side of Carmel. Carmel Valley Road leads to rushing rivers, shopping, and dining. For breakfast, stop in at the Wagon Wheel restaurant. After you grab a bite, chances are Tancredi and Morgan will be open and you can peruse their antiques. Make a stop at Earthbound Farms to create your own organic picnic. Then head to Garland Ranch Regional Park for endless hiking adventures. You can tromp around as long as you like with trails that run along the Carmel River and the chaparral hills.

For dinner, Baja Cantina is the place for some local flavor. The summer nights on the patio are pleasant with the warm valley breeze at your back.

Day 3

Start the morning at the Carmel Roasting Company, recognized for their locally roasted

Enjoy wine tasting under the sun in Carmel Valley.

Fall is a beautiful time to visit the vineyards of Carmel Valley.

beans, in Crossroads Shopping Village (off of Rio Rd.) for a bite to eat. Spend a leisurely morning admiring the fairy-tale homes of Carmel-by-the-Sea.

Get fired up for an afternoon of wine tasting. (If the kids are along, skip the wine tasting and head to Holman Ranch for horseback riding). The Monterey-Salinas Transit system's Grapevine Express, line 24, departs daily every hour with stops all along of Rio Road and Carmel Valley Road.

Begin your tasting at Château Julien, visible from the road, a European-style estate known for chardonnay, cabernet, syrah, and merlot. Call ahead to reserve a spot on the twice-daily complimentary vineyard and winery tours, given when weather permits.

A smaller vineyard in the valley is Parsonage Village Vineyard, an unpretentious little winery with some of the best syrah in California. Heller Estate Organic Vineyards is certified organic and produces exceptionally age-worthy cabernet franc,

cabernet sauvignon, chardonnay, chenin blanc, merlot, malbec, petit verdot, and pinot noir. At Robert Talbott Vineyards, expect to taste exceptional chardonnay and pinot noir on the lovely garden patio.

Gold-medal merlot, pinot noir, cabernet, syrah, chardonnay, and Pudding Wine are found at Joyce Vineyards, with tasting outside in the garden. At Bernardus Winery, have lunch in style and do a little more wine tasting in the luxurious restaurant. It is known for Bordeaux-style blended red Marinus Vineyard as well as chardonnay, pinot noir, and sauvignon blanc.

End the day with something a little different at the Running Iron Saloon, with all-American cuisine with a coastal flair. The menu includes local snapper and a fantastic beef sandwich. If you are up for it, round out the day with a seaside fire at Carmel Beach. Make a quick stop at Bruno's Market on Junipero Avenue to load up on firewood and marshmallows. The beach closes at 10 P.M.

▶ SANTA CRUZ: COAST AND MOUNTAINS

Day 1

From Highway 17, take the Half Moon Bay exit and make a left on River Street to get to Pacific Street, where there is street parking. Wander Pacific Street, stopping in unique thrift stores, bookshops, and boutiques. Be sure to stop into Streetlight Records, Thrift Center Thrift Store, Camouflage, Retro Paradise, and Graffix Pleasure. Grab lunch at Rosie McCann's Irish pub, a laid-back spot, before heading to the Santa Cruz Beach Boardwalk.

First things first: Get everybody the un-limited-ride wrist bands and make your way to the Giant Dipper (if everyone makes the height requirement). Explore 35 thrill rides, an expansive arcade, peewee golf, and beach-side bliss. Hitting the rides in the afternoon and into the night is possible mid-June–early-September, as the boardwalk is open until 11 P.M. and hosts free concerts Friday night.

Grab dinner on the Boardwalk with carnival favorites like funnel cakes, corn dogs, and burgers, or take a walk to the Santa Cruz Municipal Wharf to dine at the Stagnaro Bros. Restaurant, known for fresh seafood from their own commercial fishing boats.

Day 2

Take Highway 9 up into the thick red-woods and the town of Felton for breakfast at Rocky's Café. Next, make your way to Roaring Camp Railroads, near Henry Cowell Redwoods State Park, where big trees and steam trains await. Hitch a ride on a steam train to explore the redwood forest. Take your time to explore the mock Western town.

Visit the Mount Herman Zip-Line Tour for an experience you will never forget as you fly over a rushing river 150 feet below.

For something tamer, make your way north to Ben Lomond and Boulder Creek, quiet mountain towns lined with antiques shops.

Santa Cruz Beach Boardwalk

KAYAKING COASTAL WATERS

Get close to local marine life at the Elkhorn Slough National Estuarine Research Reserve.

The waterways throughout Monterey Bay, Carmel, and beyond to Morro Bay are perfect for kayaking expeditions. You'll have the chance to see marine life up close and get spectacular views of the region's diverse landscapes.

- **Elkhorn Slough National Estuarine Research Reserve** in Moss Landing near Monterey is teeming with local wildlife. Expect to see sea otters, sea lions, spotted seals, pelicans, blue herons, and snowy egrets.

- Monterey's **Coast Guard Wharf** to **Monterey Bay Aquarium** is a popular paddle. Weave around the moored boats and caress the breakwater to view harbor seals, pelicans, kelp beds, and sea otters. Enjoy the view of Cannery Row from a different perspective.

- **Point Lobos State Natural Reserve** is

an exceptional way to experience Monterey Bay. Whalers Cove is a pristine place to launch, and you can paddle south, hugging the shoreline, to Blue Fin Cove to view the landscape from a different vantage point.

- **Natural Bridges State Park** in Santa Cruz has an impressive rock arch. Follow the rugged coastline south all the way to the Boardwalk. See kelp beds with napping sea otters, surfers at Steamers Lane, and the Santa Cruz Municipal Wharf.

- **Morro Bay Estuary** has an abundance of sealife, including snowy egrets that are attracted by the shallow water, seals barking near the shoreline, sea otters, and sandpipers. Launch access is best at Morro Bay State Park in the marina, where there is a ramp.

Cowboy Cabin at Wilder Ranch State Park near Santa Cruz

Drop into Boulder Creek Brewing Company for a local beer and lunch before heading to Big Basin Redwoods State Park, where you'll spend the afternoon in the forest. Big Basin is located off Highway 236, and trails weave through the dense redwoods for access to waterfalls, creeks, and mountains.

At the end of the day, stop at Ben Lomond's Tyrolean Inn for a German-style family meal.

Day 3

Rise and shine with breakfast at Emily's Good Things To Eat, a bakery on Mission Street in Santa Cruz. Head north out of Santa Cruz and make a stop at Natural Bridges State Park to walk the beach, or tour the Monarch Butterfly Sanctuary (Oct.-mid Feb.).

Head north on Highway 1 to Wilder Ranch State Park, a historic dairy farm. Tour the restored ranch houses and the barn where the livestock resides. Take a short hike along the sage-filled bluffs overlooking the ocean, or follow the dusty path to the Cowboy Cabin.

Before continuing north to Davenport Landing, stop at the Dream Inn's restaurant, Aquarius.

After lunch, keep driving north to Año Nuevo State Reserve and view the elephant seals. Take the six-mile round-trip hike to view these vocal creatures with guided walks along the dunes.

Make your way back to Santa Cruz and stop for dinner at Henflings Tavern in Boulder Creek for some traditional pub fare and live music.

HIT THE TRAIL

Take in the beauty of Monterey at Point Lobos State Natural Reserve.

Throughout Monterey and Carmel, there are ample opportunities to get off the road and hike trails through stunning landscape.

- **Jacks Peak** in Monterey has over eight miles of shaded hiking trails that lead to spectacular views overlooking Monterey Bay.

- **Point Lobos State Natural Reserve,** just south of Carmel, has more than nine miles of hiking trails along the rugged coastline and among ancient cypress trees. The Cypress Grove Trail leads to one of only two remaining naturally growing stands of Monterey cypress on earth.

- **Ventana Wilderness** in Big Sur is a vast landscape of shaded redwood groves and steep canyons in the Los Padres National Forest. With nearly two million acres of coastal mountain terrain with dramatic coastal views, this is a great location for any level of hiker; trails offer easy hikes for families or more challenging terrain for serious backpackers.

- **Pinnacles National Monument,** southeast of Salinas, is an otherworldly landscape of ancient volcanic rock formations that have been shaped by thousands of years of shifting tectonic plates and wind erosion. The park is open year-round for hiking, rock climbing, picnicking, and camping. Climbers know this park for its rugged pinnacles and balconies, and hikers can explore two caves and several miles of hiking trails.

- **Año Nuevo State Reserve,** north of Santa Cruz, is home to the constant echoing snarls and snorts of enormous elephant seals. The reserve is home to the largest mainland breeding colony in the world, and young males come to the tumultuous shoreline to molt. Shedding their outer layer of skin and fur, which can take 4-6 weeks, young males stay in May-June, and the older males arrive in July and stay through August. A four-mile hiking trail winds along the bluffs of the steep shoreline through a grassy field and into the sand dunes.

▶ BIG SUR TO MORRO BAY ROAD TRIP

Day 1

Along the dramatic winding drive down Highway 1, massive cliffs drop to the Pacific and the horizon blurs into a haze of ocean and sky. South from Carmel, you'll soon approach Bixby Bridge, one of the most photographed bridges in the country.

Wend your way to Andrew Molera State Park, about 20 miles south of Carmel, and take the 1.5-mile hike out to the beach. If you take a left just before the kiosk, you'll find Molera Horseback Tours (mid-Mar.-Dec. 1). Sign up and hop on for an exciting ride along the beach, across the Big Sur River, through meadows, with a rest in the shade of the forest.

When you're getting hungry for lunch, head to the River Inn, and relax in the chairs set right in the Big Sur River for cooling down with an afternoon beer.

When you're ready to explore some more, head to Pfeiffer Beach and take a walk on the swirling purple sand. Grab dinner at Nepenthe while you enjoy the roar of the fire

and dramatic views perched on the edge of a cliff high above the sea. Set up camp at Big Sur State Park or hunker down in a rustic cabin at Glen Oaks.

Day 2

Start out early, grab breakfast to go at the Big Sur Bakery, and follow Highway 1 south to Julia Pfeiffer Burns State Park. Take the one-mile round-trip hike to the breathtaking McWay Falls.

Stop at Willow Creek to hunt for jade, and Sand Dollar State Beach, where you climb down stairs to reach the sand. During low tide, a cave is accessible to the right of the stairs.

The drive from here to San Simeon is about 67 miles and takes about 90 minutes. Stop along Highway 1 to see the elephant seals at Piedras Blancas. Arrive at Hearst Castle and take a tour of the legendary castle grounds (advance reservations are recommended to ensure a spot). Grab lunch at the snack bar in the visitors center. Plan on spending at least 3-4 hours at the castle, including lunch.

the stunning McWay Falls at Julia Pfeiffer Burns State Park

Roman Pool at Hearst Castle

After the tour, head across the highway to William Randolph Hearst Memorial State Beach. If you are camping, set up for the night at San Simeon Creek Campground within Hearst San Simeon State Historic Monument on serviced RV sites or primitive tent campsites. Ragged Point Resort is another lodging option with a resort restaurant. If you are staying in San Simeon, grab a bite with an ocean view at the Beach Bar and Grill.

Day 3

Grab breakfast on the way out at Sebastian's Café before heading south. It is less than seven miles down to Moonstone Beach in Cambria for a morning walk. Then peruse some of the 30 art galleries on Main Street.

Make your next stop in Cayucos, another 13 miles south. You can get lunch at Ruddell's Smokehouse, where outdoor seating with a scenic view is available. The Old Cayucos Tavern is another option for an authentic taste of the Wild West. Drop into Cayucos Cellars for a taste of some local vintages before taking a walk along Cayucos State Beach. Next, head to Morro Bay, another 7.5 miles farther south.

Morro Bay State Park and the foot of Morro Rock is the first stop. Watch local surfers, kayakers paddling the bay, rafts of seals, and playful sea otters. The park extends to the south end of the bay, where there is an 18-hole golf course, a marina equipped with a launch ramp, kayak rentals, a restaurant, a large campground, a natural history museum, Morro Rock Natural Preserve, and Heron Rookery Natural Preserve. If you are camping, make this your base, or stay indoors at Anderson Inn on Embarcadero Road.

Spend the early evening exploring the town on Morro Bay Boulevard or Embarcadero Road, or head to Morro Bay State Park. Grab dinner at the Galley Seafood Grill & Bar for the best surf-and-turf in town.

Take a long walk along Moonstone Beach in Cambria.

► CENTRAL COAST WINE TASTING

Take a few days to explore the Central Coast wine region. You can make your wine-tasting adventure into a road trip along the coast, or you can explore wineries in whichever region you are staying. There is no shortage of vineyards and tasting rooms, and the wines produced throughout the Central Coast are among the best in California.

Santa Cruz

The vineyards in the mountains alone are worth a visit to Santa Cruz. In Watsonville, the Alfaro Family Vineyards takes pride in crafting chardonnay, merlot, pinot noir, and syrah. In the heart of the Santa Cruz Mountains in the historic Vine Hill District is the Vine Hill Winery, specializing in chardonnay, pinot noir, and syrah. Also in the mountains is Cooper-Garrod Estate Vineyards, specializing in chardonnay, viognier, cabernet sauvignon, cabernet franc, merlot, syrah, and blends. Hallcrest Vineyards and The Organic Wine Works are known for cabernet sauvignon and riesling.

You can taste the vintages of the Santa Cruz Mountains in downtown Santa Cruz at Bonny Doon Vineyard's Cellar Door; they produce a variety of reds, whites, rosés, and dessert wines.

Carmel

Carmel is a beautiful setting for a day of wine tasting in the sun-drenched valley. You will find Bernardus Winery, focusing on chardonnay, pinot noir, and sauvignon blanc; and Château Julien, with a light, airy tasting room pouring chardonnay, cabernet, syrah, and merlot. Tiny Parsonage Village operates on just nine acres crafting fine syrah. Robert Talbott is known in the area for chardonnay and pinot noir, and Heller Estate Organic Vineyards has been pouring age-worthy wines for 40 years.

If you're up for more walking, make your way to Carmel Beach for an evening stroll. Bernardus

Vineyards are sprinkled throughout the Salinas Valley.

has lodgings with a spa and an incredible restaurant, and Edgemere Cottages offers cozy guest rooms and adorable cottages near the ocean.

Salinas and Inland Monterey

There is no better place to taste wine than among the bountiful vineyards of the Salinas Valley. From Carmel, take Highway 1 north and turn onto Highway 68. Exit south to River Road, where there are 20 vineyards along the River Road Wine Trail. Stop at Hahn Winery for a delightful picnic spot in the shade of rustling oak trees, especially nice in the fall.

San Simeon, Cambria, and Morro Bay

Follow the endless trail of vineyards west along Highway 46, where you will find plenty of tasting rooms. Eagle Castle is a unique winery known for producing several reds, whites, and dessert wines that include petite syrah, cabernet sauvignon, and zinfandel.

You can't miss Grey Wolf, right along the highway, which offers reds such as Barton Family Reserve Zinfandel, Alpha Cabernet, and Meritage. Lone Madrone focuses on collecting grapes from vineyards that are dry-farmed and head-trained to produce remarkable wines. At Jack Creek Cellars you can sample chardonnay, pinot noir, and syrah.

Four miles north on Highway 1, finish the day in Cambria. Visit Black Hand Cellars for red wines. At Moonstone Cellars, sample an array of wines including albariño, viognier, chardonnay, syrah, tempranillo, cabernet sauvignon, merlot, zinfandel, and adularia. Fermentations is the place to sample a variety of local vintages in one spot.

MONTEREY

Home to the Monterey Bay Aquarium, plenty of ocean-side fairways, and world-class restaurants, the city of Monterey brings marine science, California history, and natural landscapes together with pampered luxury and gourmet cuisine. Destination restaurants are found alongside the favorite local doughnut shop. And just beyond where the land ends, world-renowned diving awaits under the surface of the bay, where rock cod dart around as you explore the underwater landscape.

Monterey has a long history as a working-class fishing town. Originally inhabited by Native Americans who fished the bay, the area became a fishing hub for European settlers in the 19th century. Author John Steinbeck immortalized the unglamorous local fish-canning industry in his 1945 novel *Cannery Row*. It wasn't until the 20th century that the city began to lean toward gentrification—the bay became a wildlife preserve, the Monterey Bay Aquarium opened, and tourism became a mainstay of the local economy. Today, Cannery Row resembles a shopping mall, and the aquarium is consistently packed with visitors.

Pacific Grove, also known as "Butterfly Town, USA," and Pebble Beach share the Monterey Peninsula. Their range of diversions includes unique shopping, horseback riding, and legendary golf. Venturing north, Moss Landing and the Elkhorn Slough National Estuarine Research Reserve offer hiking and sea

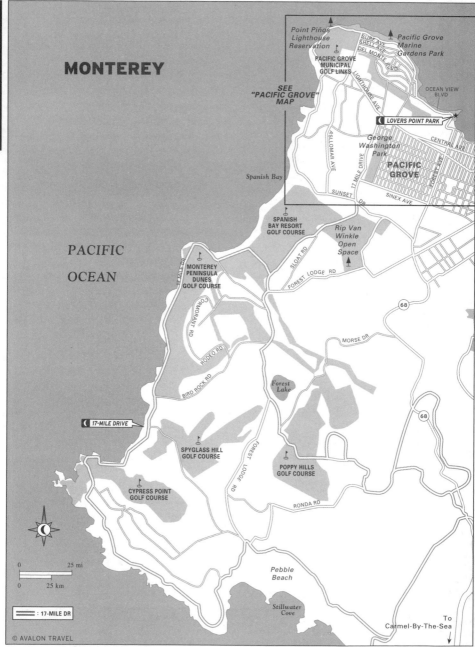

MONTEREY

Point Piños
Lighthouse
Reservation

SURF AVE.
SHELL AVE.
DEL MONTE BLVD.

Pacific Grove
Marine
Gardens Park

PACIFIC GROVE
MUNICIPAL
GOLF LINKS

OCEAN VIEW
BLVD

SEE
"PACIFIC GROVE"
MAP

LIGHTHOUSE AVE.

(LOVERS POINT PARK ★

ASILOMAR AVE.

17-MILE DRIVE

George
Washington
Park

CENTRAL AVE.

PACIFIC
GROVE

FOREST AVE.

Spanish Bay

SUNSET DR.

SINEX AVE.

PACIFIC

OCEAN

SPANISH
BAY RESORT
GOLF COURSE

Rip Van
Winkle
Open
Space

SLOAT RD.

MONTEREY
PENINSULA
DUNES
GOLF COURSE

17-MILE DR.

FOREST LODGE RD.

68

CORMORANT RD.

RODEO RD.

MORSE DR.

BIRD ROCK RD.

Forest
Lake

68

(17-MILE DRIVE

FOREST LODGE RD.

SPYGLASS HILL
GOLF COURSE

POPPY HILLS
GOLF COURSE

CYPRESS POINT
GOLF COURSE

RONDA RD.

| 0 | 25 mi |
| 0 | 25 km |

Pebble
Beach

Stillwater
Cove

To
Carmel-By-The-Sea

▬▬▬ : 17-MILE DR

© AVALON TRAVEL

MONTEREY

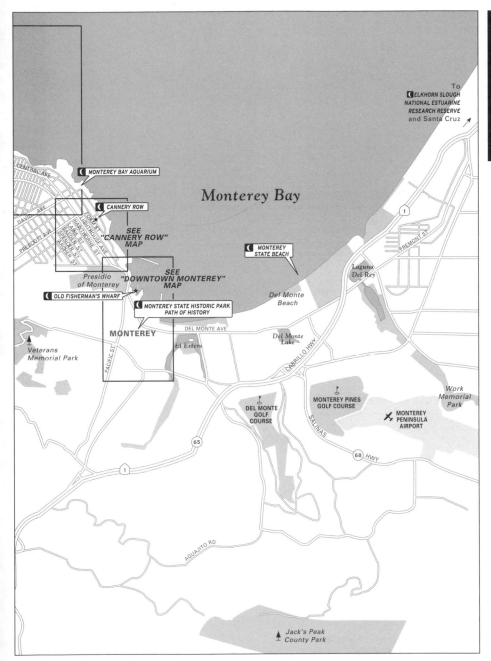

To
❰ELKHORN SLOUGH
NATIONAL ESTUARINE
RESEARCH RESERVE
and Santa Cruz

CENTRAL AVE

❰ MONTEREY BAY AQUARIUM

Monterey Bay

❰ CANNERY ROW

DAVID AVE

PRESCOTT AVE

LIGHTHOUSE AVE
HAWTHORNE ST
IRVING AVE
BARGER ST
SPENCER ST
ARCHER ST

**SEE
"CANNERY ROW"
MAP**

**❰ MONTEREY
STATE BEACH**

FREMONT ST

Laguna
Del Rey

Presidio
of Monterey

**SEE
"DOWNTOWN MONTEREY"
MAP**

Del Monte
Beach

❰ OLD FISHERMAN'S WHARF

**❰ MONTEREY STATE HISTORIC PARK
PATH OF HISTORY**

MONTEREY

DEL MONTE AVE

Del Monte
Lake

PACIFIC ST

El Estero

⚓
Veterans
Memorial Park

CABRILLO HWY

Work
Memorial
Park

**DEL MONTE
GOLF
COURSE**

**MONTEREY PINES
GOLF COURSE**

✈ **MONTEREY
PENINSULA
AIRPORT**

SALINAS

65

68 HWY

1

AGUAJITO RD

▲ Jack's Peak
County Park

HIGHLIGHTS

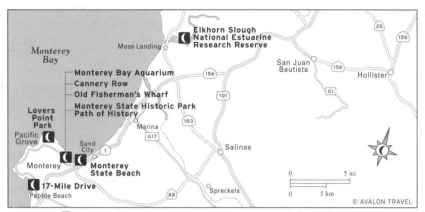

LOOK FOR **(** TO FIND RECOMMENDED SIGHTS, ACTIVITIES, DINING, AND LODGING.

(**Monterey Bay Aquarium:** The number-one attraction in Monterey, the aquarium brings the majestic world of the sea to a place where everyone can experience its raw beauty (page 29).

(**Cannery Row:** A hot spot for visitors, this historic area offers shops, restaurants, oceanfront hotels, and the Monterey Bay Aquarium (page 31).

(**Old Fisherman's Wharf:** Walk the length of the wharf while sampling clam chowder and browsing the souvenir shops, and take a fishing charter, whale-watching trip, or sailing excursion (page 31).

(**Monterey State Historic Park Path of History:** Step back in time on this 2.5-mile walk that takes you to many of Monterey's most significant historical sights (page 31).

(**Monterey State Beach:** Take a swim or catch some waves. The surf is appropriate for beginning and intermediate surfers (page 40).

(**Lovers Point Park:** One of the most beautiful spots on the Peninsula, the beach at Lovers Point is great for soaking in the sun, kayaking, or enjoying a picnic (page 63).

(**17-Mile Drive:** The ultimate scenic drive, 17-Mile Drive offers hidden coves, surf spots, beaches, and modern-day castles (page 72).

(**Elkhorn Slough National Estuarine Research Reserve:** Hitch a ride on a slough safari, sailing excursion, or fishing voyage, or rent a kayak to view the wildlife (page 79).

otter-spotting. This is Monterey's marine sanctuary at its best, where you can interact with local wildlife up close. After a full day of exploring, you can look forward to the ultimate local seafood-and-steak dinner at celebrated places like Roy's, the Whaling Station, or Sardine Factory and then hunkering down at a picturesque bed-and-breakfast or the InterContinental's Clement Monterey on Cannery Row.

PLANNING YOUR TIME

At a bare minimum you can stop by Monterey for the day and visit some of the attractions in the center of town. Monterey's Wharf, the famed Cannery Row, and the outstanding Monterey Bay Aquarium are all next to each other and within easy walking distance. A full day's entertainment will require careful planning as there are many diversions. You will want to devote at least 2-3 hours to the Monterey Bay Aquarium; whale watching can last 3-4 hours; and fishing will consume half a day, beginning before the sun rises. Just walking around the Wharf and Cannery Row can easily consume an entire day as well.

If you want to explore beyond the main attractions, spend the weekend; for a more leisurely visit you can easily spend up to a week; the entire arc of the bay and the peninsula serve up countless adventures. From Moss Landing down to Pebble Beach, you can spend at least a day in each town to experience the history, epic beauty, and plethora of rich wildlife on land and sea. North Monterey is lined with beaches, bike trails, and local eats. The downtown sector is teeming with historical buildings, shopping, dining, and museums. You can also spend the day on the sea or on the bay. You can find a variety of companies that take visitors out on the water, which can fill most of a day. Start from Monterey's Wharf or harbor, where you can go whale watching, sailing, diving, or fishing.

Moss Landing is the place to pick up tours by kayak or for fishing and whale-watching excursions. In this the tiny fishing village you can snag some local produce, throw down a bucket-size margarita, buy live Dungeness crabs or other seasonal seafood, and stop into an antiques shop or two. The neighboring towns of Marina and Seaside have some local flavor with endless beaches perfect for surfing, body boarding, kite flying, walking, running, and general beach activities.

At Pacific Grove you can scuba dive from the shore, bike along the coast, wander the shops along Lighthouse Avenue, and play golf between the sea and a historic lighthouse. Pebble Beach is the peninsula's golf haven and is home to five world-class courses. There are also extravagant accommodations, fine dining, and several shops run by the Pebble Beach Company.

Sights

◖ MONTEREY BAY AQUARIUM

A magical dreamlike experience can be found at the Monterey Bay Aquarium (866 Cannery Row, 831/648-4800, www.montereybay-aquarium.org, daily 10 A.M.-6 P.M., $30). With plenty of windows onto the world below the waves, visiting the depths of the ocean is a tranquil experience that provides an educational opportunity as well as a vacation. You can also experience the aquarium hands-on through their adventure programs, which include sailing, diving, and sleepovers.

From its beginning, the aquarium's mission has been conservation, including custodianship of the coast and the ocean in Monterey County south to Big Sur. It takes an active role in conservation of at-risk wildlife in the area, and most of the animals in the aquarium's tanks were rescued; many will eventually be returned to the wild. Most of the exhibits in this mammoth complex contain only local sealife.

One of the main attractions is the **Kelp Forest.** Beams of light pierce the water through the rich stands of kelp as leopard sharks and a school of sardines swim around. Rockfish hide at the sides of the tank and in clumps of rock. The forest rises all the way to the second floor, where you can get close to the surface for a new perspective.

Everyone seems to marvel at the **giant octopus** before being lured into the **Deep Reef.** Skates curl their winged bodies as they glide through the water past enormous sturgeons. On the opposite side of the big tanks, sand dollars are displayed; these are great for snapping black-and-white pictures. The smaller displays offer a closer look as the denizens of the deep reef: huge pink and neon-green anemones, creatures hiding beneath the sand, plenty of shrimp, and tiny fish.

In the **Wharf** exhibit, perches dart around

and sea stars, California mussels, and green anemones have attached themselves to the pilings. After a study of the wharf, you may want to take a seat at the **Real Coast Café** exhibit to see what's being served. Here you learn about sustainable seafood and what you can do to help save the oceans through your food choices. The aquarium provides *Seafood Watch,* a pocket guide to sustainable seafood choices.

Examine the high tide feast along the **Sandy Shore** as you check out the filter feeders in the surge channels. You can see the jeweled top snail and spiny brittle star up close, and standing underneath the glass bubble as the tide rushes over is a unique experience. You can pet bat rays, feel the weight of a sea cumber, pick up a knobby sea star, and slide your fingers along bull kelp.

Before you enter the **Aviary,** learn about the local wetlands, such as Elkhorn Slough, at the nature center. You can view leopard sharks from above while ruddy ducks swim fearlessly above the stingrays, and walk along the sandy shore to watch the tide roll in as birds roam the coastal wetlands.

The most popular personalities at the aquarium are the **sea otters,** and the group of five is absolutely adorable. The exhibit has two levels to provide a good look at the sea otters from above and below the surface as they play, eat, and nap. Feeding times are action-packed, and visitors crowd in like sardines; get here early if you want a clear view.

Within the **Open Sea** area are several must-see exhibits. Sardines swirl like a chandelier over the entrance to the tanks of **jellyfish,** the best photography subjects in the aquarium as they move slowly and intricately dance together. The lobed comb jellyfish are electrifying and nearly invisible. Their sides surge up and down with light in the colors of the rainbow.

The Open Sea is the largest tank in the aquarium. Scalloped hammerhead sharks circle, a sea turtle combs the surface, pacific bluefin tuna hustle in small schools, and barracudas

© KRISTIN LEAL

Discover another world within the walls of the Monterey Bay Aquarium.

group together. Upstairs, you can sit and marvel at the creatures in the tank and be hypnotized by the huge yellowfin tuna circling alongside Galápagos sharks.

The aquarium's special exhibits are always a splendid surprise. Time slows as you enter the dreamy world of the **Secret Lives of the Seahorses.** Lit in blues and greens, more typical seahorses are displayed along with more unusual species. The sheer variety of species is amazing; some resemble pieces of kelp and others look like long tubes.

For bird lovers, the **Hot Pink Flamingos** exhibit features ocean travelers such as pink flamingos, penguins, tufted puffins, and sea turtles. The color of the flamingos is stunning next to the roseate spoonbills. The newest residents are the puffins, short birds with bright yellow beaks and elegant feathers that walk around their habitat.

Splash Zone is where kids can roll up their

sleeves and get their hands wet. You can walk under the arching kelp, touch sea grapes, hold a starfish, and handle a rainbow star. Small children can crawl through many of the exhibits. This is also home to the **penguins,** entertaining as they dive into the pool and waddle around on the rocks; their feeding time is always fun.

The aquarium is not only about the exhibits. It offers opportunities to discover the wildlife of Monterey Bay in a hands-on way through the **Aquarium Adventures** programs. Board the aquarium's research vessel for an excursion on the bay to become a scientist for an afternoon. **Underwater Explorers** (mid-June-early Sept.) is for kids ages 8-13 and offers an unforgettable experience: a chance to surface-dive with the staff in the Great Tide Pool, where they float above anemones, find starfish, and learn about Monterey's marine environment. Another program, the **Behind the Scenes Tour,** gives you a backstage pass to discover the secrets of the aquarium. Trek through the employee only areas for an hour to see what it takes to care for all these animals. **Summer Sleepovers** are the ultimate slumber party for children as they bunk next to the exhibits and are lulled to sleep by the deep sea.

If you get hungry, tucked behind the Real Coast Café exhibit is the **Portola Restaurant** ($15-25), with fine sustainable dining beside large bay windows that overlook the ocean. Check out the sealife as you dine through the binoculars provided at every table along with an information card about the local creatures.

◖ CANNERY ROW

Famous for its rich fishing history and as the setting for one of John Steinbeck's classic novels, Cannery Row (831/649-6690, www.canneryrow.com) conveniently hugs the shores of the harbor. In the early 20th century it was an ideal setting to support the growing fishing industry on Monterey Bay, and it became home to 16 canning plants and 14 reduction plants that produced thousands of tons of sardines every year. The fishing industry collapsed in the mid-1950s, and today, Cannery Row serves visitors with waterfront accommodations, numerous restaurants, diving operators, jewelry shops, clothing stores, a wax museum, wine-tasting, and, of course, the Monterey Bay Aquarium. There is also a beach with a tide pool and a chance to chase the waves.

◖ OLD FISHERMAN'S WHARF

The location of Old Fisherman's Wharf (1 Old Fisherman's Wharf, 831/649-6544, www.montereywharf.com) dates back to 1770, when the harbor was discovered by Spaniard Gaspar de Portolà. The whaling industry took off in Monterey by the 1840s, and the Wharf was a major hub of action. It was also home to a booming fishing industry through the mid-20th century. Today, you can walk the planks of the 1845 pier and enjoy its historic nautical charm. Inspired by the past, the Wharf has entertainment for everyone: Seafood restaurants hand out clam chowder samples, whale-watching tour operators promise adventure, fishing charters return with their bounty from the sea, souvenir shops are filled with amusing treasures, and, unexpectedly, a preforming arts theater sits near the end of the Wharf.

DOWNTOWN MONTEREY

Downtown Monterey is roughly bounded by El Estero Park and the Presidio of Monterey. The area is filled with restaurants, bars, art museums, shops, historic buildings and gardens, the local library, a post office, and a number of hotels. Alvarado Street is the hub of the action, where the weekly farmer's market is held Tuesday evenings and weekend nights are filled with dinner out, barhopping, and dancing.

◖ Monterey State Historic Park Path of History

Take a walk and get a California history lesson

MONTEREY

SEAFOOD WATCH AND SUSTAINABILITY

© KRISTIN LEAL

Leopard sharks dart through the kelp forest at the Monterey Bay Aquarium.

Today, the health of our oceans is at risk. Around the world, 75 percent of fisheries are overfished or fished to capacity, causing many species to become endangered or extinct. What we choose to eat has a direct impact on the world around us, and Monterey Bay Aquarium has developed a program to help us take action ourselves.

Our daily food choices affect the fishing industry, and sustainability is the key to ensuring the health of the oceans. The primary mission of the **Monterey Bay Aquarium Seafood Watch** program is promoting sustainable fishing to allow ecosystems to survive and remain diverse and productive for the future. Seafood Watch is an inclusive vision of keeping the ocean sustainable by considering species, habitat, management, government reports, journal articles, and sustainability criteria to classify which seafood has the least impact on marine ecosystems.

The Seafood Watch program has a pocket guide to assist us in making sustainable seafood choices, with seafood items ranked for their sustainability as "Best Choices," "Good Alternatives," and "Avoid." Carrying it with us can help us reduce the impact of our food choices on the environment. Visit the aquarium online at www.montereybayaquarium.org and download the Seafood Watch pocket guide.

on the Monterey State Historic Park's Path of History (831/649-7118, tour reservations 831/649-7172, www.parks.ca.gov, daily, free). There is a collection of 55 historic sites along the 2.5-mile trek. Many people find Colton Hall (570 Pacific St.) or Pacific House (Custom House Plaza) nice entry spots to the Path of History, as there are parking garages at both.

The walk is self-guided, but guided tours can be purchased by calling the park office in advance. Enter the path at any point by simply looking for the round yellow tiles set in the

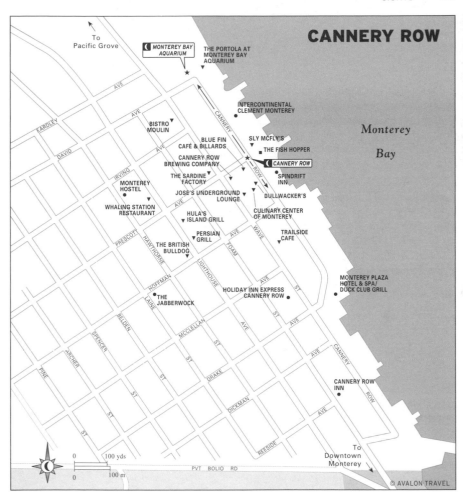

sidewalks, and begin your journey back in time. Free maps can be found at most of the historic sites along the way, or print one from the website.

CUSTOM HOUSE PLAZA

The Custom House Plaza (831/646-3866, www. mtycounty.com, daily) provides just a sample of the 55 historic sites along Monterey's Path of History. Located between downtown and Old Fisherman's Wharf, the plaza serves as the focal point of large public events throughout the year.

The **Custom House** (Custom House Plaza, 831/649-7118, www.parks.ca.gov, Sat.-Sun. 10 A.M.-4 P.M., free) was first used by the Mexican government, and it wasn't until 1846 that Commodore John Drake Sloat raised the American flag and claimed it for the United States. The museum is styled as it would have been in the 1840s, and you can examine a variety of goods and tools that were used at the port. Through the windows upstairs you can watch as boats enter and leave the harbor.

© MONTEREY COUNTY VISITORS CENTER

Cannery Row is lined with shops, restaurants, and accommodations.

Constructed in 1847, **Pacific House** (Custom House Plaza, 831/649-7181, www.parks.ca.gov, Sat.-Sun. 10 A.M.-4 P.M., free) was used as a hotel, Army storage facility, courthouse, offices, and tavern. Today, it showcases exhibits that tell the story of Monterey Bay from the time when Native Americans were the only residents through the present day. Explore Monterey's rich history on the two floors, and don't forget to head out back to the garden.

Formally known as the Maritime and History Museum, the new **Monterey History and Art Association and Museum of Monterey** (5 Custom House Plaza, 831/372-2608, www.museumofmonterey.org, Tues.-Sun. 10 A.M.-5 P.M., $5) is filled with various permanent exhibits and showcases new exhibitions as well. Nicknamed MOM, it was renovated in 2011. The museum's permanent collections include Costumes and Textiles, Decorative Arts, Model Ships, Monterey History Archive, Historical Objects, and Photography.

PERRY HOUSE

View the Perry House (201 Van Buren St., 831/641-0114, www.parks.ca.gov), a beautifully crafted Victorian home built in 1860 by whaling captain Manuel Perry, from the curb, as it is one of the many historic locations on the Path of History that is privately owned. Currently it can be rented for weddings and other events.

OLD WHALING STATION

Originally built as a home for David Wright and his family in 1847, it wasn't until 1855 that the Monterey Whaling Company used the Old Whaling Station (391 Decatur St., 831/375-5356, www.parks.ca.gov, daily 9 A.M.-5 P.M., free) as an employee residence and headquarters. Today, the building is a museum known for its whalebone walkway. Take a quick tour of the small structure and learn about the bay's whaling history.

MONTEREY

WHALING AND FISHING HISTORY

© KRISTIN LEAL

the Monterey Bay Harbor today

The cool waters of Monterey Bay have a history of providing the bounty of the sea. First Native Americans and later 19th-century European settlers made it a hub for fishing, and whalers flocked here in the early days of the whaling industry. Sardines became a popular target and made Cannery Row famous.

Whaling started in California at Monterey in the 1850s, when Captain John P. Davenport opened the first whaling company on the bay, and the Old Monterey Whaling Company began harvesting the massive beasts in 1855 from Old Fisherman's Wharf. The whales were harvested for their blubber, which was boiled at a processing station on shore and made into oil. Whaling continued in the bay until the late 1880s, when the oil became obsolete for lighting and was replaced with fossil fuel.

Chinese Americans began fishing in Monterey Bay in the early 1850s, playing a key role in developing the city and Cannery Row as a successful fishing port. By 1853 there were hundreds of experienced Chinese people working in fishing, and they opened the first commercial fishing company. By 1900 up to 800 pounds of fish per day was sent to the fishmongers on Clay Street in San Francisco. Italian Americans also began fishing the waters in the late 1800s as the industry began to boom.

The canning industry continued at Cannery Row until the mid-1950s, when fish populations collapsed. The demand for sardines rose, leading to overfishing, and new fishing technologies enabled huge harvests. Fishing boats soon found their nets coming up empty every day. The last cannery in Monterey closed in 1973.

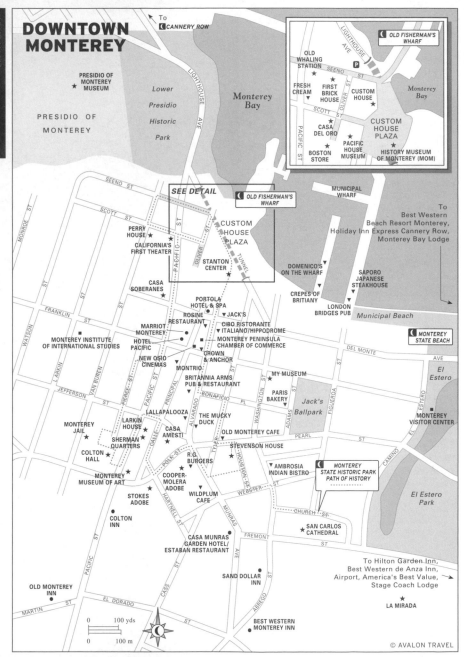

DOWNTOWN MONTEREY

To CANNERY ROW

PRESIDIO OF MONTEREY MUSEUM

Lower Presidio Historic Park

Monterey Bay

PRESIDIO OF MONTEREY

Detail inset:
OLD FISHERMAN'S WHARF
OLD WHALING STATION
FRESH CREAM
FIRST BRICK HOUSE
CUSTOM HOUSE
Monterey Bay
CASA DEL ORO
CUSTOM HOUSE PLAZA
BOSTON STORE
PACIFIC HOUSE MUSEUM
HISTORY MUSEUM OF MONTEREY (MOM)

SEE DETAIL

OLD FISHERMAN'S WHARF

MUNICIPAL WHARF

To Best Western Beach Resort Monterey, Holiday Inn Express Cannery Row, Monterey Bay Lodge

CUSTOM HOUSE PLAZA

PERRY HOUSE
CALIFORNIA'S FIRST THEATER
STANTON CENTER

DOMENICO'S ON THE WHARF
SAPORO JAPANESE STEAKHOUSE
CREPES OF BRITIANY
CASA SOBERANES
PORTOLA HOTEL & SPA
ROSINE RESTAURANT
JACK'S
LONDON BRIDGES PUB
Municipal Beach

MARRIOT MONTEREY
MONTEREY INSTITUTE OF INTERNATIONAL STUDIES
HOTEL PACIFIC
NEW OSIO CINEMAS
CIBO RISTORANTE ITALIANO/HIPPODROME
MONTEREY PENINSULA CHAMBER OF COMMERCE
CROWN & ANCHOR
MONTRIO
MY MUSEUM
MONTEREY STATE BEACH
DEL MONTE AVE
El Estero

BRITANNIA ARMS PUB & RESTAURANT
PARIS BAKERY
Jack's Ballpark
MONTEREY VISITOR CENTER

MONTEREY JAIL
LARKIN HOUSE
LALLAPALOOZA
THE MUCKY DUCK
CASA AMESTI
OLD MONTEREY CAFE
STEVENSON HOUSE

SHERMAN QUARTERS
COLTON HALL
R.G. BURGERS
AMBROSIA INDIAN BISTRO
MONTEREY STATE HISTORIC PARK PATH OF HISTORY

MONTEREY MUSEUM OF ART
COOPER-MOLERA ADOBE
WILDPLUM CAFE
STOKES ADOBE
COLTON INN
CASA MUNRAS GARDEN HOTEL/ ESTABAN RESTAURANT
SAN CARLOS CATHEDRAL
El Estero Park

OLD MONTEREY INN
EL DORADO ST
MARTIN ST

SAND DOLLAR INN
LA MIRADA
To Hilton Garden Inn, Best Western de Anza Inn, Airport, America's Best Value, Stage Coach Lodge

0   100 yds
0   100 m

BEST WESTERN MONTEREY INN

© AVALON TRAVEL

CALIFORNIA'S FIRST THEATRE

Due to structural damage, California's First Theatre (Pacific St. and Scott St., www.parks. ca.gov) is closed to the public most of the year. Once a year, in early December, the theater's tavern opens its doors for the Christmas in the Adobes event. It was originally built as a tavern and lodging house for sailors in 1847 by Jack Swan; in 1850, U.S. Army officers began producing plays as a moneymaking venture. The first night pulled in $500.

CASA DEL ORO

Home of the Boston Store and Picket Fence Garden Shop, Casa del Oro (210 Olivier St., off Pacific St., 831/649-3364, www.parks.ca.gov, Thurs.-Sun. 11 A.M.-3 P.M.) was constructed by Thomas O. Larkin in 1845 and served as a general store in 1850. Monterey's first safe was installed here in Joseph Boston & Co., and as the story goes, miners returning from the gold fields would store their assets in the safe, earning the two-story adobe the nickname "Casa del Oro" (House of Gold). The store and garden shop, offering fresh herbs, seeds for planting, silverware, coffee mills, teas, and soaps, are operated by the Historic League of Monterey.

FIRST BRICK HOUSE

Visiting the First Brick House (20 Custom House Plaza, 831/649-7118, www.parks.ca.gov) has to be a walk-by visit, as it is closed until further notice due to state budget cuts. In 1874 Gallant Duncan Dickenson arrived in California and introduced his fired clay bricks, which were much stronger and more durable that mud adobe. He never finished construction of his brick home, as the gold in the Sierras was calling him; he abandoned the structure, and the unused bricks were auctioned off for $1,000 in 1851.

COLTON HALL

Visit the site where the first California Constitution was drafted, Colton Hall (351 Pacific St., 831/646-5640, www.monterey.org, daily 10 A.M.-4 P.M., closed holidays, free). The large building also served as a courthouse and public school for many years before becoming a museum. The large lawn in front is perfect for setting out a blanket, having a picnic, and letting the kids run wild. Located behind the building is the Old Monterey Jail, which brings the Wild West to life. Used as a jail for more than 100 years, it dates to 1854. Walking into the tiny jail and looking into the cells is a chilling experience.

CASA SOBERANES

Casa Soberanes (Pacific St. and Del Monte Ave., 831/649-7118, www.parks.ca.gov, daily 9 A.M.-5 P.M., free) is an adobe with a blue gate leading to the garden. It was home to many families since the 1840s, with the Soberanes family being the longest residents, from 1860 to 1922. The garden is layered with pieces of Monterey: whalebones, wine bottles, and abalone shells line the garden path. You can also tour the interior, which is filled with modern Mexican folk art, Chinese trade pieces, and early New England furnishing.

COOPER MOLERA ADOBE

The Cooper Molera Adobe (525 Polk St. at Alvarado St. and Munras St., 831/649-7118 or 831/649-7111, www.parks.ca.gov, daily 9 A.M.-4 P.M., free) is another garden and museum, with two acres to explore, including the museum, barns, gardens, and a gift shop. It was the 19th-century home of the Cooper family, headed by Captain John Rogers Cooper, who was in the business of trading items like hides, otter pelts, tallow, and general merchandise.

LARKIN HOUSE

The first two-story building in California is the Larkin House (464 Calle Principal, 831/646-3991, www.parks.ca.gov, daily 9 A.M.-5 P.M., free), built by the merchant Thomas Oliver Larkin in 1835 as his home and storefront; later

© KRISTIN LEAL

Colton Hall in Old Monterey

it was the headquarters for the U.S. military governor of California. It has a beautiful garden and two floors to tour inside. Many of the pieces inside originate with Alice Larkin Toulmin after she acquired the adobe from her grandfather in 1922 and furnished it with early-19th-century antiques from around the world.

SHERMAN QUARTERS

A favorite subject for photographers is Sherman Quarters (Calle Principal, next to Larkin house, 831/649-7118, www.parks.ca.gov, daily 9 A.M.-4 P.M., free). The building is closed but can be viewed from the gardens of Larkin House. In 1847 it served as the living quarters of Lieutenant William T. Sherman, later General Sherman of Civil War fame, who was in charge of the troops constructing the Presidio of Monterey.

STOKES ADOBE

The focus of many social events in the early days of Monterey was the Stokes Adobe (500 Hartnell St., 831/373-1110, www.mtycounty. com), one of the most pretentious homes in Monterey. In its heyday, the most important events were the cascarone balls, festive events where eggshells were smashed between dances. During the 1840s the adobe was the home of Monterey mayor and physician James Stokes. Today, visitors enjoy walking the around the property to admire the roses and possibly catch a glance of a ghost: Employees have reported seeing the lights turn on in the early morning hours when no one is inside. Others have heard the voices of children and the sound of heavy footsteps in empty upstairs rooms. Through the years it has served as an officers' garrison and a series of restaurants.

STEVENSON HOUSE

Once a rooming house and later the French Hotel, Stevenson House (530 Houston St., 831/649-7118, www.parks.ca.gov, daily 9 A.M.-5 P.M., free) was where famed author

Robert Louis Stevenson stayed in the 1870s while courting his future wife, Fanny Osbourne. Today, it is restored to what it would have looked like in Stevenson's era, with many rooms devoted to the author. The two-story adobe is worth a visit for the lovely gardens as well. In the 19th century, the adobe was owned and run by a devoted mother and warm grandmother named Manuela Giradin. It is suspected that her spirit still roams the structure, caring for her sick grandchildren. Visitors have said they have seen a woman in a black dress walk into the nursery; a rocking chair has been known to rock with no one in it; and the aroma of sickroom disinfectant is sometimes present, with the smell of carbolic acid throughout the house.

SAN CARLOS CATHEDRAL

California's first cathedral and the birthplace of the Carmel Mission is the San Carlos Cathedral (500 Church St., 831/373-2628, www.sancarloscathedral. net), founded by Father Junípero Serra in 1770. A year later, the mission was moved to Carmel, leaving the church behind as a royal chapel for the soldiers; the structure seen today was completed in 1774.

Beautifully built in the Spanish colonial style with ornamental arches and fine sandstone molding throughout, the cathedral was associated with the new Spanish Presidio. It is currently one of the oldest functioning churches in California. The **Heritage Center Museum** (2nd and 4th Mon. 10 A.M.-noon and 1:15-3:15 P.M., Wed. 10 A.M.-noon, Fri. 10 A.M.-3 P.M., Sat. 10 A.M.-2 P.M., Sun. 1-3 P.M., donation) offers docent-led tours that explore a relic of the Vizcaíno-Serra Oak, old photos and drawings of the chapel, pieces of the whalebone sidewalk that led to the Church, and other pieces recently recovered in an archaeological dig. The museum is on the east side of the chapel in the Parish Offices Building.

Monterey Museum of Art

The Monterey Museum of Art (559 Pacific St., 831/372-5477, www.montereyart.org, Wed.-Sat. 11 A.M.-5 P.M., Sun. 1-4 P.M., closed holidays, $10) is a treasure trove in the downtown area, with eight galleries in a three-story structure that features rotating exhibits. You can admire photography, contemporary and early American art, and California paintings.

My Museum

The place for the whole family to come and play is at My Museum (425 Washington St., 831/649-6444, www.mymuseum.org, Mon.-Tues. and Thurs.-Sat. 10 A.M.-5 P.M., Sun. noon-5 P.M., $7). Interactive educational exhibits include My Day at the Beach for the little ones and My Go-Fore Golf for bigger kids. There are always 75 bins filled with art and craft supplies, both recyclable and nonrecyclable, to create masterpieces. The staff are also experts at hosting special events, and it is a popular birthday-party spot.

PRESIDIO OF MONTEREY

From the time Europeans first saw Monterey Bay in 1602, the military has played a vital role that continues today. The Presidio of Monterey (between Hwy. 68/Holman Hwy. and Lighthouse Ave., 831/242-5555, www. monterey.army.mil) is a U.S. Army base known for its Defense Language Institute Foreign Language Center. The original Presidio building was located near Lake Estero in today's downtown area. In 1792, a small fort equipped with 11 cannons, El Castillo, was built to protect the original Presidio.

Within the Presidio today are two public attractions for visitors. The 26-acre **Lower Presidio Historic Park** has markers with information about the military presence in Monterey through the Spanish, Mexican, and American periods. Views of the bay abound throughout the park. All that remains of the Rumsen Native American village here is their burial grounds and a large ceremonial rain rock that was used to grind acorns. The 31-foot-tall granite Sloat Monument marks the location of Fort Mervine, which stood here during the Civil War era.

Located in Lower Presidio Historic Park is the **Presidio of Monterey Museum** (Bldg. 113, Corporal Ewing Rd., off Artillery St., 831/646-3456, www.monterey.org, Mon. 10 A.M.-1 P.M., Thurs.-Sat. 10 A.M.-4 P.M., Sun. 1-4 P.M., free), with information on Monterey's military history in a series of exhibits that includes the Rumsen people through the present-day military presence. Parking at the museum and park is free, but make sure to bring a picture ID, as you are entering a military base.

Sports and Recreation

BEACHES
◖ Monterey State Beach

Stretching from the southern reaches of Seaside to the Monterey Municipal Wharf, the Monterey Bay shoreline has numerous access points and arcs west to the Monterey Municipal Wharf. Three separate beaches shared by Seaside and Monterey make up Monterey State Beach (west of Hwy. 1 Seaside exit 218, 831/649-2836, www.parks.ca.gov, free), the spot for surfing, body boarding, surf kayaking, kite flying, running, and shore fishing. This strip of shoreline is known for its fantastic beginning surfer waves with long flat rollers. The Monterey Junior Lifeguards find the conditions ideal and use these beaches for their yearly summer programs. On the Seaside-Monterey border, this is the only beach that has an occupied lifeguard tower throughout summer; the state beaches from Marina to Monterey are patrolled by lifeguards in a truck during summer. Locals love to surf the waters along the section known as Del Monte Beach off of Casa Verde Way. The waves are consistently changeling and get mellower farther west toward the wharf.

Other Beach Access

The Coast Guard Pier, between downtown and Cannery Row, has a small cove called **San Carlos Beach,** perfect for the little ones to get their toes wet or wrestle in the large grassy area. There is a secluded cove behind **Monterey Plaza** where you can avoid the crowds. **McAbee Beach** is along Cannery Row, with stairs next to the Fishhopper Restaurant (700 Cannery Row) that lead to the pale beach and a cluster of tide pools. If you like to snorkel, McAbee Beach has kelp mazes, rocky mounds, tiny pink starfish, quick rock cod, and the occasional harbor seal to swim around.

SURFING

Whether you're just learning to harness the power of the ocean or are a longtime ripper, the Monterey Bay coastline offers gleaming shores with year-round endless waves.

A great spot to avoid the weekend crowds is at **Marina State Beach** (Reservation Rd., off Hwy. 1, 831/649-2836, www.parks.ca.gov, free). Steady winds help to create moderate-to-hard surf that tends to be filled with strong riptides among heavy undertows. Be prepared with a full wetsuit, hoodie, and booties on windy days.

Surf Shops

Get fully geared up for beach fun on Lighthouse Avenue. The local choice surf and skate shop on the peninsula is **Sunshine Freestyle Sports** (443 Lighthouse Ave., 831/375-5015, www.sunshinefreestyle.com, Mon.-Sat. 10 A.M.-6 P.M., Sun. 11 A.M.-5 P.M.). Officially the sponsor and creator of the Annual Surf About in Carmel, the shop has been owned by local surfers since the early 1980s.

A little more on the hip and trendy side is

© KRISTIN LEAL

Monterey State Beach

On the Beach Surf Shop (693 Lighthouse Ave., 831/646-9283, www.onthebeachsurfshop.com). It has a bit of everything, including surfboard and ski rentals, to prepare you for the surf or the snow. There is also a full line of clothing and accessories for the rider lifestyle.

FISHING AND WHALE WATCHING

Randy's Whale Watching and Fishing Trips (66 Fisherman's Wharf, 831/372-7440, www.randysfishingtrips.com) offers tours year-round. The fishing voyages last about seven hours and have seasoned captains at the helm. They know the hot fishing spots for fishing rock cod, Dungeness crab, albacore, Humboldt squid, salmon, and more. Trip prices vary and can include rod and reel rentals along with a daily fishing license. Three-hour whale-watching tours ($30) head out daily year-round and are packed with adventure. Views are continuously spectacular, with the coastline and a plethora of wildlife to observe; don't forget your

camera. The unique canyon and upwelling deep below the bay is rich with plant growth, making Monterey Bay an ideal spot for migratory and year-round species. Look forward to seeing gray (Dec.-Apr.), blue, and humpback (May-Nov.) whales along with porpoises and the fearsome killer whales that are known to hunt in Monterey waters.

Chris's Fishing and Whale Watching Trips (48 Fisherman's Wharf 1, 831/375-5951, www.chrisfishing.com or www.chriswhalewatching.com) has been fishing Monterey Bay since the 1940s, and the skippers know the local waters well, hitting the water at sunrise to return by early afternoon on the hunt for rock cod, albacore, salmon, crab, and Humboldt squid (prices vary; rod and reel rentals available). The whale-watching adventure ($32) starts at the mouth of the harbor, where the sea lions like to play on the rocks, practically posing for photos. Various whales and dolphins make an appearance throughout the year as different species migrate.

Keeping a lookout for whales year-round is

the **Monterey Bay Whale Watch Center** (84 Fisherman's Wharf, 831/375-4658, www.montereybaywhalewatch.com, morning trip $47, afternoon trip $38). Hitting the seas for 4-5 hours, there are many chances to get up close to these massive creatures. The whale-watching is not all about spotting whales, as the tour focuses on the vast variety of marine animals within the bay above and below the surface. A naturalist is on board to educate you on the sea otters, harbor seals, minke whales, fin whales, pacific white-sided dolphins, Risso's dolphins, northern right whale dolphins, bottlenose dolphins, Dall's porpoises, harbor porpoises, and a vast variety of sea birds all known to make an appearance in the bay.

The largest whale-watching vessel on the Wharf is the **Princess Monterey Whale Watching** (96 Fisherman's Wharf 1, 831/372-2203, www.montereywhalewatching.com, $40), and it is strictly dedicated to following the massive mammals, watching for the whales' breath to spot them from afar. The boat's captains are experts at searching out the spouting whales, and the various companies keep in contact with each other to report where the elusive beasts have been sighted during the day, making the chances of sighting whales high.

SAILING

Year-round adventures within the bay and beyond can be had with **Monterey Bay Sailing** (78 Fisherman's Wharf 1, 831/372-7245, www.montereysailing.com, one hour $39, $25 children). With a fleet of seven sailboats, the options are numerous, from daily cruises to weeklong trips. Monterey Bay Sailing is a member of the American Sailing Association Academy (ASA), where all captains are certified instructors and teach a variety of sailing classes for any level. Check out the deals throughout the year and receive half-price sailing lessons on selected Wednesday nights.

Aboard the *Bella on the Bay* (32 Cannery Row, Suite 8, 831/822-2390, www.bellamonterey.com, $79 pp, free for 2 kids under age 11 per family), Captain Christian Hestness loves to sail and delivers a high-speed hunt for heavy winds and the big puffs. Sailing is a stunning way to take in the beauty of Monterey; the buzz of the city fades as the shoreline becomes distant. There are a variety of daily cruises to choose from.

For adrenaline junkies, sailing action is available year-round and voyage options are plentiful, from two-hour trips to overnight stays in Stillwater Cove.

SCUBA DIVING

The world below the ocean's surface is a bounty to explore. Past the kelp zone, "God beams" of sunlight shoot through the deep blue. Giant garnet pinnacles appear, fish hide among the rocks and corals, sponges attach to the garnet walls, and wolf eels are known to hide in the many dark caves. Monterey Bay and Carmel offer a unique opportunity to experience an underwater habitat within a marine sanctuary, and several companies offer the chance to dive from shore or from a boat. All dive boats depart from the Monterey Harbor and Marina between Old Fisherman's Wharf 1 and 2, on K Dock.

Dive Spots

Below the surface of Monterey Bay and the clear waters of Carmel, diving offers a wide variety of territory to explore. The water in the bay and at Carmel tends to range from the high 40s to the mid-50s Fahrenheit.

Eric's Pinnacle is best accessed by boat, off the shore of 17-Mile Drive. It is an 80-105-foot dive with lots of rock slivers shooting up. Most sealife is seen on the rocks, as many other animals bury themselves in the sand.

Farther south, **Aumentos Reef** has everything Monterey has to offer. The pinnacles are a lush carpet, and strawberry anemones cover the rocks.

Break Water is a great beginner spot, with nice walls that drop off quickly. **Tankers**

Reef off Del Monte Beach is another location in the bay that offers a bounty of discovery. Monastery Beach at Carmel is a nice location with beach entry.

Point Lobos State Natural Reserve (831/624-4909) offers diving access to Whalers Cove and Blue Fish Cove, with many access points by boat or from shore. Inside the park is a boat ramp to launch kayaks or boats up to 18 feet long. The reserve is filled with large pinnacles emerging from the sandy ocean floor. A winding maze of giant kelp is seen along the middle reef. The shoots can grab rocks as deep as 130 feet. Wolf eels, rockfish, and lingcod hide among the rocks and plantlife. Giant sunflower stars hunt for crabs, abalones, urchins, sea cucumbers, and other stars.

Dive Shops

Aquarius Dive Shop (2040 Del Monte Ave., 831/375-1933, www.aquariusdivers.com) offers everything you'll need to go diving in Monterey Bay: air and nitrox fills, equipment rentals, certification courses, and help booking trips on local dive boats. Aquarius works with four boats to create great trips for divers of all interests and ability levels. Call or check the website for current local dive conditions.

A local favorite is **Bamboo Reef Enterprises** (614 Lighthouse Ave., 831/372-1685, www.bambooreef.com), a full dive shop with lessons and certification courses. They do clean repairs at a fair price and have all the latest dive equipment for purchase.

Get suited up at **Monterey Bay Dive Company** (225 Cannery Row, 831/656-0454, www.mbdcscuba.com) and take a shore dive at the neighboring Coast Guard Wharf. It is a full-service dive shop and dive-chartering service; hitch a ride on their dive boat for a two-tank tour ($75). Sitting in the middle of Cannery Row, you can take dive classes year-round, get certified, rent equipment, and fill your own tanks.

Charters

For serious technical diving and photography,

Under Water Company (831/915-6600) is an off-the-radar business offering special deepwater trips and technical expeditions. Phil Sammet, the owner and sole instructor, is one of the most respected technical divers on the peninsula. Advanced reservations are a must.

Another popular dive boat is the **Monterey Bay Express** (831/915-0752, www.montereyexpress.com, $90). The morning and afternoon charters include two dives, and the Saturday-night trip has one. Depending on the surface conditions, trips head to the pinnacles off the shores of Pacific Grove or down to Point Lobos State Natural Reserve.

If you're looking for a dive in Point Lobos State Natural Reserve, sign up with the **Beachhopper II** (408/463-0585, www.beachhopper2.com, 6:30 A.M.-7:30 P.M., $90). It runs south to Point Lobos for a two-tank dive in the reserve and its natural glory.

Explore the natural beauty of the underwater world from Monterey to Big Sur with **Sanctuary Charters** (866/737-3483, www.sanctuarycharters.com, $90), which offers standard two-tank dives; it is the only limited-load dive boat in the bay and focuses on small groups and more diving.

Offering diving access at all the premier spots in Monterey and Carmel is **Dive Central** (831/465-1185, www.divecentral.com, $85). Hit the water in style aboard a custom 38-foot dive boat while you're getting ready for a two-tank dive. Each dive is different, and you never know what you'll encounter in the cool depths, from large sunfish to elusive wolf eels.

KAYAKING

With all the focus in Monterey on sustainable tourism, coupled with the lovely recreation area of Monterey Bay, it's no wonder that sea kayaking is popular here. Whether you want to try paddling for the first time or you're an expert with your own gear, you'll find a local outfit ready to hook you up.

Kayaking Spots

Monterey Bay offers many sites for open-water kayaking. The bay is teeming with wildlife on the liquid trails in the changing ocean. **Moss Landing** is a wonderful location for first-time kayakers. The harbor offers a calm ride with plenty of marine life to encounter. Just beyond the launch ramps, harbor seals sun themselves on the beaches beside plucky pelicans. Rafts of sea otters scatter in the water. Massive sea lions outline the mouth of the harbor. While paddling, you'll encounter the ocean tides, and the push and pull of the ocean directs the path of the kayak. Sea otters are often seen floating on their backs breaking open clam shells on their bellies. Tiny Dungeness crabs hide in grubby caves along the waterline. Various seabirds cruise the surface in search of their next meal.

Fisherman's Wharf offers both beginner and intermediate paddles. This launch location begins with an easy paddle through the harbor, where bronzed sea lions balance on buoys and harbor seals blend into the rocks. The harbor at the Wharf is filled with curious seals that tend to follow kayakers.

Dolphins are also known to show off near **Cannery Row.** Crossing through the canopy of kelp where sea otters rest slows the kayak, and paddles can become entangled. During the spring, mother sea otters can also be seen holding baby pups on their bellies. Gaining a different perspective on a highly visited place, the ride through Cannery Row is tranquil.

Beyond Cannery Row to **Lovers Point,** the bay begins to open up to the sea. Currents start to churn, and waves gain height and momentum as the trip becomes a little more exciting. Digging in deep with every stroke provides a more strenuous workout and a more successful ride in this kind of challenging surf.

Launch ramps are not the only way to access the ocean by kayak. I have seen more

The back side of Cannery Row is a popular paddling spot.

FUN OTTER FACTS

© KRISTIN LEAL

The Monterey Bay is famous for its large sea otter population.

- In one square inch, a sea otter has more hair than a human does on his or her entire head.

- Sea otters are known as the wolves of the sea: They eat sea urchins, crabs, clams, mussels, octopuses, other marine invertebrates, and fish.

- Sea otters mate year-round, and pups can be seen on their mother's bellies throughout the year.

- Sea otters usually do not migrate and only travel if the area is overpopulated or food sources are scarce.

experienced paddlers and thrill-seekers go for the fun rush of launching into the surf. **Del Monte Beach** off Casa Verde is a challenge, and many local paddlers compete for the waves alongside the surfers. **Monterey State Beach** is another great spot to paddle in the foamy surf; the waves are not huge but offer a mixed challenge.

Kayak Rental and Tour Companies
Throughout the Monterey Bay area, several kayaking companies offer rentals and tours for any level of paddler. They have all the proper gear, and the guides are familiar with the local waters and wildlife. If you have never been kayaking or are unfamiliar with Monterey, it is best to take a tour.

To go out on your own or to take a tour, a good place to start is **Adventures by the Sea** (299 Cannery Row, 831/372-1807, www.adventuresbythesea.com, daily 9 A.M.-sunset, tours $50 pp, rentals $30 per day). All-day kayak rentals allow you to choose your own route in and around the magnificent Monterey Bay. If you're not confident enough to go off on your own, the tour of Cannery Row (2.5 hours, $50 pp) is filled with wildlife sightings: harbor seals, sea otters, pelicans, seagulls, and dolphins. The sit-on-top tandem kayaks make it a great experience for school-age children. Also ask about the tour of Stillwater Cove at Pebble Beach for a whole new view of the world-class resort. Reservations are recommended for all tours, but during summer the Cannery Row tour leaves daily at 10 A.M. and 2 P.M., so you can stop by unannounced to see if there's a spot available.

Monterey Bay Kayaks (693 Del Monte Ave., 831/373-5357, www.montereybaykayaks. com, tours $50-60 pp) specializes in tours of both central Monterey and Elkhorn Slough to the north. You can choose between open-deck and closed-deck tour groups, beginning tours perfect for kids, romantic sunset or full-moon paddles, or even long paddles designed for more experienced sea kayakers. Check the website for specific tour prices, times, and reservation information. If you prefer to rent a kayak and explore the bay or Elkhorn Slough on your own, Monterey Bay Kayaks can set you up. If you really get into it, you can also sign up for closed-deck sea kayaking classes to learn about safety, rescue techniques, tides, currents, and paddling techniques.

AB Seas Kayaks of Monterey (32 Cannery Row, Suite 5, 831/647-0147, www.montereykayak.com, tours $60 pp, rentals $30 per day), also has plenty of sit-on-top single or double sea kayaks for rent, or take a tour of Monterey Bay with an experienced guide.

PARKS
El Estero
Everyone has a chance to be a kid where the world of Dennis the Menace comes to life. Nestled in the center of Monterey, the El Estero complex (Pearl St. and Camino El Estero, www.montery.org) is a multiuse recreation area that includes the Dennis the Menace

Park, perfect for tiny tikes. Teenage skaters tear up the skate park, and there is a ball park, fishing piers, an exercise course, and paddleboat rentals. Grab a bite at the El Estero Snack Bar, next to the steam engine.

Jacks Peak County Park
Within the city of Monterey, a ridge-top reserve awaits the outdoor addict. Hidden among thick pine forest, Jacks Peak County Park (25001 Jacks Peak Dr., off Hwy. 68, 831/372-8551, www.co.monterey.ca.us, $5) is a perfect escape for an afternoon ramble. Stunning wide views overlook Monterey Bay through the shaded woods.

The is an exceptional location for some hiking or horseback riding, with over eight miles of trails. There are picnic sites available, wildlife and foliage, and great photo ops.

BIKING
Bike Trails
Hopping on a bike and heading out to the **Monterey Bay Coastal Bike Trail** (www. mtycounty.com) is a fantastic way to take in the sights of the bay. As the trail runs through Monterey, it follows the shore of the bay through the sandy dunes, crosses Old Fisherman's Wharf, and leads into Pacific Grove. Ocean views are pretty much constant. The northern leg of the trail presents plenty of challenging hills, and anyone can enjoy the flat stretch from the Naval Postgraduate School to Asilomar State Beach. The full trail runs 29 miles from Castroville to Pebble Beach.

There are many paved and dirt trails in **Fort Ord Dunes State Park** (Hwy. 1 Lightfighter exit, 831/649-2836, www.parks.ca.gov, free). The trails roll through the dunes for miles, with many dirt paths branching off. Beware that this is the site of an old military base, and there may undetonated explosives in the area; stay on the trails and do not tamper with metal objects buried in the ground or in the sand.

There is also a newly opened paved bike trail beginning here that runs to Monterey. A nice alternative to the Monterey Bike Trail, it cuts through the dunes toward the ocean.

Bike Shops

A full-service bike shop that specializes in everything from BMX and triathlon to family fun is **Joselyn's Bicycles** (398 E. Franklin St., 831/649-8520, www.joselynsbicycles.com, Mon.-Fri. 9:30 A.M.-6 P.M., Sat. 9:30 A.M.-5 P.M., Sun. 11 A.M.-5 P.M., $20 per hour, half day $60, full day $100). Rent a road or mountain bike and check out Monterey from a new perspective.

In operation for 29 years is **Aquarian Bicycles** (486 Washington St., 831/375-2144, www.aquarianbicycles.com, Sun.-Mon. noon-5 P.M., Tues.-Sat. 10 A.M.-5:30 P.M., $8 per hour, 4 hours $24, 24 hours $36). It is not just about rentals here; it is a full-service shop with knowledgeable technicians.

Take the family to **Bay Bikes** (585 Cannery Row, 831/655-2453, www.baybikes.com) and put them on a surrey for a splendid ride to Lovers Point and beyond. Bay Bikes offer a full line of rental bikes, including surreys, tandem bikes, Trail-a-Bikes, street bikes, mountain bikes, and accessories.

GOLF

Yes, you can play golf in Monterey, and it's often much cheaper here than on the hallowed courses of Carmel or the pricey greens of Pebble Beach. The public **Monterey Pines Golf Course** (1250 Garden Rd., 831/656-2167, Mon.-Fri. $18-34, Sat.-Sun. $20-37) has 18 holes for a comparatively cheap greens fee. It's a short par-69 course with four levels of tee to make the game fun for players of all levels. Monterey Pines was originally built as a private Navy course for the pleasure of the officers at the major naval installation north of town; today, it is open to all. Call ahead for tee times.

A bit more pricey but still not Poppy Hills or Pebble Beach, **Del Monte Golf Course** (1300 Sylvan Rd., 831/373-2700, reservations 800/877-0597, www.pebblebeach.com, $195) is part of that legendary set of courses. This historic 18-hole, par-72 course, along with two other courses, still plays host to the Pebble Beach Invitational each year. You won't get the ocean views of Pebble Beach, but you will be treated to lovely green mountains surrounding the course as you play through. The property includes a full-service pro shop and the Del Monte Bar & Grill. You can check available tee times online, and then phone to book your preferred time.

Entertainment and Events

BARS AND CLUBS

The after-dark scene in Monterey is hopping: From downtown Alvarado Street to Cannery Row, there are several spot to quench your thirst and even get your groove on or enjoy some local bands.

A hip young hangout with a full bar and live entertainment is **The Mucky Duck** (479 Alvarado St., 831/655-3031, www.muckyduck-monterey.com, daily 11 A.M.-2 A.M.). Under new ownership, the digs have been upgraded with a new menu filled with local seafood and produce. The recent facelift is popular with locals, and the Duck is better than ever.

A favorite of locals and visitors alike is **Britannia Arms Pub and Restaurant** (444 Alvarado St., 831/656-9543, www.britanniaarmsofmonterey.com, daily 11 A.M.-2 A.M.), just the stop for a dark brew and a bite to eat. Look forward to local bands and DJs every Friday and Saturday night, and check out the game on one of the many TV screens.

A British-style pub known for aged bourbons and vintage ports is **Crown & Anchor** (150

W. Franklin St., 831/656-9543, www.crown-andanchor.net, daily 11 A.M.-2 A.M.). The best part of this pub is the patio, a perfect place to mingle throughout the day and into the night. The full food menu is served until midnight, and appetizers are available until closing time, making it a great late-night stop.

If you're looking for a modern disco, look no farther than the **Hippodrome** (321 Alvarado St., 831/262-2704, www.hippclub.com, Thurs.-Mon. 9 P.M.-2 A.M.) This is the place to get your groove on, with four dance floors, go-go cages, and 13 bar stations. An outside deck is the perfect cooling-off space to grab a smoke and a little conversation. Live bands frequent the stages, and DJs rock the night away year-round.

Grab a steak or feast on seafood while you sip a signature martini at **Lallapalooza** (474 Alvarado St., 831/645-9036, www.lallamonterey.com, daily 4 P.M.-midnight), a hip contemporary restaurant and bar with extra-large beers that locals flock here for on weekends. The large TV above the bar is great for game nights with friends.

Live music and dancing is what's happening at **Cibo Ristorante Italiano** (301 Alvarado St., 831/649-8151, www.cibo.com, Tues.-Sun. 7-10:30 P.M.). On Sunday night, dinner is always accompanied by the sweet sound of light jazz music. Things heat up the rest of the week, with dancing to Latin jazz, R&B, salsa, soul, funk, and swing. Both the decor and the menu are Italian, with soft Tuscan-yellow walls creating a nice environment for enjoying pizza, pastas, and scampi along with the music.

To shoot some pool, the **Blue Fin Café & Billiards** (685 Cannery Row, 831/717-4280, www.bluefinbillards.com, daily noon-2 A.M., table rates $12 per hour) is the place to be, with 11 tournament-size pool tables as well as arcade games, darts, and even a small dance floor. And for beer lovers, there are 16 draft varieties on tap.

There is never a cover charge at **Sly McFly's** (700 Cannery Row, 831/649-8050, www.slymcflys.net, daily 11:30 A.M.-2 A.M.). It is one of the best venues for live music on Cannery Row, bringing in a wide variety of artists, some very well known, to play rock, blues, and soul seven nights a week. The stage is small, and the ambience is a little tired, but the music and the crowds spill out into the streets.

If you want a late-night brew, the **Cannery Row Brewing Company** (95 Prescott Ave., 831/643-2722, www.canneryrowbrewingcompany.com, Mon.-Thurs. 11 A.M.-11 P.M., Fri.-Sun. 11 A.M.-midnight) is a choice spot, with nearly 75 beers on tap and 25 in bottles. The industrial decor and concrete floors give it a bit of a rough feel, and it can also be quite loud inside.

Live music on the weekends is on at **Captain Bullwackers Restaurant & Patio Pub** (653 Cannery Row, 831/373-1353, www.bullwackers.com, daily 11 A.M.-10:30 P.M. or later when busy). It typically features local bands playing a little of everything, so jam to reggae beats, rock out, or tap your foot to the blues. Inside is a full bar and restaurant, making it a great place to tip back a few and have a bite to eat. Do it Monterey style with a beer and a bowl of clam chowder.

Live bands rock the house Thursday-Saturday nights at **Jose's Underground Lounge** (638 Wave St., 831/655-4419, daily 11 A.M.-10 P.M. or later). The inside or outdoor seating is intimate to listen to rock, punk, and indie jams, and there is a full bar mixing drinks along with beer on tap and by the bottle.

A popular hangout where locals come to unwind with a few brews is **The British Bulldog** (611 Lighthouse Ave., 831/658-0686, daily 11:30 A.M.-2 A.M.), pouring several beers on tap and with a full bar. The bartenders are always friendly, and though the food isn't the best, if it's the last stop of the night, that won't matter much.

For a beer and great clam chowder, stop by the **London Bridges Pub** (Fisherman's Wharf 2, 831/372-0581, www.lbpmonterey.com, daily 11:30 A.M.-2 A.M.). Weekends heat up in the little pub with live music on Friday-Saturday night. You can take in views of the marina while tasting a bit of London flavor, and the outdoor patio and fire make it a great place to gather with friends or make some new ones.

ART GALLERIES

Housed in an old green-shingled home, the **Monterey Peninsula Art Foundation** (425 Cannery Row, 831/655-1267, daily 11 A.M.-5 P.M.) is a cooperative of about 30 local artists. Their pieces are in watercolors, acrylics, ceramics, jewelry, and sculpture. It's one of the few Monterey galleries that exhibits exclusively local art, and there is also a classy selection of greeting cards featuring works by the artists.

If you're looking for a piece depicting the Monterey area, **Venture Gallery** (260 Alvarado St., 831/372-6279, www.venturegallery.com, daily 10 A.M.-6 P.M.) is the place to go. It is owned and operated by local artists who specialize in capturing scenes of the Monterey Peninsula. The gallery is ever-changing as the artists manipulate a variety of media, including ceramics, sculptures, paintings, jewelry, and pottery.

Fine-art photography by Russell Levin can be found at the **Levin Gallery** (408 Calle Principal, 831/649-1166, www.russlevin.com, Mon.-Fri. 11 A.M.-4 P.M.). A California native and local photographer, Levin brings his love of art to Monterey. His passion lies in capturing people, action images, simple nudes, and environmental nudes. Come in for a look; you may want to take one of his works home with you.

If you have an interest in 19th-century photographs, **Willem Photographic** (426 Calle Principal, 831/648-1050, www.willemphotographic.com, Sat.-Sun. and by appointment) is the place to visit. The gallery contains an eclectic mix of 19th- and 20th-century photographs; artists include Ansel Adams, Norman Parkinson, Alvin Booth, and Ruth Orkin.

The place for Swarovski Crystal in Monterey is at **Crystal Fox Gallery** (381 Cannery Row, 831/655-3905, www.crystal-fox.com, Mon.-Sat. 10 A.M.-6 P.M., Sun. 10 A.M.-5 P.M.). It really is all about crystal and glass art. Enjoy the Richard Satava jellyfish, art glass sculptures, and bronzed sculptures, many with marine inspiration.

THEATER

For live performances, check out the **Bruce Ariss Wharf Theatre** (Old Fisherman's Wharf 1, 831/649-2332, www.mctaweb.org, $25 adults, $10 under age 13), which has been putting on lighthearted shows and musicals for 35 years, with occasional dramas and Broadway reviews. Community-based shows run Thursday-Friday evenings with a Sunday matinee.

If you are looking to catch an older film, you'll want to see what's playing at the **Golden State Theater** (417 Alvarado St., 831/372-4555, www.goldenstatetheater.com). What was once one of the coolest rock venues in the region has been restored and shows classic films like *Jaws* and *Indiana Jones*. The interior feels like a temple to cult classics.

A favorite among locals in the heart on Monterey's downtown district is the independent art theater **Osio 6 Cinema** (350 Alvarado St., 831/644-8171, www.osiocinemas.com), which has that small-town appeal and features mostly indie films in cozy theaters that seem to date back to the 1970s.

Located in the Del Monte Shopping Center is the **Century Cinemas** (1410 Del Monte Court, 800/326-3264, www.delmontecenter.com). A large state-of-the-art movie theater, it shows current wide-release films, including 3-D movies, with stadium seats and rocking chairs; there is good access for wheelchairs.

If you are looking for Extreme Digital Cinema, you are in luck: The **Cinemark Monterey Cannery Row XD** (640 Wave St., 831/372-4645, www.cinemark.com) is located in the heart of Monterey with two shows daily, an older movie and one of the latest blockbusters. The movie house is large with comfortable seating and an excellent picture.

FESTIVALS AND EVENTS

The Monterey region hosts numerous festivals and special events through the year. Whether your pleasure is fine food or funky music, you'll probably be able to plan a trip around a multiday festival with dozens of events and performances.

Spring

Celebrate the days of Dixieland and swing music with **Dixieland Monterey** (831/657-0298, www.dixieland-monterey.com). The three-day event is held at the Portola Hotel in early March and welcomes anyone who has a little rockabilly in them. Check out all the venues along Old Fisherman's Wharf and Downtown Monterey while you listen to local youth bands and top national jazz bands.

The weekend festival to catch in early April is the **Next Generation Jazz Festival** (831/373-3366, www.montereyjazzfestival.org, free) at the Monterey Fair Grounds. Sit back and be astonished as you're serenaded by all the up-and-coming young jazz musicians.

Come to the Monterey Bay Aquarium in late May for a food and wine adventure with **Cooking for Solutions** (831/644-7561, www.montereybayaquarium.org). One of the hottest tickets in town, this is an all-out fabulous event. World-renowned top chefs host live demonstrations in support of the aquarium's Seafood Watch program, and you get a chance to wander the aquarium's exhibits as you sample some fine sustainable dishes.

For two days in late May at the Monterey County Fairgrounds, the **Monterey Rock & Rod Festival** (831/649-0102, www.monterey-rockrod.com) is a classic and custom car show along with an oldies rock festival. The festival benefits the Gateway Center of Monterey County, a nonprofit serving the needs of developmentally disabled adults.

Summer

In keeping with the Central Coast's epicurean obsession, the annual **Monterey Wine Festival** (800/422-0251, www.montereywine.com) in early June has a number of tasting events during about a week, including a major event at the fairgrounds and a swank soiree at the Monterey Bay Aquarium. There are also a few private events and parties at participating wineries and restaurants. Check the website for this year's venues, dates, times, and ticket prices. The festival offers the perfect introduction to Monterey and Carmel wineries, many of which have not yet made big news in wine circles. The Wine Festival is just one of several similar events in the region each year, so if you can't make it, there are plenty of other opportunities to enjoy the area's best cuisine and vintages.

Beer fans can practice their skills at the **Monterey Beer Festival** (831/521-7921, www.nightthatneverends.com), also in early June, which features more than 70 breweries with tastings, live music, a short-film festival, and good grub. Held at the Monterey County Fairgrounds, tickets are $30 in advance and include all the beer you can drink.

In late June, blues lovers kick off the summer with a weekend at Monterey County Fairgrounds for the **Monterey Bay Blues Festival** (831/394-2652, www.montereyblues.com), a three-day event with a sizzling lineup of artists from around the world; visit the website for an update on the performers. The large venue has multiple stages for varied entertainment and plenty of space to walk around.

A much loved tradition in Monterey is the **Fourth of July Lawn Party** (831/624-2522, www.monterey.org). Locals and visitors make their way to the lush lawns of Colton Hall for this outdoor barbecue and live-music event that spills into the wider downtown area. Bring the family for a fun-filled day.

The Mazda Raceway U.S. Grand Prix attracts more than 5,000 riders to Laguna Seca, east of town, for high-speed battles in late July. Racers show off their goods in town at **Race**

Nights on the Row (www.canneryrow.com), when the streets fill with gleaming bikes and the restaurants and bars are hopping.

The summer jam tradition at the end of July is one of the largest reggae festivals in California, **Monterey Bay Reggaefest** (831/394-6534, www.mbayreggaefest.net), held at the Monterey County Fairgrounds. More than 25 bands, including star performers, dancers, and dancehall acts, take to the stages. The event is a family-friendly celebration, with an entire area set aside for kids to play, including a bouncy house and a giant slide.

The rich and fertile land of Monterey County has an ideal climate to cultivate grapes. At the mid-August **Winemaker's Celebration** (831/375-9400, www.montereywines.org), 45 local wineries come together at the Custom House Plaza to pour new releases and special vintages. It is a mellow way to spend the day at the historic plaza with fine wine, music, and food.

A nice way to end the summer is a visit to the **Monterey County Fair** (831/372-5863, www.montereycountyfair.com, $9 adults, $8 seniors, $5 children 6-12, free children 5 and under) in late August-early September. It is a nice outing for the whole family just before heading back to school. Held at the Monterey County Fairgrounds, there are carnival rides and games, livestock auctions, live music, face painting, and cotton candy. The local Costco in Sand City can provide discounted admission.

Fall

One of the biggest music festivals in California is the **Monterey Jazz Festival** (2000 Fairground Rd., 831/373-3366, www.montereyjazzfestival.org), which is also the longest-running jazz festival in the world, attracting top performers. Concerts are held over a long weekend each September—the month that offers the best chance for beautiful weather on Monterey Bay—at the Monterey County Fairgrounds, allowing visitors to enjoy all the

concerts without switching venues. Nine stages host acts day and night, making it easy to settle in for multiple acts or wander the grounds to sample performances at each venue.

History comes to life at the **Monterey HistoryFest** (831/372-2608, www.historicmonterey.org) at Custom House Plaza in October. The full-day event is a fun way for the whole family to experience the bay's lush historic resources and diverse cultural heritage.

The **Great Wine Escape** (831/375-9400, www.montereywines.org) in mid-November is hosted by the InterContinental Hotel Monterey to introduce guests to the thriving wines of Monterey County. There are food-and-wine integration seminars, live music, self-guided and narrated wine-country tours, and winery open houses.

Live music kicks off the holiday season in November during the **Cannery Row Tree Lighting Ceremony** (www.canneryrow.com). This annual event, held at Steinbeck Plaza, features the lighting of the tree accompanied by Santa Claus, so bring the little ones with their wish lists at the ready. This is a free event that the whole town enjoys and loves to share with visitors.

Winter

Get in the Christmas mood at the **Monterey Cowboy Poetry & Music Festival** (800/722-9652, www.montereycowboy.org) in early December at the Monterey Conference Center, an all-ages tribute to Monterey's Western heritage. Get geared up for live music, cowboy poetry, and the Christmas Western Art and Gear Show.

Christmas in the Adobes (831/649-7118, www.parks.ca.gov) in mid-December is a seasonal celebration with period dance lessons, cookies, refreshments, and games at 20 of the historic adobes, glowing with flickering candlelight and bagpipe music. Begin your journey at Custom House Plaza and walk the Path of History to enjoy the festive decorations.

Ring in the New Year on December 31 with

the **First Night in Monterey** (831/373-4778, www.firstnightmonterey.org), a celebration at Custom House Plaza in which more than 30 venues hold activities for adults and children. At midnight everyone moves to the plaza for the special moment.

Shopping

DOWNTOWN MONTEREY

Officially known as Alvarado Mall, **The Portola Plaza Mall** (Portola Plaza and Alvarado St.) has many specialty shops in the open air on either side of the promenade. There are several independent clothing stores, jewelry shops, art galleries, wine and gift shops, restaurants, brewpubs, a spa, and more. Many of the shops are independent.

Lizzie G and Me Boutique (490 Alvarado St., 831/373-3100, www.lizzigandme.com, daily 10:30 A.M.-5:30 P.M.) carries women's goodies like handbags, jewelry, jeans, dresses, and suits. Lizzie G is always up for the challenge of helping you find what you're looking for.

If you want to go home with a nice bottle of wine or do a little afternoon tasting, stop in at **Wine from the Heart** (241 Alvarado St., 831/641-9463, www.winefromtheheart. com, daily 10 A.M.-6 P.M.), which specializes in California and Monterey wines from small family wineries, artisanal wineries, and limited-edition or small-production vintages. They also carry gourmet foods and gifts, and you can put together elegant gift baskets.

A fine shop to search for treasure is **Monterey Antiques** (449 Alvarado St., 831/372-5221, daily 11 A.M.-4:30 P.M.). New riches are constantly being brought in, so no two visits are the same. Buying large and small estates, they fill the store with fine period furniture, jewelry, rugs, art, coins, bronzes, and other collectables.

Monterey presents a plethora of photography opportunities, and the place to pick up photography equipment is at **Green's Camera World** (472 Alvarado St., 831/655-1234, www. greenscameraworld.com, daily 10 A.M.-6 P.M.).

Green's provides photo preservation, canvas printing, greeting cards, repairs, and equipment rentals and is also a source for prints, from wallet-size to posters, all on high-quality paper.

DEL MONTE CENTER

For the mall scene, head to Munras Avenue and Del Monte Center (1410 Del Monte Center, 831/373-2705, www.shopdelmonte.com, Mon.-Fri. 10 A.M.-9 P.M., Sat. 10 A.M.-7 P.M., Sun. 11 A.M.-5 P.M.), a chic outdoor mall with fountains placed among the heavy hitters like Macy's, Williams-Sonoma, Century Theaters, Victoria's Secret, the Apple Store, Whole Foods, and Forever 21. With over 75 stores on 675,000 square feet, you can get your shopping on in this parklike setting; trendy dining and coffee shops abound as well.

OLD FISHERMAN'S WHARF

As in the past, Monterey is still about fishing, but today the prey are the two-legged type. Using beach souvenirs and saltwater taffy as bait, Old Fisherman's Wharf (Fisherman's Wharf 1, www.montereywharf.com) nets visitors with tightly packed stores flanking creaky wooden planks.

The **Harbor House** (1 Fisherman's Wharf 1, 831/372-4134, www.montereywharf.com, daily 10 A.M.-10 P.M.) can be seen all the way from the parking lot, a bright-pink building at the entrance to the Wharf. Inside, tiny trinkets and goodies wait for a good home. In business since 1950, it is a traditional stop for returning visitors.

For swashbuckling sailors, **Pirates Cove Gifts and Things** (42 Fisherman's Wharf 1, 831/372-6688, daily 10 A.M.-10 P.M.) is the place to make port and secure that Jolly Roger T-shirt or warm Monterey sweatshirt.

As the fog comes and goes unpredictably in Monterey, an extra layer of clothing is always a good idea. Stay warm and pick up a souvenir at the **Ocean Front Sea and Tree Gallery** (15 Fisherman's Wharf 1, 831/649-6426, daily 10 A.M.-10 P.M.), with a comfy selection of fleeces, perfect protection from the chill.

Kids of all ages will love the handcrafted sweets at **Carousel Candies** (31 Fisherman's Wharf 1, 831/646-9801, www.carouselcandies. com, daily 10 A.M. 10 P.M.), serving up candy on the Wharf since 1960 and specializing in chocolates, caramel apples, and saltwater taffy.

CANNERY ROW AND LIGHTHOUSE AVENUE

Like sardines in a can, Cannery Row (www. canneryrow.com) and Lighthouse Avenue are crammed with shopping possibilities. More than 85 stores carry everything from home decor to souvenir key chains. Clothing shops feature beachwear and Monterey-branded garments.

On the border of Monterey and Pacific Grove is the **American Tin Cannery** (125 Ocean View Blvd., 831/372-1442, www.americantincannery.com), a retail and entertainment center with over 20 merchants that include Reebok, Rockport, Factory Brands Shoes, Mr. Z's Fine Jewelry, and Captain Ben's Antiques.

If you're looking for a killer shark T-shirt, **Sharky's Shirts** (685 Cannery Row, 831/655-0743, daily 10 A.M.-10 P.M.) is the place to shop. It is bursting with everything shark-themed, such as hilarious T-shits and tiny shark trinkets. You can also purchase a light jacket at a decent price if you're feeling the damp chill.

Treasures of Monterey (700 Cannery Row, Suite H1, 831/375-1437, daily 10 A.M.-10 P.M.) has postcards, shot glasses, key chains, and magnets.

Across the street from the Aquarium with a pirate guarding the door is **Mackerel Jacks Trading Company** (799 Cannery Row, 831/655-2399, daily 9 A.M.-7:30 P.M.), carrying everything from treasure maps to books on local folklore. There is an extensive collection of local books, T-shirts, shells, rubber sharks, and plenty of Jolly Roger flags.

If you're looking for antiques, the **Cannery Row Antique Mall** (471 Wave St., 831/655-0264, Mon.-Fri. 10 A.M.-5:30 P.M., Sat. 10 A.M.-6 P.M., Sun. 10 A.M.-5 P.M.) combines 150 vendors in a massive two-story warehouse filled with sterling silver, vintage dolls, china, and furniture in mission, country, and art deco styles.

For nautical fashions, look no farther than **Monterey Bay Boatworks Company** (400 Cannery Row, 831/643-9482, daily 10 A.M.-7 P.M.), where you can find fairly conservative men's and women's resort wear with a nautical bent from names like Tommy Bahama and Bugatchi. There are also hats, sweaters, books, and gifts.

One of the many places selling clothing with Monterey and California motifs is **California Classics** (750 Cannery Row, 831/324-0528, daily 9 A.M.-9 P.M.), where you can buy souvenir sweatshirts and T-shirts.

Don't forget to stop by **Book Buyers** (600 Lighthouse Ave., 831/375-4208, www.bookbuyers.com) on Lighthouse Avenue. Sadly, it is one of the last independent used bookstores in the area. There are over 30,000 titles in hardbacks and paperbacks. The tight maze of books is a surprisingly well-organized and diverse selection that includes a large children's section.

Accommodations

CAMPING

Within the City of Monterey are a few out-of-the-way campgrounds that welcome tents, RVs, and trailers. **Monterey Veteran's Memorial Park** (Veterans Dr. and Skyline Dr., 831/646-3865, www.monterey.org, $27, first-come, first-served) is located one mile up the hill from Cannery Row and Fisherman's Wharf in a quiet spot with wide views of the bay. Within the 50-acre park are hiking trails, a playground, a basketball court, picnic areas, barbecue pits, lawn areas, restrooms, and a dump station.

A little-known spot to park the RV with full hookups is the **Monterey County Fairgrounds RV Camping** (2004 Fairgrounds Rd., 831/372-5863, www.montereycountyfair.com, $40), a lovely spot if you're coming for an event at the fairgrounds or just want to get away from the crowds.

CANNERY ROW
Under $150

The **Monterey Hostel** (778 Hawthorne St., 831/649-0375, http://montereyhostel.com, $23-64) offers inexpensive accommodations within walking distance of the aquarium, Cannery Row, and the Monterey Bay Coastal Bike Trail. Rates include a pancake breakfast every morning, linens are included with your bed, and there are casual common spaces with couches, musical instruments, and monthly potluck dinners with guest speakers. There's no laundry on-site, and the dorms can be crowded, so if you like a little space, opt for a private room.

Slightly inland from Steinbeck's infamous factories is the **Cannery Row Inn** (200 Foam St., 831/649-8580, www.canneryrowinn.com, $89-399). It is well within walking distance of historic Cannery Row, Old Fisherman's Wharf, and downtown, making it a great base. Overlook Monterey Bay from a modern guest room with a private balcony and enjoy free Wi-Fi.

In the heart of Cannery Row is the charming Victorian **Best Western Victorian Inn** (487 Foam St., 831/373-8000, www.victorianinn.com, $99-599). Guest rooms are equipped with marble fireplaces and private balconies, patios, or window seats. Check out the various package deals that can include tickets to local attractions like the aquarium.

Clean and centrally located on the north end of Cannery Row is the **Holiday Inn Express Cannery Row** (443 Wave St., 831/372-1800, www.hiexpress.com, $139-399). The breakfast bar, with hot and cold items, is included, a great way to save on dining.

$150-250

Be sure to call in advance to get a room at the popular **Jabberwock Inn** (598 Laine St., 831/372-4777, www.jabberwockinn.com, $169-299), a favorite with frequent visitors to Monterey. This *Alice in Wonderland*-themed B&B is both whimsical and elegant; expect to find a copy of an *Alice* novel in your tastefully appointed guest room. Be sure to take the owners up on their daily wine-and-cheese reception in the afternoon-they have extensive information about the area and will be happy to recommend restaurants and activities for all tastes. Although it is located up a steep hill, the Jabberwock is within walking distance of Cannery Row and its adjacent attractions, and it's worth the extra exercise to avoid the cost and hassle of parking in the crowded visitor lots.

Guest rooms at the European-style **Spindrift Inn** (652 Cannery Row, 831/646-8900, www.insofmonterey.com, $199-459) are cozy and have wood-burning fireplaces and king canopy beds. Enjoy the nightly wine-and-cheese reception that features local wines before you head out for the evening. Within walking distance is plenty to keep you busy day and night.

Over $250

To stay right on Cannery Row in a guest room

overlooking the bay, you'll pay handsomely, but it's worth it at the **Monterey Plaza Hotel & Spa** (400 Cannery Row, 831/646-1700, www.montereyplazahotel.com, $250-3,500). The atmosphere is traditionally elegant and comfortable, and views of the ocean are the centerpiece from the moment you enter the lobby plaza. Guest rooms are spacious, and many have ocean views and balconies. There is a relaxing spa and four restaurants on-site.

The **InterContinental Clement Monterey** (750 Cannery Row, Monterey, 831/375-4500, www.ichotelsgroup.com, $250-1,300) is a comfortable minimalist hideaway. The modernist Asian-inspired interior belies the pragmatic Cannery Row exterior. Tiles and wood blend with fabric and inset rugs to create a dynamic play of materials and surfaces that honor the cannery past. Every guest room has its own orchids, and the furnishings are clean and sleek. There are 110 rooms on the bay side and another 98 on the inland side, connected by a covered walking bridge. The hotel includes a full-service spa, a Kids Club with supervised day care so parents can slip away for a while, and a 350-car covered garage. This is the newest and probably last oceanfront hotel that will be built on Cannery Row due to stringent building regulations.

DOWNTOWN MONTEREY
Under $150

A small cute budget motel, the **Monterey Bay Lodge** (55 Camino Aguajito, 831/372-8057, www.montereybaylodge.com, $79-349) brings a bit of the Côte d'Azur to the equally beautiful coastal town of Monterey. With small guest rooms decorated in classic yellows and blues, a sparkling pool with a fountain in the shallow end, and an on-site restaurant serving breakfast and lunch, the Lodge makes a perfect base for budget-minded families.

A European-style property that has been updated as a modern hotel with a turn-of-the-20th-century handcrafted ambiance is the **Monterey Hotel** (406 Alvarado St., 831/375-3184, www.montereyhotel.com, $89-309). Built in 1904, the hotel is elegantly furnished with pieces from that era, and the guest rooms and suites have been lavishly restored.

Offering guests amenities that are a cut above a standard beach-town motel is the **Colton Inn** (707 Pacific St., 831/649-6500, www.coltoninn.com, $99-279), located in the middle of downtown Monterey. The queen and king guest rooms boast attractive fabrics, designer baths, and pretty appointments. While you'll find restaurants and historic adobe buildings adjacent to the Colton, expect to drive or take public transit to Cannery Row and the aquarium.

A historic hotel in the center of downtown is the **Casa Munras Hotel and Spa** (700 Munras Ave., 831/375-2411, www.hotelcasamunras.com, $129-449), a beautifully restored building and one of the sights on the Path of History. There is an outdoor heated pool, a fitness center, and bikes available to borrow. Look forward to relaxing after a long day of exploration at the spa and restaurant.

Ocean views downtown can be found at the **Monterey Marriott Hotel** (350 Calle Principal, 831/649-4234, www.marriotthotels.com, $109-320), which is within walking distance to nightlife on Alvarado Street and Old Fisherman's Wharf. Guest rooms are sizable, and the property has a relaxing spa.

Within driving distance of Cannery Row and downtown is the **Best Western De Anza** (2141 Freemont St., 831/646-8300, www.bestwesterncalifornia.com, $79-389), one of the least expensive and nicest hotels in town. Located away from the touristed parts of town, you can get a taste of local life. The 43 guest rooms have microwaves, fridges, and coffeemakers, and there's an outdoor heated pool and hot tub.

Closer to the ocean, the **Inn at Del Monte Beach** (1110 Del Monte Blvd., 831/655-0515, www.theinnatdelmontebeach.com, $66-120) offers 15 guest rooms in a unique boutique property with a 1960s-meets-beaux arts feel. Amenities include Wi-Fi in the guest rooms, DVD players, electric fireplaces, a full breakfast in the communal dining room, afternoon tea, and wine and cheese in the early evening on the deck overlooking the Pacific, all included in the room rates. You can park on the street or pay a small fee for the valet. A nice rooftop deck offers great views to the bay and downtown, which is just a five-block walk.

$150-250

Minutes from Monterey's primary attractions is the **Hotel Pacific** (300 Pacific St., 831/373-5700, www.hotelpacific.com, $159-429). All the guest rooms are luxurious suites with fireplaces in an authentic Spanish-style adobe. With its lovely gardens it may exceed your expectations, and it is one of the few pet-friendly hotels on the peninsula. It makes a great getaway for a romantic weekend.

Although the ◖ **Portola Hotel** (2 Portola Plaza, 831/649-4511, www.portolahotel.com, $189-550) is a big hotel, it feels smaller. About 40 percent of its 379 guest rooms offer prime views of the bay. There is also an on-site fitness room, a large round outdoor pool, and a hot tub. The hotel is conveniently located between downtown and Cannery Row; the walk downtown is about five minutes, and to Cannery Row about 20 minutes along the coast (more if you stop to watch the sea lions). The guest rooms and baths are large and comfortable with in-room coffeemakers and fridges on request. Many packages include local restaurants and attractions, but parking and Wi-Fi cost extra.

An escape from the heavy summer traffic and a short drive to Cannery Row, downtown, and Old Fisherman's Wharf is the **Hyatt Regency Monterey Hotel and Spa on Del Monte Golf Course** (1 Old Golf Course Rd., 831/372-1234, www.hyattregencymonterey.com, $99-2,500). You can experience the luxury of Monterey with newly renovated guest rooms and a seductive spa. Bring your golf clubs, as the fairways are just steps from your room.

Over $250

Monterey visitors looking for elegant accommodations will love the ◖ **Old Monterey Inn** (500 Martin St., 831/375-8284, www.oldmontereyinn.com, $250-449). The lovely old building stands in mature gardens that blossom all spring and summer, showing their sedate green side in fall and winter. Inside, the garden motif echoes in the upscale bed linens and window treatments that complement the pretty furnishings and cozy fireplaces. Spa bathtubs pamper guests. Additional amenities include a full breakfast (often served in the garden) and a menu of spa treatments that can be enjoyed downstairs in the serene treatment room.

Food

The organic and sustainable food movements have caught on in the Central Coast region, with many eateries serving local produce and sustainable seafood. The Monterey Bay Aquarium is a leader in this movement, creating the Seafood Watch program (www.montereybayaquarium.org), a definitive resource for consuming sustainable seafood.

CANNERY ROW AND OLD FISHERMAN'S WHARF
American

For coffee, espresso, and home-baked beignets, head to the delightful little ◖ **Trailside Café** (550 Wave St., 831/649-8600, www.trailsidecafe.com, daily 8 A.M.-4 P.M., $15-20). This Cannery Row restaurant offers breakfast, lunch, and dinner on a heated patio overlooking the bay.

◖ Jacks (2 Portola Plaza, 831/649-2698, www.portolahotel.com, daily 6-10:30 A.M., 11:30 A.M.-2 P.M., and 5-9 P.M., $30) is located in the Portola Plaza Hotel and Spa and serves up a fresh California coastal fare with sustainable ingredients. Dine fireside on the outdoor patio or enjoy the nautically themed interior.

Cheap Eats

On the far south end of Cannery Row, the **Cannery Row Delicatessen** (101 Drake St., 831/645-9549, daily 7 A.M.-5 P.M., $10) offers massive breakfast burritos stuffed with eggs, chorizo, and potatoes as well as pancakes; lunch options like tuna melts and tofu pita; and hot and iced coffee drinks. The space is tiny, with just three small tables, but the wooden deck outside facing the bike path and surrounded by ivy makes for a nice respite.

The **Fishhopper** (700 Cannery Row, 831/372-8543, www.fishhopper.com, daily 10:30 A.M.-8 P.M., $10), a to-go chowder cart, is the spot to grab a fresh fruit cup, ceviche, prawns and cocktail sauce, and, of course, clam chowder in a bread bowl. Take your food down to the beach for a picnic.

Open for breakfast, lunch, and dinner is **Loulou's Griddle in the Middle** (Old Fisherman's Wharf 2, 831/372-0568, Mon. 7:30 A.M.-3 P.M., Tues.-Sun. 7:30 A.M.-7:30 P.M., $10). A quaint hut on the Wharf 2, Loulou's serves local treats like fresh seafood and produce. The attire is casual, and the kids will love the chocolate-chip pancakes.

The place to indulge in authentic Breton-style French crepes is on Old Fisherman's Wharf at **◖ Crepes of Brittany** (6B Old Fisherman's Wharf 1, 831/601-4847, www.vivelacrepemonterey.com, daily 8:30 A.M.-about 4 P.M., $10). Whether it's sweet or savory, they are made to satisfy. Grab a seat outside, marvel at the sleepy seals as the tide pushes in, and listen to the mast bells of the sailboats chime.

French

You'll think you're in France at the **Bistro Moulin** (867 Wave St., 831/333-1200, www.bistromoulin.com, daily 5-9 P.M., $20). Just steps away from the Monterey Bay Aquarium, it is a true European bistro with intimate tables, a casual environment, and a menu that includes classics like coq au vin, crepes, and pâté. The wine list showcases the local wineries but has a good selection of French wines too.

Fusion

The Duck Club Grill (400 Cannery Row, 831/646-1706, daily 6:30 A.M.-9:30 P.M., $30) feels like a comfortable club where you want to become a member. Low-backed wooden chairs and wood accents don't distract from the views of the bay. The menu is limited mainly to fish and meat entrées. Start with the tuna *poke* tacos with a wasabi mayo dipping sauce; it comes with avocado and ginger in a crispy sesame taco and has a nice kick to it. Follow the terrific clam chowder, made with heavy cream and sherry, with the flagship roast duck, glazed four times with a soy, ginger, and *yuzu* sauce. Consider a cocktail like the Patio Boss, the powerful signature margarita voted "Best in the Bay" in a local magazine poll.

A tropical Hawaiian fusion restaurant in the heart of Monterey is **Hula's Island Grill** (622 Lighthouse Ave., 831/655-4852, www.hulas-tiki.com, Tues.-Sat. 11:30 A.M.-4 P.M., Sun.-Mon. from 4:30 P.M., $30), known for featuring island fish, prime steaks, juicy burgers, and creative salads. There is a full bar that features fruity cocktails that come with a heavy punch.

Mediterranean

Appetizing aromas greet you as you walk in the door at the **Persian Grill** (675 Lighthouse Ave., 831/372-3720, www.persiangril.com, Wed.-Mon. 11:30 A.M.-2 P.M. and 5:30-9:30 P.M., $20). Potent kebabs, lamb, walnut stew, feta cheese, herbs, and stuffed grape leaves are augmented by traditional belly dancing Friday-Saturday night, adding to the authentic atmosphere.

Amir's Kabob House (794 Lighthouse Ave., 831/642-0231, lunch Mon.-Sat. 11:30 A.M.-2 P.M., dinner daily 5-9 P.M., $15-35) has a variety of kebabs that will tempt everyone. Check out the belly dancers on Saturday night.

Seafood

Kicking off the resurgence of Cannery Row over four decades ago and still a must-stop is **(** **The Sardine Factory** (701 Wave St., 831/373-3775, www.sardinefactory.com, daily 5 P.M.-midnight, $40-50). There are several dining rooms: The Captain's Room pays tribute to brave sailors, the Conservancy is a glass room surrounded by greenery, and the Wine Cellar is the more exclusive private dining room downstairs. The abalone bisque, served at both of Ronald Reagan's presidential inauguration dinners, is a must, and the fish entrées are tremendous; consider Alaskan salmon topped with artichoke hearts and hollandaise sauce. Wine enthusiasts won't be disappointed, as the Sardine Factory has received many awards for its impressive wine list from a collection of over 35,000 bottles. The cellar below the dining room includes the only vertical collection of Inglenook cabernet sauvignons from 1949 to 1958 (No, you can't buy them, but you can take a peek.) Nearby are the private wine lockers of Clint Eastwood and Arnold Schwarzenegger, among others, who have their wines pulled out when they dine here. Desserts are simple: Skip the ice cream, take the cannoli.

If sushi is more to your liking, **(** **Crystal Fish** (514 Lighthouse Ave., 831/649-3474, lunch Mon.-Fri. 11:30 A.M.-2 P.M., dinner daily 5-9 P.M., $25) is the place. From rolls to *nigiri* and sashimi, the fish is fresh and artfully prepared and served, and there is a selection of vegetarian rolls. There are noodles and tempura as well, but stick with the sushi and you won't go wrong. The *bento* boxes are a nice size and provide a sampling of everything.

The newest addition to the Cannery Row dining scene is also one of the best: **C Restaurant** (750 Cannery Row, 831/375-4500, www.thecrestaurant-monterey.com, daily 6:30 A.M.-10 P.M., $25). The sleek minimalist interior offers unencumbered views of the bay. The clean lines also extend to the menu, heavy on seafood but also including rack of lamb and pasta mixed with local sardines. The lobster bisque is the creamiest you'll find in the county. Also worthwhile is the angel-hair pasta with local red abalone, harvested just steps from the restaurant. All of the fish is sustainable in accordance with the Monterey Bay Aquarium's seafood watch list, and fresh local ingredients rotate seasonally.

Located in one of the original sardine cannery buildings, **The Fish Hopper** (700 Cannery Row, 831/372-8543, www.fishhopper.com, daily 10:30 A.M.-9 P.M., $25) is right over the bay with a great deck that gets crowded quickly. Fifteen daily specials include fresh fish, pasta, and steaks; there is also a sizable kids menu.

For some fine steaks and seafood, make reservations at the **(** **Whaling Station Restaurant** (763 Wave St., 831/373-3778, www.whalingstationmonterey.com, dinner daily 5-9:30 P.M., $35-45). John Pisto, an international TV chef, brings his talents to Monterey with a casually sophisticated dining experience. The Whaling Station is famous for its beautiful thick cuts of meat, and waitstaff brings a tray of the cuts around to tempt the carnivores.

A reliable Wharf staple for both seafood and the views over the harbor is the **Old Fisherman's Grotto** (39 Fisherman's Wharf, 831/375-4604, daily 11 A.M.-10 P.M., $35). The menu focuses on fresh seafood and Italian standards, and the restaurant has a full bar. If you sample it outside, you may be lured in by the signature clam chowder.

With a fresh Italian spin on seafood with prime steaks, **Domenico's on the Wharf** (50 Fisherman's Wharf, 831/372-3655, www.

domenicosmonterey.com, daily 10:30 A.M.-10 P.M., $30) is all about the panoramic view of the harbor. It features locally caught seafood and fresh local produce from the owner's farm.

DOWNTOWN MONTEREY
American

Housed in an old firehouse, 【 **Montrio** (414 Calle Principal, 831/648-8880, www.montrio.com, 4:30 P.M. till close, $15-20) has high ceilings, graceful curved walls, and custom lighting. The menu emphasizes local sustainable and organic food in dishes like artichoke ravioli, seared diver scallops on parsnip puree, rosemary-roasted portobello mushroom, and the legendary crab cakes. It gets very busy and so can be noisy; reservations are recommended. Ask about the dinner-and-a-movie deal and catch a flick at the Osio Theater afterward.

Locals love the family atmosphere of 【 **Rosines Restaurant** (434 Alvarado St., 831/375-1400, www.rosinesmonterey.com, daily 8 A.M.-9 P.M., $10-15). It is the place for large plates and a menu that has a bit of everything. You can't leave without sharing a piece of cake, layered a mile high, which will catch your eye on the way to your table.

A good old American burger joint is 【 **r.g. Burgers** (570 Munras Ave., 831/372-4930, www.rgburgers.com, daily 11 A.M.-8 P.M., $15). Make it a frosty shake and a double cheese burger, or try one of the more creative combinations from the all-embracing menu. The setting is comfortable, and dress is casual.

A hip hangout with a modern contemporary feel is **Lallapalooza** (474 Alvarado St., 831/645-9036, www.lalla-palooza.com, daily 4 P.M.-midnight, $30). It features an all-American menu that includes steaks, seafood, and Monterey's best martini. They tend to cater to a younger crowd, and it is a good place for elegant late-night eats, as food is served until midnight.

Wild Plum Café and Bakery (731 Munras Ave., Suite B, 831/646-3109, Mon.-Fri.

7 A.M.-7 P.M., Sat. 7 A.M.-5:30 P.M., $25) focuses on breakfast and lunch and has some of the finest quick organic eats in town. There is limited seating inside and a few tables on the sidewalk, so it may have to be a grab-and-go stop.

Breakfast

For 60 years people have been coming to **Reds Donuts** (433 Alvarado St., 831/372-9761, daily 6:30 A.M.-1:30 P.M., $2) in downtown Monterey to grab an old fashioned, a bear claw, or any of 20 other varieties. This is a local classic, with old yellow Formica countertops, simple stools, and walls lined with old photos and paintings of clowns. There are no complex coffee drinks or French pastries-nothing but doughnuts and basic coffee. Sometimes all you need is a glazed doughnut to go.

Around the corner is the **East Village Coffee Lounge** (498 Washington St., 831/373-5601, daily 7 A.M.-9 P.M., $7), which has a comfortable lounge vibe as well as outdoor seating. There are plenty of coffee and tea drinks, and they use organic milk. Pastry options include a tasty and moist chocolate scone and organic peach coffeecake. Parfaits, ham and cheese croissants, and tomato and basil panini are also available. Free Wi-Fi means lots of people hunker down with their laptops.

British

About as British as it gets in downtown Monterey is the 【 **Crown and Anchor** (150 W. Franklin St., 831/649-6496, www.crownandanchor.net, daily 11 A.M.-2 A.M., $12). It is located below street level, and as you walk downstairs you'll see walls lined with images of kings, queens, lords, and guns. Twenty British and international beers are on tap to complement lamb shanks, cottage pie, corned beef and cabbage, and, of course, fish-and-chips. It's very popular with a mainly older local crowd.

Britannia Arms Pub and Restaurant (444 Alvarado St., 831/656-9543, www.britanniaarmsofmonterey.com, daily 11 A.M.-2 A.M.,

$15) is the pub to stop in for a dark brew and a bite to eat. Watch the game on one of the many TVs tuned to various sports year-round, as enjoy the 24 different draft beers, ales, and hard ciders available.

Cheap Eats

Have a little taste of Italy right near Cannery Row at the **Pino's Café** (211 Alvarado St., 831/649-1930, daily 6:30 A.M.-9 P.M., $8), with daily-changing pasta dishes and traditional salads like chicken and tuna as well as Italian meatball, salami, and turkey sandwiches. They also have 16 different kinds of gelato. The simple interior makes it a great spot for kids or for a grab-and-go breakfast.

For a quick cheap bite, try the **Old Monterey Café** (489 Alvarado St., 831/646-1021, daily 6:46 A.M.-2:30 P.M., $10). The café is known to college kids for its filling breakfast and casual

© KRISTIN LEAL

At the local farmers markets, fresh artichokes are a delight.

atmosphere. Sit back and enjoy the cozy cottage decor and friendly service, or get food to take out.

Visit **Paris Bakery** (271 Bonifacio Place, 831/646-1620, daily 6 A.M.-6 P.M., $8) for real French pastries, just the place to jump-start your morning with an espresso and stuffed croissant. They also serve a fast lunch that you can take to go, or eat in the bustling café. Kids will love the large selection of colorful sweets.

Making tasty New York-style bagels and pleasant breakfast sandwiches in downtown Monterey is the **Bagel Bakery** (452 Alvarado St., 831/372-5242, daily 6 A.M.-5 P.M., $3). The staff are always friendly, and the coffee is perking all day. It is a great place for a pick-me-up breakfast or afternoon snack.

Tantalize your taste buds at the lunch buffet at **Ambrosia Indian Bistro** (565 Abrego St., 831/641-0610, www.ambrosiaib.com, daily 11:30 A.M.-close, $10, Sun. lunch buffet $12), one of the best deals in town. The Sunday brunch buffet includes champagne or another beverage. Regular dishes include flavorful butter chicken and tandoori chicken, and vegetarians will find many options.

Mexican

The colorful cafeteria-style eatery **Turtle Bay Taqueria** (431 Tyler St., 831/333-1500, daily 11 A.M.-9 P.M., $13) focuses on the cuisine and flavors of coastal Mexico with a focus on seafood. You'll find Yucatán-style soups, charbroiled tilapia, *carnitas,* tacos, and burritos. The very good salsa, as well as the Mayan chocolate mousse, are made in-house.

Seafood

Seafood choices downtown are limited, since much of the seafood action is at Old Fisherman's Wharf and Cannery Row. Located north of downtown and away from the touristed area, **Monterey's Fish House** (2114 Del Monte Ave., 831/373-4647, lunch daily 11:30 A.M.-2:30 P.M., dinner Mon.-Fri.

5-9:30 P.M., $20) has long been a local favorite, serving up sole, oysters, calamari, and swordfish. The best versions of any of the fish are oak-grilled and have a delicate smoky note. Reservations are a good idea, and the tiny dining room ensures a social atmosphere.

Spanish

Inside the Casa Munras Hotel is **Estéban** (700 Munras Ave., 831/375-0176, daily 5-10 P.M., $18). It focuses on tapas (small plates) and has many other choices: Traditional Spanish serrano ham shares the spotlight with crab cakes, chorizo dishes, and paella. Dining outdoors in the large wood chairs near the fire pit is best, but the interior, all sleek and sophisticated, offers views of the kitchen.

FARMERS MARKETS

Showcasing more than 50 farmers and other vendors is the **Monterey Peninsula College**

Farmers Market (980 Fremont St., www. montereybayfarmers.org, year-round Thurs. 2:30-6:30 P.M.), with fresh produce, flowers, and plants.

At Monterey Peninsula College is the **Monterey Farmers Market** (930 Fremont St., www.montereybayfarmers.org, year-round Fri. 10 A.M.-2 P.M.), founded in 1978 and currently featuring 49 local farmers and other vendors with a bountiful selection of produce and flowers.

Three blocks of Alvarado Street close to traffic for the ◖**Old Monterey Market Place** (Alvarado St., 831/655-8070, www.oldmonterey.org, winter Tues. 4-7 P.M., summer Tues. 4-8 P.M.). The street fills with an organic rainbow of vendors and shoppers with over 150 stands lining the street. Produce vendors from all over California have sold their certified organic goods here, rain or shine, since 1991.

Information and Services

VISITOR INFORMATION

In Monterey, the **El Estero Visitors Center** (401 Camino El Estero, 877/MONTEREY, www.montereyinfo.org, summer: Mon.-Sat. 9 A.M.-6 P.M., Sun. 9 A.M.-5 P.M., winter: 9 A.M.-5 P.M., Sun. 10 A.M.-4 P.M.) is the local outlet of the Monterey Country Convention and Visitors Bureau. They put out a comprehensive annual guide to Monterey County; you can download the guide from the website or call the office to have one mailed. They also have loads of local flyers promoting many local business and activities.

MEDIA AND COMMUNICATIONS

The local newspaper is the *Monterey County Herald* (www.montereyherald.com), a daily that has a weekly "Go" section featuring all

the current local happenings. The *Monterey County Weekly* (www.montereycountyweekly. com) is the alternative paper for area happenings, with a "Club Grind" section and a daily events calendar. It also features local news, sports, art, and entertainment.

Looking to send those majestic postcards? **Post offices** are located at 565 Hartnell Street and at 686 Lighthouse Avenue.

MEDICAL AND EMERGENCY SERVICES

The **Community Hospital of the Monterey Peninsula** (CHOMP, 23625 Hwy. 68/Holman Hwy., 831/624-5311) provides emergency services to the area. Open daily 24 hours is the **Monterey Police Department** (3151 Madison St., 831/646-3914). In case of emergency, dial 911.

MONTEREY

Getting There and Around

GETTING THERE

By Car

Having a car while you're in Monterey is key if you want to discover the outlying areas on your own schedule. Most visitors drive to Monterey via the scenic Highway 1. Twenty miles inland, U.S. 101 runs north-south through Salinas. From Salinas, Highway 68 runs west to Monterey.

If you are coming from San Jose (1.5 hours), take U.S. 101 south to Highway 156 west. Turn south at Highway 1 toward the Monterey Peninsula. From San Francisco (2.5 hours), another option is to take U.S. 101 south to San Jose, then Highway 85 south, and then Highway 17 south toward Santa Cruz. Eventually you merge on to Highway 1 heading south to Monterey.

From Los Angeles (6 hours), head north on U.S. 101. As you approach Salinas, from the Spreckels exit merge onto Abbott Street, turn left on Blanc Road, and then head left on Main Street (Highway 68) west to Monterey.

To make your way to Big Sur (45 minutes) from Monterey, take Highway 1 south for about 30 miles. The route to Santa Cruz (50 minutes) from Monterey is easy: Take Highway 1 north all the way. You can get off at the Santa Cruz exit, where you can head to the beach or farther north toward Half Moon Bay.

RV Rentals

The RV rentals closest to Monterey are in Santa Cruz at **Cruise America** (1186 San Andreas Rd., Watsonville, 800/671-8042, www.cruiseamerica.com). They offer large and standard vehicles perfect for the road trip along the coast. Rental quotes are based on the type of RV and approximate mileage. Between Monterey and Santa Cruz are many RV-friendly camping locations, some nearly right on the beach.

Airports

There are two major airports in the Monterey area, in Monterey and in San Jose. The small and convenient **Monterey Peninsula Airport** (MRY, 200 Fred Kane Dr., 831/648-7000, www.montereyairport.com) has service by United, Allegiant, American Eagle, and America West along with car-rental companies. Taxi service is available through Central Coast Taxi (831/626-3333), or hire a limo through Arrow Luxury Transportation (831/646-3175).

San Jose International Airport (SJC, 2077 Airport Blvd., San Jose, 408/277-4859, www.sjc.org) is about 90 minutes inland along U.S. 101 in Silicon Valley. All major U.S. airlines serve this airport, and there are flights to Mexico as well. Hop on the Monterey-Salinas Air Bus (831/373-7777, http://montereyairbus.com, $30-40) from San Jose Airport to Monterey, or rent a car from the one of the many providers.

Train

For a more leisurely ride, **Amtrak**'s Seattle-Los Angeles *Coast Starlight* train travels through Salinas (Station Place and Railroad Ave., Salinas, daily 8 A.M.-10 P.M.) daily in both directions. For Amtrak travelers, there is free bus service (30 minutes) to downtown Monterey.

Bus

You can take **Greyhound** (19 W. Gabilan St., Salinas, 831/424-4418, www.greyhound.com, daily 5 A.M.-11:30 P.M.) from just about anywhere in the country to the transit station in Salinas and make your way to Monterey.

To Monterey from San Jose or Salinas, **Monterey-Salinas Transit** (MST, 831/899-2555, www.mst.org) serves both Monterey and Santa Cruz Counties. The Monterey San Jose Express route 55 (2.25 hours, one-way $5, round-trip $10) runs Monterey. If you're coming to Monterey from Salinas, take Monterey-Salinas bus route 20 (50 minutes, $1-3.50).

GETTING AROUND

Downtown at the end of Alvarado Street is the Monterey **Transit Plaza**, where you can pick up a full bus schedule; you can also view bus routes, prices, and times on the Monterey-Salinas Transit website (www.mst.org). Exact change is required on buses, and fares range $1.50-2. You can also take advantage of the free **WAVE Trolley** (Memorial Day-Labor Day daily 9 A.M.-7:30 P.M.), which loops between downtown Monterey and the aquarium.

Pacific Grove

Pacific Grove, also known as Butterfly Town USA, is one of the hidden gems of the Monterey Peninsula. This small town has special attractions, including a monarch butterfly sanctuary, golf fairways on the ocean, a historical lighthouse, museums, and shopping, to fill a day and tempt you to extend your stay for a weekend. Around Mother's Day at the height of spring, ice plants burst into glowing crimson blooms, turning the landscape into a blast of color. With charming Victorian homes and bed-and-breakfasts, Pacific Grove is great for a romantic getaway. Families aren't left out either; the surf is always up, and tide pools and sand castles draw little ones to Asilomar State Beach.

The first inhabitants of Pacific Grove were the Rumsen people, hunters and fishers who flourished in the rich environment of Monterey Bay. In 1875 a group of Methodists settled in the area and named it Pacific Grove. It did not take long for others to come to the area for retreats, and many chose to stay. Today, the town remains a quiet retreat, and the past is relived through a variety of celebrations throughout the year.

SIGHTS
Point Piños Lighthouse

Within the Pacific Grove city limits is Point Piños Lighthouse (Lighthouse Ave. and Asilomar Ave., 831/648-3176, www.ci.pg.ca.us/lighthouse, Thurs.-Mon. 1-4 P.M., $5 donation). This was the second lighthouse built on the West Coast constructed from a lighthouse kit shipped from the East. It has operated since 1855 and is the oldest extant lighthouse on the West Coast. The U.S. Coast Guard is in charge of the light, and volunteers operate the day-use facilities.

Inside, the early 1900s come back to life. Pacific Grove's Museum of Natural History restored the location to model the living conditions of Emily Fish, one of the few women who worked as lighthouse keeper in that era. The original bathtub still sits on its sturdy metal feet, and the tea set Fish once owned is stored inside. She was known as a socialite and hosted many events at the lighthouse.

◖ Lovers Point Park

Located near Cannery Row in Pacific Grove, Lovers Point Park (630 Ocean View Blvd., daily dawn-dusk) juts out to offer views of Monterey to the right, Pacific Grove to the left, and Santa Cruz across the bay. It is one of the most beautiful spots on the peninsula. There's access to sandy coves and stunning granite rock formations. Climb up for even more spectacular views of the coastline. It's a great spot for a picnic, with a large grassy area, tables, a beach volleyball court, and restrooms just above the water. It's also a popular location for weddings. A walking and cycling path leads to the Monterey Bay Aquarium and Asilomar State Beach.

Museum of Natural History

Prepare for discovery both indoors and out at the Pacific Grove Museum of Natural History

Wander among the many tide pools along Pacific Grove's shoreline.

© KRISTIN LEAL

(165 Forest Ave., 831/648-5716, www.pgmuseum.org, Tues.-Sun. 10 A.M.-5 P.M., closed holidays, donation $3 pp, $5 family). The museum displays native wildlife, including giant pelicans and falcons, and outside, local plantlife fills the botanical gardens. You can't miss the massive piece of locally harvested jade on display. With more than 100 native plants and a "spirit nest" (a giant bird's nest created by a Big Sur artist), there is enough to entertain both adults and children. A large sculpture of a whale is at the front entrance, enticing little ones to climb on it.

Monarch Sanctuary

As winter approaches, majestic monarch butterflies make their way to Pacific Grove, nicknamed Butterfly Town USA, and specifically to the Monarch Sanctuary (end of Ridge Rd. off Lighthouse Ave.). The trailhead is next to the Butterfly Grove Inn. Monarch season runs early November-late February. The fog-shrouded eucalyptus and pine forest is the best place to watch these magnificent creatures, and the trees seem to come alive with their fluttering wings.

Docents offer free guided tours (Sat.-Sun. noon-3 P.M., peak season daily noon-3 P.M.) during the migration season, providing a behind-the-scenes look at the butterflies. Tours are run by the **Pacific Grove Museum of Natural History** (831/648-5716, www.pgmuseum.org).

SPORTS AND RECREATION
Beaches

Asilomar State Beach (800 Asilomar Blvd., parking along Sunset Dr., 831/372-8016, www.visitasilomar.com, free) is a narrow mile-long strip of sandy dunes and rocky coves with a conference center and accommodations options. Dirt paths and boardwalks lead through the dunes, and the coves have some good tide pools. On the main beach the surf is consistently high, providing intermediate to expert

MONTEREY

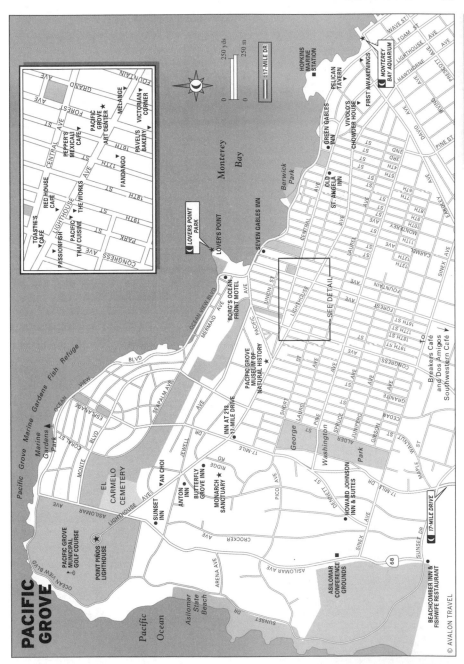

PACIFIC GROVE

250 yds
250 m

17-MILE DR

Map labels:

GRAND AVE
FOUNTAIN AVE
MELANGE
VICTORIAN CORNER
PACIFIC GROVE ART CENTER
PEPPER'S MEXICAL CAFÉ
PAVEL'S BAKERY
FOREST AVE
CENTRAL AVE
16TH ST
FANDANGO
17TH ST
TOASTIE'S CAFÉ
RED HOUSE CAFÉ
THE WORKS
PASSIONFISH
PACIFIC THAI CUISINE
LIGHTHOUSE AVE
18TH ST
19TH ST
PARK ST
CONGRESS AVE

Monterey Bay

Berwick Park

GREEN GABLES INN
VIVOLO'S CHOWDER HOUSE
OLD ST. ANGELA INN
HOPKINS MARINE STATION
PELICAN TAVERN
FIRST AWAKENINGS
MONTEREY BAY AQUARIUM
WAVE ST
FOAM ST
LIGHTHOUSE AVE
HAWTHORNE AVE
PRESCOTT AVE
IRVING AVE
DAVID AVE
PINE ST
2ND ST
3RD ST
4TH ST
5TH ST
6TH ST
7TH ST
8TH ST
9TH ST
10TH ST
11TH ST
12TH ST
13TH ST
CARMEL AVE
SINEX AVE
FOUNTAIN AVE
FOREST AVE
16TH ST
17TH ST
18TH ST
19TH ST
CONGRESS AVE
GRANITE ST

LOVERS POINT PARK
LOVER'S POINT
SEVEN GABLES INN
LIGHTHOUSE AVE
LAUREL AVE
CENTRAL AVE
MONTEREY AVE

OCEAN VIEW BLVD
MERMAID AVE
BORG'S OCEAN FRONT MOTEL
PACIFIC ST
UNION ST

PACIFIC GROVE MUSEUM OF NATURAL HISTORY

SEE DETAIL

Breakers Café and Dos Amigos
Southwestern Café

BLVD
OCEAN VIEW
Pacific Grove Marine Gardens Fish Refuge
Marine Gardens
CORAL ST
MONTE AVE
SEA PALM AVE
ESPLANADE
JEWELL AVE
INN AT 213 17-MILE DRIVE
17-MILE DR
GEORGE
LAUREL
PINE
SPRUCE
ALDER
JUNIPERO
SHORT ST
Washington Park
GIBSON ST
CEDAR
WALNUT ST
MAPLE ST

EL CARMELO CEMETERY

AN CHOI
ANTON INN
BUTTERFLY GROVE INN
MONARCH SANCTUARY
SUNSET INN
RIDGE RD
LIGHTHOUSE AVE
ASILOMAR AVE
PICO AVE
DENNETT ST
HOWARD JOHNSON INN & SUITES
17-MILE DR
17-MILE DRIVE

POINT PIÑOS LIGHTHOUSE
PACIFIC GROVE MUNICIPAL GOLF COURSE
OCEAN VIEW BLVD

CROCKER AVE
ARENA AVE
ASILOMAR AVE
68
SINEX AVE
SUNSET DR

Pacific Ocean

Asilomar State Beach
SUNSET DR

ASILOMAR CONFERENCE GROUNDS

BEACHCOMBER INN & FISHWIFE RESTAURANT

© AVALON TRAVEL

© KRISTIN LEAL

Point Piños Lighthouse

waves. On rare flat days, this is an ideal location for beginners, as the breakers push for a good distance.

Surfing

The place for the fearless to catch the big waves is at **Lovers Point** (630 Ocean View Blvd.) in Pacific Grove. The surf breaks near the rugged coastline, and some navigation skills are definitely required. This spot offers an intense rush, and the waves, rated moderate to hard, are among the most massive on the peninsula. In winter the waves are huge and epic.

A nice location where the surf is almost always up is at **Asilomar State Beach** (south end of Sunset Dr. near Asilomar Blvd., 831/646-6440, www.parks.ca.gov, free) in Pacific Grove. The breakers are continuous, and the ride is moderate. The wide beach has a nice cove to walk along, and you can hang out all day. Parking is limited to the street, so check the tide table and arrive early.

Kayaking

Get geared up for great paddling on Pacific Grove's shores at **Adventures By the Sea** (Lovers Point Park, 831/372-1807, www.adventuresbythesea.com, daily 9 A.M.-sunset, $30 pp), offering single and double kayaks to explore the coves of Asilomar, the back side of the aquarium, Cannery Row, and Monterey Harbor. Along the rocky shoreline you'll see spotted harbor seals sunning themselves and snoozing. Mother sea otters hold their young pups on their bellies for a nap while older juveniles roll around in the thick kelp beds. You may even catch sight of migrating whales spouting in groups in the distance.

Biking

The **Monterey Bay Coastal Bike Trail** runs to Pebble Beach and 17-Mile Drive, with countless turquoise coves, beach access, and tide-pool combing along the way. Through Pacific Grove the trail is mostly flat with a few small hills

MONTEREY

© KRISTIN LEAL

Spotted harbor seals are often seen at Lovers Point.

that are barely noticeable. Bikes can be rented at Lovers Point Park through **Adventures By the Sea** (Lovers Point Park, 831/372-1807, www.adventuresbythesea.com, daily 9 A.M.-sunset, $7 per hour, half day $20, full day $25). Besides the ocean views, you can make your way inland and bike through neighborhoods of unique Victorian homes on the way to Lighthouse Avenue, where there are worthy eats and pleasurable shopping.

Golf

Tee time in Pacific Grove is dreamy and an affordable alternative to Pebble Beach. **Pacific Grove Municipal Golf Links** (77 Asilomar Blvd., 831/648-5775, www.pggolflinks.com, day $40-48, twilight $20-25) is an 18-hole, par-70 course with a Scottish links experience. Views on the back nine are incredible as the salty shoreline and Point Piños Lighthouse come into sight, and the greens seem to extend nearly into the surf.

ENTERTAINMENT

Pacific Grove is all about wholesome fun, and the **Lighthouse Cinema** (525 Lighthouse Ave., 831/643-1333, www.entertainmentgrp.com) is just the thing for the whole family or a date night. Showing blockbuster hits on four screens, it has the charm of a small-town theater.

Pacific Grove Art Center (568 Lighthouse Ave., 931/375-2208, Wed.-Sat. noon-5 P.M., Sun. 1-4 P.M.) provides free concerts, poetry readings, a variety of art classes, and local art exhibits. There are four galleries with exhibits that change every six weeks.

FESTIVALS AND EVENTS

Pacific Grove has an array of town gatherings year-round. Drift back into the past at **Pacific Grove Good Old Days** (downtown, 831/373-3304, www.pacificgrove.org, Apr. 9-10, free). The streets close to traffic and the good old days come back to life with live entertainment, music, crafts, art, games, contests, and a parade down Pine Avenue.

The largest in the Central Coast region, the **Wildflower Show** (165 Forest Ave., 831/648-5716, www.pgmuseum.org, Apr. 15-17) has growers bringing more than 600 species for public display both inside and outside the museum. It is a colorful event the whole family will enjoy. For cyclists, the **Butterfly Criterium** (Lighthouse Ave., www.ghosttreeracing.com) in May is a 1970s Prestige Classic bicycle race, perfect for a weekend getaway before the summer rush. Spend your time watching the races and relaxing in picturesque Pacific Grove during some of the best weather of the year.

Kick off the summer with **Pacific Grove City Fourth of July BBQ** (Caledonia Park, Caledonia Ave. between Central Ave. and Jewell Ave., 831/373-3304, www.pacificgrove. org). In the good old American tradition, July 4 is a day filled with an old fashioned barbecue and live entertainment.

The **Feast of Lanterns** (831/649-8737, www.feast-of-lanterns.org, July 29-30) has been a citywide celebration for the last 100 years that grants scholarships to local female students. There is a lantern parade to the beach and a fireworks show in the evening. Lovers Point Park is the site of live music throughout the day.

The **Triathlon at Pacific Grove** (Lovers Point Park, 831/373-0678, www.tricalifornia. com, Sept. 9-11) is a weekend with two days of racing and a three-day Health and Fitness Expo. Athletes do the Kelp Crawl swim and run and cycle on the trails looping the park.

Bask in the faultless fall weather while taking the **Pacific Grove Historic Homes Tour** (831/373-3304, www.pacificgrove.org, Oct. 2). This one-day event allows inside views of many Victorians and other historic homes.

The holiday season is a big deal in Pacific Grove, and there are several celebrations and extravagant decorations in December. Through the holiday season, residents along several streets transform their front yards into winter wonderlands for **Candy Cane Lane** (area bounded by Beaumont Dr. and Morse Dr.).

The **Parade of Lights** (downtown, 831/373-3304, www.pacificgrove.org, Dec. 1) is an annual event with marching bands, holiday floats, dance teams, equestrian groups, and, of course, the star, Santa Claus. Kids will enjoy the carolers, wagon rides, and a chance to tell Santa what they want for Christmas; stores remain open with plenty of gifts for sale.

Take a day off, and then gather the kids for **Stillwell's Fun in the Park** (Caledonia Park, Caledonia Ave. between Central Ave. and Jewell Ave., 831/373-3304, www.pacificgrove. org, Dec. 3), where Caledonia Park is transformed into the Arctic, blanketed in snow and twinkling with lights. Santa makes his grand entrance in style as local firefighters give him a lift in their shiny fire engine; hang out with Frosty the Snowman and the Snow Queen or take a hayride. Kids love the petting zoo.

Get tickets early for **Christmas at the Inns** (downtown, 831/373-3304, www.pacificgrove. org, Dec. 6-7), an exploration of 10 Victorian bed-and-breakfasts around Pacific Grove. The inns are decadently decorated to bring the holiday season to life, and light refreshments and entertainment are provided.

Helping you keep fit during the holidays is the **Jingle Bell Run** (Lovers Point Park, 831/373-3304, www.pacificgrove.org, Dec. 10). This 5K walk or run raises funds for the Arthritis Foundation while partaking in some outdoor exhilaration with Santa.

SHOPPING

You'll find a trove of antiques-Tiffany lamps, 18th- and 19th-century furniture, porcelain dolls-at **Trotters Antiques** (590 Lighthouse Ave., 831/373-3505, Mon.-Sat. 11 A.M.-5 P.M.). Owner Lee Trotter has been in the business for 46 years, and her reputation for delivering unique finds is impeccable. Formerly known as Diamonds and Rust, **Pacific Grove Antiques** (472 Lighthouse Ave., 831/658-0488, daily 10 A.M.-5 P.M.) still carries unique vintage furnishing and accessories on two floors. Overflowing with antiques is **Blessings Boutique** (620 Lighthouse Ave., 831/641-0813, daily 10 A.M.-5 P.M.), specializing in local art, seaside souvenirs, and vintage furnishings. A mermaid guards the entrance and tempts pedestrians to stop in for a closer look.

As the name suggests, **Carried Away** (612 Lighthouse Ave., 831/656-9063, www.carried-awayboutique.com, daily 10 A.M.-5 P.M.) is the place for bright, colorful handbags from designers like Vera Bradley. Hats and outerwear are on offer as well. Contemporary feminine clothing for women can be found at **Marita's Boutique** (551 Lighthouse Ave., 831/655-3390, daily 9 A.M.-5 P.M.), which carries sizes ranging from XS to 3X. You can also drop into her shoe shop (547 Lighthouse Ave., 831/373-4650, daily 9 A.M.-5 P.M.), just a few doors down, where you'll find style with comfortable soles for women and men.

Local art is celebrated at the **Sunstudios** (208 Forest Ave., 831/373-7989, daily 9 A.M.-5 P.M.), featuring a collection of artwork, crafts, and jewelry handcrafted by local artisans. If you're looking for that special card that no one will have, look no farther than **The Quill** (217 Grand Ave., 831/373-8189, daily 9 A.M.-5 P.M.), a unique stationery and gift store specializing in individual orders for special occasions and holidays.

The Works (667 Lighthouse Ave., 831/372-2242, www.theworkspg.com, Mon.-Sat. 7 A.M.-6 P.M.) is one of the last local bookstores, a hip place to pick up some hot beverages, purchase local art, and catch some live entertainment. Locals love it for its small-town bookstore qualities.

ACCOMMODATIONS
Under $150

A sweet little hideaway in Pacific Grove just across the street from the ocean is the ◖ **Borg's Ocean Front Motel** (635 Ocean View Blvd., 831/375-2406, www.borgsocean-frontmotel.com, $65-165). The views from the guest rooms are breathtaking, Lovers Point Park is nearby, and the Monterey Bay Coastal Bike Trail is steps from your room. The price, the view, and the location are hard to beat.

An affordable option is the **Beachcomber Inn** (1996 Sunset Dr., 831/373-4769, www.montereypeninsulainns.com, $50-100), just steps from Asilomar State Beach and a great base for a surf vacation. Next door is a local favorite eatery, The Fish Wife. There is a pool on the grounds, and many of the guest rooms have ocean views.

Marking the entrance to the Monarch Butterfly Sanctuary is the **Butterfly Grove Inn** (1073 Lighthouse Ave., 831/373-4921, www.butterflygroveinn.com, $79-319). The trail to the sanctuary starts beside the inn. Located in a quiet part of town, you can truly relax, take a few laps in the pool, and unwind in the hot tub. The guest rooms are clean and cozy.

For an ocean view at a fair price, book a room at **Lovers Point Inn** (625 Ocean View Blvd., 831/373-4771, www.loverspointinn.com, $69-159). The guest rooms are equipped basic amenities, including TVs and phones. The included continental breakfast is a great way to get a quick start to the day.

Pacific Grove Inn (581 Pine Ave., 831/375-2825, www.pacificgroveinn.com, $119-379) is a romantic bed-and-breakfast blending Old World charm with modern-day luxury. There are 16 guest rooms and suites, many with ocean views. Wine and cheese is served daily, as are cookies and milk before bed.

$150-250

Designed by architect Julia Morgan of Hearst Castle fame, ◖ **Asilomar Conference Grounds** (800 Asilomar Ave., 888/635-5310, www.visitasilomar.com, $175-750) was originally commissioned as a YWCA by William Randolph Hearst's mother. The original 65 rooms, built between 1913 and 1928, are true to their historic roots: They're small-quaint, really-and face an outdoor courtyard. Built separately from the original structure, 259 larger, more modern guest rooms are Spartan, with no telephones or TVs. There is an outdoor pool and Wi-Fi in the common areas along with a business center. The overall vibe is log-cabin rustic: A park ranger offers talks around a campfire in the early evenings. It's a short walk across the dunes to the beach in Pacific Grove, and it's not unusual to see deer wandering among the pines that grow throughout the property.

The woodwork is spectacular at the **Inn at 213 Seventeen Mile Drive** (213 17-Mile Dr., 800/526-5666, www.innat17.com, $200-280 d), a classic craftsman home built in 1925. There are four upstairs guest rooms in the house, with an additional 10 in the separate coach house. Breakfast is served at 9 A.M., and each evening wine and hors d'oeuvres are served at 5 P.M., all prepared by a Cordon Bleu-trained chef. The guest rooms are large, each with its own theme. Parking is off-street, and other amenities include Wi-Fi and a small hot tub in the garden.

Get cozy at the historic Victorian-style **Green Gables Inn** (301 Ocean View Blvd., 831/375-2097, www.greengablesinnpg.com, $135-275) bed-and-breakfast, with views of the ocean. Guest rooms are snug, and the suites are roomy for a romantic escape.

An elegant bed-and-breakfast overlooking the ocean is **Martine Inn** (255 Ocean View Blvd., 831/373-3388, www.martineinn.com, $169-499). The landscaped courtyard has several rose gardens and wide bay views. It is centrally located just four blocks from the Monterey Bay Aquarium.

The **C Seven Gables Inn** (555 Ocean View Blvd., 831/372-4341, www.thesevengablesinn.com, $199-559) is a massive bed-and-breakfast on the shores of Monterey Bay. Every guest room has scenic ocean views, and a walk along the shore is only steps away.

FOOD
American

There are plenty of good eats in Pacific Grove, and one of my favorite hangouts is **C The Red House Café** (662 Lighthouse Ave., 831/643-1060, breakfast Sat.-Sun. 8-11 A.M., lunch Tues.-Sun. 11 A.M.-2:30 P.M., dinner Tues.-Sun. 5 P.M.-close, $20). Offering New American cuisine with a European flavor and a strong emphasis on fresh, seasonal ingredients, it shows off the bounty of the region. Order a locally brewed Sparkies Root Beer; it packs a bite.

A fun bar with decent food overlooking Monterey Bay is the **Pelican Tavern** (125 Ocean Ave., 831/647-8200, www.thepelicantavern.com, daily 11 A.M.-11 P.M., $12-18). Sports are always on TV, and the waitstaff are always friendly. This is a hot spot on the edge of Cannery Row with a daily happy hour and live music.

Asian

The best place on the peninsula to get a steamy bowl of sukiyaki is at **Takara Sushi** (218 17th St., 831/655-2730, daily 5-9 P.M., $20-30); the Japanese soup will calm any cold. They offer takeout, have a cozy sushi bar, and welcome small children. The fish is always fresh, authentically prepared, and presented with flair.

The moment you walk into **C Pacific Thai Cuisine** (633 Lighthouse Ave., 831/646-8424, www.pacificthaicuisine.com, Mon.-Thurs. 11 A.M.-3 P.M. and 5 P.M.-close, Fri.-Sun. 11:30 A.M.-close, $20-30), the aroma will make your mouth water. This is my top stop for Thai iced tea and red curry, and the chicken satay and scrumptious salads are great starters.

Breakfast

When the professional surfer Kelly Slater is in town, he has been known to dine at **First Awakenings** (125 Ocean View Blvd., Suite 105, 831/372-1125, www.firstawakenings.net, daily 7 A.M.-2:30 P.M., $12) before teeing up at the Pacific Grove Municipal Golf Links. Located in the American Tin Cannery across from the Monterey Bay Aquarium, the restaurant is well-known for its distinctive and bulky pancakes. Choices are numerous for breakfast and lunch, with fat sandwiches and hearty salads.

If you're looking for an extensive breakfast menu, the **Victorian Corner** (541 Lighthouse Ave., 831/372-4641, www.victoriancorner.com, Mon.-Sat. 7:45 A.M.-3 P.M. and 5-9:30 P.M., $10). There are plenty of "Victorian corner classics" (varied cuisine) along with the traditional pancakes, omelets, and waffles.

There is nothing fancy about **【 Toasties Café** (702 Lighthouse Ave., 831/373-7543, Mon.-Sat. 6:30 A.M.-3 P.M., Sun. 7 A.M.-2 P.M., $12), but the food is very good, and the line out the door all day long, seven days a week speaks for itself. Locals and visitors love this place.

Before an early morning surf at Asilomar State Beach, stop for a bite at **【 Breakers Café** (1126 Forest Ave., 831/375-8484, daily 7:30 A.M.-2 P.M., $8-12), away from the busy part of town and a local favorite. traditional breakfast and lunch café favorites are served in sizable portions.

Cheap Eats

Visit **【 Pavel's Bakery** (219 Forest Ave., 831/643-2636, daily 6:30 A.M.-2:30 P.M., $5) for a steaming cup of coffee as well as savory and sweet treats. Get here early, as the display case gets picked over by noon. The smell of hot fresh bread will lure through the front door. You can pick up food on the way to the beach for a picnic.

Goodies Deli (518 Lighthouse Ave., 831/655-3663, www.goodiesdeliblogspot.com, Mon.-Sat. 9:30 A.M.-4 P.M., $6-10) has everything from pastries to homemade soups and puts together bulky sandwiches large enough to share. The salads are gourmet quality.

Mediterranean

Since 1984 **Petra** (477 Lighthouse Ave., 831/649-2530, Mon.-Thurs. 11 A.M.-9 P.M.,

Fri.-Sat. 11 A.M.-9:30 P.M., $15) has been making kebabs, gyros, lentil soup, and stuffed grape leaves. The interior has an upscale cafeteria vibe, but the Mediterranean menu is packed with flavor. A separate entrance, just to the left of the main door, serves take-out orders.

Feast on a variety of Mediterranean delights at **Fandango** (223 17th St., 831/372-3456, www.fandangorestaurant.com, Mon.-Sat. 11:30 A.M.-2:30 P.M. and 5-9:30 P.M., Sun. 10 A.M.-2 P.M. and 5-9:30 P.M., $25), including rack of lamb, fresh seafood from the open grill, and regional dishes like pastas and couscous.

Mexican

Dos Amigos Southwestern Café (1184 Forest Ave., Suite H, 831/646-8888, daily 11 A.M.-9 P.M., $20) is an authentic Mexican restaurant known for serving delightful traditional tacos, enchiladas, and burritos. The layout is laid-back, with a small bar and a wide-screen TV.

Grab a table early to dine with the locals at **Peppers MexiCall Café** (170 Forest Ave., 831/373-6892, Mon.-Thurs. 11:30 A.M.-9 P.M., Fri.-Sat. 11:30 A.M.-10 P.M., Sun. 4-9 P.M., $15). The decor is Southwestern, and the food is Latin American with an emphasis on seafood. Everything is made in-house with a spicy pepper kick.

An affordable choice for Mexican food is **Michael's Grill and Taqueria** (179 Country Club Gate Center, 831/647-8654, Mon.-Sat. 10 A.M.-9 P.M., Sun. 10 A.M.-8 P.M., $8), preparing authentic carne asada, rocking burritos, and saucy enchiladas.

Seafood

Vivolo's Chowder House (127 Central Ave., 831/372-5414, www.vivoloschowderhouse.com, Mon.-Fri. 11 A.M.-3 P.M. and 5 P.M.-close, Sat.-Sun. 11 A.M.-close, $14-23) brings the Italian seafood experience to Pacific Grove with a variety of decadent fresh fish, pastas, and steaks; lunch has seafood sandwiches.

There's no need to pull out your *Seafood*

Watch card at **(Passionfish** (701 Lighthouse Ave., 831/655-3311, www.passionfish.net, daily 5 P.M.-close, $30) as they pride themselves on serving only sustainable seafood. The menu changes regularly as Chef Ted Walter and his wife, Cindy, choose the finest ingredients according to local harvests.

The flavor of the **(Fish Wife** (1996 ½ Sunset Dr., 831/375-7107, www.fishwife.com, daily 11 A.M.-9 P.M., $12-25) is all California seafood with a twist of the Caribbean. The chef uses local produce from the Salinas Valley to present colorful daily specials, seafood, and pasta dishes. The atmosphere is casual, and there is a full bar.

Farmers Market

Rain or shine, the **Pacific Grove Farmers Market** (Lighthouse Ave. between Forest Ave. and 18th St., 831/384-6961, www.everyonesharvest.org, year-round Mon. 4-8 P.M.) is always a fun time. A modest market, it features mostly organic vendors and local bakeries. There are some amazing deals, delightful eats, and a street performer or two.

INFORMATION AND SERVICES

A quick stop at the **Pacific Grove Chamber of Commerce** (Forest Ave. and Central Ave., 831/373-3304, www.pacificgrove.org, Mon.-Fri. 9:30 A.M.-5 P.M.) and the **Tourist Information Center** (100 Central Ave., 831/373-3304, www.pacificgrove.org, daily 10 A.M.-5 P.M.) will get you a rundown on all the attractions of Pacific Grove. The **U.S. Post Office** (680 Lighthouse Ave., 831/373-2271) is centrally located.

For medical needs, the **Community Hospital of the Monterey Peninsula** (CHOMP, 23625 Hwy. 68/Holman Hwy., 831/624-5311) provides emergency services in the area. The main office of the **Pacific Grove Police Department** (580 Pine Ave., 831/648-3143) is open daily 24 hours. In an emergency, dial 911.

GETTING THERE AND AROUND

There are two ways to enter Pacific Grove: Highway 1 to Highway 68 heading northwest to Sunset Boulevard; or get off at Highway 1's "Monterey Aquarium" exit and follow the signs to Cannery Row and the Monterey Bay Aquarium, where you will eventually run into Ocean View Boulevard in Pacific Grove. Alternately, once you reach Lighthouse Avenue, stay on it; it runs through both Monterey and Pacific Grove.

Pebble Beach

While Pebble Beach's reputation is all about its championship golf course, there's a lot more to this small unincorporated town than golf greens and sand traps. A gated community surrounding the course and spreading back into the trees has some of the most expensive homes in California with some of the most majestic views of the Pacific. Some of the main attractions within Pebble Beach include picturesque 17-Mile Drive, the famed Lone Cypress, the multitude of multimillion-dollar homes, an extensive equestrian center, and, of course, the renowned golf courses.

SIGHTS
(17-Mile Drive

If you are a first-time visitor to the Monterey area, 17-Mile Drive (starts at Sunset Dr./Hwy. 68 and 17-Mile Dr. in Pacific Grove, www.pebblebeach.com, daily sunrise-sunset, cars $10, motorcycles not allowed) can introduce you to some of the most beautiful views on the

MONTEREY

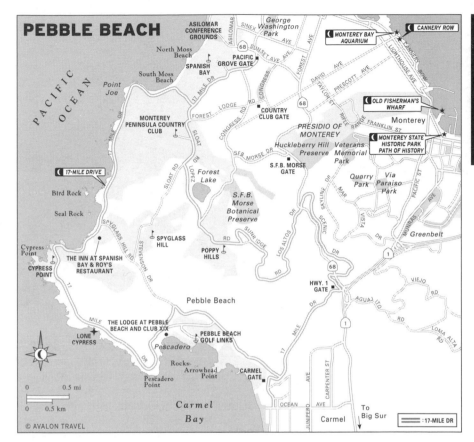

Central Coast. Long ago, the locally all-powerful Pebble Beach Corporation realized what a precious commodity this road was and began charging a toll. The good news is that when you pay your fee at the gatehouse, you'll get a map of the drive that describes the parks and sights that you pass. These include the much-photographed **Lone Cypress,** the beaches of **Spanish Bay,** and Pebble Beach's **golf course,** resort, and housing complex. There are plenty of turnouts where you can stop to take photos of the stunning ocean and the iconic cypress trees. You can picnic at many of the formal beaches. **Bird Rock** has basic restroom facilities and an ample parking lot. The only food

and gas are at the Inn at Spanish Bay and the Lodge at Pebble Beach.

The best time to view this scenic seascape is at dusk, when the pinks of the fading sun accent the blues of the ocean. If you're in a hurry, you can get from one end of 17-Mile Drive to the other in 20 minutes—but that would defeat the main purpose of the drive, which is to enjoy the beauty of the area. If you take your time and bring a picnic, it will take about two hours. The best picnic spots are between **Point Joe** and **Seal Rock**.

Spanish Bay

Spanish Bay (2700 17-Mile Dr., 831/647-7500,

the Lone Cypress on 17-Mile Drive

Pebble Beach, www.pebblebeach.com) is the first resort you'll see when you enter Pebble Beach from the Sunset Drive Gate in Pacific Grove, and it offers posh services for residents, members, and visitors. The Links at Spanish Bay is a traditional Scottish-style golf course, topped off with a bagpiper playing a distinct melody nightly on the greens. The Inn at Spanish Bay is contemporary and elegant with captivating views of the golf course and the crashing surf. The featured restaurant is Roy's at Pebble Beach, where you can watch the beauty of the ocean while dining on Hawaiian fusion creations. Be sure to make dinner reservations to catch the bagpiper and the sunset.

The Lodge at Pebble Beach

From 17-Mile Drive, turn onto the lodge's lengthy driveway to visit the ultra-high-end resort (2700 17-Mile Dr., 831/647-7500, www. pebblebeach.com). Nonguests can park and walk into the main lobby of the hotel. Most visitors walk through onto the immense multilevel patio area to take in the priceless and oft-photographed views. Whether you stay on the flagstones and enjoy a drink from the lobby bar or take a walk on the wide lawns, you can see the dramatic cliffs plummeting to the small blue-gray bay. The golf course draws right up to the lawns, allowing nonguests to check out a couple of the hallowed greens and fairways dotted with cypress trees. The lodge itself is worth touring; you can take the paths to see the exterior of the accommodations, walk into the lobby of the exclusive spa, and see the dining room.

SPORTS AND RECREATION
Golf

There's no place for golf in California like Pebble Beach. You can play courses trodden by Tiger Woods and Jack Nicklaus, pause a moment before you putt to take in the sight of the stunning Pacific Ocean, and pay $300 or more for a round. Golf has been a major pastime

© KRISTIN LEAL

Pebble Beach Golf Links

here since the late 19th century, and today avid golfers come from around the world to tee off beside the ocean. The golf scene here is the driving force behind what makes the peninsula what it is today. Pebble Beach is home to five golf courses, with the Pebble Beach Company running four of them.

The 18-hole, par-72 **Pebble Beach Golf Links** (The Lodge at Pebble Beach, 1700 17-Mile Dr., 831/622-8723, $495, cart rental included for guests) is the priciest fairway in the county and what many consider to be the best course in the country. You can feel the energy of golf's greats, who have played here since 1919. Events include the annual AT&T Pebble Beach National Pro-Am and five U.S. Open Championships, with a return engagement scheduled for 2019.

One of the Pebble Beach Resort courses, the 18-hole, par-72 **Spyglass Hill** (1700 17-Mile Dr., 800/654-9300, www.pebblebeach.com, $360, cart rental included for guests) gets its name from the Robert Louis Stevenson novel *Treasure Island*. But don't be fooled—the holes on this beautiful course may be named for children's characters, but that doesn't mean they're easy. Spyglass Hill boasts some of the most challenging play in the course-laden Carmel region. Expect a few bogeys, and tee off from the Championship level at your ego's own risk.

Designed in the image of true Scottish play from over 500 years ago is the 18-hole, par-72 **Links at Spanish Bay** (The Inn at Spanish Bay, 2700 17-Mile Dr., 800/654-9300, www. pebblebeach.com, $260, cart rental included for guests). A bagpiper closes each evening with whimsical music, and the greens will impress. You'll have to hit your ball in a steady breeze, as the Scottish term *links* actually means a sandy wasteland near the sea with bristly grasses and ever-prevailing winds.

The best deal and the easiest course in Pebble Beach is the nine-hole, par-27 **Peter Hay Golf Course** (The Lodge at Pebble Beach,

© KRISTIN LEAL

Links at Spanish Bay

1700 17-Mile Dr., 831/622-8723, www.pebblebeach.com, $30 adults, $10 ages 13-17, free under age 13 with an adult). This is the place to take the kids for a lesson, and as it's just across the way from the Pebble Beach Golf Links, your little one will feel like a pro. It is the only public course on the peninsula, and it could not be in a better location; it is a good spot to work on your short game.

Another favorite with the golf crowd is the famed 18-hole, par-72 **Poppy Hills Golf Course** (3200 Lopez Rd., 831/622-8239, www.poppyhillsgolf.com, day $200, twilight $65). Although it's not managed by the same company, Poppy Hills shares amenities with Pebble Beach golf courses, so you can expect the same level of care and devotion to the maintenance of the course and your experience as a player. If you're looking to improve your game, check out the two-day program that gets you onto both Poppy and Spyglass Hill for a chance to pick up some new skills and enjoy the incidentally gorgeous views.

Beaches

On 17-Mile Drive, **Point Joe** is a secluded site to catch some waves. The surf tends to be moderate. The parking lot is sizable and frequented mostly by picnickers and surfers. This beach is easy to recognize as it has countless piles of rocks scattered on the shore.

Just a little farther south on 17-Mile Drive, you can build a bonfire or hop in the water on a sunny day for dazzling snorkeling at **Seal Rock.** There are two fire pits in the sand with tables; the pale sandy beach is sheltered, with a stream cutting through in the winter. The reflective blue-green water is conducive to snorkeling, with plenty of scattered rock mounds with tiny creatures to float over, including gripping starfish, sea grasses, fish hiding in the sand, and speedy rock cod.

Surfing

In Pebble Beach on 17-Mile Drive, **Point Joe** is a good place for surfing. The waves tend to be moderate. The cove is nice and protected and typically glows a magnificent turquoise. The beach gradually descends into the sea, making it a favored spot for local surfers. Usually you can expect to tackle three to four sets of breakers before making it out to the deep water. It's one of the spots to hit up on flat days. The parking lot is sizable and frequented by surfers.

Horseback Riding

The **Pebble Beach Equestrian Center** (Portola Rd. and Alva Lane, 831/624-2756, www.ridepebblebeach.com) has options that include pony rides, lessons, and trail rides that head out four times daily. The trail rides provide views of the secluded golf courses, thick forests, the ocean, and the backs of beachfront houses along 17-Mile Drive. The horses are very mellow and are great on the trails, following each other nicely and rarely needing much direction.

Biking

A beautifully challenging bicycle route in Pebble

Beach is **17-Mile Drive.** Cyclists can follow the road and enjoy the spectacular scenery in a way that drivers just can't. Expect fairly flat terrain with lots of twists and turns and a ride that runs about 17 miles. Foggy conditions can make this ride a bit slippery in summer, but spring and fall weather are perfect for pedaling here. Just be aware that you're sharing a narrow road with distracted visitors and rushing locals. Wander off the main route at your own risk; the area's roads are very convoluted with steep inclines.

Spas

Relax your mind and body where the Del Monte pine forest converges with the Pacific Ocean at **The Spa at Pebble Beach** (1700 17-Mile Dr., about 400 yards from The Lodge at Pebble Beach, 888/565-7615, www.pebblebeach.com). An array of treatments for both men and women are available, including day packages with extensive pampering.

EVENTS

Held in mid-April, in a few short years the **Pebble Beach Food & Wine** (26364 Carmel Rancho Lane, 800/907-3663, www.pebblebeachfoodandwine.com) has become the predominant culinary event between Los Angeles and San Francisco. Master chefs and high-end winemakers from across the nation converge on Pebble Beach for a three-day celebration of eating and drinking with cooking demonstrations, wine symposia, and vertical tastings of rare vintages, all against the gorgeous backdrop of Pebble Beach and the Pacific Ocean.

During the first two weeks of August, the **Concours d'Elegance** (1700 17-Mile Dr., www.pebblebeachconcours.net) celebrates the automobile. Hundreds of cars-vintage, unusual, and just plain beautiful-congregate on the 18th green at Pebble Beach, while others line the streets of Carmel. Cars are judged for their historical accuracy; you'll see some stunning and valuable mint-condition vehicles; some have

sold at auction for $500,000. This is one of the largest events in the area, second only to the Monterey Jazz Festival, with nearly 10,000 people swamping the hamlet of Carmel. Getting reservations anywhere during this time is nearly impossible unless you plan well in advance.

There are three major annual golf events at Pebble Beach that bring in the pros, celebrities, and up-and-coming juniors. The **AT&T Pebble Beach National Pro Am** (1700 17-Mile Dr., www.pebblebeach.com) in early February brings professional team talent to the greens; Hollywood celebrities, world-famous musicians, and captains of industry compete for a sizable purse.

The second event is the **First Tee Open at Pebble Beach** (Peter Hay Golf Course, 1700 17-Mile Dr., www.pebblebeach.com) in early July, which brings past champions to the peninsula to golf alongside up-and-coming juniors.

The **Callaway Pebble Beach Invitational** (1700 17-Mile Dr., www.pebblebeach.com) in mid-November is a unique tournament that brings together professionals from PGA, LPGA, Championships, and National Tours for fierce competition.

SHOPPING

The Lodge at Pebble Beach and **The Inn at Spanish Bay** (2700 17-Mile Dr., 831/647-7500, www.pebblebeach.com) have everything from golf and tennis pro shops to fashion boutiques, and not to worry, the kids won't be left out, as there are specialty shops just for them. Visit the website for a full list of the Pebble Beach Company's stores and the general inventory, which even includes housewares and souvenirs.

ACCOMMODATIONS

Pebble Beach has three elegant resorts that will pamper you with their legendary service. **The Inn at Spanish Bay** (2700 17-Mile Dr., 831/647-7500, Pebble Beach, www.pebblebeach.com, $595-3,450). Take in views of the golf course with the ocean as the backdrop in the secluded

© KRISTIN LEAL

You can find shopping just across from the Lodge at Pebble Beach.

bay. The decor is contemporary, and the accommodations are lavish. All guest rooms feature fireplaces, modern baths, included wireless Internet access, and flat-panel TVs. The magnificent and spacious suites come in five styles, with the Presidential suite the most luxurious.

The place to stay for ultimate decadence is [**The Lodge at Pebble Beach** (2700 17-Mile Dr., 831/647-7500, www.pebblebeach.com, $675-3,275). Since it opened in 1919, the Lodge has been legendary; guest rooms and suites feature private patios or balconies, fireplaces, flat-panel TVs, plush towels, and fine linens.

Just beyond the Lodge entrance is **Casa Palmero Pebble Beach** (1700 17-Mile Dr., 831/622-6650, www.pebblebeach.com, $845-2,750), an estate with the flair of Mediterranean architecture. There are 24 suites, a heated outdoor pool, a billiards room, and a library. Views overlook the Pebble Beach golf courses. Each guest room has a fireplace, an oversize soaking tub, and heavenly mattresses.

FOOD

Pebble Beach has a handful of dining options at The Inn at Spanish Bay and The Pebble Beach Lodge. **The Pebble Beach Market** (2184 Sunset Dr., 831/625-8528, www.pebblebeach. com, daily 7:30 A.M.-7 P.M.) is the place to grab a picnic lunch or wine to go. They offer a fine selection of wines from around the world, including local vintages. You can also find fine gourmet cheeses, meats, and other goodies.

The Lodge at Pebble Beach (2700 17-Mile Dr.) has four restaurants: The **Stillwater Grill** (831/625-8524, www.pebblebeach.com, daily breakfast, lunch, and dinner, $30) serves sizzling sustainable seafood and organic produce. At **The Tap Room** (831/625-8535, www.pebblebeach.com, $40-60) you will find a classic American-style tavern open for dinner and late-night dining. Fill up on tasty spirits and fine cuts of meat after a day of golf. The **Gallery Café** (831/625-8577, www.pebblebeach.com, daily breakfast and lunch, $12) is a cheap place for home-style meals in a casual atmosphere; expect burgers, deli sandwiches, and the best milk shake in town. **The Terrance Lounge** (831/625-8524, www.pebblebeach.com) is the place to congregate for cocktails and close conversation. Come in to enjoy the full bar and cushy oversize chairs while you watch the sunset over Carmel Bay.

The Inn at Spanish Bay (2700 17-Mile Dr.) is home to five restaurants and bars: **Peppoli at Pebble Beach** (831/647-7433, www.pebblebeach.com, daily 6-10 P.M., $50) serves bold northern Italian seafood and meat dishes and features traditional pastas. **Roy's at Pebble Beach** (831/647-7423, www.pebblebeach.com, daily breakfast, lunch, and dinner, $40-60) brings Hawaiian fusion to the table as you take in the beauty of the ocean view. Big flavor in a casual atmosphere is at **STICKS** (831/647-7470, www.pebblebeach.com, daily breakfast, lunch, and dinner, $30) for sports, food, and fun. **Taps** (831/647-7500, www.pebblebeach.com), a sports bar, has a full bar and serves dinner and late night meals of favorites like hot wings, burgers, fried chicken, and delectable desserts. **The Lobby Lounge** (831/647-7500, www.pebblebeach.com, daily lunch, dinner, and evening) has a full cocktail bar and food menu where you can enjoy a drink and snack on appetizers.

GETTING THERE AND AROUND

There are five entry gates to Pebble Beach, which can make things confusing. Stick to the main gates: the Pacific Grove Gate (Sunset Dr./Hwy. 68 and 17-Mile Dr.) and the Carmel Gate (N. San Antonio Ave. and 2nd Ave., Carmel). The best way to navigate Pebble Beach is by car ($10), but you can also hitch a ride with one of the many tour companies that travel 17-Mile Drive. If you are feeling bold, you can hop on a bicycle and navigate this narrow road as well.

Northern Monterey County

To reach the northern part of Monterey County, drive north on Highway 1. The small towns and villages here include Moss Landing, 20 miles from the city of Monterey; Marina, about 10 miles away; and Seaside, at the northern border of the county.

MOSS LANDING

Moss Landing is a sleepy fishing village between Monterey and Santa Cruz that is teeming with wildlife at Elkhorn Slough, the second-largest estuary in California. It stretches for 17 miles on more than 5,000 acres and provides homes for 340 bird species and hundreds of marine mammals. This is the place to get up close to the wildlife of Monterey Bay.

Elkhorn Slough National Estuarine Research Reserve

The Elkhorn Slough National Estuarine Research Reserve (1700 Elkhorn Rd., 831/728-2822, www.elkhornslough.org, day-use $2.50) has five miles of hiking trails that weave along the edges of the estuary, where fingers of green land stretch into the gleaming blue still saltwater. The reserve, which includes beaches, marshes, and woodlands, is an excellent place for viewing wildlife. In spring you can see seal pups trying out new feats under the careful watch of their mothers. Spring is also an excellent time for bird-watching, although the bird population flourishes year-round.

From Highway 1 in Moss Landing you can take a two-hour sightseeing tour with **Elkhorn Slough Safari** (Moss Landing Harbor, across from the Whole Enchilada, 831/633-5555, $35 adults, $26 children). Bring your camera, and be sure to make reservations well in advance, as the tours sell out early.

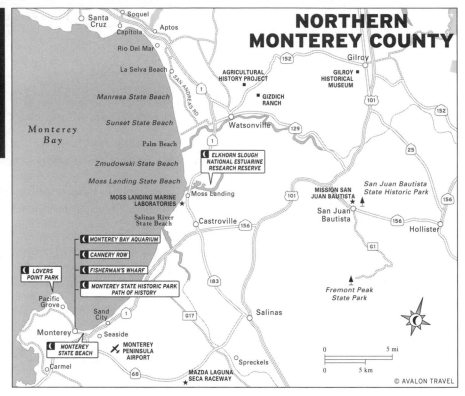

Moss Landing State Beach

The surf is up at Moss Landing State Beach (end of Jetty Rd., 831/649-2836, www.parks.ca.gov, free). It has moderate to difficult waves throughout the year and attracts avid surfers and body boarders. Fishing from the shore for striped bass is popular here as well.

Kayaking

Take a wildlife paddle with **Kayak Connection** (2370 Hwy. 1, 831/724-5692, www.kayakconnection.com, single or double kayak $30 pp) and **Monterey Bay Kayaks** (Moss Landing Harbor, 800/649-5357, www.montereybaykayaks.com, single or double kayak $30 pp), both of which offer rentals and tours of Elkhorn Slough.

Whale Watching

Whale watching is always in season, and two companies run daily tours from Moss Landing: **Blue Ocean Whale Watching** (7881 Sandholdt Rd., 831/600-5103, www.blueoceanwhalewatch.com) and **Sanctuary Tours** (Moss Landing Harbor, 831/917-1042, www.sanctuarycruises.com). Both offer 4-5-hour tours that seek the elusive beasts for a close encounter. There is nothing quite like floating alongside a pod of migrating or feeding whales.

Fishing

Geared up year-round to fish the depths of Monterey Bay is **Kahuna Sports Fishing** (Moss Landing Harbor, 831/633-2564, www.kahunasportfishing.com), with seasonal fishing trips for

© KRISTIN LEAL

Elkhorn Slough National Estuarine Research Reserve

salmon, rock cod, and albacore. Make sure to call ahead for reservations, and dress in warm waterproof layers, as the sea can be rough and wet.

Shopping

On the last Sunday of July every year, Moss Landing becomes an antiques mecca, hosting a street fair with the five local antiques shops along with hundreds of other booths. Many of the shops on Moss Landing Road and Sandholdt Road are open year-round; **Hamlin Antiques** (8070 Moss Landing Rd., 831/633-3664, daily 10 A.M.-5 P.M.) and **Promenade Deck** (7902 Sandholdt Rd., Suite D, 831/633-6122) are both worth a stop as they carry all kinds of cool old stuff, including furniture and antique jewelry.

Accommodations

If you want to stay the night in Moss Landing, the best bet is **Captain's Inn** (1822 Moss Landing Rd., 831/633-5550, www.captainsinn.

com, $149-255). Each guest room is decorated with antique nautical pieces and has modern amenities such as a fireplace and an updated bath. Since this is a bed-and-breakfast, services include a home-cooked breakfast and freshly baked cookies before bed. You can book a room in the main house or in the boat house, where the bed is fashioned after a boat.

Food

Get fresh local seafood entrées at **Phil's Fish Market** (7600 Sandholdt Rd., 831/633-2152, www.philsfishmarket.com, daily 11:30 A.M.-9 P.M., $20). Featured on the Food Network several times, including on *Throwdown! with Bobby Flay,* Phil makes the best cioppino on the West Coast (and Phil totally beat Bobby). This is also an actual fish market as well, selling fresh seafood to go.

Seafood Mexican-style is at the **Whole Enchilada** (Hwy. 1 and Moss Landing Rd., 831/633-3038, www.wenchilada.com, $25),

© KRISTIN LEAL

seals loafing along the shore at Moss Landing

with *grande* margaritas that will quench your thirst. A local favorite for the live music, it is also a hip place for dinner and dancing.

PRODUCE STANDS

There are many small produce stands at the southern end of Moss Landing that feature local produce such as artichokes, pumpkins, cherries, and strawberries. Before leaving Moss Landing, you may want to grab some local goodies from the largest stand in the area, **Farm Fresh Produce** (next to Whole Enchilada, 831/633-3636, daily 24 hours); prices are unbelievably reasonable, and the fruit is delectable. The produce is primarily California-grown with a focus on local fare, so what you find here is literally farm-fresh.

MARINA

There are only a few reasons to make a stop in the city of Marina: cheaper accommodations, Marina State Beach, and **California State University**

Monterey Bay (CSU, 100 Campus Center, Hwy. 1 Imjin Rd. exit, 831/582-3000, www.csubm.edu).

Sports and Recreation

The waves are consistently up for surfing at **Marina State Beach** (end of Reservation Rd., 831/649-2836, www.parks.ca.gov, daily 8 A.M.till 30minutes after sunset, day-use free). The easiest way to access the beach is just off of Highway 1 on Reservation Road at the main state park entrance; the parking lot is on a dune right above the beach.

The reach of Marina State Beach is vast and can also be accessed from other locations: across the street from Marina Dunes RV Park (3330 Dunes Dr.) and across the street from the Marina City Animal Shelter (211 Hillcrest Ave.), both of which grant a secluded escape to the dunes and surf mostly frequented by local residents. Parking is free, and finding a spot to park is stress-free at any time of year.

Steady winds help to create moderate to hard

surf with strong riptides. Flying a kite from the dunes is a popular activity because of the constant winds, and you can stroll the beach as far as Monterey Wharf. This beach is for day use only, and dogs are not allowed.

For wide-open dune exploration and endless beach access, visit **Fort Ord Dunes State Park** (Light Fighter Dr., at 8th St. and Hwy. 1 near CSU campus, 831/649-2836, www.parks.ca.gov, daily 8 A.M. till 30 minutes after sunset, day-use free), with plenty of space to cycle, long-board, or jog with your dog along the old military roadways that meander through the park. The Monterey Bay Coastal Bike Trail, and the alternate bike trail that opened in 2011 to allow a closer look at Monterey Bay's majestic coastline, both begin here. The new trail heads out to the dunes just above the beach and hugs the coast until it joins the main Monterey Bay Coastal Bike Trail.

From the parking lot you can access all the paved paths that meander among the sage and the sand. The paths are peaceful, and cars are not allowed. The rolling hills invite some speed when cycling, and the flats offer nice glides. The stunning views from the park's paths encompass the ocean, Monterey, and Pacific Grove. The sandy dunes, filled with ice plants and sage, create calm and desolate atmosphere.

Above the beach at the west end of the parking lot is a short boardwalk along the crest of the dunes that leads to a viewing platform with 360-degree views of the peninsula. Informational panels flank the path.

Getting to the beach is an easy short walk through a small canyon in the dunes. Four miles of open beach are perfect for fishing for striped sea bass from the shore, picnicking in numerous private nooks, and jogging surfside on sand that is especially hard-packed at low tide.

Accommodations
CAMPING
A nice spot for camping is the **Marina Dunes RV Park** (3330 Dunes Dr., off Reservation Rd., 831/384-6914, www.marinadunesrv.com, $45-65), just beyond the dunes and steps from the shore. Experience the beauty of the bay away from the crowds. The park has full-hookup sites and is an all-service facility.

UNDER $150
Reasonable rates and simple guest rooms can be found at **Laguna Lodge** (430 Reservation Rd., 831/384-5248 or 800/594-5552, www.lagunalodge.com, $39-120). Room size is cozy, and the location is near Marina State Beach. All guest rooms are nonsmoking, although smoking is permitted outside; room amenities include mini fridges, microwaves, coffeemakers, and hair dryers.

Another affordable option is **Old Marina Inn** (3110 Del Monte Blvd., 831/384-9401, www.oldmarianinn.com, $39-159), a modest family-run motel just one mile from the beach. Room size is just big enough to fit the furniture, and room amenities include mini fridges, microwaves, and coffeemakers; some rooms have three beds. Wireless internet access is included, and downtown Monterey is seven miles away.

Just steps from Marina State Beach is the **Quality Inn-Monterey Beach Dunes** (3280 Dunes Dr., 831/384-1800 or 800/550-0055, www.qualityinnmarina.com, $69-350), with 114 guest rooms and several family suites neutrally decorated in blues and light reddish-browns. Guest rooms have a small table with chairs or a desk, and continental breakfast is included.

Just down the street and across from the beach is the **Best Western Beach Dunes Inn** (3290 Dunes Rd., 831/883-0300 or 800/550-0055, www.beachdunesinn.com, $79-375). Guest rooms are spacious, with plenty of room to spread out, including a small sitting area. The location is great if you're looking for a quieter stay, about 10 minutes' drive from the Laguna Seca racetrack and 20 minutes from Cannery Row.

Situated between the CSU Monterey Bay campus and Marina State Beach is the **Holiday**

MONTEREY

Inn Express Marina (189 Seaside Circle, 831/884-2500 or 800/465-4329, www.hiexmarina.com, $102-350). Guest rooms are substantial, and the suites having mini kitchens and an additional seating area. The beach is a short walk away, where you can admire hang gliders and surfers taking advantage of the consistent wind. If you are into flying kites, bring one along; the dunes provide the perfect launch.

Located near the center of Marina is the Ramada Inn (323 Reservation Rd., 831/582-9100 or 800/272-6232, $75-400), where you can enjoy a quiet stay just beyond the more heavily touristed area. The beach is only a few miles away, and Monterey and Carmel are a short drive. Guest rooms are modern and spacious; standard rooms have a desk and a table, and the suites have a good-size sitting area with a couch. You can also get in a workout at the on-site fitness center.

$150-250

If you want a full-service hotel on the beach and out of the main traffic, stay at the Sanctuary Beach Resort (2600 Sand Dunes Dr., 831/394-3321 or 800/242-8627, www.thesanctuarybeachresort.com, $199-449), where you can marvel at the stunning ocean view and the city lights against the sunset. Amenities include the Serenity Spa and the local favorite steak house, Kula Ranch Restaurant.

Food
CASUAL DINING

For the authenticity of Thailand with a California twist, D'Anna Thai Kitchen (210 Reindollar Ave., 831/883-9399 or 831/883-9339, www.dannathaikitchen.com, daily lunch and dinner, $10-15) makes every dish fresh to order: mild, medium, or spicy. On a warm night or a sunny afternoon the outside deck is inviting. The lunch specials (Mon.-Fri. 11:30 A.M.-3 P.M.) are the best deals and include hot soup, salad, steamed rice, and a choice of entrée.

Decade-old Nak Won Korean BBQ House (330 Reservation Rd., Suite A, 831/883-2302, Mon.-Sat. 11 A.M.-9 P.M., $10-15) is one of the few authentic Korean restaurants in the area. The lunch specials are filling, and dinner is a fun experience with the traditional side dishes. Try the barbecue table.

Serving fresh Mexican food for over 25 years, the fare at Sarita's Mexican Restaurant (342 Reservation Rd., 831/384-1318, www.saritasmexicanrestaurant.com, daily 8 A.M.-9 P.M., $4-17) is hearty, and you won't leave hungry. Breakfast is on all day, the chips and salsa are addicting, and the combo plates are outstanding. Relax with a cold beer and enjoy the colorful decor.

For a traditional Italian meal with plenty of seafood, try Francisco's Restaurant (262 Reservation Rd., Suite B, 831/883-9115, daily 11 A.M.-9 P.M., $9-28). It is a great secluded foodie spot in Marina that is worth the trek. Warm art graces the walls, and the extensive menu has a fine dessert selection, perfect for a romantic meal or family fun.

CHEAP EATS

Grab a quick bite and a hot cup of joe at Marina Donuts & Bagels (266 Reservation Rd., Suite H, 831/883-4527, Mon.-Fri. 5 A.M.-3 P.M., Sat.-Sun. 6 A.M.-2 P.M., $2-6). Locals have made this a morning stop ever since this family-owned bakery first opened. The breakfast and lunch sandwiches are a huge improvement on fast food, and the doughnuts and bagels are always fresh; get here early if you want to try the buttery and flaky croissants.

For gourmet take-out breakfast and lunch items that won't break the bank, the Wild Thyme Deli & Café (445 Reservation Rd., 831/884-2414, www.wildthymedeli.com, Mon.-Sat. 10 A.M.-5:30 P.M., $6-13) specializes in soups, salads, sandwiches, and baked goods. Offerings include marinated tri-tip, house-roasted turkey, a Salinas Valley iceberg lettuce wedge, and the hot soup of the day.

For a taste of traditional German food, stop in at **Mecca Delicatessen** (215 Reservation Rd., Suite N, 831/384-7821, Mon.-Fri. 10 A.M.-6 P.M., Sat. 10 A.M.-5 P.M., $11-15), serving homemade bratwurst, fresh German meats, and a sweet selection of German beers since 1970. The food is satisfying, the service charming, and the atmosphere welcoming.

FINE DINING

Dive into the Pacific Rim cowboy-style at **Kula Ranch Island Steakhouse** (3295 Dunes Dr., 831/883-9479, www.kula-ranch.com, Tues.-Thurs. and Sun. noon-9 P.M., Fri.-Sat. noon-10 P.M., Mon. 4:30-9 P.M., $17-28). The menu is inspired by exotic islands and the Wild West and features fresh seafood, juicy steaks, a sushi bar, colorful salads, and excellent desserts. Enjoy dining by the fire outdoors or relax indoors in the modern dining room. If you like a cocktail with your meal, try the legendary mai tai.

For something a little more than casual, grab a table at **Dishes Bistro and Grill** (330 Reservation Rd., 831/883-1207, Mon.-Sat. 5-9:30 P.M., $11-30). Belying its strip-mall location, the food is delicious and the menu is mostly Italian and red-meat options, with wood-fired pizzas and an extensive selection of imported beer and wine. Children are welcome, and save room for dessert, as the tiramisu is outstanding.

SEASIDE

Visitors find themselves in Seaside for beach fun and as a base for exploring the area. Numerous events are held year-round at Laguna Seca Raceway, a few miles away along Highway 68. Although downtown Monterey and Carmel are also nearby, in Seaside you can escape the hustle of those more heavily visited areas and experience the local vibe on the sunny side of the bay.

Sports and Recreation

There are plenty of secluded coves along the beaches of Seaside. **Monterey State Beach** (Del Monte Ave. and Park Ave., 831/624-3407, daily 8 A.M. till 30 minutes after sunset, free) and **Fort Ord Dunes State Park** (Hwy. 1 Lightfighter exit, 831/649-2836, www.parks.ca.gov, daily 8 A.M. till 30 minutes after sunset, day-use free) provide miles of open beaches perfect for fishing, surfing, sunbathing, flying kites, and windsurfing. Access to the beach is along the coast off the frontage road. The southern reaches of the beach tend to have a mellow swell perfect for kids and beginning surfers. Farther north, the swell picks up and the ocean floor drops much more drastically, providing sizable waves most of the year. Know your limits, and always swim with caution.

Bayonet and Black Horse (1 McClure Way, 831/899-7271, www.bayonetblackhorse.com, daily 7 A.M.-4:30 P.M., $100-120 plus cart fees) are two great golf courses in one lovely location overlooking Monterey Bay. Both courses were redesigned in 2007 by award-winning golf-course architect Gene Bates to provide new and inspiring challenges. Bayonet is tree-lined and showcases Bates' bunkering and charming greens. There are expanded views, and the order of the holes has changed, including a new ninth hole. The longest green on the course is 613 yards, and the new finisher is a par-4 uphill 476 yards. Par-72 Black Horse has had its tree-lined challenges removed and has new fairways, greens, trees, and bunkering throughout, and views of the bay have expanded.

Accommodations

Located near the County Fairgrounds is **Pacific Best Inn** (1141 Fremont Blvd., 831/899-1881, www.pacificbestinn.com, $39-100). Smoking or nonsmoking guest rooms are simple and have TVs and free local phone calls, and some have microwaves and fridges. Bed options are king, queen, or two doubles.

Located on Highway 1 just a block from the beach is the **Seaside Inn** (1986 Del Monte

Blvd., 831/394-4041 or 800/399-4212, www. seasideinnmonterey.com, $49-179). Guest rooms are tasteful and modest with patios on the first floor and balconies on the second floor. Amenities include a small table and chairs, a fridge, included Internet access, in-room microwaves, and included continental breakfast.

The newly refurnished **Magic Carpet Lodge** (1875 Fremont Blvd., 831/899-4221, www. magiccarpetlodge.com, $59-149) offers casual guest rooms at good rates; continental breakfast is included. Guest rooms have TVs with HBO and a few extended channels, coffeemakers, and hair dryers; outside is a heated swimming pool.

Just next door is another fine lodging operation at the **Holiday Inn Express at Monterey Bay** (1400 Del Monte Blvd., 831/394-5335, www.hiexpress.com, $89-309), offering clean midsize guest rooms and a family-fun outdoor pool. The hot or cold express breakfast is included in the room rates.

Accommodations at the **EconoLodge Bay Breeze** (2049 Fremont Blvd., 831/899-2700, www.econolodgebaybreeze.com, $39-260) are straight out of the 1950s. The hotel has 50 spacious guest rooms with cable TV with HBO, and some rooms have fridges and microwaves. Continental breakfast is included, and an inviting outdoor picnic area is perfect for having breakfast outside. There are restaurants nearby.

For great room rates near Monterey, **Discovery Inn of Monterey** (1106 Fremont Blvd., 831/394-3113, www.discoveryinnmontereybay.com, $39-269) is only blocks from Del Monte Beach and a short drive to the Monterey Wharf and Pebble Beach, the airport, and the County Fairgrounds. You will feel comfortable in the large, simply decorated guest rooms.

Close to the beach and near the major shopping area of Sand City is the **Sandcastle Inn** (1011 Autocenter Pkwy., 831/394-6556, www. sandcastleinnseaside.com, $49-249), a great

location outside the heavily touristed area. Fast food and cheap eats are all within walking distance, and local attractions are a short drive away. Guest rooms are modern with a beachy feel and are equipped with fridges, microwaves, tubs and showers, included Wi-Fi, cable TV, and included continental breakfast.

The most upscale accommodations in town are the **Embassy Suites Monterey Bay-Seaside** (1441 Canyon Del Rey Blvd., 831/393-1115, www.embassysuites1.hilton.com, $129-399). Many of the suites have ocean views, and the hotel is only three blocks from the beach. Guest rooms are fully equipped and quite spacious, with more than enough room to stretch out.

Food

There are a few good eats in Seaside: **The Breakfast Club** (1130 Fremont Blvd., Suite 201, 831/394-3238, www.breakfastclubrestaurant.com, daily 6 A.M.-2 P.M., $10-15) is locals' preference when it comes to breakfast. Weekends are always hopping; be prepared to get on the waiting list and have a cup of coffee outside while you wait.

The authentic Thai restaurant **Bann Thai** (1769 Fremont Blvd., Suite F-1, 831/394-2996, www.bannthaiseaside.com, Mon.-Fri. 11 A.M.-3:30 P.M. and 5-9 P.M., Sat. noon-9 P.M., $10-18) has chicken rice soup, pad thai, and various curries that are unparalleled in the area. Order the excellent Thai iced tea.

For the best Vietnamese in the area, make your way to the **Pho King** (1153 Fremont Blvd., 831/899-1424, daily 11:30 A.M.-9 P.M., $8-15). The spring rolls, cold noodle bowl, and rice bowls are more than filling, and you can plan on taking home leftovers. It is definitely a local hot spot, and the staff wear warm smiles.

GETTING THERE AND AROUND

Getting to Northern reaches of Monterey County is easy. Simply follow Highway 1; either head south from Santa Cruz or north from

Monterey. It is about miles 34 from Santa Cruz to Marina and just under 10 miles to go from Marina to Monterey. Seaside borders Monterey on the north side, and Moss Landing is 18 miles from Monterey. You can either drive, hop on the local **Monterey-Salinas Transit** bus (MST, 831/899-2555, www.mst.org), or take the **Santa Cruz METRO,** 831/425-8600, www.scmtd.com).

CARMEL

Carmel's landscape is divided into two distinct sections: Carmel-by-the-Sea, with quaint homes and small shops alongside sprawling estates and designer boutiques; and Carmel Valley, conjuring images of the Wild West with dusty hills and windswept seaside forests.

The main drag through Carmel-by-the-Sea, Ocean Avenue, is lined with art galleries, couture shops (including fashion for your beloved pet), fine dining, and occasional but discreet souvenir shops. A leisurely stroll along Ocean Avenue's shops and galleries is a must. Favorite stops along the way include Cottage of Sweets, a mouthwatering candy shop, and Mountain Song Galleries, a laid-back art gallery that's all about California. Carmel is known as a dog-friendly town: You'll see water bowls set out along the street, and many restaurants, shops, and hotels allow you to bring your furry friend. But the charm of the town extends beyond Ocean Avenue. Make time to walk or drive through some of the winding streets of Carmel to see fairy-tale bungalows and gingerbread-style houses next to secret gardens and tiny castles.

If you find yourself on the peninsula on a foggy day, head inland to the chaparral landscape of Carmel Valley. Vineyards, tasting rooms, and the pioneering organic farm and restaurant Earth Bound serve up a more rustic California atmosphere. Outdoors fans will enjoy Garland Ranch Regional Park, with miles of trails for working up a sweat.

HIGHLIGHTS

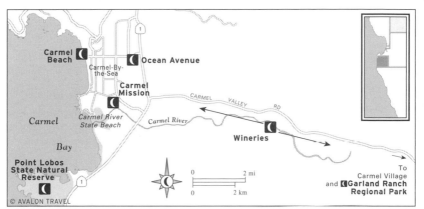

© AVALON TRAVEL

LOOK FOR **(** TO FIND RECOMMENDED SIGHTS, ACTIVITIES, DINING, AND LODGING.

(Carmel Mission: Father Junípero Serra's crown jewel of the Spanish Mission system in Carmel-by-the-Sea is still a functioning church as well as a school and museum (page 91).

(Point Lobos State Natural Reserve: The reserve showcases the natural treasures of the Monterey Bay, including an ancient cypress grove, China Cove, and a spellbinding coastline (page 92).

(Carmel Beach: Also known as the hamlet-by-the-sea, this is the spot to do some surfing, take the dogs for a trot, snuggle up by an evening beach bonfire, or entertain the kids for the day (page 93).

(Ocean Avenue: Whether you're in the mood for window-shopping, browsing in art galleries, or sampling local cuisine, walking the avenue and adventuring down its side streets is a charming experience (page 98).

(Wineries: Carmel Valley is the perfect place to taste some of Central California's most delicious wines (page 109).

(Garland Ranch Regional Park: The granddaddy of the Monterey County Regional Park System, Garland has 4,462 acres for hiking, biking, fishing, and picnicking (page 112).

CARMEL

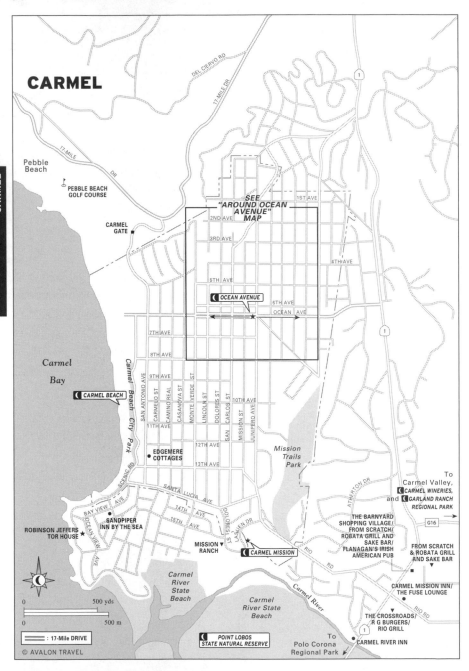

CARMEL

SEE "AROUND OCEAN AVENUE" MAP

Pebble Beach

PEBBLE BEACH GOLF COURSE

CARMEL GATE

1ST AVE
2ND AVE
3RD AVE
4TH AVE
5TH AVE

OCEAN AVENUE

6TH AVE
OCEAN AVE

7TH AVE
8TH AVE

Carmel Bay

CARMEL BEACH

9TH AVE

SAN ANTONIO AVE
CARMELO ST
CAMINO REAL
CASANOVA ST
MONTE VERDE ST
LINCOLN ST
DOLORES ST
SAN CARLOS ST
MISSION ST
JUNIPERO AVE

10TH AVE
11TH AVE

Carmel Beach City Park

SCENIC RD

EDGEMERE COTTAGES

12TH AVE
13TH AVE

Mission Trails Park

SANTA LUCIA AVE

BAY VIEW AVE

14TH AVE
15TH AVE

DOLORES ST
LASUEN DR

SANDPIPER INN BY THE SEA

ROBINSON JEFFERS TOR HOUSE

OCEAN VIEW AVE

MISSION RANCH

CARMEL MISSION

RIO RD

Carmel River State Beach

Carmel River State Beach

Carmel River

ATHERTON DR

To Carmel Valley, CARMEL WINERIES, and GARLAND RANCH REGIONAL PARK

THE BARNYARD SHOPPING VILLAGE/ FROM SCRATCH/ ROBATA GRILL AND SAKE BAR/ FLANAGAN'S IRISH AMERICAN PUB

G16

FROM SCRATCH & ROBATA GRILL AND SAKE BAR

CARMEL MISSION INN/ THE FUSE LOUNGE

RIO RD

THE CROSSROADS/ R G BURGERS/ RIO GRILL

CARMEL RIVER INN

0   500 yds
0   500 m

POINT LOBOS STATE NATURAL RESERVE

To Polo Corona Regional Park

: 17-Mile DRIVE

DEL CIERVO RD
17-MILE DR.
17-MILE DR

© AVALON TRAVEL

PLANNING YOUR TIME

A day trip is possible but a weekend is preferred to discover all the charming touches of Carmel from the sea to the valley, exploring wine, fine art, live performances, outdoor attractions, distinctive shopping, epicurean dining, and historic sites.

Carmel-by-the-Sea

Carmel-by-the-Sea quickly charms with whimsical cottages, a historic mission, big-city entertainment, shopping galore, and outdoor fun. You can spend a day perusing the unique shops in search of treasure, or make a day of exploring the terrain of Point Lobos State Natural Reserve. Grab the family and head to the beach, rounded out with a sunset fire at the ocean. The area is known as a haven for artists, and there are a number of interesting galleries.

SIGHTS
◖ Carmel Mission

Carmel Mission (3080 Rio Rd., 831/624-3600,

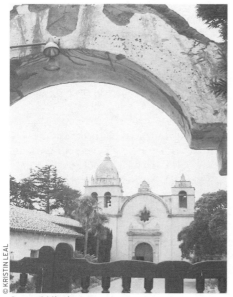

© KRISTIN LEAL

Carmel Mission

www.carmelmission.org, Mon.-Sat. 9:30 A.M.-5 P.M., Sun. 10:30 A.M.-5 P.M., $6.50 adults, $4 seniors, $2 ages 7-17, free under age 7), formally called Mission San Carlos Borroméo de Carmelo, was Father Junípero Serra's personal favorite among his California missions. He lived, worked, and eventually died here, and visitors today can see a replica of his cell.

A working Catholic parish remains part of the complex, so be respectful when taking the self-guided tour. The rambling buildings and courtyard gardens show some wear, but enough restoration work has been done on the church and living quarters to make them attractive and easy to visit. The Carmel Mission has a small memorial museum inside off the second courtyard, but this small dated space is not the only historical display; exhibits run through many of the buildings, illustrating the lives of the 18th- and 19th-century friars.

The highlight of the complex is the church, with its gilded altar, shrine to the Virgin Mary, the grave of Junípero Serra, and an ancillary chapel dedicated to his memory. Round out your visit by walking in the gardens among the flowers and fountains, and read the grave markers in the small cemetery.

Fairy Tale Homes of Carmel

House numbers are not used on the twisting streets of Carmel-by-the-Sea; rather, homes are named for locations from fairy tales. Today, the village still represents the original intention of its bohemian creators as a haven for artists, and the dwellings themselves are artworks. Many of the cottages are the original structures from Carmel's early days, and newer dwellings are

CARMEL

NATIVE AMERICANS AND THE MISSIONS

Beginning in 1769, Native Americans throughout California's Central Coast region were forcefully converted to Christianity by the Spaniards in the hopes of securing a Spanish colony along the western coast of the New World. The goal was to convert Native Americans into loyal Spanish subjects, and they were used as forced labor to build and maintain the missions along the California coast. By 1823 the Spaniards had established 21 missions, from San Diego to Sonoma, and had converted thousands of Native Americans. Brutal tactics forced them into farm labor and domestic service at the missions.

This interaction with the Spanish would change life for Native Americans forever. Many were never able to return to their previous way of life and would provide labor for the large ranchos, working as vaqueros herding cattle, on farms, and as domestic servants.

built to mirror the whimsical forerunners. Along any street in the one-square-mile village, walking or driving reveals interesting houses.

Robinson Jeffers Tor House

Robinson Jeffers, the "dark prince of poetry," built a rugged-looking castle on the Carmel coast in 1919 and named it Tor House (26304 Ocean View Ave., 831/624-1813, www.torhouse.org). It was constructed from boulders unearthed on the shore of Carmel Bay. The house and its Hawk Tower look medieval, and the structure is a fitting monument to his work and poetry, which often dealt with dark and controversial topics in heavy blank verse. There is a fragrant, layered English cottage garden, and docents lead tours (Fri.-Sat. 10 A.M. to 3 P.M. on the hour, $10 adults, $5 students).

Carmel Art Association

Of the many galleries in Carmel, the one with the greatest breadth of local talent is the Carmel Art Association (Delores St. between 5th Ave. and 6th Ave., 831/624-2176, www.carmelart. org, daily 10 A.M.-5 P.M.), a co-op of over 120 talented artists, all of whom live within 30 miles of town. The association was founded in 1927 and bought this space in 1933. The majority of pieces are oils and pastels, but there are other media, including wood and sculpture. Artists bring in new works on the first Wednesday of each month, ensuring constant rotation.

PARKS
◖ Point Lobos State Natural Reserve

Five miles south of Carmel is Point Lobos State Reserve (Hwy. 1 at Riley Ranch Rd., 831/624-4909, www.pointlobos.org, year around daily 8 A.M.-sunset, day-use $10), a stunning piece of land abutting the ocean. The rugged, ragged cliffs and rocks, beautiful and malformed, are dotted with pine and cypress trees and scented by the pines and the fresh ocean breeze. Spanish moss hangs languidly from tree branches.

Replete with hiking and diving prospects, the reserve has 12 hiking and walking trails on nine square miles. You can access the water or climb into the hills on wide dirt paths (it's important to stay on the paths to avoid the plentiful poison oak). Rough trails hug the ridged rocks and wander through ancient cypress groves. Meander farther along, and graceful secluded beaches become visible. There is a convenient launch ramp for diving and kayaking in Whalers Cove.

Within the sheltered coves and twisting forests, history runs deep. Europeans arrived in the area at Point Lobos in 1796 and used this location as a whaling station, a shipping port, a cannery, a pasture for livestock, and residential lots. The whaler's cabin at the bottom of Whalers Cove was built by Chinese fisherman in the 1850s and is now a cultural history museum; adjacent to it is the whaling station museum.

Hiking trails within the park stretch for miles

© KRISTIN LEAL

Stop by the Tor House to marvel at its gothic tower.

along the weathered coastline and wind among ancient cypress trees. Cypress Grove Trail is less than one mile long and is home to one of only two naturally occurring stands of Monterey cypress trees that exist. Pine Ridge Trail is about 0.5 miles long and runs through open woods filled with coast live oaks and Monterey pines. A favorite path starts at South Shore Trail, hugs the beach for one mile, and runs into Bird Island Trail, which about one mile into China Cove and Gibson Beach. Maps are available at the entrance for $2.

Point Lobos is fantastic for technical diving as there is an abundance of deep water with pinnacles emerging from the sandy ocean floor. A winding maze of giant kelp is seen along the middle reef, and the shoots can grab rocks as deep as 130 feet. Wildlife that can be seen includes wolf eels, rockfish, and lingcod hiding among the rocks and plantlife; giant sunflower stars hunt crabs, abalone, sea urchins, sea cucumbers, and other starfish.

Cycling is allowed on all the paved roadways, and parking areas are available to lock up your bicycle if you want to continue on the dirt paths on foot. It is a great way to see the majestic park with the wind in your hair. Motorized vehicles are limited to 15 mph in the park, making cycling feel safer.

Palo Corona Regional Park

Entry to Palo Corona Regional Park (200 yards south of the Carmel Bridge on Hwy. 1, 831/372-3196, www.mprpd.org, daily sunrise-sunset, free) is only possible if you obtain a permit on the website 2-3 days in advance. The park has several trails for backcountry access to disused livestock corrals, a worn-out barn, and rusting machinery that evoke the Wild West. Rich green rolling hills dotted with groves of oaks reach into Carmel Valley, and the entrance is lined with an old wooden fence that sways in the wind. The park is great for a family picnic or an afternoon hike.

BEACHES
◖ Carmel Beach

At the west end of Ocean Avenue is the sparkling white sand of Carmel Beach (Ocean Ave., 831/624-4909, daily 6 A.M.-10 P.M.). This lovely south-facing stretch allows off-leash dog visitors, and bonfires are allowed south of 10th Avenue until 10 P.M. Surfing, wading, and sunbathing are especially popular in the summer and fall. Enjoy the beautiful cypress trees and consider bringing a kite as this beach is often windy. A nice walking trail above the beach at street level provides views of Carmel Bay. Parking is generally easy along Scenic Drive for instant access to the sandy shore.

This is the only beach in Carmel that is safe enough to surf and body board, and the waves are appropriate for beginners and intermediates. Be aware of the strong riptides and that the waves tend to crash in the shallows. Check the tide table ahead of time as the water gets

HOUSE NUMBERS

As you see mailing addresses in Carmel-by-the-Sea and begin to explore the neighborhoods, you'll realize something interesting: There are no house numbers. Some years ago Carmel residents voted not to allow door-to-door mail delivery, and thus saw no need for numeric addresses on buildings. So you have to pay close attention to the street names and the block you're on. To make things even more fun, street signs can be difficult to see in the mature foliage, and a dearth of streetlights can make them nearly impossible to find at night. If you can, come during the day to get the lay of the land before trying to navigate after dark.

flat at high tide. Within the cove the water is generally clear, and the kelp tends to grow some distance offshore.

Carmel River State Beach

A mile-long beach and lagoon, Carmel River Beach (end of Carmelo St., 831/649-2836, www.parks.ca.gov, free) is perfect for building sandcastles, and when the river is high, it cuts right through the beach to empty vigorously into the sea. Part of Carmel River State Beach is the dangerous **Monastery Beach** (just north of Point Lobos State Natural Reserve). A popular site for shore divers, the waters can be unforgiving to recreational swimmers or waders; the undertow is swift, and the ocean floor drops quickly near shore.'

SURFING

Carmel Surf Lessons (831/915-4065, $100 pp includes equipment) meets daily at Carmel Beach and has professional lessons for all skill levels and ages. Owner Noah Greenberg has been catching waves for over 20 years and is the surf instructor at California State University Monterey Bay. Known locally as "the dude who can teach you

everything you need to know about the local surf," he is also great at teaching kids.

ENTERTAINMENT

Events and entertainment in Carmel tend to focus on art and food. This town loves its haute culture, so you won't find sports bars or generic movie theaters; instead, enjoy classical music, a wealth of live theater, and a glass of wine on mild evenings.

Bars

The population of Carmel is mostly wealthy seniors, hence the nightlife isn't too hopping, and live music in bars was illegal until 2006—seriously. Most of the drinking happens in restaurants and a few hotel lounges. If you're looking for an evening out within the city limits, try a night at the theater.

Younger locals hang out at **Ody's Tavern** (San Carlos St. between Ocean Ave. and 7th Ave., 831/626-6821, daily 6 P.M.-2 A.M.). The late-night crowd can get pretty rowdy (well, rowdy for Carmel), so on the weekend be prepared for a bumping time. The food is typical bar grub, and after a few cocktails it won't matter what you're eating anyway.

The General Store, also known as **Forge in the Forest** (Junipero St. and 5th Ave., 831/624-2233, www.forgeintheforest.com, Sun.-Thurs. 11:30 A.M.-9 P.M., Fri.-Sat. 11:30 A.M.-10 P.M.) has a rustic pioneer bar in the heart of Carmel-by-the-Sea. Enjoy a frothy brew or a classy cocktail next to the actually flaming forge or outside in the patio.

The place for a breakfast mimosa or Bloody Mary is **Il Fornaio** (Ocean Ave. and Monte Verde St., 831/622-5100, www.ilfornaio.com, daily 9 A.M.-10 P.M.), one of the few bars in Carmel open all day and into the evening. It is busy most of the day, and weekend and summer nights are hopping.

Enjoy sipping a cocktail while listening to piano melodies at **Mission Ranch** (26270 Dolores St., 831/625-9040, www.missionranch.

CARMEL

© KRISTIN LEAL

Take in the breathtaking views of Point Lobos State Natural Reserve.

com, from 4 P.M.). The atmosphere is relaxed California and you may catch a glance of Clint or Dina Eastwood; as this is their digs.

The bar is comfortable and the fire is cozy at **The Fuse Lounge** (Carmel Mission Inn, 3665 Rio Rd., 831/624-1841, www.carmelmissioninn.com, daily 5-10 P.M.). There is never a cover charge, and make sure to wear your dancing shoes: The weekend music will get you out on the dance floor in no time.

Art Galleries

Carmel boasts more art galleries per capita than any other town in the United States. Accordingly, shopping in the downtown pedestrian area means "checking out the galleries." **Gallery Diamante** (Dolores St. between 5th Ave. and 6th Ave., 831/624-0852, www.gallerydiamante.com) is representative, with a large collection of landscape paintings by different artists, interesting sculptures, and the most popular modern styles in painting,

sculpture, and even art glass and jewelry on display. The jewelry can be reasonably priced, but expect to spend more for paintings.

Bucking the current trends in Carmel art is Boban Bursac, sole owner of the tiny **EX-tempore Gallery** (Dolores St. between 5th Ave. and 6th Ave., 831/626-1298, bobanart@yahoo.com). Bursac's amazing large-format paintings evoke emotional reactions from even the most casual passerby; lucky visitors might even get to meet the artist. Sadly, these works of art do not come cheap, which is understandable given their size and the skill and devotion it takes to paint them.

For something altogether different and perhaps less intimidating, the **Sports Gallery** (Dolores St. between Ocean Ave. and 6th Ave., 831/624-6026, www.sportsgalleryweb.com) is a more casual and down-to-earth space with sports memorabilia, signed photos, and even paintings of favorite sports heroes and legends, many at reasonable prices. It is a great spot to look for a gift for a sports fanatic.

Carmel Beach

Trotter Galleries (San Carlos St. between Ocean Ave. and 7th Ave., 831/625-3246, www.trottergalleries.com) is the place to look for local and California art. It has specialized in early California and Americana with many featured Carmel artists since 1980.

Mountain Song Galleries (Ocean Ave., just south of Mission St., 831/620-0600, www.mountainsonggalleries.com) is a quintessential California art gallery. Displaying an array of art that includes handblown glass, surfboards, sculpture, paintings, and guitar art from all over the state, the vibe is laid-back as you are welcomed with a free cup of coffee.

Winfield Gallery (Dolores St. between 7th Ave. and Ocean Ave., 831/624-3369, www.winfieldgallery.com) is hands down the finest art gallery on the peninsula. Artist Chris Winfield and his wife offer a sophisticated collection of contemporary artists, including Andrea Johnson, Jack Zajac, and Bruce Beasley.

Perfect for the seaside town of Carmel is a branch of the **Wyland Galleries** (Ocean Ave., north of Mission St., 831/626-6223, www.wylandgallerycarmel.com). Wyland is an accomplished photographer, writer, painter, and sculptor, and his shops are always worth a visit. Stunning artworks capture the treasures of the world under the sea.

Theater

Despite its small size, Carmel has nearly a dozen live theater groups. In a town that defines itself by its love of art, performing arts are important; don't hesitate to ask local people what's playing when you're in town.

The **Pacific Repertory Theater** (PacRep, 831/622-0100, www.pacrep.org) is the only professional theater company on the Monterey Peninsula, performing all over the region but most often in the Golden Bough Playhouse (Monte Verde St. and 8th Ave.), the company's home theater. Other regular venues include the Forest Theater (Mountain View St. and Santa

© KRISTIN LEAL

the lobby at the Sunset Center

Rita St.) and the Circle Theater (Casanova St. between 8th Ave. and 9th Ave.), in the Golden Bough complex; also watch for their plays at Monterey State Historic Park and in Pebble Beach. The company puts on classic and new dramas, comedies, and musicals. You might see John Patrick Shanley's *Doubt,* enjoy songs in *The Fantasticks,* or sing along to *High School Musical.* Check the website for upcoming shows, and buy tickets online or by phone to guarantee seats. Each fall, PacRep puts on the **Carmel Shakespeare Festival,** a short showing of Shakespeare that even draws the notice of Bay Area theater aficionados. Check the website for information on this year's shows and venues.

Nestled among the fairy-tale cottages of Carmel, the lights dim and the intimate audience quiets as the **Sunset Center** (San Carlos St. and 9th Ave., 831/620-2040, www.sunsetcenter.org) brings numerous big-city performances to its stage year-round. Annual events by the four major presenting partners

include the Carmel Bach Festival, Carmel Music Society concerts, Chamber Music Monterey Bay concerts, and performances of the Monterey Symphony. Sunset also brings popular headline acts that include comedians, musicians, dance companies, and more.

FESTIVALS AND EVENTS

Famous for the Carmel Bach Festival and the Carmel Art Festival, Carmel hosts a variety of annual events, focused on the arts, classic cars, music, and family fun.

Spring

Celebrate the bounty of spring in May with the **Robinson Jeffers's Tor House Garden Party** (Tor House, 831/624-1813, www.torhouse.org), an afternoon-long celebration of Carmel, architecture, and Jeffers that includes music and poetry.

In a town famed for art galleries, one of the biggest events of the year is the **Carmel Art Festival** (Mission St., www.carmelartfestival.org) in May, a four-day event celebrating visual arts in a variety of media with shows by internationally acclaimed artists at galleries, parks, and other venues around town. The festival also sponsors here-and-now contests, including the prestigious plein air (outdoor painting) competition. Visitors get a rare opportunity to witness the artists working outdoors, engaging in the creative process with Carmel's scenery for inspiration.

Round out your festival experience by bidding on paintings at the auction at the end of the event. You can get a genuine bargain on original artwork while supporting both the artists and the festival. Perhaps best of all, the Carmel Art Festival is a great place to bring the family—a wealth of children's activities encourages the budding artist in even the youngest festivalgoers.

Summer

Kick off summer with the **Carmel Fourth of July Celebration** (Davendorf Park,

CARMEL

831/624-2522, www.carmelcalifornia.org). Join the annual gathering to mark the country's independence.

A classical music experience and one of the most prestigious festivals in Northern California is the **Carmel Bach Festival** (Sunset Center, www.bachfestival.org). For three weeks in July-August, Carmel-by-the-Sea and surrounding towns host dozens of classical concerts. Of course, the works of J. S. Bach are featured, but you can also hear Mozart, Vivaldi, Handel, and other heavyweights of the genre. You can choose among big concerts in major venues or intimate performances in smaller spaces. Concerts and recitals are held every day, and budget-conscious music lovers can just as easily enjoy the festival midweek as on the weekends.

Fall

Celebrate the fall equinox in late September with the **Carmel Authors and Ideas Festival** (Sunset Center, www.carmelauthors.com), an intimate event where you can meet authors and attend lectures and book signings.

Get a **Taste of Carmel** (Carmel Mission, 831/624-2522, www.tasteofcarmel.com) in early October, when more than 30 restaurants come together to tempt your palate with local produce paired with wines from 20 local vineyards. You can get to know local winemakers while mingling with area residents.

A weekend in October is filled with music and poetry for the **Robinson Jeffers Fall Festival** (Tor House, 831/624-1813, www.torhouse.org). Enjoy a weekend of readings by Taelen Thomas along with lectures on Jeffers, a gathering at Carmel Mission, and a poetry walk to Carmel River Beach.

The **Carmel Art and Film Festival** (Sunset Center, www.carmelartandfilm.com) in mid-October is a five-day event showcasing groundbreaking art and exclusive film premieres. The event provides the opportunity to mingle with leading artists, filmmakers, and industry professionals.

Winter

The holiday season is a magical time in Carmel-by-the-Sea as **Carmel's Holiday Tree Lighting** (Devendorf Park, 831/620-2000, www.ci.carmel.ca.us) fires up the beacon on Ocean Avenue. The magnificent pine is lit in a kaleidoscope of color, a charismatic sight twinkling brightly against the backdrop of the ocean.

SHOPPING

There are three distinct shopping areas in Carmel: the tight cluster of shops on Ocean Avenue, the country-themed Barnyard mall, and the classy Crossroads mall.

◖ Ocean Avenue

Downtown Carmel-by-the-Sea is a great place to get out of your car and stroll among the boutiques and numerous galleries. The main shopping street is Ocean Avenue and its side streets all the way to the ocean. There are antiques shops, unique gifts, typical souvenirs, and clothing along with the jewel in the crown, **Carmel Plaza** (Ocean Ave. and Mission St., 831/624-0138, www.carmelplaza.com, Mon.-Sat. 10 A.M.-6 P.M., Sun. 11 A.M.-5 P.M.), a mall with 40 high-end chain stores on three levels. The **Carmel Bay Company** (Ocean Ave. and Lincoln St., 831/624-3868, www.carmelbaycompany.com, daily 10 A.M.-5 P.M.) is an adorable home store with accessories, purses, and hats as well as treasures for every room of your home.

Some of the grandest antiques on the peninsula are for sale at **Jan de Luz Boutique** (Dolores St., 831/622-7621, www.juandeluz.com, daily 10 A.M.-6 P.M.), a French-inspired collection with everything from fireplaces to linens. You'll find two floors of furniture for sale at **Carmel Antiques** (Ocean Ave. and Dolores St., 831/624-6100, www.carmelantiques.net, daily 10 A.M.-6 P.M.), including wardrobes, desks, and sideboards, many of them French and English pieces from the 1930s. Lamps and other small items round out an overall good

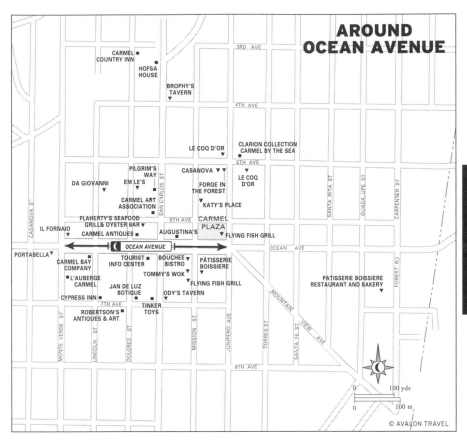

AROUND OCEAN AVENUE

© AVALON TRAVEL

CARMEL

selection. The focus at **Robertson's Antiques & Art** (Dolores St. and 7th Ave., 831/624-7517, Mon.-Sat. 10 A.M.-5 P.M., Sun. 11 A.M.-5 P.M.) is pieces from the mid-19th to mid-20th centuries. You'll find lots of porcelain and silver plates, but there are more unusual items, including Asian pieces, small sterling tea sets, and even a small collection of swords. Robertson's has a strong reputation, having been in business for 20 years. You'll love **Carrigg's of Carmel** (Ocean Ave. and San Carlos St., 831/601-0613, daily 9 A.M.-5:30 P.M.), with home furnishings from around the world. It is the oldest design store in Carmel, and its eye candy is worth at least a walk through.

Augustina's (Ocean Ave. between Mission St. and San Carlos St., 831/624-2403, www.augustinaleathres.com, daily 9:30 A.M.-6 P.M.) is the ultimate stop for fine furs, leather, sterling silver buckle sets, and jewelry. The window displays are fantastic and will lure you in from across the street. Fine-tune your Wild West look at **Burns Cowboy Shop** (Ocean Ave. between Lincoln St. and Dolores St., 831/624-4014, www.burnscowboyshop.com, daily 10 A.M.-6 P.M.), a six-generation family business that has been bringing the Western way of life to consumers since 1876. They carry an extensive line of Lucchese Boots, William Henry knives, silver buckles, and other Western fashions. **Rittmaster** (Pine Inn, Ocean Ave. and Monte Verde St., 831/624-1147, www. rittmastercarmel.com, Mon.-Sat. 10:30 A.M.-5:30 P.M.) is for the modern woman, with racks of cleverly displayed clothing and accessories. The place men come to dress is at **Robert Talbott** (Ocean Ave. between Dolores St. and Lincoln St., 831/624-6604, www.roberttalbott. com, daily 10 A.M.-6 P.M.). It is all about looking great with fine fabrics, hand-sewn neckwear, and silk accessories.

If you're looking for something different, you'll find unusual paper products, handcrafted cards and candles, distinctive collectable pieces, and rich jewelry at **Piccolo** (Dolores St. between Ocean Ave. and 7th Ave., 831/624-4411, www.piccolocarmel.com, daily 10 A.M.-5:30 P.M.). **Thinker Toys** (7th Ave. and San Carlos St., 831/624-0441, www.thinkertoys. com, Sun.-Thurs. 10 A.M.-6 P.M., Fri.-Sat. 10 A.M.-8 P.M.) is a Carmel tradition where kids jump for joy at the hands-on toys that encourage thinking and imagination. Conveniently located **Carmel Forecast** (Ocean Ave. and Dolores St., 831/626-1735, daily 8 A.M.-10 P.M.) is all about casual wear, the best place to buy a gift for someone who wants the word *Carmel* emblazoned on a hat. There are two floors of hats, sweatshirts, flip-flops, and jeans, along with mugs and knickknacks.

Founded in 1969, **Pilgrim's Way** (Dolores St. between 5th Ave. and 6th Ave., 800/549-9922, www.pilgramsway.com, Mon.-Thurs. 11 A.M.-6 P.M., Fri.-Sat. 11 A.M.-7 P.M.) is the only remaining bookstore in Carmel. It has a good selection of books with spiritual themes as well as current best-sellers and biographies. Take a peek at the secluded garden in back, filled with water fountains, wind chimes, and plants-as well as peace and quiet.

The Barnyard Shopping Village

The Barnyard Shopping Village (831/624-8886, www.thebarnyard.com, daily

You can walk along Ocean Avenue in Carmel and find a seemingly endless variety of shops.

10 A.M.-6 P.M.) is a whimsically well-designed two-story complex with bike shops, women's clothing, sparkly treasures, and full salons.

You will most certainly find something sparkly at **Jewel Boutique** (831/625-1016), which sells certified diamonds, estate jewelry, antiques, and original designs. **Bellagio** (831/622-7117, daily 9 A.M.-5 P.M.) provides full-service salon care for men and women. It's best to make an appointment, but walk-ins are welcome.

People gather at the window of **Pieces of Heaven** (831/625-3368, Sun.-Thurs. 10 A.M.-6 P.M., Fri.-Sat. 10 A.M.-8 P.M.) to watch owners Peg and Bob Whitted make candy and pull taffy. Everything is made onsite, and they've been turning out two dozen kinds of truffles, English toffee, caramel-covered marshmallows, and more since 1995. Real cream and butter make the taste far superior to factory-manufactured chocolates.

DOG-FRIENDLY CARMEL

Dogs are a big part of the charm of Carmel, embraced and invited into many stores, restaurants, and the beach. Water bowls are set out for thirsty canines, and biodegradable poop bags can be found in dispensers around town. To visit Carmel with your dog, here is a list of canine-friendly accommodations and restaurants.

ACCOMMODATIONS

There are many pet-friendly lodgings in Carmel, including **Hofsas House** (San Carlos St. and 3rd Ave., 831/624-2745, www.hofsashouse.com, $120-260), **Edgemere Cottages** (San Antonio St. between 13th Ave. and Santa Lucia Ave., 866/241-4575, www.edgemerecottages.com, $129-299), **Carmel Mission Inn** (3665 Rio Rd., 831/624-1841, www.carmelmissioninn.com, $99-499), **Carmel River Inn** (2600 Oliver Rd., 831/624-1575, www.carmelriverinn.com, $80-369), **Carmel Country Inn** (Dolores St. and 3rd Ave., 831/625-3263, www.carmelcountryinn.com, $195-395), and **Cypress Inn** (Lincoln St. at 7th Ave., 831/624-3871, www.cypress-inn.com, $225-575, dogs $30 extra).

RESTAURANTS

Bringing your furry pal along to a meal is easy in Carmel, and several local eateries cater to both your needs. Check out **Katy's Place** (Mission St. and 6th Ave., 831/624-0199, www.katysplacecarmel.com, daily 7 A.M.-2 P.M., $13-25), **From Scratch** (3626 The Barnyard, 831/625-2448, daily 7:30 A.M.-2:30 P.M., $10-15), **Forge in the Forest** (5th Ave. and Junipero St., 831/624-2233, www.forgeintheforest.com, Sun.-Thurs. 11:30 A.M.-9 P.M., Fri.-Sat. 11:30 A.M.-10 P.M., brunch Sun. 11 A.M.-2:30 P.M., $25), **Tommy's Wok** (Mission St. and Ocean Ave., 831/624-8518, Tues.-Sun. 11:30 A.M.-2:30 P.M. and 4:30-9:30 P.M., $12-25), **Casanova** (5th Ave. between San Carlos St. and Mission St., 831/625-0501, www.casanovarestaurant.com, daily 11:30 A.M.-3 P.M. and 5-10 P.M., $25), **Da Giovanni** (Lincoln St. between 5th Ave. and 6th Ave., 831/626-5800, www.dagiovannis.com, daily 5-9 P.M., $25-40), **Cypress Inn Restaurant and Lounge** (Lincoln St. and 7th Ave., 831/624-3871, www.cypressinn.com, 11:30 A.M.-4 P.M. 5-10 P.M., $9-26), and **Flaherty's Seafood Grill & Oyster Bar** (6th Ave. between San Carlos St. and Dolores St., 831/625-1500, www.flahertysseafood.com, daily 11 A.M.-9:30 P.M., $30).

SHOPPING

Dogs and felines can get all their specialty needs taken care of in Carmel, from fashionable outfits to healthy snacks. **Diggidy Dog** (Ocean Ave. and Mission St., 831/625-1585, www.diggidydogcarmel.com, daily 10 A.M.-6 P.M.) serves the posh desires of your pets with distinctive clothing, tasty treats, and toys.

The Raw Connection (26549 Carmel Rancho Rd., 831/626-7555, www.therawconnection.com, Mon.-Sat. 9 A.M.-6 P.M., Sun. 10 A.M.-6 P.M.) is the place to fill furry bellies with raw and grain-free food and provides nutrition consulting, vitamins, treats, toys, training supplies, and on-site training classes for both cats and dogs.

CARMEL

Bay Bikes (831/624-7433, www.baybikes.com, daily 9 A.M.-5 P.M.) is a full-service shop that supplies cyclists with the latest gear and rides. There is a huge inventory of mountain bikes, road bikes, hybrids, and comfort bikes; you may fall in love as you walk through the door. Rent a bike here to head to Point Lobos or into Carmel-by-the-Sea.

The Crossroads

Crossroads Shopping Village (Hwy. 1 and Rio Rd., 831/625-4106, www. crossroadsshoppingvillage.com, Mon.-Sat. 10 A.M.-6 P.M., Sun. noon-5 P.M.) is the place for practicality and specialized stores. The mall contains over 50 stores, making it easy to lose track of time while wandering and browsing.

For basic toiletries, cosmetic items, and picnic fixings, make your way to **Safeway** (831/625-8820, daily 24 hours) or **CVS Pharmacy** (831/624-0195, daily until 10 P.M.).

"Clean sportswear" is the motto at **Pacific Tweed** (831/625-9100, www.pacifictweed.com,

© KRISTIN LEAL

Visit the farmers market at The Barnyard Shopping Village for a taste of Monterey's local bounty.

daily 10 A.M.-6 P.M.), one of the best-known clothing stores in Carmel. The clothes are slightly traditional, slightly trendy, casual, and subdued. For women's wear made for comfort in the coastal climate, check out the airy threads at **Carmel Apparel Company** (831/626-7777), with delicately detailed garments and cozy loungewear. Wearable art is what's sold at **Exotica** (831/622-0757), with colorful clothing from the Pacific Rim and Asia and accessories for accent. Get colorful and get comfortable at the same time.

For a full stock of hand-chosen books, look no farther than **River House Books** (831/626-2665), with an assortment of foreign and domestic magazines as well as art, cooking, fashion, and reference books, children's classics, and best-selling fiction and nonfiction.

ACCOMMODATIONS
Under $150
The exterior of **C Hofsas House** (San Carlos St. and 3rd Ave., 831/624-2745, www.hofsashouse.com, $120-260) evokes a quaint Dutch country inn, but Hofsas House is in a quiet residential neighborhood within easy walking distance of downtown Carmel-by-the-Sea. Guest rooms in the rambling multistory structure are surprisingly spacious, with nice furniture and linens that show just a touch of wear, along with adequate baths. If you can, get an ocean-view room with a patio or balcony, buy a bottle of wine, and spend some time sitting outside looking over the town of Carmel and the distant Pacific.

Edgemere Cottages (San Antonio St. between 13th Ave. and Santa Lucia Ave., 866/241-4575, www.edgemerecottages.com, $129-299) is removed from the hustle of downtown Carmel and only two minutes from the beach. There are three cottages behind a private residence and one guest room inside the house; all the guest rooms are reasonably large, with

© KRISTIN LEAL

CARMEL

the meadows at Mission Ranch

comfortable everyday furnishings. The three cottages have kitchenettes, and all guest rooms have Wi-Fi access. Breakfast is served 8:30-10 A.M. in the dining room. Edgemere is pet-friendly, but the two house cats, Riff-Raff and Magenta, rule the backyard, so dogs beware.

The **Carmel Mission Inn** (3665 Rio Rd., 831/624-1841, www.carmelmissioninn.com, $99-499) provides a central base in town just outside the heavily touristed area. It is easy to find, right off of Highway 1, and has several room choices.

Owned by Carmel's movie-star former mayor, Clint Eastwood, ◖ **Mission Ranch** (26270 Dolores St., 831/624-6436, www.missionranchcarmle.com, $120-310) is a high-end place to stay with wide views of the grassy ranch leading to the ocean. Postcard-worthy sheep graze, and the fog burns off slowly, exposing gaps of blue sky. There are tennis courts on-site, and guest rooms are country elegant with room to spread out.

At the **Carmel River Inn** (2600 Oliver Rd., 831/624-1575, www.carmelriverinn.com, $80-369), the spacious and comfortable guest rooms are equipped with kitchenettes, fireplaces, and in-room jetted tubs, with a pool on-site. The inn is perfect if you have a lot a gear and need to stretch out.

The **Sandpiper Inn-by-the-Sea** (2408 Bay View Ave., at Martin Way, 831/624-6433, www.sandpiper-inn.com, $129-280) is a small inn steps from the pale sand and cooling sea. Guest rooms are decorated in modern country-cottage style, reflecting the surrounding story-book village atmosphere.

$150-250

Travelers with dogs and cats are welcome at **Carmel Country Inn** (Dolores St. and 3rd Ave., 831/625-3263, www.carmelcountryinn.com, $195-395), but as it is a romantic getaway, children under age 6 are not allowed. Guest rooms and suites boast comfortable furnishings that feel more like a home than a generic hotel; some have fireplaces, reading nooks, and jetted tubs.

Staying at the all-inclusive resort ◖ **Hyatt Carmel Highlands** (120 Highland Dr., 831/620-1234, www.highlandsinn.hyatt.com, $225-695) feels like staying near edge of the world. Guest rooms have dramatic views of the rugged coastline and Point Lobos in the distance. The pool is delightful, and the hot tub feels great after a long day of hiking or horseback riding in the valley.

Despite its ghastly name, the cliff-top **Tickle Pink Inn** (155 Highland Dr., 831/624-1244, www.ticklepinkinn.com, $231-559) offers tasteful luxury. Each guest room has a view of the ocean, an array of high-end furniture and linens, and the top-end amenities you'd expect from a distinctive Carmel hostelry. For a special treat, shell out for the spa-bath suite and watch the ocean while you soak in the tub with your sweetie.

Doris Day is one of the owners of the ◖ **Cypress Inn** (Lincoln St. at 7th Ave., 831/624-3871, www.cypress-inn.com, $225-575, pets $30 more), one of the oldest and classiest places to stay in Carmel. Day's Hollywood memorabilia is on display throughout the property, and given her love of animals, it's no surprise that the inn is pet-friendly. The midsize rooms are well appointed, with fresh flowers, fruit, and cream sherry to welcome you. Many guest rooms have jetted tubs, and all have Wi-Fi. You can hear the ocean, four blocks away, from the charming outdoor patio.

Over $250

The **Holly Farm** (9200 Carmel Valley Rd., 831/625-1926, www.hollyfarm.com, packages from $500) is a great place to get married, and you can celebrate all evening just steps from your honeymoon bed. Packages range from two-night stays to weeklong escapes. The farm is rustic with elegant gardens and room for your wedding guests.

Built in 1929, **L'Auberge** (Monte Verde St. and 7th Ave., 831/624-8578, www.lauberge-carmel.com, $425-700) defines luxury. This is the place to stay if you like to be pampered;

virtually anything you want will be provided. The brick courtyard where horses were once brought after riding is the best feature of this European-style hotel. The furnishings are beautiful but not stuffy, and all 29 guest rooms have fridges and Wi-Fi access. Pets are not allowed.

FOOD
American

For a traditional home-cooked meal, **Em Le's** (Dolores St. between 5th Ave. and 6th Ave., 831/625-6780, www.em-les.com, Mon.-Tues. 7 A.M.-3 P.M., Wed.-Sun. 7 A.M.-3 P.M. and 4:30-8 P.M., $20) focuses on comfort foods like meatloaf, Caesar salad, pasta dishes, triple-decker clubs, and patty melts. The food is simple but fresh and fairly inexpensive compared to surrounding restaurants. Unfortunately, the wine list doesn't match the food. The decor is country comfortable, and the service attentive. This is one of the oldest restaurants in Carmel, dating to 1955.

Outdoor seating in a garden with heaters will lure you into the ◖ **Forge in the Forest** (5th Ave. and Junipero St., 831/624-2233, www.forgeintheforest.com, Sun.-Thurs. 11:30 A.M.-9 P.M., Fri.-Sat. 11:30 A.M.-10 P.M., brunch Sun. 11 A.M.-2:30 P.M., $25). Get a hot dog and a beer or saddle up for a juicy steak. The menu will satisfy the hungry, with nicely crafted salads to tempt smaller appetites.

Asian

For the best Japanese food on the peninsula, go to ◖ **Robata Grill and Sake Bar** (3658 The Barnyard, 831/624-2643, lunch Mon.-Sat. 11:30 A.M.-2 P.M., dinner Sun.-Thurs. 5-8:30 P.M., Fri.-Sat. 5-9:30 P.M., $20-30). The sushi is fantastically creative but isn't really a menu staple; there is a full selection of hot items. Highlights include the barbecue ball and steamed vegetables with special sauce. Happy hour is Monday-Tuesday 5-7 P.M. for half-price appetizers, and Wednesday-Thursday for half-price house wine, draft beer, and hot sake.

For a more authentic hole-in-the-wall local dining experience, try **Tommy's Wok** (Mission St. and Ocean Ave., 831/624-8518, Tues.-Sun. 11:30 A.M.-2:30 P.M. and 4:30-9:30 P.M., $12-25). All the veggies are fresh and organic, and the food is consistently good whether you dine in or take it out.

Breakfast

Katy's Place (Mission St. and 6th Ave., 831/624-0199, www.katysplacecarmel.com, daily 7 A.M.-2 P.M., $13-25) is a self-described "Carmel tradition" that can get quite crowded on weekend mornings. Breakfast, including heavy eggs Benedict or light Belgian waffles, is available whenever it's open.

As the name implies, breakfasts at **◖ From Scratch** (3626 The Barnyard, 831/625-2448, daily 7:30 A.M.-2:30 P.M., $10-15) are made from scratch. Specialties include corned beef and hash, cheese blintzes, crab eggs Benedict, granola, and oatmeal. There's a country feel to the small dining room, tucked downstairs from street level, but the best seats are out front under the vine-covered arbor.

The **◖ Tuck Box** (Dolores St. between Ocean Ave. and 7th Ave., 831/624-0440, www. tuckbox.com, daily 7:30 A.M.-2:30 P.M., $12) reflects the storybook atmosphere of Carmel-by-the-Sea. Celebrated as a historical landmark and serving hot meals for the last 70 years, generations of visitors have made it a stop. A full line of groceries, including fruit spreads and scone mix, is available.

Cheap Eats

When you just want a good burger, go to **r.g. Burgers** (201 Crossroads Village, 831/626-8054, daily 11 A.M.-8:30 P.M., $12). Any burger can be made with beef, bison, turkey, chicken, or veggie falafel in variations that include the black and bleu, jalapeño cheddar, and even a Reuben. The 20-plus varieties of milk shake include mint chip, strawberry, banana, and

mocha; while they aren't thick, they are flavorful. Since it gets loud inside, the few tables outside are a better choice.

Kick back and hang out at **Brophy's Tavern** (4th Ave. and San Carlos St., 831/624-2476, daily 11:30 A.M.-11 P.M., $12), serving basic pub food such as potato skins, sliders, BLTs, french dip sandwiches, and hot dogs smothered with sauerkraut, all in a golf-themed wood-paneled environment. There's a good selection of beers as well as tequilas, and unusually for Carmel, it's open late.

Happy-hour action at **Flanagan's Irish American Pub** (3772 The Barnyard, 831/625-5500, www.flanagancarmel.com, daily 11:30 A.M.-2 A.M., $12) includes $3 pints (Mon.-Fri. 4-6:30 P.M.). Among its traditional pub grub items, you can always count on the fish-and-chips. There is a pool table inside and a fire burning outside, making it a comfortable place to spend some time.

French

Belying the "fancy" stereotype of French restaurants are the country-style meals at the decidedly unstuffy **Le Coq d'Or** (Mission St. and 4th Ave., 831/626-9319, www.lecoqdor.com, daily 5-10 P.M., $35). Order a classic French beef stew or a German schnitzel, and perhaps share a juicy morsel with your canine companion, who is welcome to dine with you on the heated porch.

Get close in a warm cottage for casual French dining at **Pâtisserie Boissiere** (Mission St. between Ocean Ave. and 7th Ave., 831/624-5008, www.patisserieboissiere.com, lunch daily 11:30 A.M.-4:30 P.M., dinner Wed.-Sun. 5:30-9 P.M., $25). The bakery case is always filled with signature pastries that include almond croissants, *pot au chocolat,* and éclairs. The cuisine is California French with french toast or brioche for Sunday brunch and beef bourguignon for dinner.

Italian

The king of Jordan has dined at **Casanova** (5th

Ave. between San Carlos St. and Mission St., 831/625-0501, www.casanovarestaurant.com, daily 11:30 A.M.-3 P.M. and 5-10 P.M., $25), a Carmel institution. It's deceptively small from the outside but unfolds into several dining areas that include a fine-dining section, a large arbor-covered outdoor patio, several small intimate spaces, and the Van Gogh room, where you eat at a table that once belonged to artist Vincent van Gogh. An excellent wine list complements the country French and Italian menu, with options like niçoise salad, linguini with lobster, bacon-wrapped rabbit, and housemade cannelloni.

Taste a bit of Italy at **Da Giovanni** (Lincoln St. between 5th Ave. and 6th Ave., 831/626-5800, www.dagiovannis.com, daily 5-9 P.M., $25-40), where Firok Shield presents his Italian dream at one of his three restaurants in town. Dishes are a fusion of family recipes and the romance of Italy.

Mediterranean

For ambiance, you can't beat the flower gardens and traditional cottage at **PortaBella** (Ocean Ave. and Monte Verde St., 831/624-4395, www.carmelsbest.com, daily 11:30 A.M.-11 P.M., $20-40). This upscale kitsch restaurant serves Mediterranean-inspired cuisine with a distinct local flair.

Seafood

The **Flying Fish Grill** (Mission St. between Ocean Ave. and 7th Ave., 831/625-1962, Sun.-Thurs. 5-9 P.M., Fri.-Sat. 5-9:30 P.M., $30-40) serves Japanese-style seafood with a California twist in the Carmel Plaza open-air shopping mall. While the food isn't universally revered, the service at the Flying Fish and the presentation of the plates makes a visit worth the time and expense.

Sate your seafood cravings at **Flaherty's Seafood Grill & Oyster Bar** (6th Ave. between San Carlos St. and Dolores St., 831/625-1500, www.flahertysseafood.com, daily

11 A.M.-9:30 P.M., $30). There are two restaurants under one roof, and a fresh catch is always on the menu. Flaherty's is known for satisfying chowders and cioppino.

Farmers Markets

You'll find fruits, veggies, honey, meats, cheeses, and flowers—many of them organically produced—at the **Carmel Certified Market** (3690 The Barnyard, www.montereybayfarmers.org, May-Sept. Tues. 9 A.M.-1 P.M.). The **Carmel Farmers Market** (City Hall, 1 Civic Square, www.carmelfarmersmarket.com, May-Sept. Sat. 8-11:30 A.M.) focuses on local products that include orchids, pastries, beeswax, poultry, and more.

INFORMATION AND SERVICES
Visitor Information

You'll find the **Carmel Visitors Center** (San Carlos St. between 5th Ave. and 6th Ave., 831/624-2522, www.carmelcalifornia.org, daily 10 A.M.-5 P.M.) right in downtown Carmel-by-the-Sea.

Media and Communications

For more information about the town and current events, pick up a copy of the local weekly newspaper, the **Carmel Pine Cone** (www.pineconearchive.com).

Medical Services

The nearest major medical center to Carmel-by-the-Sea is in nearby Monterey. For minor issues, head for the **Community Hospital of Monterey** (23625 Holman Hwy., Monterey, 831/622-2746, www.chomp.org).

GETTING THERE AND AROUND

The most direct driving route from San Francisco to Carmel takes 2.5 hours, and about 117 miles. Get on U.S. 101 south, exit onto Highway 156 west, and then get onto Highway 1 south.

From Los Angeles, the drive takes 5.5-6

PREPARING THE PERFECT PICNIC

Throughout Carmel you can embark on adventures that pair perfectly with a picnic. There are quite a few places to fill your basket with gourmet goodies in Carmel-by-the-Sea, and if you don't want to bother putting one together, stop by a local eatery for a freshly prepared picnic to go.

MARKETS

You can easily fill your picnic basket at **Bruno's Market and Delicatessen** (Junipero St. and 6th Ave., 831/624-3821, www.brunosmarket.com, daily 7 A.M.-8 P.M.), where you will find a full-service deli that makes great sandwiches to order along with a large selection of premade salads, barbecue ribs, and roasted chicken. They will even grill you up a fresh burger if you have time to wait. You will also find fine cheeses, a whole isle of wine, crackers, a small produce corner, sweets, and just about anything else you'd will want to snack on. Keep an eye out for the hot-food carts at the front doors and near the deli counter; they serve up Chinese and Mexican food. This is also the place to pick up bottled soda pop. The selection is massive, and you'll find your old-time favorites alongside newer brands.

Create your own gourmet picnic basket at **Nielsen Bros. Market** (San Carlos St. and 7th Ave., 831/624-6441, www.nielsenmarket.com, daily 8 A.M.-7 P.M.). The wine section has over 10,000 bottles from around the world, including fine Carmel Valley wines and half-size bottles ideal for picnicking. There is an extensive deli with freshly made salads and sandwiches made to order, epicurean cheeses galore, fresh produce, cases of cold beverages, snacks, crackers, cured meats, and tasty local sweets.

RESTAURANTS

Treat yourself to a French-inspired picnic at the **Pâtisserie Boissiere** (Mission St. between Ocean Ave. and 7th Ave., 831/624-5008, www.patisserieboissiere.com, daily 11:30 A.M.-4:30 P.M., $8-14). You can find a picnic menu filled with appetizers, salads, soups, sandwiches, and freshly baked desserts. The best deal on the menu is the eight different sandwiches ($7.50-8), which come with a pleasant salad.

A quick and easy place to pick up a picnic is at **5th Avenue Deli & Catering** (5th Ave. between San Carlos St. and Dolores St., 831/625-2688, www.5thavedeli.com, Sun.-Mon. 7 A.M.-6 P.M., Sat. 9 A.M.-6 P.M., $10-15), with sandwiches, salads, and baked goods. The goodies in the Lovers Lunch basket ($75) include smoked salmon, fresh fruit, two deli salads, an assortment of cheeses, two desserts of your choice, and a bottle of Korbel champagne or a split of Ventana Gold Stripe chardonnay.

Carmel Belle (Doud Arcade, San Carlos St. south of Ocean Ave., 831/624-1600, www.carmelbelle.com, daily 8 A.M.-5 P.M., $5-18) has a large to-go menu of country-fresh and organic items. Traditional picnic items include cheese platters and savory sandwiches, but more adventurous is a morning excursion with some breakfast sandwiches or green eggs and ham.

Whether you are in the mood for an afternoon outing or a dinner picnic with a bonfire on the beach, the **Forge in the Forest** (5th Ave. and Junipero St., 831/624-2233, www.forgeintheforest.com, Sun.-Thurs. 11:30 A.M.-9 P.M., Fri.-Sat. 11:30 A.M.-10 P.M., brunch Sun. 11 A.M.-2.30 P.M., $10-25) has it covered: The entire menu is available to take out, including hearty sandwiches, salads, hot dogs, pasta, pizza, and steaks cooked to perfection.

Stop at **Il Fornaio Café** (Pine Inn Hotel, Ocean Ave. between Lincoln St. and Monte Verde St., 831/624-3821, www.ilfornaio.com, daily 8 A.M.-5 P.M., $6-12) for some fine Italian food to take out, along with authentic pastries, steaming-hot coffee, crisp salads, freshly baked cookies, and house-made breads. It is an ideal stop for a beach picnic as it is located just before the beach near the bottom of Ocean Avenue.

While you are picnicking at the beach, don't be surprised if encounter a local artist; this is a local hangout for creative minds.

CARMEL

hours and about 336 miles. Get onto U.S. 101 north, exit onto Highway 68 west, and then take Highway 1 south.

Car

The slow but incredibly beautiful and much preferred coastal routes into Carmel are via Highway 1, which runs north-south. From Highway 1, take Ocean Avenue to downtown Carmel. A more expensive but even more beautiful route is 17-Mile Drive ($10 per car). To reach it from north-south U.S. 101, at Salinas take Highway 68 toward Monterey. This can be a slow road and is heavily congested during weekends and on peak summer days.

Bus

Monterey-Salinas Transit (MST, 888/678-2871, www.mst.org) has service all around the peninsula and can transport you from Monterey to Carmel. They also operate a shuttle service through Carmel, a green-and-wood-colored bus that operates every 30 minutes.

The **Carmel Valley Grapevine Express** (888/678-2871, www.mst.org, year-round daily 11 A.M.-6 P.M.) shuttle bus stops at Cannery Row, downtown Monterey, and the Barnyard Shopping Center in Carmel and takes you to the Carmel Valley wineries for just $6 round-trip. Buses run every hour. This is a great way to avoid the hassle of driving and finding parking.

Taxi

Carmel Taxi (26080 Carmel Ranch Blvd., 831/624-3885) can take you anywhere on the peninsula.

Train

Amtrak's (800/872-7245, www.amtrak.com) Seattle-Los Angeles *Coast Starlight* train travels through Salinas (Station Place and Railroad Ave., Salinas, daily 8 A.M.-10 P.M.) daily in both directions. To reach Carmel, first take the free shuttle bus to the Aquarium Bus Stop in Monterey, which is a curbside-only stop. From there, switch to the Monterey-Salinas Transit (MST, 888/678-2871, www.mst.org) bus to Carmel.

Air

The **Monterey Peninsula Airport** (MRY, 200 Fred Kane Dr., Monterey, 831/648-7000, www.montereyairport.com) has nonstop flights by United, Allegiant, American Eagle, and America West from Los Angeles, San Diego, Phoenix, Denver, Las Vegas, and San Francisco, but airfares are much higher than flying into the larger **San Jose International Airport** (SJC, 2077 Airport Blvd., San Jose, 408/277-4859, www.sjc.org), which is 90 minutes' drive north.

Carmel Valley

If you're chasing the sun, you can almost always find it in Carmel Valley. The hills, evergreen oak trees, and mild climate give way to vineyards and more outdoor recreation opportunities. The cluster of villages in the valley offers a glimpse into the past; time moves at slower pace out here.

SIGHTS
Earthbound Farms

One of the largest purveyors of organic produce in the United States, Earthbound Farms (7250 Carmel Valley Rd., 831/625-6219, www.ebfarm.com, Mon.-Sat. 8 A.M.-6 P.M., Sun. 10 A.M.-5 P.M.) offers visitors access to its small-ish facility in the Carmel Valley. Drive up to the farm stand and browse a variety of organic fruits, veggies, and flowers. Outside, you can walk into the fields to inspect the chamomile labyrinth and the kids garden (yes, kids can look and touch). Select and harvest your own fresh herbs from the cut-your-own garden, or leave the cooking to the experts and purchase delicious prepared organic dishes at the farm stand. If you're interested in a more in-depth guided tour of the farm, check the website for a schedule of walks in which an expert guide-perhaps a chef or locally famous foodie-leads a group out into the fields for a look at what's growing and how to use it.

Carmel Valley Village

The laid-back side of Carmel is a 20-minute drive inland from the coast. The scenery shifts to wide ranches, rows of grapevines arcing over the hills, and the cool Carmel River. Carmel Valley Village (Carmel Valley Rd. and Esquiline Rd.) is an unincorporated little town with wine tasting, shopping, outdoor action, and good eats. You can easily fill a day wandering the tiny village. Most of the valley's tasting rooms are here, and you can walk from one to the next. Famed antiques shop Jan De Luz is in the center, and you can find an assortment of Western-inspired restaurants as well as the old-fashioned Running Iron Saloon. Cool off and take a dip with the locals in The Bucket, or gather the family for a hike to the Los Padres Reservoir and Dam or a picnic in Carmel Valley Community Park.

◖ WINERIES

Its small size means there are a limited number of vineyards in the Carmel Valley, but it is a charming place for a wine-tasting day trip from Carmel, Monterey, or even Big Sur. Traffic is lighter and crowds are smaller than in larger wine districts, and many of the wineries are still family-owned. You'll get personal attention and delicious wines in a gorgeous rural setting.

Bernardus Winery (5 W. Carmel Valley Rd., 800/223-2533, www.bernardus.com/winery, daily 11 A.M.-5 P.M., tasting $5-10) sits is at a vineyard that also has a luxurious lodge and a gourmet restaurant. The short list of wines made from the grapes grown on the estate includes Marinus Vineyard, a Bordeaux-style blended red. Chardonnay, pinot noir, and sauvignon blanc varietals come from cooler coastal vineyards. If you're lucky, you might get to sip some small-batch vintages of single-vineyard wines that are available only in the tasting room.

The biggest name in the Carmel Valley is **Château Julien Wine Estate** (8940 Carmel Valley Rd., 831/624-2600, www.chateaujulien.com, Mon.-Fri. 8 A.M.-5 P.M., Sat.-Sun. 11 A.M.-5 P.M.). The European-style white estate building with a round turret is visible from the road. The light, airy tasting room is crowded with barrels, wine cases, souvenirs, and tasting glasses. You can taste a wide selection of chardonnays, cabernets, syrahs, merlots, and more. If you're lucky, you might be able to

CARMEL

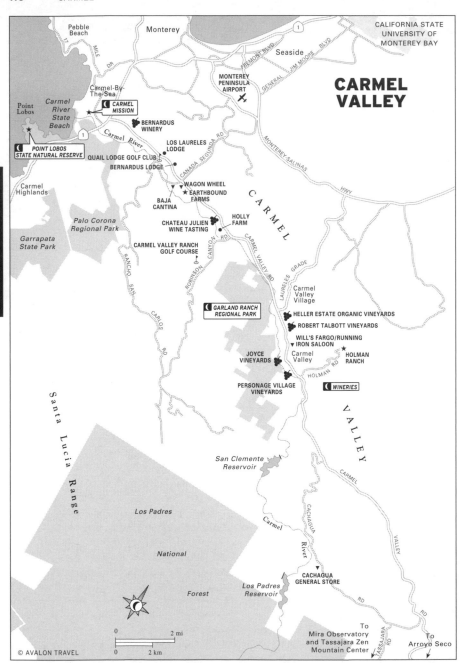

CARMEL VALLEY

© AVALON TRAVEL

0 _____ 2 mi

0 _____ 2 km

©KRISTIN LEAL

Château Julien Wine Estate

taste a rare reserve blended red or a 10-year-old port. For a treat, call ahead and reserve a spot on the twice-daily free vineyard and winery tours. When weather permits, these tours conclude with a special tasting outside on the flagstone patio.

On the other end of the size spectrum, tiny **Parsonage Village Vineyard** (19 E. Carmel Valley Rd., 831/659-7322, www.parsonagewine.com, daily 11 A.M.-5 P.M., tasting $8) often doesn't make it onto Carmel Valley wine maps—which is a shame, because arguably some of the best syrah in California comes from this unpretentious winery's nine-acre vineyard. The tasting room is along a tiny strip of shops in a glowingly lit space with a copper-topped bar. On the walls are quilts made by co-owner Mary Ellen Parsons. At the bar, you can taste wonderful syrahs, hearty cabernet sauvignons, and surprisingly deep and complex blends—the Snosrap (that's "Parsons" spelled backwards) table wine is inexpensive for the region and very tasty. If you find a vintage

you like at Parsonage, buy it then, since they sell out of many of their wines every year.

Heller Estate Organic Vineyards (69 W. Carmel Valley Rd., 831/659-6220, www.hellerestate.com, daily 11 A.M.-5 P.M.) has been making wines for over 40 years, and the vineyard has been certified organic since 1996, producing exceptionally age-worthy wines. There is a picnic area in the sculpture garden where you can nibble on gourmet samples and a boutique for gifts. Among the hills overlooking the Cachagua area, Heller's mountain vineyard grows cabernet franc, cabernet sauvignon, chardonnay, chenin blanc, merlot, malbec, petit verdot, and pinot noir.

At **Robert Talbott Vineyards** (53 W. Carmel Valley Rd., 831/659-3500, www.talbottvineyards.com, daily 11 A.M.-5 P.M., tasting $7.50), sample some of the featured chardonnay and pinot noir made from grapes grown on Talbott's 565-acre Sleepy Hollow Vineyard, in the Santa Lucia Mountains, and the 14-acre

Diamond T Vineyard in Carmel Valley. The garden patio is lovely, and you are welcome to bring a picnic while you enjoy a tasting.

Handcrafted gold-medal wines are found at **Joyce Vineyards** (6 Pilot Rd., 831/659-2885, www.joycevineyards.com, Fri.-Sun. 11 A.M.-5 P.M.), with a newly renovated tasting room and outdoor garden and featuring merlot, pinot noirs, cabernets, syrahs, chardonnays, and Pudding Wine.

An easy way to explore the wine tasting in the valley is the **Carmel Valley Grapevine Express** (888/678-2871, www.mst.org, year-round daily 11 A.M.-6 P.M., $6 round-trip), a shuttle bus that can be boarded throughout Carmel and at the Monterey Transit Plaza (every hour at quarter past the hour). Tours Monterey (831/624-1700, www.toursmonterey.com) has a relaxing **Wine Trolley** ($99) that includes a box lunch and a five-hour tour. Advanced reservations are required, and tours start at 11 A.M. sharp at Portola Plaza in Monterey.

SPORTS AND RECREATION
Hiking
◀ GARLAND RANCH REGIONAL PARK

Slightly inland and along the Carmel River, adventure awaits for outdoors enthusiasts at Garland Ranch Regional Park (Carmel Valley Rd., 8 miles east of Hwy. 1, 831/372-3196, www.mprpd.org, daily sunrise-sunset, day-use free), with 4,462 acres of mountain biking and hiking trails, fishing, and picnicking. Horse trails are accessible to hikers, and dogs are welcome throughout the park. The latest addition to the park, Kahn Ranch, added 1,100 acres and many more trails to discover. Get access the park by visiting the website for a permit, or call 831/372-3196, ext. 108; access is via a private easement on Hitchcock Canyon Road.

LOS PADRES RESERVOIR

Deep in Carmel Valley are freshwater adventures along the Carmel River. Backcountry access, day hikes, and swimming are possible at off-the-beaten-path Los Padres Reservoir (end of Nason Rd., off Cacagua Rd., www.fs.fed.us). The drive is breathtaking as the road climbs high into the coastal range above the vineyards of Carmel Valley and down into the forest.

Two miles along Nason Road, the land becomes part of the Los Padres National Forest. There are four main hiking trails; the 0.5-mile Big Pine Trail leads to the dam. The Carmel River Camp and Miller Canyon Trail is 4.5 miles long, the Pine Valley Trail is 13 miles, and Church Creek Divide Trail is 15 miles. Dogs are welcome on the trails, and there are many spur paths that lead through the high dry grass to the Carmel River, where you can swim.

ARROYO SECO

One of the county's lesser-known hiking spots is Arroyo Seco (Arroyo Seco Rd., just outside Greenfield, 831/674-5726, camping reservations 877/444-6777, www.rockymountainrec. com, www.fs.fed.us, day-use $7, camping $20, primitive sites $15), with a trail to the bottom of a massive gorge and the river cutting through it. Arroyo Seco is in the Los Padres National Forest in the Santa Lucia Mountains, and besides camping and hiking, it provides opportunities for swimming, seasonal fishing, and jumping off cliffs into the river.

For white-water aficionados, the rapids here on the Arroyo Seco River are rated Class III. You can do a full run of 14.5 miles if you put in at the Willowcreek Bridge and stop at the Arroyo Seco picnic area; a three-mile stretch has Class IV-V rapids. The river is not always navigable for kayaks and rafts; Riverfacts.com (http://riverfacts.com) can provide information on current conditions.

Parks

Plan a day of outdoor fun at **Carmel Valley Community Park** (Carmel Valley Village, 831/659-3983, www.mtycounty.com), with large grassy areas, barbecues, playground equipment, and a swimming pool. Locals like to pack a picnic, bring the kids, and spend the day in the sun and resting in the shade under the oak trees.

Golf

Rancho Cañada Golf Course (4860 Carmel Valley Rd., 800/536-9459, www.ranchocanada. com, $40-70) has two 18-hole courses known as the East Course and the West Course. The East Course is longer, but both have wide and narrow fairways that cross the Carmel River. At a mere $39, Twilight Thursdays (from 2:30 P.M.) are the least expensive rounds available. There's a pro shop, dining, and bunkered chipping greens.

A par-71 course tucked in the hills of Carmel Valley is the **Quail Lodge** (8205 Valley Greens Dr., 831/620-8866, www.quaillodge.com, $100-150). Verdant greens are sited between the mountains rising on either side. It's quiet despite being close to Highway 1. This is a traditional course, with three sets of tees at each hole and a seven-acre driving range. The 10 lakes on the property and the Carmel River provide some challenges. PGA-certified pros are available to help improve your game.

Carmel Valley Ranch Golf Course (1 Old Ranch Rd., 831/620-6406, www.carmelvalleyranch.com, $100-195) is a semiprivate course in a warm part of the valley that gets an average of 300 sunny days each year. Scenic views of the Santa Lucia Range can be had throughout the par-70 course, which recently underwent a multimillion-dollar enhancement, now featuring a layout restored to Pete Dye's original design with T1 bentgrass, enlarged greens, improved tee boxes, and a renovated clubhouse.

Horseback Riding

The historic hacienda, stables, and vineyard of Holman Ranch, once an escape for Hollywood celebrities, offers an escape into the quiet countryside of the Carmel Valley. **Holman Ranch**

Equestrian Center (60 Holman Rd., 831/659-2640, www.holmanranch.com) provides boarding opportunities and guided tours during the summer months. English and Western lessons are available by reservation, and children will love the pony rides.

Off-Roading

Open year-around for private and group adventures, the **Land Rover Driving School** (8205 Valley Greens Dr., 831/620-8854, www.landroverusa.com) brings four-by-four driving to the peninsula. This is one of the three locations in the United States and the only Land Rover School on the West Coast. The five-mile technical course, on the grounds of Quail Lodge golf course, is tight and steep, with natural and artificial obstacles. Mossy oak trees restrict the trail, and huge mounds of soil like moguls on a ski hill create uneven obstacles.

Swimming Holes

Klondike Canyon Private Road, on Carmel Valley Road past Carmel Valley Village to the left of the vineyard, is a dusty trail that leads to a secluded clothing-optional swimming hole known as **The Bucket.** The entrance to the trail was once the site of the Bloody Bucket Saloon, notorious for its rough bar brawls and gun fights. The swim hole takes its name from the saloon. Parking is a little tricky-watch for the "No Parking" signs, as the police are known to ticket heavily along this roadway; plan on hiking in from a turnout.

FESTIVALS AND EVENTS

Sun-drenched Carmel Valley has several events through the year. The **Quail Motorcycle Gathering** (831/620-8887, www.quaillodgeevents.com) in mid-May is a one-day display of world-class classic sports and racing bikes. Grab a plate and enjoy the barbecue.

A Carmel tradition is the **Art and Wine Celebration** (831/659-4000, www.

carmelvalleychamber.com) in early June, with an open-house event in Carmel Valley Village that features live music. Stop into the fine art galleries, country antiques shops, cafés, and restaurants.

¡Olé! The **Carmel Valley Fiesta** (831/644-6180, www.cvkclub.org) in early August is a full-blown two-day festival with a parade, a dog show, dancing, and delicious traditional Latin food.

In mid-August, gourmet food and ferocious cars attract crowds to the valley for **The Quail, A Motorsports Gathering** (831/620-8887, www.quaillodgeevents.com). This one-day event combines displays of landmark vehicles with a culinary extravaganza.

The fall season is all about the harvest, and in Carmel Valley at the end of September it kicks off with the **Harvest to Table Festival** (831/622-7770, www.harvestcarmel.com). Over 50 chefs show off their culinary skills with delectable bites to sample, and over 100 wineries gather to pour their creations.

SHOPPING

The valley has fine antiquing prospects that are worth traveling inland for. The country charm of **Tancredi and Morgan** (Valley Hills Shopping Center, 7174 Carmel Valley Rd., 831/625-4477, www.tancredimorgan.com, Mon.-Sat. 10 A.M.-5 P.M., Sun. 11 A.M.-4 P.M.) includes continuously replenished antiques from Europe, unique paper art, and jewelry.

Classic French style is at **Jan de Luz** (4 E. Carmel Valley Rd., 831/659-7966, www.jandaluz.com, Mon.-Sat. 9 A.M.-5 P.M.). Alongside linen and interior products are one-of-a-kind French antiques, wall fountains, fireplace hearths, statues, cast-iron firebacks, and furniture.

ACCOMMODATIONS
Under $150

If you come to Carmel to taste wine, hike in the woods, and enjoy the less-expensive golf courses, **Country Garden Inns** (102 W. Carmel Valley Rd., 831/659-5361, www.

countrygardeninns.com, $109-179) is a perfect spot to rest and relax. Comprising two inns, the Acacia and the Hidden Valley, this small B&B has violet and taupe French country-style charm as well as a pool, a self-serve breakfast bar, and strolling gardens. Guest rooms run from romantic king-bed studios up to large family suites, and most sleep at least four, with daybeds in the window nooks.

An affordable full-service place in the valley is ◖ **Los Laureles Lodge** (313 W. Carmel Valley Rd., 831/659-2233, www.loslaureles. com, $125-650). Once a historic ranch, it was converted into a resort in the late 1930s. Amenities include free Internet access, family suites, a pool, in-room jetted tubs, fireplaces, and kitchenettes; pets are welcome. The guest rooms are spacious and rustic, and there is a restaurant and saloon on-site. Several room-and-wine-tasting packages are available.

The best deal in the valley for accommodations is **Blue Sky Lodge** (10 Flight Rd., 831/659-2256, www.blueskylodge.com, $95-169). There are patio rooms, sundeck rooms, and suites. The decor is a little outdated, but the size of the even the standard guest rooms compensates. The pool and hot tub outside are nice for an afternoon swim and tanning session or a cool evening gazing at the stars.

$150-250

A peaceful retreat where dogs are always welcome is **Carmel Valley Lodge** (8 Ford Rd., 831/659-2261, www.valleylodge.com, $169-359). Located at the edge of Carmel Valley Village, the simple country charm runs throughout the 31-unit complex. The outdoor pool is big enough to do short laps, with a cozy hot tub just adjacent. Guest rooms are spacious, and the cottages are the right size for families.

Over $250

Set amid seven acres of grapevines, the ◖ **Bernardus Lodge** (415 W. Carmel Valley

Rd., 888/648-9463, www.bernardus.com, $295-1,970) is one of the nicest properties in Carmel Valley, with first-rate service and furnishings. Small bottles of Bernardus wines welcome you to your room along with complimentary bottled water, a small fridge, and a spacious bed. Some guest rooms overlook the pool; others face the bocce and croquet lawn. There are two restaurants on-site; go for the Chef's Table, a small booth right in the kitchen where the chef prepares your meal in front of you. The walls have been signed by well-known guests, including Julia Child. This is one of those places you just don't want to leave.

If you love to golf and enjoy the sun, book a room at the **Carmel Valley Ranch** (1 Old Ranch Rd., 831/625-9500, www.carmelvalleyranch.com, $359). Tucked amid stands of oak trees in the Santa Lucia Mountains, it is a peaceful location with over 500 acres to explore as well as a pool, a golf course, the Land Rover Driving School, and a spa. Views from the balconies are of Garland Ranch and the Santa Lucia Mountains.

A nice romantic getaway is the **Stonepine Estate Resort** (150 E. Carmel Valley Rd., 831/659-2245, www.stonepinecarmel.com, $300-3,000), with world-class packages for equestrians, massages, and wine tasting. Guest rooms are well decorated with modern charm throughout. The gardens are romantic and perfect for a morning or evening stroll.

FOOD
American

The funky **Cachagua General Store** (18840 Cachagua Rd., 831/659-1857, dinner Mon., $25) defies description. The location is a run-down old general store, a piecemeal building that you wouldn't notice driving by. Not that you would drive by it, since it's in the middle of nowhere—it will take you at least 45 minutes to drive here from Carmel, past Carmel Valley up and down winding mountain roads. Dinner is served only on Monday nights, and reservations have to be made three weeks in advance. Menus are printed as guests show up and are sometimes incomplete. There are two seatings, at 6:30 P.M. and 8:30 P.M., but the times are only approximate; if the kitchen isn't ready to serve, you wait. Is it worth all the trouble? Michael Jones's food is superb, and the ever-changing menu offers dishes like rabbit five ways, pumpkin basil ravioli, or local sardines, and many of the ingredients come from the surrounding farms. Sometimes there's live music. There's no decor to speak of, the chairs are mismatched, and servers wear whatever suits them, but that's all part of the charm.

The outdoor patio at **Corkscrew Café** (55 W. Carmel Valley Rd., 831/659-8888, Wed.-Mon. 11:30 A.M.-3 P.M., Wed.-Sun. 5-9 P.M., $20), with its brightly colored chairs and umbrellas, is perfect on spring days. The interior has a soft Tuscan feel, with tiled floors and ocher-colored walls. The menu is limited but good: Meals begin with hummus and toasted bread and continue with items like calamari, halibut tostadas, sandwiches, and salads. They make a terrific *croque monsieur* dished up on hearty nut bread. They also carry a decent list of Monterey County wines.

Step back into the classy West at the ◖ **Will's Fargo** (16 W. Carmel Valley Rd., 831/659-2774, www.bernardus.com, daily 4:30 P.M.-close, $28), a steak house and saloon that will drive carnivores wild with meat choices that include fish, veal, pork, lamb, quail, and chicken. The surf-and-turf as well as the top sirloin and quail combo pack are all meat. For veggie eaters, the lasagna and goat-cheese ravioli are mouthwatering.

For a good old country breakfast or lunch, the ◖ **Wagon Wheel** (7156 Carmel Valley Rd., 831/624-8878, daily 6:30 A.M.-2 P.M., $10-15) is a must. Wake up early to get a seat or be ready to wait for one. The oatmeal pancakes and corned beef and hash are excellent. The atmosphere is totally country-western with a side order of rodeo. Enjoy the valley air at one of the small tables outside.

California

For a taste of wine country cuisine, reserve a table at **Marinus at Bernardus Lodge** (415 W. Carmel Valley Rd., 831/658-3550, www. bernardus.com, daily 6-10 P.M., $45-80). The exquisite California cuisine features the produce, fish, and meat of local producers, and it has been served to celebrities that include Julia Child and Leonardo DiCaprio. Choose a three-, four-, or five-course meal, or go for broke and get the chef's tasting menu.

With boots, saddles, and other Western paraphernalia hanging from the ceiling, the **C Running Iron Saloon** (24 E. Carmel Valley Rd., 831/659-4633, Mon.-Fri. 11 A.M.-10 P.M., Sat.-Sun. 10 A.M.-10 P.M., $20) is true to its name even if it's rather out of place in the upscale Carmel Valley. Of course, that's partly the point. There is live music on Friday and karaoke on Tuesday.

Open for breakfast, lunch, and dinner is the **Carmel Valley Ranch Lodge Restaurant** (1 Old Ranch Rd., 831/625-9500, www.carmel-valleyranch.com, Mon.-Sun. 7 A.M.-10 P.M., $13-30). The food is local, organic, sustainable, and very good. Executive chef Tim Woods loves to play with his foods, and you can taste his sense of adventure in every bite. Enjoy tasty grill items and sandwiches on the patio or inside.

Mexican

The walls and ceilings at **C Baja Cantina** (7166 Carmel Valley Rd., 831/625-2252, Mon.-Fri. 11:30 A.M.-10 P.M., Sat.-Sun. 11 A.M.-9 P.M., $20) are decorated with everything imaginable, like walking into a festive yard sale. It's an upbeat environment with an outside deck that's perfect for sunny days and a fireplace near the bar that's perfect when the fog rolls in. Most shots in the tequila selection are in the $10 range. Menu favorites include the rosemary chicken burrito, mango chicken enchiladas, and halibut fish tacos. The chips and salsa are excellent.

GETTING THERE AND AROUND

To get to the Carmel Valley, take Highway 1 to Carmel Valley Road, a major intersection with a stoplight, and signs point the way. The **Carmel Valley Grapevine Express** (888/678-2871, www.mst.org, year-round daily 11 A.M.-6 P.M.) shuttle bus stops at Cannery Row, downtown Monterey, and the Barnyard Shopping Center in Carmel and takes you to the Carmel Valley wineries for just $6 round-trip. Buses run every hour. This is a great way to avoid the hassle of driving and finding parking.

SALINAS AND INLAND MONTEREY

The inland reaches of Monterey County are worth a day trip or a stop on the way through to the peninsula. Made famous by John Steinbeck's *East of Eden*, this region has the rich soil and climate to make it "the salad bowl of the world," with a rainbow of fresh fruits and vegetables growing in the farmland. Temperatures are generally hotter than on the peninsula, and life is a bit more rugged.

Salinas has an annual rodeo and is known as Steinbeck country, home to the National Steinbeck Center. Pinnacles National Monument presents opportunities to explore caves, rock climb, camp, and take in sweeping views of the Salinas Valley. The Laguna Seca Raceway in Hollister is a dusty, dirty haven for

ATV fans, and mountain bikers will find challenging trails in the surrounding recreation area.

For more peaceful pursuits, step back in time in the old California town of San Juan Bautista, with an early-1800s mission and plaza. Along the San Benito Wine Trail, friendly tasting rooms welcome you, including Robert Talbott and its "Wrath" wines.

PLANNING YOUR TIME

The inland part of Monterey County is worth at least an afternoon, if not an entire day. You can easily fill a day wandering the Western town of San Juan Bautista or hiking in Pinnacles National Monument. Some sites are good to visit on the drive to the peninsula

© THE NATIONAL STEINBECK CENTER/KIRK KENNEDY

HIGHLIGHTS

© AVALON TRAVEL

LOOK FOR ◖ TO FIND RECOMMENDED SIGHTS, ACTIVITIES, DINING, AND LODGING.

◖ **National Steinbeck Center:** The museum is a tribute to the life and work of legendary local author John Steinbeck. Learn all about Steinbeck and see this complex part of the world through his eyes (page 120).

◖ **River Road Wine Trail:** There are many vineyards in the valley and several places to stop in for tastings; River Road off Highway 68 is the primary route (page 120).

◖ **Mazda Laguna Seca Raceway:** Race fans, start your engines, and get ready to feel the rumble of historic-car races, superbikes, speed festivals, and an array of Grand Prix events (page 121).

◖ **Mission San Juan Bautista:** One of the lesser-known California Missions, Mission San Juan Bautista is in the center of an authentic Western town (page 126).

◖ **San Juan Bautista Old Town:** The area remains much as it was in the days of the gun slingers. Wander along 3rd Street for antiques, saloons, and many historic sites (page 126).

◖ **Fremont Peak State Park and Observatory:** The night sky comes alive, and Fremont Peak affords spectacular views from the ocean to the Sierra Nevada Range (page 128).

◖ **Pinnacles National Monument:** Replete with massive rock formations, caves, and water displays, the park offers hiking, rock climbing, picnicking, and camping (page 132).

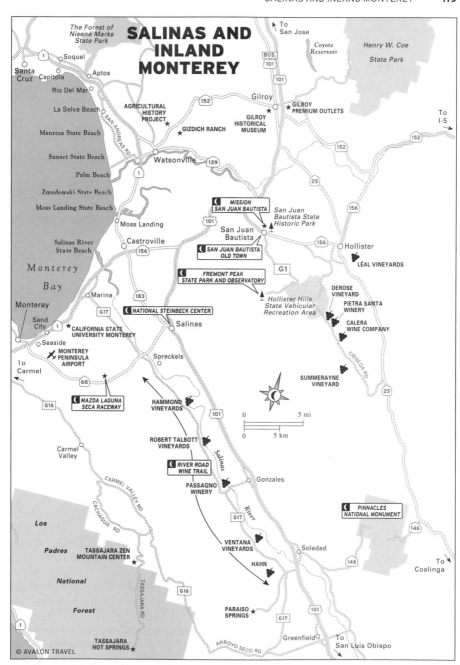

SALINAS AND
INLAND
MONTEREY

or on the way home, including Gilroy's Outlet Mall and the National Steinbeck Center. To get a feel for the area and see all the sights, plan on staying overnight.

Salinas

East of Eden, the title of John Steinbeck's novel set in the area, says it all when it comes to describing the city of Salinas, an agricultural town with a rich history. The Mazda Laguna Seca Raceway, National Steinbeck Center, and Pinnacles National Monument are major attractions.

SIGHTS
(National Steinbeck Center
In the heart of Old Town Salinas is the National Steinbeck Center (1 Main St., 831/775-4721, www.steinbeck.org, daily 10 A.M.-5 P.M., $11 adults, $9 seniors and students, $8 ages 13-17, $6 ages 6-12, free under age 6), where you can explore Steinbeck's life and famous works. The interactive museum brings his writing to life and gives visitors a full sensory experience walking in the author's footsteps. You can get an interactive understanding of Monterey County's agriculture, art, history, and literature. The $15-million complex comprises two permanent exhibits, the John Steinbeck's Exhibition Hall and the Rabobank Agricultural Museum.

The six themed galleries of the **John Steinbeck's Exhibition Hall** showcase the life and times of Steinbeck through artifacts, film clips, photography, and interactive exhibits. Take a journey into the life of Salinas's native son and discover his inspiration for works that include *The Grapes of Wrath, Tortilla Flat, East of Eden,* and *Cannery Row.*

As you wander **The Rabobank Agricultural Museum,** you will learn why the Salinas Valley is considered the salad bowl of the world. The land is fertile and the weather ideal for growing everything from lettuce to strawberries. See how California's produce is brought from seed to table, and learn about the culture and history of Salinas's farming industry through the exhibit's many artifacts.

(RIVER ROAD WINE TRAIL
Toast the vintages of the Monterey County along the **River Road Wine Trail** (along River Rd. and Foothill Rd., Hwy. 68 Spreckels exit, www.riverroadwinetrail.com) as you travel into the heart of the Salinas Valley. You will find the tasting rooms charming and intimate, with many opportunities to taste and purchase limited-release wines.

One of the newer vineyards in Monterey County is **Hammond Vineyards** (655 River Rd., 831/455-8173, www.hammondvineyards.com, Sat.-Sun. 11 A.M.-5 P.M., tasting $5). Releasing its first vintage in January 2011, they specialize in chardonnay and pinot noir. Tastings here are all about showcasing the character and flavor of each wine.

Featuring estate-grown chardonnay and pinot noir is **Robert Talbott Vineyards** (1380 River Rd., 831/675-0942, www.talbottvineyards.com, Thurs.-Mon. 11 A.M.-5 P.M., tasting $7.50), featuring chardonnay and pinot noir made from grapes grown on Talbott's 565-acre Sleepy Hollow Vineyard, on River Road in the Santa Lucia Mountains, and the 14-acre Diamond T Vineyard in Carmel Valley.

Hahn (37700 Foothill Rd., Soledad, 831/678-4555, www.hahnestates.com, Mon.-Fri. 11 A.M.-4 P.M., Sat.-Sun. 11 A.M.-5 P.M., tasting $5) is a delightful spot for a picnic and wine tasting. Take your wine outside to relax in the shade of the rustling oak trees, or stay inside and mingle while you learn about the vineyard.

For over 20 years, **Pessagno Winery** (1645 River Rd., 831/675-9463, www.pessagnowines.

National Steinbeck Center

com, Mon.-Thurs. 11 A.M.-4 P.M., Fri.-Sat. 11 A.M.-5 P.M., tasting $5) has been producing award-winning wines. The tasting room has tables and plenty of space; this is a must-stop if you are traveling with a large group or are in the mood to make some new friends. Winemaker Steve Pessagno presents limited quantities of exclusive and single-vineyard wines from Monterey and San Benito Counties.

Monterey County's rising wine star is **Ventana Vineyards** (38740 Los Coches Rd., Soledad, 831/372-7415, www.ventanawines.com, Sat.-Sun. 11 A.M.-5 P.M., tasting fee waived with $15 purchase). Founded in 1974 by legendary viticultural expert Doug Meador, the winery has earned more medals and awards than any other vineyard in the country. Known for its white wines and unique sustainable planting style, this is a must-see on a wine tour.

SPORTS AND RECREATION
Toro Regional Park
Between Salinas and Monterey on Highway 68 is the wide-open space of Toro Park Regional (501 Hwy. 68, 831/775-4899, www.co.monterey.ca.us, $6-8), a 4,756 acre retreat known to locals but not to most visitors. Miles of paved roads and dirt trails allow for off-road biking, hiking, and horseback riding, and dogs are welcome. There are also wide swaths of manicured grass with playgrounds for the kids, softball diamonds, basketball hoops, and barbecues.

Many of the trails in Toro Park allow vigorous exercise, including 20 miles of hiking trails to seven fantastic mountain peaks and five springs. Look for the variety of wildlife, which includes coyotes, deer, golden eagles, and mountain lions.

◖ Mazda Laguna Seca Raceway
If you're feeling the need for speed, you can get lots of it at the Mazda Laguna Seca Raceway (1021 Monterey-Salinas Hwy., 831/242-8201, www.laguna-seca.com), one of the country's premier road-racing venues. Monterey has had a love affair with fast sexy cars and the

STEINBECK'S SALINAS

© NATIONAL STEINBECK CENTER

Celebrate Steinbeck's dedication to Monterey County at the National Steinbeck Center.

Steinbeck is one of California's most illustrious 20th-century literary products, and Salinas became famous for inspiring his work. In the pages of the 1952 novel *East of Eden* are the smells, flavors, colors, sights, sounds, and texture of the Salinas Valley. It is the tale of two real-life families and the California experience in an agricultural community. Many say it is an autobiography of Salinas told through the eyes of common people. In broader terms it is a story of life's extremes, the battle between good and evil, strength and weakness, love and hate, beauty and ugliness.

The book is dedicated to Steinbeck's two young sons. He wanted them to know his beloved valley as he did, and one of the proposed titles for the book was *My Salinas Valley.*

You'll find a variety of Steinbeck maps online at www.mtycounty.com that offer self-guided tours of Salinas. Serious Steinbeck scholars prefer the **National Steinbeck Center** (1 Main St., 831/796-3833, www.steinbeck.org, daily 10 A.M.-5 P.M., $11) and the **Steinbeck House** (132 Central Ave., 831/424-2735, www. steinbeckhouse.com, summer daily, tours $10), both in the still-agricultural town of Salinas. If the museums aren't enough, plan to be in Monterey County in early August for the annual **Steinbeck Festival** (www.steinbeck.org), a big shindig put on by the Steinbeck Center in order to celebrate the great writer's life and works.

obsession to race them since the Pebble Beach Road Races of the 1950s. Today, the races have expanded to several events year-round, including the Red Bull U.S. Grand Prix, Ferrari Racing Days, superbikes, and stock-car races, to name a few. The major racing season runs May-October most years. In addition to the big events, Laguna Seca hosts numerous auto clubs and smaller sports-car and stock-car races. If you've ever wanted to learn to drive race car-style, check the schedule to see if one of the track classes is being held during your visit. These often happen in the middle of the week, nearly every day in the off-season (Nov.-Apr.).

Be sure to check the website for parking directions specific to the event you plan to attend—this is a big facility. You can camp here, and there are plenty of food concessions during big races.

ENTERTAINMENT AND EVENTS

Several annual events around the Salinas Valley are worth a visit, including celebrations of favorite son John Steinbeck and the big event of the summer, California Rodeo Salinas.

Spring

The largest cycling festival and trade show in North America is at the **Sea Otter Classic**

(800/218-8411, www.seaotterclassic.com) in mid-April. The expo features over 250 vendors, races for all ages and skill levels, the latest gear, demos, stunt shows, activities for kids, and a bike playground.

King City in the south end of the valley is the host for the annual **Salinas Valley Fair** (831/385-3243, www.salinasvalleyfair.com) in mid-May. An old-fashioned county fair, this event has traditional carnival games, bull-riding, crafts, 4-H exhibits, music, and the Monterey Wine Competition Grand Wine Tasting. Bring the kids, grab some funnel cake, and have some wholesome fun.

Ladies and gentlemen-prepare yourself for some car-crushing action at the **Monster Truck Jam** (831/775-3100, www.salinassportscomplex.com). Held in mid-May at the Salinas Sports Complex, this affair typically sells out, so get tickets early. This is a family-friendly event with food, drinks, and souvenirs, and you can look forward to an afternoon of flying mud and mangled cars.

Summer

Check out the modern-day cowboys in late July at **California Rodeo Salinas** (831/775-3100, www.carodeo.com). Preserving the traditions of the West, the California Rodeo Association has put on this rodeo annually for over 100 years at the Salinas Sports Complex. Activities include the Miss California Rodeo competition, professional bull riding, chuck-wagon races, and other rodeo events.

The world's premier Grand Prix motorcycle racing championship in the MotoGP class is the annual **Red Bull U.S. Grand Prix** (www.mazdaraceway.com), held at Laguna Seca Raceway in late July. Top manufacturers that participate include Honda, Suzuki, Ducati, Yamaha, Kawasaki, and Aprilia.

Steinbeck fans can mark the calendar for early August for the **Steinbeck Festival** (831/775-4721, www.steinbeck.org), an annual

event that has been inspiring young and old for over 30 years. The four-day event has films, guest speakers, panels, performing arts, and bus and walking tours of Steinbeck's home turf.

Get a feeling for Ireland and Scotland in early August at the **Scottish Games** (831/633-4444, www.montereyscotgames.com), a Celtic celebration held every year at Toro Regional Park. The energized weekend is full of dancing, athletic competitions, and music.

Formerly known as the Historic Races, the **Rolex Monterey Motorsports Reunion** (831/242-8201, www.mazdaraceway.com) is a late-August annual event celebrating important race cars through history. This event provides an opportunity to get up close to some of the most stunning race cars in the world.

The **Concours d'LeMons** (916/207-4645, www.concoursdlemons.com) in late August is a spoof of the peninsula's celebrated Concours d'Elegance motorsports gathering. It is a family-friendly one-day celebration of weird, odd, and absolutely awful automobiles, held at Toro Regional Park on Highway 68.

Fall

It wouldn't be fall in Monterey County without the **Cherry's Jubilee Motorsports Festival** (831/759-1836, www.cherrysjubilee.org), held in September with handsome hot rods, wicked motorcycles, and the Mazda Laguna Seca's famous Corkscrew racetrack.

You can watch racing into the night with the **American Le Mans Series** (831/242-8201, www.mazdaraceway.com) at Laguna Seca in mid-September. Top car companies in attendance include Acura, Mazda, Porsche, Dodge, Ferrari, Jaguar, and more. The six-hour race keeps the audience amped with exhilarating competition.

For over 30 years, the annual late-September **California International Airshow** (831/754-0808, www.salinasairshow.com) has entertained fans. Kids will love the high-flying action and daring maneuvers, and walking around the parked planes is an amazing experience. Check out the many booths and grab a hot dog or two.

Winter

Celebrate the holiday season with the **Salinas Holiday Parade of Lights** (www.salinasparade. com). South Main Street through Old Town to the National Steinbeck Center becomes the stage for a kaleidoscope of lights, handcrafted floats, Santa riding a fire engine, and dance performances.

Grab your sweetheart and celebrate passion with the **River Road Wine Trail Valentine's Passport** (www.riverroadwinetrail.com, Feb. 12 11 A.M.-5 P.M.). Twelve artisanal vintners pour tantalizing creations, and good food is on offer.

Steinbeck's Birthday Celebration (831/775-4721, www.steinbeck.org) is a day-long event in late February at the National Steinbeck Center in recognition of the beloved local author. Family-friendly fun includes

Sample some of Monterey County's lush strawberries at the local farmers markets.

© KRISTIN LEAL

reading circles, author talks, book signings, cultural presentations, and birthday cake.

SHOPPING

For mall fans, Salinas's **Northridge Mall** (N. Main St. and Boranda Rd., 831/449-7226, Mon.-Sat. 10 A.M.-9 P.M., Sun. 11 A.M.-7 P.M.) has 125 stores along with a food court, movie theater, department stores that include Macy's and Sears, specialty shops, electronics, a pharmacy, and fashion for the whole family.

Another good bet for some shopping is **Old Town Salinas** (Main St., www.oldtownsalinas. com, www.salinaschamber.com), with a handful of boutiques, shops, and salons along the main drag.

FARMERS MARKETS

Because the Salinas Valley is known as "the salad bowl of the world," you can find farmers markets with all the fresh delights of the valley. Prepared food vendors are usually included.

Count on **Old Town Salinas Farmers Market** (Monterey St. Parking Garage, Alisal St. and Monterey St., 831/904-1407 or 831/920-1088, www.oldtownsalinas.com, year-round Sat. 9 A.M.-2 P.M.) to have the freshest local produce. Other vendors carry fresh fish, baked items, local restaurant food, arts and crafts, and jewelry, and there is live family-oriented entertainment.

The **Natividad Farmers Market** (1441 Constitution Blvd., 831/755-4111, www.natividad.com, Mar.-Nov. Wed. 11:30 A.M.-5:30 P.M.) is part of Natividad Medical Center's commitment to promoting wellness. The weekly market features fresh fruit, vegetables, eggs, flowers, and unique gifts.

Go organic at the **Salinas Alisal Certified Market** (E. Alisal St. and S. Pearl St., 831/796-2861, Aug.-Oct. Thurs. 9:30 A.M.-5:30 P.M.), one of the smaller markets but worth a walk through. Participants are local Salinas Valley farmers and those from other parts of California.

Bringing organic products to the table for

more than five years is the **Soledad Farmers Market** (Encinal St., May-Sept. Thurs. 4-8 P.M.), with a variety of fresh produce and prepared foods. Just south of Salinas, this is a little-known treasure and a nice spot for a fresh snack.

For over 30 years, the **Greenfield Certified Farmers Market** (Green Village Park, El Camino Real and Park Ave., www.greenfieldfarmersmarket.com, May-Aug. Sun. 9:30 A.M.-3 P.M.) has provided fresh local products with a serious focus on organically grown goods. This is a big event, and vendors sell just about everything from hand-thrown pottery to portable chicken coops, not to mention the fresh fruits and veggies from the surrounding farms.

INFORMATION AND SERVICES

The best place to visit for a guide to the area and event information is the **Salinas Valley Chamber of Commerce** (119 E. Alisal St., 831/424-7611, www.salinaschamber.com, Mon.-Fri. 9 A.M.-5 P.M.), which is also an official Monterey County Convention and Visitors Bureau, so they know their way around the county. The **Old Town Salinas Association** (831/758-0725, www.oldtownsalinas.com) is here as well and can provide information on downtown events, shopping, and activities.

Salinas has seen a rise in crime and gang activities in recent years. There are some crime hot spots in the city, so it is not wise to wander too far from the main attractions.

GETTING THERE AND AROUND

Salinas is on U.S. 101 for easy driving access from the Bay Area or Los Angeles. From Monterey, take Highway 68 east.

Amtrak's Seattle-Los Angeles *Coast Starlight* train travels through Salinas (Station Place and Railroad Ave., daily 8 A.M.-10 P.M.) daily in both directions. For Amtrak travelers, there is free bus service (30 minutes) to downtown Monterey.

If you arrive on **Greyhound** (19 W. Gablin St., 831/242-4418 or 800/231-2222, www.greyhound.com), you can catch local buses to all the sights. **Monterey-Salinas Transit** (1 Ryan Ranch Rd., Monterey, 831/899-2555 or 831/242-7965, www.mst.org) has bus routes throughout the peninsula; check online for fares and schedules.

Salinas Municipal Airport (SNS, 30 Mortesen St., 831/758-7214, www.ci.salinas.ca.us) has no commercial flights but welcomes small aircraft. The major airlines have regularly scheduled flights to the **Monterey Peninsula Airport** (MRY, 200 Fred Kane Dr., Monterey, 831/648-7000, www.montereyairport.com) and the larger **San Jose International Airport** (SJC, 2077 Airport Blvd., San Jose, 408/277-4859, www.sjc.org), just over an hour's drive north.

SALINAS

Inland Monterey

The inland reaches of Monterey County are rich with lavish farmland and small Western towns. Spend an afternoon exploring the area as you pass through, or devote an entire day to discovering this unique region. You will find a historic mission, an off-road recreation area, and several wine-tasting stops.

SAN JUAN BAUTISTA

A visit to the quiet town of San Juan Bautista is like a trip back in time. Visit the Mission San Juan Bautista and the San Juan Bautista State Historic Park for a glimpse of the Old West, then go antiquing and visit the local saloon. In the evening, gaze at the stars from Fremont Peak State Park and Observatory.

◖ Mission San Juan Bautista

The San Juan Bautista area was originally inhabited by the Mutsun people until the Spanish arrived and began building the mission in 1797. The location of Mission San Juan Bautista (406 2nd St., 831/623-4528, www.oldmissionsjb.org, daily 9:30 A.M.-4:30 P.M., donation) was chosen because of the fertile local soil and the distance of a day's walk nearby missions. The Spanish forced the Mutsun people to build the mission, and at one time there were 1,200 Native Americans working and living on the compound. There is a mass grave beside the mission with more than 4,300 Native Americans interred. You can see this area at the back of the mission, and some claim to feel the energy of these departed souls.

Mission San Juan Bautista is beautiful but modest compared to the Carmel Mission. The chapel is small, but the grounds are extensive. Inside is a small gift shop. The mission puts on an annual Christmas play with the chapel as the stage. It is a wonderful experience as the actors' voices echo in the chapel, telling a dark holiday tale in Spanish.

◖ San Juan Bautista Old Town

Just across from the mission is the Plaza Hotel and **San Juan Bautista State Historic Park** (2nd St. between Washington St. and Mariposa St., 831/623-4526, www.parks.ca.gov, Tues.-Sun. 10 A.M.-4:30 P.M., $3 adults, free children 16 and under). The park is a tour through the San Juan Bautista Old Town, once the largest city in central California and a stop along the Camino Real, the historic Spanish colonial route connecting San Francisco and Los Angeles. The tour includes four historic museums. The **Plaza Hotel** is an adobe structure that once served as barracks for soldiers and later as a hotel during the 19th century. **Plaza Hall-Zanetta House** displays furnishings from the 1800s along with many children's toys from the era. Spanish pueblos were usually built around a central plaza, and San Juan Bautista's plaza was used for bear fights, bull fights, cock fights, parades, social gatherings, baking bread, and drying large cowhides. Wagons and stagecoaches were common, and the horses were housed in the **Plaza Stables and Blacksmith Shop.** Today, the exhibit includes stagecoaches, a fire wagon, carriages, and wagons. The **Castro-Breen Adobe** was owned by General José Castro in the early 1840s, but his duties kept him elsewhere. Castro was notorious for an incident on Fremont Peak, where he demanded Kit Carson and John C. Frémont leave Mexican territory. He soon sold his newly built adobe to the Breen family, who survived the 1846 Donner Party incident. Castro had a soft spot for the family and allowed them to live in the house until they could afford to buy it. The Breen family eventually bought the adobe and 400 acres after John Breen returned from the gold fields in 1848. The land and the adobe stayed in the Breen family until it 1933, when California State Parks acquired the land.

SALINAS

© KRISTIN LEAL/SCULPTURE BY THOMAS MARSH

Visit one of California's earliest missions in San Juan Bautista.

Guided walking tours of San Juan Bautista Historic Park can be reserved in advance; prices are $70 for groups of 1-10 plus $4 pp to tour the mission, and $7 pp for groups of 11-25 plus $3 pp to tour the mission.

Antiques Shopping

San Juan Bautista's antiques shops line both sides of 3rd Street in a cluster, where over a dozen stores provide plenty of treasure-hunting opportunities. Each shop has its own inspiration, so it never gets dull.

Z-Place Mrs. B's (306 3rd St., 831/623-8880, daily 10 A.M.-5 P.M.) has antiques as well as shoes, apparel, dolls, small gifts, and jewelry. You might just find that wild top you've been looking for among the vintage garb.

From the home to the garden, **Once Upon a Time Vintage** (107 The Alameda, 831/623-4219, daily 11 A.M.-5 P.M.) has over 10,000 square feet of unique treasures for decorating,

including large architectural pieces, stained glass, jewelry, estate pieces, and furniture. Located in the historic Dobbs and Chevrolet building, they also buy antiques.

In the heart of downtown San Juan Bautista is **Bluebird Antiques and Collectibles** (401 3rd St., 831/623-4017, daily 11 A.M.-5 P.M.), with treasures such as complete sets of vintage jewelry and cute housewares.

The place to stop for vintage pieces created by a local artist as well as large furniture is **Attic Angels** (410 3rd St., 831/623-9234, Thurs.-Sun. 11 A.M.-5 P.M.). Also specializing in restoration and repair, they know their antiques.

Find cottage and Victorian items at **Sweet Pea Antiques** (404 3rd St., 831/623-1053, Mon. and Wed.-Thurs. 11 A.M.-4 P.M., Fri.-Sun. 10 A.M.-5 P.M.), a cozy shop stuffed with perfect items the home or garden, including hard-to-find dishware, linens, jewelry, pottery, and small furniture pieces.

The Little Red Barn Antiques (405 3rd St., 831/623-4792, daily noon-5 P.M.) is filled with every kind of antique: glassware, housewares, vintage books, furniture, clothing, and an extensive jewelry collection.

Accommodations
UNDER $150

Count on a reasonably priced stay any time of year at the **San Juan Inn** (410 The Alameda, Suite 156, 831/623-4380, www.sanjuaninnca.com, $69). The guest rooms are simple and spacious, and all have Wi-Fi, phones, cable TV, fridges, microwaves, and coffeemakers. You can relax at the outdoor spa and pool, or take a walk around the landscaped garden and grassy areas.

At the **Posada de San Juan** (310 4th St., 831/623-4030, www.sjbposadadesanjuan.com, $105-235), find a range of guest rooms to fit your budget. Standard rooms and Queens Quarters have fireplaces, shower-baths, and cozy beds; VIP Rooms have California king beds, large baths with oversize whirlpool tubs, fireplaces, and large balconies.

SALINAS

© KRISTIN LEAL

San Juan Bautista State Historic Park

Food

Locals love to eat at **Jardines de San Juan** (115 3rd St., 831/623-4466, www.jardinesrestaurant.com, Sun.-Thurs. 11:30 A.M.-9 P.M., Fri.-Sat. 11:30 A.M.-10 P.M., $7-12). There are tables outside on nice days in the exceptional garden, and on weekends a local musician performs. Did I mention that the authentic Mexican food is to die for, and comes in hefty portions?

La Casa Rosa (107 3rd St., 831/623-4563, www.lacasarosarestaurant.com, Thurs.-Sun. 11:30 A.M.-3 P.M., $15) provides Basque comfort cooking for lunch. Open since 1935, La Casa Rosa keeps things simple with a small menu, with just four entrées: Old California Casserole, New California Casserole, Chicken Soufflé, and Seafood Soufflé.

For an authentic taste of Germany, get a table at **Joan & Peter's German Restaurant** (322 3rd St., 831/623-4521, Tues.-Sun. 11 A.M.-9 P.M., $8-14). There is some wonderful German beers on tap, the hot food is filling.

You can also get sandwiches to take out for a picnic. If you didn't get enough of that tasty bread before your meal, you can get a fresh loaf to take with you.

◖ FREMONT PEAK STATE PARK AND OBSERVATORY

About 11 miles south of San Juan Bautista, 159-acre Fremont Peak State Park (park info 831/623-4255, observatory info 831/623-2465, www.parks.ca.gov, daily 8 A.M. till 30 minutes after sunset) is easily accessible from Highway 156. Five hiking trails make nice day hikes: Fremont Peak Trail is an easy one-mile round-trip with mild elevation gains that leads up the peak for a 360-degree view. On a clear day, it's possible to see Monterey Bay, the Salinas Valley, the San Benito Valley, the Santa Cruz Mountains, the Diablo Range, the Gabilan Range, the Santa Lucia Mountains, and the Sierra Nevada Mountain Range from atop the 3,169-foot peak.

You can also drive to the top of the peak on the San Juan Canyon Road. The views along the drive are spectacular, as the valleys below open up and the ocean appears beyond the rolling coastal range. There are also plenty of opportunities for picnicking at sites equipped with tables and barbecues.

The park is known for awe-inspiring stargazing at the Fremont Peak Observatory (Apr.-Oct. moonless Sat.). The peak is high above the surrounding towns and away from urban lights, so the night sky glitters. Check the website to be sure of when the observatory is open.

The peak is named for Army Captain John C. Frémont, leader of an expeditionary force that surveyed the area in 1846. He used the peak as a strategic location to watch for anyone approaching. He is well-known for raising the U.S. flag with Kit Carson; the Mexican Army subsequently demanded that Frémont and his group leave Mexican territory. In a later incident in 1847 he was found guilty of mutiny, but was pardoned by President James K. Polk.

CAMPING

For camping with great views, try **Fremont Peak State Park** (park info 831/623-4255, reservations 888/444-7275, www.parks.ca.gov, www.reserveamerica.com, $25), with 25 campsites nestled among the pine and oak trees. Trailer, RV, tent sites available, and water hookups and washrooms are nearby. There are 20 primitive campsites available on a first-come, first-served basis. The views are stunning from every site day and night.

HOLLISTER

Among the hills of Hollister is much to discover, from outdoor attractions to the San Benito wineries. The climate tends to be warm year-round and the summers are hot. It is a perfect day trip destination if you are staying on the peninsula, and because it is off most visitors' radar, it is worth making the trek.

Sports and Recreation
HOLLISTER HILLS STATE VEHICULAR RECREATION AREA

Like a ski resort, Hollister Hills SVRA (7800 Cienega Rd., 831/637-3874, www.parks.ca.gov, daily sunrise-sunset, day-use $5, camping $10) has beginner, intermediate, and expert trails for off-road vehicles. Located on the outskirts of Hollister, this 3,200-acre playground has sensational landscapes ranging from oak forests to rolling grasslands and chaparral. Trails challenge your driving skills with tight twists and turns, ruts created by runoff create obstacles throughout, and mogul-like mounds of dirt add a little bounce. Pay attention to the signs; intermediate and expert trails are mixed, and sometimes a green route turns into more difficult terrain.

Elevation gain on the trails ranges 660-2,425 feet. There are two major sections: The Lower Ranch is for motorcycles and ATVs and has about 64 miles of trails; the Upper Ranch is strictly for four-by-fours and has about 24 miles of drivable terrain.

RIDGEMARK GOLF AND COUNTRY CLUB

The pace of play at Ridgemark Golf and Country Club (3800 Airline Hwy., 831/637-8151, www.ridgemark.com, $24-59 includes cart) is brisk, and you can easily fit both 18-hole courses into a full day of golf. The courses are tucked between the mountains and foothills of the Gabilan and Diablo Ranges. The Gabilan course is the longer and more challenging, and the Diablo course is more scenic. Either way, you are in for a beautiful day, as the sun shines nearly every day.

Accommodations
CAMPING

If you have an ATV or four-by-four, you can camp deep in the rolling chaparral hills at **Hollister Hills SVRA** (7800 Cienega Rd., 831/637-3874, www.parks.ca.gov, year-round daily, camping $10). Campsites are spacious,

© KRISTIN LEAL

Spend some time in the terrain parks improving your off-road techniques.

SALINAS

suitable for RVs and tents, and facilities include running water and showers; there are also many group campsites.

UNDER $150

The whole family will enjoy staying at the **Best Western San Benito Inn** (660 San Felipe Rd., 831/637-9248, www.bestwesternhollister.com, $82-138). There are 42 guest rooms, continental breakfast and high-speed Internet access included in the room rates, and an outdoor swimming pool the kids will love. The atmosphere is laid-back, and the guest rooms are spacious and have comfortable beds.

Ridgemark Golf and Country Club (3800 Airline Hwy., 831/637-8151, www.ridgemark.com, $88-120) has 32 guest rooms with king beds and patios. Amenities include irons, TVs, whirlpool tubs, air-conditioning, fridges, phones with voice mail, blow-dryers, microwaves, and coffeemakers.

Food

For Japanese food, you can't go wrong with **Miyako Japanese Restaurant** (321 San Felipe Rd., 831/635-0800, www.miyakojapanese.com, daily 11 A.M.-2 P.M. and 5-9 P.M., $10-20), with a full sushi bar serving lunch and dinner, sizable specials, and any roll the way you want it. The expansive menu includes hot items as well.

Breakfast, lunch, and dinner is on at **Ella's Italian Restaurant** (1709 Airline Hwy., 831/638-0338, www.cafe-ella.com, Mon.-Sat. 10 A.M.-9 P.M., $5-20), proudly serving fine local ingredients on a menu that changes seasonally.

Hollister's **Maverick BBQ** (35 5th St., Suite A, 831/635-8000, www.maverickbbq.com, lunch Wed.-Fri. 11:30 A.M.-1:30 P.M., dinner Mon.-Tues. 5-8 P.M., Wed.-Thurs. 5-9 P.M., Fri.-Sat. 4-9 P.M., Sun. 4-8 P.M., $10-25) is a finger-licking Western barbecue experience famous for the tri-tip, ribs, slow-smoked pulled pork, barbecue chicken, and mouthwatering steaks. The sandwiches are a good deal at under $10. There is also a special gluten-free menu.

THE PINNACLES AND NEENACH VOLCANO

© KRISTIN LEAL

Climb around the red rocks of Pinnacles National Monument.

The Pinnacles rocks are believed by geologists to be part of the historic Neenach Volcano that existed 23 million years ago. The rocks are supposedly a broken chunk of the volcano dragged northward over millions of years. The Pinnacles are located near the San Andreas Fault, the boundary of the Pacific North American Tectonic Plates.

Today, the other half of the extinct Neenach Volcano can be found near Lancaster, California. Scientists say the San Andreas Fault split the volcano, and as the Pacific Plate crept north, it carried the Pinnacles over 195 miles. Over time, water and wind eroded the volcanic rocks, forming the unusual rock structures we see today throughout the park. Even now, the lava formation is traveling north at the rate of about an inch every year.

SAN BENITO WINERIES

Throughout the inner reaches of the Salinas Valley, grapes are grown to be crushed and fermented. The sun's heat and the ocean breeze create especially superb grape-growing conditions in San Benito, a region known for producing exceptional syrah and pinot noir. There are nine wineries along the San Benito Wine Trail (www.sbcwinegrowers.org), four with tasting rooms and five that can be visited by appointment.

Start east of San Juan Bautista and on the outskirts of Hollister at **Léal Vineyards** (300 Maranatha Dr., 831/636-1023, www.lealvineyards.com, daily 11 A.M.-5 P.M., tasting $10), where you can taste current releases that include award-winning chardonnay and cabernet sauvignon as well as the more exotic flavors of Threesome and Carnavál.

The oldest vineyard in California is said to be the **DeRose Vineyard** (9970 Cienega Rd.,

831/636-9143, www.derosewine.com, Sat.-Sun. 11 A.M.-4 P.M., tasting $5), with vines dating back to the late 1890s. Winemaker and vineyard manager Pat DeRose focuses on traditional farming methods and contemporary cellar practices to create big, bold, rustic wines from handpicked grapes with native yeasts and little or no filtration.

Experience award-winning wine and olive oil at **Pietra Santa Winery** (10034 Cienega Rd., 831/636-1991, www. pietrasantawinery.com, Wed.-Sun. 11 A.M.-5 P.M., tasting $5-10). A family-owned estate since the 1850s, this mission-style vineyard has 450 acres of wine grapes and 25 acres dedicated to olive trees. The oldest vines date to 1905 and consist of a cherished zinfandel block.

At **Calera Wine Company** (11300 Cienega Rd., 831/637-9170, www.calerawine.com, daily 11 A.M.-4:30 P.M., tasting $5), it is all about the limestone. Specializing in pinot noir, winemaker Josh Jensen is no stranger to experimentation, as he was the first in California to plant viognier, in 1983; today, you can enjoy a wide variety of blends, among them aligoté, viognier, pinot noir, and chardonnay.

Summerayne Vineyard (770 Limekiln Rd., 831/902-5638) produces only organic white zinfandel, and tastings are by appointment only, but it is worth setting one up. The tasting is in a parklike setting in the countryside, and the tasting fee counts toward any purchase made.

【 PINNACLES NATIONAL MONUMENT

The 26,000 acres of rugged territory at Pinnacles National Monument (5000 Hwy. 46, 831/389-4485, www.nps.gov, day-use $5, camping $23 tents, $36 RVs) has hiking and plenty of steep rock walls to climb. Camping is a possible year-round but most popular in the summer.

The terrain of the park looks like another planet. Huge rocks shoot into the sky, boulders protrude from massive cracks, and there is much evidence of volcanic activity. Narrow trails traverse the sides of the monument and allow access to a dormant volcano. Be sure to bring plenty of water, as it is generally warm and dry year-round; expect blazing heat in the summer.

There are two sets of caves in the reddish rocks. The **Bear Gulch Cave** is located along the **Moses Spring-Rim Trail Loop** on the east side of the monument. This uphill hike gains 500 feet in elevation as it climbs through the forest, with lush moss covering the boulders, passing the dark cave system and leading to a reservoir. Open seasonally (mid July-mid-May), only some sections of the cave system can be explored; this is to protect the resident rare Townsend's big-eared bats. The bats leave their caves completely for short periods in October and March, when the entire cave system is open, so be sure to check the status of the caves before you depart.

At the west entrance to the monument, the easy-to-moderate **Old Pinnacles Trail to Balconies Caves** is a 2.4-mile loop with an elevation gain of 100 feet; hiking it counterclockwise is less strenuous. The trail has sections of talus to get through, and bring a flashlight along to look inside the **Balconies Caves**.

All facilities at Pinnacles, including the campground, are accessed via the east entrance in Paicines, which is south of Salinas and east of Soledad. No road traverses the park. Visitors wishing to camp or use the visitors center must either hike through the park or drive around to the east side (2 hours, 100 miles).

GILROY

As you pass through the aromatic garlic fields of Gilroy on U.S. 101, you may want to stop at the **Gilroy Premium Outlets** (681 Leavesley Rd., 408/842-3729, www.premiumoutlets.com, Mon.-Sat. 10 A.M.-9 P.M., Sun. 10 A.M.-6 P.M., check website for holiday hours). More than 150 stores include Ralph Lauren Polo, Calvin Klein, Juicy Couture, Saks Fifth Avenue Off 5th, Billabong, Forever 21, Lids, Vans, and DKNY.

GILROY GARLIC

During the 19th century, thriving Gilroy farms produced apples, apricots, cherries, peaches, pears, plums, and all kinds of nut crops. At the turn of the 20th century, row-crop farming techniques were introduced by Italians and other southern Europeans, who grew, canned, or dehydrated crops of tomatoes, peppers, onions, and garlic. With the arrival of Japanese farmers during World War I, garlic began to boom as a crop, and the stinky rose was grown for the commercial market in massive quantities. Not until the late 1970s was the garlic harvest officially celebrated as a community event, attracting over 130,000 visitors annually.

The **Gilroy Garlic Festival** (Christmas Hill Park, 7100 Miller Ave., 408/842-1625, www. gilroygarlicfestival.com, one-day admission $17 adults, $8 over age 59 and ages 6-12, free under age 6). is held for three days on the last full weekend in July and features flaming cook-offs, family fun, live entertainment, and more. Vendors sell their wares and lure you in with the aroma of garlic; you may go home with some tasty Gilroy garlic souvenirs. Watch for Miss Gilroy Garlic, rock out to live concerts all day long, and visit over 100 fine arts and crafts merchants.

The heart of the event is at Gourmet Alley, where chefs gather to showcase their garlic culinary techniques in an all-out competition that features pepper steak, stuffed mushrooms, calamari, garlic bread, fries, pasta con pesto, scampi, chicken stir-fry, combo plates, Italian sausage, and even some garlic-free grub.

GETTING THERE

To San Juan Bautista from Monterey, take Highway 1 north to Highway 156 east, then U.S. 101 north to Highway 156 east to San Juan Bautista. To get to Hollister, continue on Highway 156 east of San Juan Bautista. From Salinas, take U.S. 101 north to Highway 156 east.

SALINAS

SANTA CRUZ

Santa Cruz is the laid-back, fun-in-the-sun, hang-loose beach town where anyone can fit in. There's no place like it: Not even in the far-out San Francisco Bay Area can you find another town that has embraced radical new ideas as a municipal cultural statement. You'll find surfers on the waves year-round, nudist beaches, environmentalists in the redwood forests, tattooed and pierced punks downtown, and families walking the dog along West Cliff Drive, all living side by side.

The quintessential Santa Cruz hippy atmosphere can be experienced along Pacific Street, the town's main drag, filled with an eclectic mix of shops that range from thrift stores to the Gap. By night, there's more action here than in Monterey or Carmel. Local bands jam at places like the Catalyst (a personal favorite), and big names stop by regularly.

Santa Cruz is also great for families. Spend the day hanging out at the beach and visiting the famous Boardwalk, with fast amusement-park rides and summer concerts. The beaches of the Santa Cruz region are for more than just lounging and strolling; campers can spend the night seaside at New Brighten State Beach, north of town along Highway 1, and surfing is big in Davenport.

Locals and students from the University of California, Santa Cruz (UCSC) tend to hang out at the Pacific Garden Mall and stroll along West Cliff Drive. The east side of town can be

© KRISTIN LEAL

HIGHLIGHTS

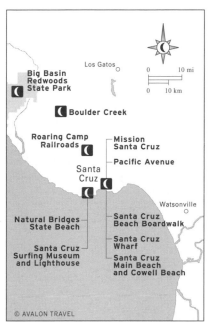

© AVALON TRAVEL

LOOK FOR **◖** TO FIND RECOMMENDED SIGHTS, ACTIVITIES, DINING, AND LODGING.

◖ Santa Cruz Beach Boardwalk: This seaside amusement park is the place to feel like a kid again. Watch the waves crash and hear the roller coaster rumble in the background (page 137).

◖ Santa Cruz Wharf: Watch the day's catch being hauled in, then dine at the seafood restaurants lining the wharf and know that your meal is as fresh as it gets (page 138).

◖ Santa Cruz Surfing Museum and Lighthouse: The museum's timeline spans over 100 years of local surfing culture. See old-school surfboards and plenty of nostalgia-inducing photos (page 139).

◖ Mission Santa Cruz: Only one building remains from the original complex of the 12th California mission, built in 1791 (page 142).

◖ Natural Bridges State Beach: Surf's up, butterfly hunting is on, and beautiful ocean views are to be had at this wonderful state beach (page 147).

◖ Santa Cruz Main Beach and Cowell Beach: The most popular stretch of sand in Santa Cruz covers Main and Cowell Beaches, running from the south end of the Boardwalk to the Wharf and beyond (page 148).

◖ Pacific Avenue: Also known as "the Mall," this area is replete with secondhand shops, cheap eats, hip clothing outlets, and rocking nightclubs (page 160).

◖ Roaring Camp Railroads: Get a taste of the Wild West along Main Street, and picnic and play nearby. Bring the dog: Canines have full access to everything in the park, even the train (page 172).

◖ Boulder Creek: Deep in the Santa Cruz Mountains, this small community is filled with charming antiques shops, a local brewery, a few winemakers, state parks, and a golf course surrounded by redwoods (page 173).

◖ Big Basin Redwoods State Park: Among the park's 80 miles of trails are some of the tallest redwoods in the world, along with gushing waterfalls, freshwater streams, steep mountain inclines, and backcountry camping (page 174).

SANTA CRUZ

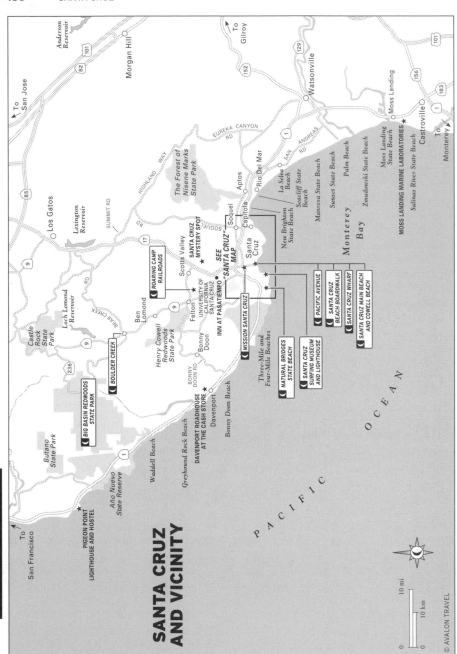

SANTA CRUZ

SANTA CRUZ AND VICINITY

© AVALON TRAVEL

dangerous, with petty crime and drug activity, while the west side is more comfortable for families with children. The restaurants in Santa Cruz offer a multitude of cuisines and prices for every budget.

Outside the city of Santa Cruz are a series of small beach towns; Aptos, Capitola, and Soquel are all south of Santa Cruz along the coast, and each has its own shopping district, restaurants, and lodgings. They've also got their own charming beaches.

Away from the beach, the Santa Cruz Mountains are home to majestic redwood forests. Take a train from the ocean to the forest, or see the trees from a high-flying zip line. Big Basin

Redwoods State Park offers hiking and backpacking opportunities, and afterward, you can fill up on a hearty German meal at the Tyrolean Inn in the mountain town of Ben Lomond.

PLANNING YOUR TIME

To get a taste of unforgettable Santa Cruz, dedicate a long weekend or at least three days. The coast is filled with pretty beaches for sun worshippers and surfers, and the coastal mountains beckon with hiking and camping prospects, a zip-line challenge, local wines, antiques shopping, and home-cooked meals. The southern agricultural part of the region offers a fantastic fruit trail, state beaches, and freshwater fun.

Sights

◖ SANTA CRUZ BEACH BOARDWALK

The Santa Cruz Beach Boardwalk (400 Beach St., 831/423-5590, www.beachboardwalk.com, daily 11 A.M.-close, parking $10), or just "the Boardwalk" as it's called locally, has an appeal that beckons young children, too-cool teenagers, and adults of all ages.

The amusement park rambles along each side of the south end of the Boardwalk. Currently the only major ocean-side amusement park on the West Coast, the Boardwalk has been a local landmark since 1907. Several of the rides extend high into the sky, affording impressive views of Monterey Bay, while others cater to younger children. Admission to the amusement park is free, but to ride the rides, you must buy per-ride tickets or an unlimited-ride wristband. There are numerous rides, including a roller coaster and the 1924 Giant Dipper or the 1911 Carousel. There is even a free summer concert series (mid-June-early Sept. Fri. evening).

The park contains 35 rides, including the Double Shot, a tower ride that launches thrillseekers 125 feet into the air. The Hurricane

creates 4.5 g's and banking angles of 80 degrees. Get caught up in the swirling Tsunami-the ride runs both forward and reverse. The newest attraction is the Sea Swings, and the Haunted Castle takes the brave deep into the dungeons below the Boardwalk. The ride has expanded its boundaries, taking horror to a new low by adding 10,000 square feet of basement space to the original site.

Twelve rides in the park are dedicated to young children, including the Cave Train, a glow-in-the-dark experience. Take a flight on the Red Baron and the Jet Copters, or have some water fun on the Sea Dragons and Starfish.

Avid gamers can choose between the lure of prizes from the traditional midway games and the large arcade. Throw baseballs at things, try your arm at skee ball, or try a classic or newer video game. The traditional carousel from 1911 actually has a brass ring that you or your children can try to grab.

After you've worn yourself out with games and rides, you can take the stairs down to the broad sandy beach below the Boardwalk. It's a great place to flop down in the sun or brave a dip

SANTA CRUZ

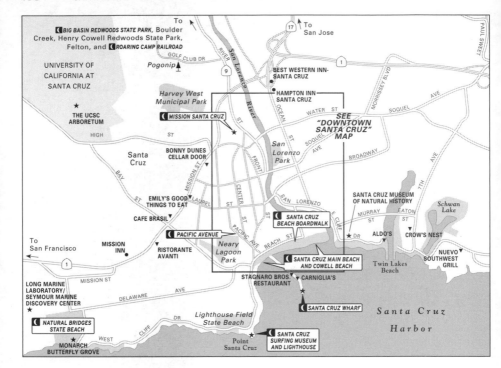

in the cool Pacific. It gets crowded in the summer, but all the services you could ever want are right here at the Boardwalk, plus the sand and the water (and the occasional strand of kelp).

There are a variety of options for something tasty to munch on or a drink to cool you off, including an old-fashioned candy shop and snack stands with corn dogs, burgers, fries, lemonade, and other traditional carnival food.

Beach volleyball is a big deal in Santa Cruz on the sand courts next to the Boardwalk. The courts are open year-round, but the summer brings plenty of action with the California Beach Volleyball Competition and amateurs at play. Court use is free, and it is usually easy to set up a match or join a team.

◖ SANTA CRUZ WHARF

Stretching half a mile out to sea is the Santa Cruz Municipal Wharf (831/420-5273 or 831/420-6025, www.santacruzwharf.com, fee for parking), an iconic landmark. It was built in 1914 as a haven for ocean travelers, and today, you can walk the length of the wharf to find caramel apples, coastal dining with the best views in town, fish markets supplied by local fisheries, boat rentals and tours, and souvenir shops filled with all the beach apparel you could need. You can even do a little fishing right off the pier.

The Lifeguard Headquarters (831/420-6015) is located on the wharf, public restrooms are at the end of the wharf and at the entrance (on the right), and a public boat landing is on the Boardwalk side of the Wharf, across from Santa Cruz Boat Rentals.

The Wharf, however, is not just about what's on the pier; the surf is always up, with summer attracting the most boarders and sun worshippers flocking to the beaches. Surfers can always

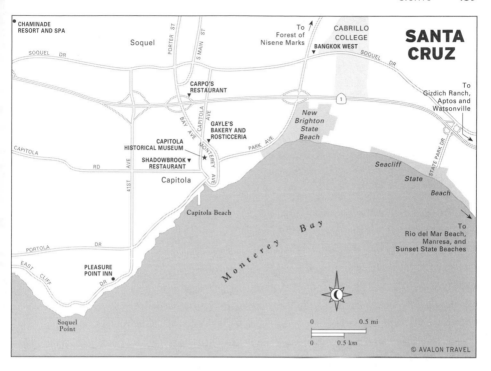

be found on the right side of the Wharf, an area known as Steamers Lane. Body boarders and swimmers tend to take advantage of the surf too. Kayakers are also known to ply these waters; launching is easy with beachside parking, and kayaks can be rented on the Wharf.

SANTA CRUZ SURFING MUSEUM AND LIGHTHOUSE

Mark Abbott Memorial Lighthouse, also known as the Santa Cruz Surfing Museum (701 W. Cliff Dr., 831/420-6289, www.santacruzsurfingmuseum.org, Sept.-June Thurs.-Mon. noon-4 P.M., July-early Sept. Wed.-Mon. 10 A.M.-5 P.M., free), is the first of its kind, opened in the summer of 1986 and celebrating more than 100 years of surfing history with a focus on local heroes. Read stories of shark attacks and surf clubs, check out old-school surfboards, boards with shark bites, and plenty of

nostalgic photos. Pick up a book of tide tables, and grab a T-shirt or a postcard on the way out.

Just below the museum, enjoy watching local surfers along Steamers Lane and the Point, and look to the sandy cove on the north end for skim boarding. The lighthouse is located just above the Boardwalk, nestled among exquisite Victorian homes and quaint beach bungalows. The size of the lighthouse is not all that impressive, but the brick construction against the backdrop of the ocean is postcard worthy.

SANTA CRUZ MUSEUM OF NATURAL HISTORY

A great place to take the whole family is the Santa Cruz Museum of Natural History (1305 E. Cliff Dr., 831/420-6115, www.santacruzmuseums.org, Memorial Day-Labor Day Wed.-Fri. 10 A.M.-5 P.M., Labor Day-Memorial Day Tues.-Sun. 10 A.M.-5 P.M., $4 adults, $2

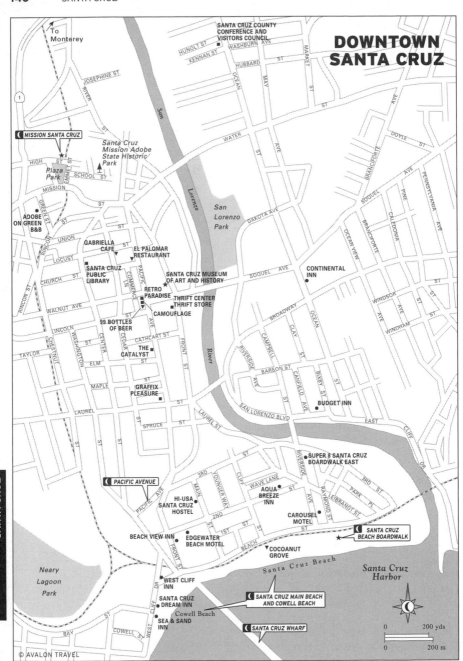

DOWNTOWN SANTA CRUZ

SANTA CRUZ

© AVALON TRAVEL

HISTORY OF THE BEACH BOARDWALK

© KRISTIN LEAL

When seen from a distance, the Santa Cruz Beach Boardwalk hasn't changed all that much in the last 100 years.

The origins of the Santa Cruz Beach Boardwalk began in 1865 with a bathhouse near the mouth of the San Lorenzo River. Soon other bathhouses opened and began to attract people by the hundreds. Visitors craved exposure to the saltwater and sea air; in the 19th century they were believed to be naturally medicinal. Soon restaurants began to open along with small shops and souvenir photo stands.

It wasn't until the end of the 19th century that grand plans for a boardwalk and casino were laid out by Fred W. Swantson, considered one of the great entrepreneurs of his time. Having grown up in Brooklyn, New York, Swantson had fond memories of the Coney Island seaside amusement park there and wanted to recreate it on the West Coast. In 1907 Swantson brought this dream to fruition, and in 1915 the Santa Cruz Seaside Company took over operations, with Swantson playing the role of an investor.

The oldest extant seaside amusement park in California, the Boardwalk today aims to stay true to the original dream while adding many new attractions. These include the Double Shot, a 125-foot tower ride, and the Fireball, a powerful spin and swing ride with strong g-forces. Landmark attractions include the 1911 Carousel and the 1924 Giant Dipper.

© KRISTIN LEAL

Santa Cruz Municipal Wharf

children and seniors), the first public museum in the city, dating to 1904. Permanent and rotating exhibits include the Native American Ohlone people, geology of the Santa Cruz region, wildlife and habitats of the Santa Cruz region, marine life of Monterey Bay, and the Garden Learning Center.

◖ MISSION SANTA CRUZ

Believe it or not, weird and funky Santa Cruz started out as a mission town. Mission Santa Cruz (126 High St., 831/426-5686, Tues.-Sat. 10 A.M.-4 P.M., Sun. 10 A.M.-2 P.M., small donation suggested) was one of the last California missions, dedicated in 1791. Today, the attractive white building with its classic red-tiled roof welcomes parishioners to the active Holy Cross church and fourth-grade students from around the Bay Area to the historic museum exhibits.

The buildings here today, like many others in the string of California missions, are not the originals built by the Spanish in the 18th century. Indeed, none of the first mission and only one wall from the second mission remains; the rest was destroyed in an earthquake. The church is the fourth one at the site, built in 1889. After you tour the complex and grounds, stop in at the Galeria, which houses the mission gift shop and a stunning collection of religious vestments-something you won't see in many other California missions.

LONG MARINE LABORATORY

If you love the sea and the critters that live in it, take a tour of the Long Marine Laboratory (Delaware Ave., 831/459-3800, www.seymourcenter.ucsc.edu, Tues.-Sat. 10 A.M.-5 P.M., Sun. noon-5 P.M., $6 adults, $4 children). The large, attractive gray building complex at the end of Delaware Avenue is on the edge of a cliff overlooking the ocean—convenient for the research done primarily by students and faculty of UCSC. The **Seymour Marine Discovery Center** is the public part of the lab; you'll be

Mission Santa Cruz

©KRISTIN LEAL

downtown Santa Cruz, the classrooms and dorms are under groves of coastal redwood trees and among tangles of ferns and vines. You can take a tour of the campus (831/459-4118, groups of six or more, reservations required). Or just find a parking lot and wander the campus and into the woods.

The UC Santa Cruz Arboretum

The UC Santa Cruz Arboretum (1156 High St., 831/427-2998, www.arboretum.ucsc.edu, daily 9 A.M.-5 P.M., $5 adults, $2 children) is a research and teaching facility, and visitors are welcome to explore the lush gardens. There are more than 300 plant varieties, including a large collection of rare and threatened species. Learn about plant diversity and conservation that you can apply in your own garden. You can call ahead to schedule a docent-led tour ($8 pp) for a behind-the-curtain experience; the cost is worth it as the guides are extremely knowledgeable.

greeted outside the door by a full blue whale skeleton that's lit up at night.

Inside, instead of a standard aquarium setup is a marine laboratory similar to those used by scientists elsewhere in the complex. Expect to see pipes and machinery around the tanks, designed to display their residents rather than to mimic habitats. Kids particularly love the touch tanks, while curious adults enjoy the seasonal tank that contains the wildlife that's swimming around outside in the bay right now.

The best way to introduce yourself to the lab is to take a tour (Tues.-Sun. 1 P.M., 2 P.M., and 3 P.M.); sign up an hour in advance to be sure of getting a slot.

UNIVERSITY OF CALIFORNIA, SANTA CRUZ

The University of California, Santa Cruz (UCSC, Bay St., 831/459-0111, www.ucsc. edu), might be the most beautiful college campus in the country. Set in the hills above

PIGEON POINT LIGHTHOUSE AND HOSTEL

Located just north of Año Nuevo State Park is the Pigeon Point Lighthouse (210 Pigeon Point Rd., 650/879-0633 or 800/909-4776, www.norcalhostels.org or www.parks.ca.gov, dorm $24-26, private room $72-98, family room $156), a great stop on a scenic drive or an overnight getaway, operating year-round as a hostel. The location is secluded, with glorious ocean views and plenty of outdoors to be explored in the vicinity.

The point is crawling with ice plants, and a protected beach can be found at the south end, where you can explore tide pools and watch the waves crash in. A wooden deck winds around the lighthouse, allowing wildlife viewing, including whales, which can be seen year-round as several species migrate through the cool waters of California's Central Coast. Look for their spouts of water blowing up into the air in the distance. California harbor seals lounge lazily on the kelp-covered rocks, and sea otters

SANTA CRUZ

dart among the pools of water diving for their dinner. Even rabbits can be seen running through the geraniums.

SANTA CRUZ MYSTERY SPOT

Since the early 1930s, visitors have been making their way to the Santa Cruz Mystery Spot (465 Mystery Spot Rd., 831/423-8897, www.mysteryspot.com, June-Aug. daily 9 A.M.-7 P.M., Sept.-May Mon.-Fri. 10 A.M.-4 P.M., Sat.-Sun. 10 A.M.-5 P.M., $6, parking $5), where gravity seems to be off-kilter. There are many theories about what makes the mystery spot so mysterious. In the 1950s, after the Roswell incident, the idea of alien intervention became popular. The cabin tends to be the highlight of the 45-minute tour. You will marvel as you walk up walls, balls roll uphill, brooms stand on end, and people seem to shrink.

CAPITOLA HISTORICAL MUSEUM

For a bit of Capitola's past, visit the Capitola Historical Museum (410 Capitola Ave., Capitola, 831/464-0322, www.capitolamuseum.org, Wed. and Fri.-Sun. noon-4 P.M., free). Inside the little red building is an assortment of historical assets, including an extensive collection of old photographs and significant artifacts from the seaside town. The museum also has a constant rotation of new exhibits that focus on the town's history and art. Some of the newer attractions include a reconstructed cottage from the early 20th century and a washhouse.

GIZDICH RANCH

It is all about fresh pickings at the Gizdich Ranch (55 Peckham Rd., 831/722-1056, www.gizdich-ranch.com, daily 9 A.M.-5 P.M.) in Watsonville, where you can pick seasonal fruit right off the vine or tree. Bring along a blanket and other picnic fixings, as the shade under the apple trees is ever so inviting after some work gathering fruit.

Countless rows apple trees and berry bushes provide four harvests, including strawberries (May-July), olallieberries (June), boysenberries (mid-June), and apples (Sept.). Make sure to call for the operating dates, as every season is slightly different, and the best time to visit is during the harvest. But if you're visiting off-season, the baked-goods shop is open year-round, with barrels of apples, freshly baked pies, boxed lunches, flavored crushed ice the kids, and homemade jellies.

HELICOPTER TOURS

Up, up, and away for a bird's eye view of Santa Cruz and Monterey Counties aboard **Specialized Helicopter Tours** (150 Aviation Way, Suite 101, 831/763-2244, www.specializedheli.com, call for reservations). Departures are from both the Watsonville and Monterey airports. Your perspective on the world changes as the helicopter rises into the air. The nose drops and the tail rises while time stops for a moment. They offer five scenic tours, custom flights, sky safaris, and aerial photography. The Sky High tour is a great quickie and perfect for first-timers. Shorter flight buzz the wide strawberry fields of the Pajaro Valley and the bay. The Santa Cruz tour is a 34-mile flight that cruses along the shoreline to Lighthouse Point, and the Monterey tour is 54 miles south to the City of Monterey. The Carmel tour is an incredible 80-mile journey, and best of all is the Big Sur tour, with a grand view of the bay and beyond.

Wineries

The rich climate of Santa Cruz County allows for many vineyards and distinctive wines. Before your wine-tasting adventure, visit the website for the **Santa Cruz Mountain Wine Growers Association** (831/685-8463, www.scmwa.com) or call for a wine trail map, a list of local growers, and a calendar of upcoming events. Wines of Santa Cruz (www.santacruzwines.com) sells Santa Cruz wines online.

WINE TOURS

If you don't feel like driving around yourself, several options are available. **White Hat Limo** (408/966-7980, rush service 480/691-5717, www.whitehatlimo.com, reservations required, call for rates) provides several coach options, including the luxury party van, and limos of all sizes, including a stretch Hummer. Whether your wine-tasting adventure is about private luxury or a casual gathering of friends, White Hat can create a unique wine tour according to your tastes. The company's limos service the San Francisco Bay Area and Northern California from Los Gatos and Mountain View.

Visit wineries that are not typically open to the public with **The Santa Cruz Experience** (831/421-9883, www.thesantacruzexperience.com, Sat.-Sun. 11 A.M.-4:30 P.M., group tours $75 pp, private outings $50-70 pp). Tours include a full day of beautiful scenery, a picnic lunch, and outstanding local wine. You'll be treated like a personal guest at the wineries and get to know the backstory of some of Santa Cruz's best. Shared group tours include visits to three wineries and lunch. Tours meet in downtown Santa Cruz; make your reservations no later than the end of day before your tour. Private tours custom-tailored to your interests are also available.

Santa Cruz Wine Tours (831/607-8784, www.santacruzwinetours.com, luxury and nonluxury vehicles $59-215 per hour) offers private tours tailored to your needs and tastes and will take you to wineries of your choice at your own pace. With so many wineries to choose from, if you can't decide, consult with the experts at Santa Cruz Wine Tours, and they will create an itinerary for you based on your their expert knowledge of the region.

ORGANIC VINEYARDS

The **Organic Wine Trail of the Santa Cruz Mountains** website (www.organicwinetrail.org) points to the certified organic vineyards in the Santa Cruz region. Begin near the town of Watsonville at the **Alfaro Family Vineyards** (420 Hames Rd., Watsonville, 831/728-5172, www.alfarowine.com, Sat. noon-5 P.M., tasting $10) in Corralitos. Once an artisanal bread baker, Richard Alfaro began making wine after 1997 when he acquired a 75-acre apple farm, which he converted into a vineyard and winery. Currently 38 acres are under vines, and in 2010 eight acres of certified organic grapevines were planted. Alfaro specializes in crafting chardonnay, merlot, pinot noir, and syrah.

The next vineyard is **Vine Hill Winery** (2300 Jarvis Rd., Soquel, 831/427-0436, www.vinehillwinery.com, 3rd Sat. of the month noon-5 P.M., tastings $5 and $10), 30 minutes' drive from Alfaro in the hills above Soquel. In the heart of the Santa Cruz Mountains in the historic Vine Hill District, which was originally established in 1867, the winery is dedicated to carrying on the tradition of creating outstanding artisanal wines while using sustainable vineyard and winery practices in crafting chardonnay, pinot noir, and syrah.

From Vine Hill Winery, continue up the mountain to **Silver Mountain Vineyards** (Silver Mountain Dr., off Miller Cutoff, 408/353-2278, www.silvermtn.com, Sat. noon-5 P.M., tasting $5, waived with wine purchase), on high land overlooking Monterey Bay and specializing in small lots of handcrafted chardonnay, pinot noir, and Alloy, a Bordeaux-style blend.

Next is the final winery on the tour, about 20 miles away: **Cooper-Garrod Estate Vineyards** (22645 Garrod Rd., Saratoga, 408/867-7116, www.cgv.com, Mon.-Fri. noon-5 P.M., Sat.-Sun. 11 A.M.-5 P.M., tastings $5 or $10 include souvenir glass), in the hills above Saratoga. The family-owned and operated estate winery has grown 28 acres of vines for over 100 years in the long growing season of the Santa Cruz Mountains. Garrod specializes in chardonnay, viognier, cabernet sauvignon, cabernet franc, merlot, syrah, and blends.

Another organic stop that did not make the organic wine trail list is **Hallcrest Vineyards and the Organic Wine Works** (379 Felton Empire Rd., Felton, 831/335-4441, www.hallcrestvineyards.com, daily noon-5 P.M., tasting $7). The vineyard was established in 1941 where the soil and climate are ideal for producing premium California varietals. Chaffee Hall, a former attorney from San Francisco, established his own vineyard and released his first vintage in 1946. Soon after, Hallcrest Vineyards became known for its cabernet sauvignon and white riesling. After Hall's death, the vineyard was purchased in 1987 by its current owner, John Schumacher, and he stays true to handcrafting fine wines in small lots the signature character of the Santa Cruz Mountain American Viticultural Area. Also known as the original producer of organic wines, Hallcrest bottles its organics under the Organic Wine Works label. They use certified organic grapes and harness an organic winemaking process that naturally avoids the use of sulfites.

OTHER WINERIES

There are several other wineries and vineyards worth looking into. **Ahlgren Vineyard** (20320 Hwy. 9, Boulder Creek, 831/338-6071, www.

ahlgrenvineyard.com, Sat. noon-4 P.M., tasting free) started in the early 1970s when Valerie Ahlgren began to craft zinfandel in her suburban Silicon Valley garage. Today, along with her husband, Dexter, she produces limited runs of fine premium wines in their rustic mountain-cottage cellar, including semillon, chardonnay, cabernet sauvignon, merlot, cabernet franc, zinfandel, nebbiolo, and syrah. They have earned a reputation for fine balance, fullness, and intensity of varietal flavor, firm structure, complex character, and extended life.

Near downtown, have a taste of the savory Santa Cruz Mountains at **Bonny Doon Vineyard's Cellar Door** (328 Ingalls St., 831/425-6737, www.bonnydoonvineyard.com, daily noon-5 P.M., tasting $5, waived with wine purchase). Known for their exceptional Rhône and Italian varietals, they craft a full line of reds, whites, rosés, and dessert wines. If you like what you taste, you can purchase from the website.

Originally established in 1863 as the Jarvis Brothers Vineyard, **Santa Cruz Mountain Vineyard** (334-A Ingalls St., 831/426-6209, www.santacruzmountainvineyard.com, Wed.-Sun. noon-5 P.M. and by appointment) is located at one of the oldest continuously operated vineyards in California. In 1975, Ken Burnap started the winery, setting out to make the finest pinot noir possible. The first release under the Santa Cruz Mountain Vineyard label was the highly regarded 1975 vintage. Today, Ken continues to craft fantastic wines and has brought the tasting room to downtown Santa Cruz.

A small winemaker in the Watsonville area is the **River Run Vintners** (65 Rogge Lane, Watsonville, 831/726-3112, www.riverrunwines.com, by appointment). It takes a bit more effort to visit River Run, but it is worth the bother if you're a fan of reds. They purchase grapes throughout the state to craft a fantastic variety of primarily red wines with a few rosés. This is a family-operated winery with an annual production of 1,000-3,000 cases.

Sports and Recreation

BEACHES
◖ Natural Bridges State Beach

At the tip of the west side of Santa Cruz, Natural Bridges State Beach (W. Cliff Dr., 831/423-4609, www.parks.ca.gov, daily 8 A.M.-sunset, $10) offers nearly every kind of beach recreation possible. The sand isn't wide but it's deep and is crossed by a creek that runs into the sea. An inconsistent break makes surfing at Natural Bridges fun on occasion, while the near-constant winds bring out windsurfers nearly every weekend. Hardy sun-worshippers brave the breezes, bringing beach blankets, umbrellas, and sunscreen on rare sunny days (usually late spring and fall).

Back from the beach, a wooded picnic area has tables and grills. Even farther back, the visitors center can provide great stories about the various natural wonders of this surprisingly diverse state park. Rangers offer guided tours of the tide pools at the west side of the beach, accessed by a scrambling short 0.5-mile hike on the rocks. These odd little holes full of sealife aren't like most tide pools; many are nearly perfect round depressions in the sandstone cliffs worn away by harder stones by the tide. Don't touch the residents of these pools, as human hands can damage the delicate creatures.

Every year October-February, monarch butterflies travel to Natural Bridges State Beach, resting among the trees with their legs intertwined to resemble leaves. You can hike behind the scenes with a docent naturalist and discover the wonders of the Monarch Grove. There are hour-long guided tours (Oct.-Jan. Sat. 11 A.M. and 2 P.M.) that depart from the visitors center, or take a self-guided tour on the boardwalk that leads directly into the grove.

Seabright Beach

At the south end of Santa Cruz, near the harbor, beachgoers flock to Seabright Beach (E. Cliff Dr. and Seabright Ave., 831/685-6500, www.santacruzstateparks.org, daily 6 A.M.-10 P.M., free) during summer. This miles-long stretch of sand, protected by the cliffs from heavy wind, is a favorite retreat for sunbathers and loungers. While there's little in the way of snack bars, volleyball courts, or facilities, there's lots of soft sand to lie in, plenty of room to play football or set up your own volleyball net, and, of course, easy access to the chilly Pacific Ocean. There's no surfing—Seabright has a shore break that delights skimboarders but makes wave-riding impossible.

Each Fourth of July, the Santa Cruz police cordon off the area surrounding Seabright Beach. No one can park nearby or even walk in after a certain time in the afternoon, which seems to change annually. But if you show up early and cart in your stuff, you can participate in the unbelievable fireworks extravaganza that starts almost as soon as the sun goes down. Although it's technically illegal, people still create professional-grade pyrotechnic productions and launch them from Seabright. The effect quickly becomes overwhelming, but for those who can handle it, the night is truly magical.

New Brighton State Beach

Down in Capitola, one of the favorite sandy spots is New Brighton State Beach (1500 Park Ave., Capitola, 831/464-6330, www.parks.ca.gov, 8 A.M. till 30 minutes after sunset, $10). This forest-backed beach has a strip of sand that's perfect for lounging and cold-water swimming, a forest-shaded campground for both tent and RV campers, hiking trails, and ranger-led nature programs. If you plan to camp, call in advance to make reservations at this popular state park, or just come for the day and set up on the sand. New Brighton can get crowded on rare sunny summer days, but it's nothing like the wall-to-wall people of popular Southern California beaches.

◖ Santa Cruz Main Beach and Cowell Beach

The most famous stretch of beach in the area is the Santa Cruz Main Beach (Beach St., 831/420-6015, www.santacruzparksandrec.com, free). Located on the back side of the Santa Cruz Beach Boardwalk, it graces countless postcards. Its reach is wide, from the Wharf to the south end of the Boardwalk. Volleyball courts are available year-round with plenty of action in the summer and on weekends, kids love to swim in the surf, the waves are just right for body boarding, and the beach beckons sun worshippers.

The section of beach that reaches north from the Wharf is known as Cowell Beach (101 Beach St.). This section tends to be less crowded and is a good spot for first-time surfers. You can also see lifeguards doing their training on this beach, as their headquarters are located on the Wharf. A small parking lot is located next to the Dream Inn. The free outdoor showers make it easy to hop in and out of the sea.

Seacliff State Beach

With more than a mile of soft sand and a shipwreck at the end of the pier, Seacliff State Beach (west end of State Park Dr., 831/685-6442, www.parks.ca.gov, daily 8 A.M.-sunset, $10) is perfect for a stroll, sunbathing, catching some waves, casting a line from the pier or the shore for striped bass, and watching the sunset. There is a snack shack and a visitors center as well as RV camping right next to the beach.

Manresa State Beach

Manresa State Beach (400 San Andreas Rd., 831/761-1795, www.parks.ca.gov, daily 8 A.M.-sunset, $10) has surfing, primitive walk-in camping, and is a pleasant location to bring

Seacliff State Beach

© KRISTIN LEAL

children. Showers in the parking lot make it easy to clean up after a day on the sand. The fishing from shore is good for starry flounder, California halibut, barred surf perch, striped bass, and surf smelt. Bring some wood to make a fire in the beach fire pits.

Sunset State Beach

A year-round destination for camping and beach fun 16 miles south of Santa Cruz is Sunset State Beach (San Andreas Rd., Watsonville, 831/763-7062, www.parks.ca.gov, 8 A.M.till 30 minutes after sunset, $10), peacefully nestled in Watsonville's farmlands. Beach access is from a parking lot next to the sand. Beach gear is available for rent, and numerous barbecues and picnic tables are useful for large groups. Fires are allowed on the beach, and if you park outside the gate and hike in, you can stay well past sunset. Bring your pole along to fish from the shore for surf perch, sardines, and the occasional striped bass.

Davenport Landing

Eleven miles north of Santa Cruz, the strong continuous wind of Davenport Landing (Hwy. 1, 831/454-7956, www.scparks.com, free) provides good opportunities to windsurf. Kayakers, body boarders, and surfers are also seen here. The beach itself is pleasant and secluded with a few picnic tables and restrooms. Dogs are welcome, and there is plenty of space for children to run around. Fishing from the shore is possible, and keep an eye on the sand for pieces of glass polished in the sea.

Waddell State Beach

High-flying madness is on display at Waddell Beach (Hwy. 1, 15 miles north of Santa Cruz, 831/427-2288, www.parks.ca.gov, 8 A.M.till 30 minutes after sunset, free) as kite surfers take flight by the dozens. Strong winds and the open ocean create a prime environment for kite surfing and windsurfing. The beach is a bit too windy for lounging but makes a nice walk. There is a large parking lot and pit toilets, with additional parking along Highway 1.

SURFING

The cold waters of Santa Cruz demand full wetsuits year-round, and the shoreline is rough and rocky, unlike the flat sandy beaches of Southern California. But that doesn't deter the hordes of locals who ply the waves every chance they get. Surfing culture pervades the town, symbolized by the cliff-top *To Honor Surfing* sculpture (W. Cliff Dr. and Pelton Ave.), which is often dressed up and usually gets a costume for Halloween.

Cowell Beach (350 W. Cliff Dr.) on the west side is all about surfing. The coastline geography and underwater features create a reliable small break that lures new surfers by the dozens. The waves are low and long, making for fun long-board rides and helpful for beginners just getting their balance. Because Cowell's break is an acknowledged newbie spot, the often sizable crowd tends to be polite to newcomers.

For more advanced surfers looking for smaller crowds in the water, **Manresa State Beach** (San Andreas Rd., Aptos, www.parks.ca.gov), several minutes' drive south of Santa Cruz, has good beach break, and the waves can get big when there's a north swell. It is also known for its great negative tide. There are fire pits on the beach and open showers in the parking lot.

Visitors who know their surfing lore may want to surf the more famous spots along the Santa Cruz shore. **Pleasure Point** (between 32nd Ave. and 41st Ave., Soquel) encompasses a number of different breaks, including The Hook (steps at 41st Ave.), a well-known experienced long-boarders' paradise. But don't mistake The Hook for a beginner's break; locals feel protective of the waves and aren't always friendly toward inexperienced surfers. The break at 36th and East Cliff (steps at 36th Ave.) is a better place on weekdays; on weekends the intense crowding makes catching your

Steamers Lane

own wave a challenge. Up at 30th and East Cliff (steps at 36th Ave.) are challenging sets and hot-dogging short-boarders.

The most famous break in Santa Cruz can also be the most hostile to newcomers. **Steamers Lane** (W. Cliff Dr. between Cowell Beach and the Lighthouse) has both a fiercely protective crew of locals and a dangerous break that actually kills someone every other year or so. But if you're into adrenaline and there's a swell coming in, you'll be hard-pressed to find a more exciting ride in California.

Farther north along Highway 1 and somewhat out of the way is a lesser-known surf spot called **Scott Creek Beach** (Hwy. 1, 3 miles north of Davenport Landing), a wide beach with parking along the highway. The surfing is engaging and the waves are generous, providing long rides for the adventurous. The winds pick up nicely, and surfers share the waves with windsurfers and kite surfers. This is a good spot for more seasoned surfers as the waves tend to be forceful with a nice overhead.

Surfing Schools

Yes, you can learn to surf in Santa Cruz, despite the distinct locals-only vibe at some of the breaks. Check out **Santa Cruz Surf School** (131 Center St., 831/345-8875, www.santacruzsurfschool.com) or **Richard Schmidt School of Surfing** (849 Almar Ave., 831/423-0928, www.richardschmidt.com) for lessons.

Surf Shops

O'Neill at the Boardwalk (400 Beach St., 831/459-9230, www.oneill.com, Mon.-Fri. 10 A.M.-5 P.M., Sat.-Sun. 10 A.M.-8 P.M.), a prefab chain, specializes in surfboards, wetsuits, skateboards, accessories, and brand-name clothing.

For 30 years, Pearson Arrow has been shaping custom high-quality surfboards at **Arrow Surf & Sport** (2322 Mission St., 831/423-8286, www.arrowsurfshop.com, Mon.-Sat. 9 A.M.-7 P.M., Sun. 9 A.M.-6 P.M.), where the emphasis is on surfboards, along with accessories and apparel.

SURF COMPETITIONS

For over 25 years, the **Santa Cruz Kayak and Surf Festival** (Steamers Lane and Cowell Beach, just north of the Municipal Wharf) in mid-March has been a celebrated event for locals and visitors. Watch stand-up paddle surfing, kayak surfing, and traditional surfing.

The West Coast's oldest and longest-running surfing competition is the **Santa Cruz Longboard Club Invitational** (Steamers Lane at Lighthouse Point, 831/324-2278, www.santa-cruz-longboard-union.com) in late May. The event features amateur and professional surfers in 11 age groups. It is a great event for the whole family with plenty of places along the coast road with a good view of the surfers.

Surf's up in Santa Cruz all year long.

From the surf to the snow, **Pacific Wave Surf Shop** (1502 Pacific Ave., 831/458-9283, www.pacwave.com, Sun.-Thurs. 10 A.M.-8 P.M., Fri.-Sat. 10 A.M.-9 P.M.) carries a little of everything-surf, skate, and snowboard apparel plus accessories as well as a limited selection of surfboards and skateboards.

WINDSURFING AND KITE SURFING

Beginning windsurfers vie with long-boarders for space at **Cowell's break** (stairs at W. Cliff Dr. and Cowell Beach), next to the City Wharf. For a bigger breeze, head up West Cliff Drive to **Natural Bridges State Beach** (W. Cliff Dr., www.parks.ca.gov), the easiest spot to set up. There are restroom facilities and ample parking.

Serious windsurfers head farther north to **Davenport Landing** (Hwy. 1, 20 miles north of Santa Cruz). You'll know you've found the right rugged and windswept stretch of coast by the endless crowd of windsurfers and kite surfers out on the waves. Parking can be a bit haphazard, but it can be worth your time even just to stop by to watch these athletes taking fast rides. The heaviest winds of the area are at **Waddell**

State Beach (Hwy. 1, 15 miles north of Santa Cruz, 831/427-2288, www.parks.ca.gov, 8 A.M.till 30 minutes after sunset, free). On a typical day, the surf is filled with dozens windsurfers and kite surfers; countless onlookers pull off Highway 1 to watch.

If you want to try windsurfing for the first time, contact **Club Ed** (831/464-0177, www.club-ed.com) to set up a lesson. They operate in the gentle breezes and small swells at Cowell's break and make it easy for first-timers to gain confidence.

KAYAKING

Santa Cruz kayaking is spectacular. There are secluded coves to discover, a wide harbor, open water near the wharf, and the possibility to fish. Bring your own gear and launch at numerous locations or pick up a rental boat. The local rental companies offer self-guided and guided tours, which can take you to some incredible locations for an alternative perspective on the coast. Tours are especially helpful for beginners and first-timers in the area.

A great beginner spot is **Santa Cruz Main Beach** (Beach St., 831/420-6015, www.santacruzparksandrec.com, free) and **Cowell Beach**

(101 Beach St.). Parking is close to the water, with easy drop-off points near Cowell's break and on the north side of the Boardwalk. The breakers tend to be smaller on Santa Cruz Main Beach and are easier to navigate through if you're looking for a relaxing paddle along the shore. If you are in the mood for a heart-pumping thrill ride, head to Cowell Beach and ride the waves. The showers in the parking lot here are particularly appreciated after a day in the sea.

Surf kayaking at **Davenport Landing** (Hwy. 1, 11 miles north of Santa Cruz, 831/454-7956, www.scparks.com, free) starts with an easy launch as parking is very close to the beach. Although it is a well-known kayaking spot, there are plenty of waves for everyone. Views of the shore reveal hidden beaches among the cliffs. This cove is good place to drop a line to fish for rock cod, sometimes lingcod, and several other tasty fish.

The easiest launch in town is at **Santa Cruz Harbor** (Santa Cruz Port District, 135 5th Ave., 831/475-6161, www.santacruzharbor.org). The launch ramps makes unloading and putting in easy, you can drive right to the water's edge. The harbor is fun to explore, as you can get a close look at the boats in port and the noisy sea lions. You can also easily head out past the breakwaters to the open sea for a more adventurous paddle.

Kayak Rentals and Tours

You can pick up a rental or a lesson at **Venture Quest Kayaking** (2 Municipal Wharf, 831/425-8445, www.kayaksantacruz.com, Mon.-Fri. 10 A.M.-7 P.M., Sat.-Sun. 9 A.M.-7 P.M., single sit-on-top kayak from $30 for 3 hours). Access to the Bay from the Santa Cruz Municipal Wharf is ideal; you don't have to break the surf, and wildlife encounters start right away with the large sea lions napping under the pier.

Kayak Connections (413 Lake Ave., Suite 3, 831/479-1121, www.kayakconnection. com, Mon.-Fri. 10 A.M.-5 P.M., Sat.-Sun. 9 A.M.-5 P.M., single $35, double $50 for 4

hours) is located on the harbor for rentals, repairs, and gear. Besides renting out kayaks, they have stand-up paddle boards, body boards, wetsuits, and other gear. Lessons are available for all skill levels on kayaks, surf kayaks, and stand-up paddle boards.

For lessons and multiple-day expeditions, try **Eskape Sea Kayaking** (740 30th Ave., Suite 117, 831/476-5385, www.eskapekayak.com). Since 1992 Eskape has paddled around Santa Cruz and knows the waters well. Eskape offers advanced and custom clinics, beginner classes, and American Canoe Association certification workshops, great for kayakers of any skill level. Classes are small, allowing for personal attention from your instructor, and kayaks are provided.

FISHING TRIPS AND CHARTERS

Deep-sea fishing happens throughout Monterey Bay, and Santa Cruz is no exception. **Stagnaro Fishing Trips** (32 Municipal Wharf, 831/427-2334, www.stagnaros.com) is a leader in charter fishing trips, with year-round excursions for commercial use and recreational fishing. Seasonal catches include salmon, sand dabs, rock cod, and albacore. Rock cod trips are the most fun for children, as they are easy to hook, and everyone usually catches their limit. Stagnaro also runs whale-watching tours (year-round daily) to look for blue, humpback, and gray whales, a variety of dolphin species, and many other sea mammals and birds.

A variety of trips can be booked through **Monterey Bay Charters** (333 Lake Ave., 831/818-8808, www.montereybaycharters. com). Depending on the season, salmon, halibut, tuna, lingcod, sea bass, and rock cod can be caught. Other options include marine-sanctuary sightseeing tours, on-the-water picnics, marine and wildlife ecotours, team building, and private "Day on the Bay" parties.

Captain Brad, owner and operator of **Ultimate Fish Charters** (departs Santa Cruz Harbor at 135 5th Ave., 831/566-9407, www.

ultimatefishcharters.com), has been fishing the waters of Monterey Bay all his life and knows where find the hot biting. His trips go into Monterey Bay, Morro Bay, and Half Moon Bay. Spring trips fish near the shore for salmon, rock cod, and halibut; in summer, trips look for albacore tuna.

WHALE WATCHING

Stagnaro Fishing Trips, also known as **Santa Cruz Whale Watching** (32 Municipal Wharf and 3640 Capitola Rd., 831/427-2334 or 831/427-0230, www.stagnaros.com or www. santacruzwhalewatching.com, $45 adults, $31 children) runs 3- to 4-hour whale-watching trips in the bay, where you will most likely encounter several whales, dolphins, seals, sea otters, and a variety of marine birds. They also offer an inner-bay calm water tour (1 hour, $20 adults, $13 children), a shorter ride along the shore that showcases some of Santa Cruz's sights from a different perspective. You can also see a plethora of marine animals, including seabirds, sea otters, harbor seals, sea lions, and possibly a dolphin or two.

SAILING

Sailing on the bay can range from a restorative excursion to full-on racing. Either way, you can view the magnificent coastline and possibly encounter some wildlife.

Set sail with **Chardonnay II Sailing Charters** (704 Soquel Ave., Suite A, 831/423-1213, www.chardonnay.com) and choose from 16 tour options for special events. Tours aboard the 70-foot *Chardonnay II* sailing yacht highlight the protected wildlife of Monterey Bay. The most exciting seat is in the bow, where you might even get wet. The Winemaker and Brew Masters excursions allow you to sample locally crafted wine or beer. Other tour options include Wednesday night races, Sunday champagne brunch, or afternoon sailing.

Lighthall Yacht Charters (934 Bay St., 831/429-1970, www.lighthallcharters.com) has

two-hour tours for as little as $40. Shared tours and private charters operate on 34- to 47-foot sailing yachts. Lighthall has taken more than 1 million passengers out on the local seas.

O'Neill Yacht Charters (2222 E. Cliff Dr., 831/457-1561, www.oneillyachtcharters.com, spring-summer, 1-hour sail $20 pp, 1.5-hour sail $30 pp) sails along the Santa Cruz shoreline while taking in the Boardwalk, the Wharf, Walton Lighthouse, local surfers, playful sea otters, and napping seals. Private charters are available year-round and can be individually tailored.

Learn to sail or take a private cruise with **Pacific Yachting Sailing** (790 Mariner Park Way, Suite 1, 831/423-7245 or 800/374-2626, www.pacificsail.com). Cruises (from $230 for 2 hours) accommodate up to six passengers and can be a leisurely sail, a whale-watching adventure, a romantic sunset getaway, an ocean picnic, a catered meal, or a special place to pop the question.

HIKING AND BIKING
West Cliff Drive

West Cliff Drive is a winding street with a full walking path and cycling trail running its length on the ocean side. It is the town's favorite walking, jogging, skating, scootering, dogwalking, and biking route. Start at Natural Bridges State Beach (west end of W. Cliff Dr.) and go for miles. The *To Honor Surfing* sculpture (W. Cliff Dr. and Pelton Ave.) is several miles along the road from Natural Bridges. There are plenty of fabulous views, so bring your camera if you're here on a clear day. Watch for your fellow path users; it can get a bit treacherous when it's busy.

Wilder Ranch State Park

Just north of Santa Cruz is a place where the flavor of the Wild West lives on. Wilder Ranch State Park (1401 Old Coast Rd., 831/423-9703 or 831/426-0505, www.parks.ca.gov, year-round daily, $10) was once home to the Ohlone people, who hunted in the hills and

SANTA CRUZ

fished in the sea for edibles like abalone. Later it became the home of the Wilder family, settlers who operated a dairy farm, and today it is a huge state park with sections of the land leased to local farmers.

On the ranch are 13 structures that can be toured (Thurs.-Sun. 1 P.M.), including an adobe homestead, a bunkhouse, a garage, a chicken coop, a horse barn, and a cowboy cottage. The Farm Animal Program has sheep, goats, chickens, barn cats, and horses. Being able to interact with them is great for kids to get some exposure to farm animals. Nature walks are held on Saturday, and there are annual events and holiday celebrations with live entertainment, crafts, and lots of fun. Call for more details on tours and upcoming events.

Wilder Ranch has hiking and horseback-riding trails that follow the rolling terrain. Ohlone Bluff Trail and the Enchanted Loop Trail evoke the time when Native Americans were the only inhabitants. The 1.25-mile Old Cove Landing Trail is one of the more popular treks and leads to the Ohlone Bluff Trail. It has broad views of the ocean and lush farmland. The trail runs above a gentle valley that leads to the coast.

Bird-watchers may catch sight of large predators such as peregrine falcons, which can reach speeds up to 200 mph as they dive after prey. Look for small seabirds along the shore, including elegant, Caspian, and Forster's terns, snowy plovers, and many more. Tiny quails scurry across the dusty paths to hide in the coyote brush.

The Forest of Nisene Marks State Park

Just south of Santa Cruz is the Forest of Nisene Marks State Park (Aptos Creek Rd. and Soquel Dr., Aptos, 831/763-7063, www.parks.ca.gov, $10), 10,000 acres of semi-wilderness redwood and Douglas fir forest with 30 miles of hiking, jogging, and biking trails that climb as high as

Wilder Ranch has many picnicking prospects.

© KRISTIN LEAL

SANTA CRUZ

2,600 feet. Ferns fan out on the forest floor, bright green moss clings to dark boulders, and sunbeams peer through gaps between the trees. Picnic tables and barbecue pits are available, and there is primitive camping deep inside the park. Dogs are welcome as long as they are on a leash.

The forest is primarily second- and third-growth redwoods and Douglas firs. It was virgin old-growth forest until 1881, when the Loma Prieta Lumber Company and the Southern Pacific Railroad got together to harvest the lumber. The railroad was built along Aptos creek, and 140 million board feet of lumber was removed over the next 40 years. By 1922 there was nothing left to cut, and a Salinas family purchased the land from the lumber company in hope of striking oil. They didn't, and in 1963 the family donated 9,700 acres to the State of California in memory of their mother, Nisene Marks. The Save-the-Redwoods League helped expand the park to 10,036 acres.

Pinto Lake

Tucked in agricultural Watsonville is a freshwater escape known as Pinto Lake (451 Green Valley Rd., Watsonville, 831/722-8129, www.pinto-lake.com; 757 Green Valley Rd., Watsonville, 831/454-7956, www.scparks.com), with two parks, one run by the city and one by the county, that have year-round access for recreation. The lake is spring-fed and covers 92 acres, reaching depths of 30 feet. The Santa Cruz County park has some decent winding hiking trails and covered barbecue pavilions near the lake.

The best time to fish in Pinto Lake is February-May, and in June-July there is nice surface bites by the rainbow trout the lake is stocked with. Other species include bluegill sunfish, catfish, carp, and lots of bass. During the summer months kids can hook bluegills from the shore of both parks.

The city park offers rowboat and paddle-boat rentals ($8) and has a launch ramp for kayaks and trolling boats. Put-in fees are $3 for craft up to 12 feet and $5 for anything larger. Personal watercraft must be inspected before entering the lake to prevent infestation by the invasive zebra mussel, so you have to arrive before 3 P.M.

SPAS

Massage choices around Santa Cruz County include sea-salt body scrubs, green tea and ginger wraps, facials, and an assortment of massage packages. Many spas have on-site steam rooms, hot tubs, and meditation areas.

High above Monterey Bay on a bluff overlooking Santa Cruz is **The Spa at Chaminade** (One Chaminade Lane, 831/465-3465, www.chaminade.com, by appointment daily), with an extensive menu of facials, pedicures, massages, aromatherapy, body scrubs, wraps, skin care, and waxing. Get ready to be pampered with all sorts of natural skin products; Chaminade takes pride in being a certified green business and uses only environmentally friendly products.

In the rustic countryside of Soquel is the country charm of **SUDzzz Eco-Friendly Lil' Day Spa** (Soquel Farm Cottage, 1221 Old San Jose Rd., Soquel, 831/476-2662, www.sudzzz.com, by appointment daily 10 A.M.-1 P.M.), with deep stainless-steel soaking tubs, antique decor, and contemporary design. A different special is offered every month, and services include an array of facials, chocolate treatments, masterful massages, vino-therapy, makeup artistry, body treatments, hair removal, and plenty of packages.

Locally owned since 1984, the Asian-inspired **Tea House Spa** (112 Elm St., 831/426-9700, www.teahousespa.com, Mon.-Sat. 11 A.M.-midnight) in downtown Santa Cruz is located in a 50-year-old grove of bamboo. Indulge in private or couples hot tub rooms, sauna, and massage. The spa has a waterfall, and you can rest in the shade under the stately cypress.

For professional massage, skin, and body care, **Well Within Spa** (417 Cedar St., 831/458-9355, www.wellwithinspa.com, daily

10 A.M.-midnight) has all kinds of massage packages, including a couples experience, aromatherapy, and prenatal treatment. Sessions last 25-80 minutes. Private indoor and outdoor hot tubs overlook the lush Japanese garden, and the private Onsen Retreat Room, the perfect size for two, is equipped with a Japanese-style soaking tub and cedar-lined sauna.

Entertainment and Events

BARS AND CLUBS

Down on Pacific Avenue, called "the Mall," walk upstairs to **Rosie McCann's** (1220 Pacific Ave., 831/426-9930, www.rosiemccanns.com) for a pint and a bite. This dark-paneled Irish-style saloon serves Guinness, black and tan, snakebites, and several tasty draft beers. Food includes sausages, mashed potatoes, and other hearty pub fare. A largely local crowd hangs out here, and you'll find the bar crowded and noisy, but the vibe is friendly and entertaining.

There is no better place in Santa Cruz for cold beer than **99 Bottles of Beer on the Wall** (110 Walnut Ave., 831/459-9999, daily 11 A.M.-midnight). Like the sign says, they serve 99 different varieties of beer and a few wine choices. Try Dutch imports or local beers such as Santa Cruz Ale Works Oatmeal Stout. The food isn't bad and pairs nicely with the brews.

Callahan's (507 Water St., 831/427-3119, www.dhcallahans.com, daily 11 A.M.-2 A.M.) is a classic bar experience with 13 cold beers on tap, pool tables, and darts. They host a pool tournament every Wednesday (sign-up 9 P.M.). Five high-definition TV screens play sports, including NFL Ticket and MLB Package offerings.

For drink specials and a dance floor grooving to DJ beats, look no farther than **Blue Lagoon** (923 Pacific Ave., 831/423-7117, www.thebluelagoon.com, daily 4 P.M.-2 A.M.). Everyday drink specials include Pabst Beer ($2), Jäger shots ($3), and Hornitos shots ($5). Thursday is stand-up comedy night with dancing to '80s music afterward. Friday music is a house and Top 40 mix. Check the website for occasional live music.

LIVE MUSIC

The Catalyst (1011 Pacific Ave., 831/423-1338, advance tickets 866/384till 3060, www. catalystclub.com, $12-35), downtown on the Mall, is *the* Santa Cruz live rock venue for big-name acts that now play clubs rather than stadiums. The Catalyst is completely democratic in its bookings—you might see Ted Nugent one week, the Indigo Girls the next, and a ska band the week after that. Catalyst also hosts DJ dance nights, teen nights, and other fun events. Check the calendar when you buy tickets; some shows are age 21 and over only. The main concert hall is a standing-room-only space while the balconies offer seating. The bar is downstairs adjacent to the concert space. The vibe tends to be low-key, but it depends on the night and the event. Some of the more retro acts definitely draw an older crowd, while the techno-DJ dance parties cater to the university crowd. You can buy tickets online or by phone; advance purchase is recommended, especially for nationally known acts.

The **Crow's Nest** (2218 E. Cliff Dr., 831/476-4560, www.crowsnest-santacruz.com) has a full bar and restaurant and functions as a venue for all kinds of live music. You might see a contemporary reggae-rock group one night and a Latin dance band the next. Lots of funk bands play, and a few tribute bands, usually to hippie '60s and '70s legends like Jimi Hendrix and Santana, perform on occasion as well. Most shows are free, but if there's a really popular act, cover charge might be $5. Check the website for a calendar of performances, and count on live musical here Wednesday-Saturday nights.

The Crow's Nest has weekly stand-up performances (Sun. 9 P.M.). Hosting comedy on Sunday allows the Crow's Nest to bring in big-name comics who have been in San Francisco or San Jose for weekend engagements, allowing headliners to perform in a more casual setting for a fraction of the admission cost of big-city clubs.

With live entertainment six nights a week, **Moe's Alley** (1535 Commercial Way, 831/479-1854, www.moesalley.com, Tues.-Sun. 4 P.M.-2 A.M.) hosts blues, salsa, ska, and hip-hop. The dance floor is spacious, and the outdoor patio has heaters and a smoking area. Check the website for a list of coming performances.

THEATER

Santa Cruz is home to several community theater groups and an outdoor summer Shakespeare festival that draws theatergoers from around the Bay Area.

The **Santa Cruz Actors' Theatre** (1001 Center St., 831/425-7529, www.sccat.org) is Santa Cruz's permanent local theater company, with a subscription season, theater arts workshops, playwriting contests for kids and adults, and improv shows. All shows are contemporary works, including plays in the full-production series. The most exciting shows, though not necessarily the best quality, are the completely new plays, mostly by local authors, that have won Actors' Theatre contests. If one of these appears during your visit, especially the "Eight Tens at Eight," consider getting tickets to see something completely different.

If you prefer historic theater to modern, UCSC puts on the annual summer **Shakespeare Santa Cruz** (831/459-2121, http://shakespearesantacruz.org, from $15 till 30 adults, $14 under age $18), a six-week festival in July-August. Both venues are on the UCSC campus: the indoor Theatre Arts Mainstage (1156 High St.) and the Festival Glen (Meyer Dr.), in a redwood forest. Each year the festival puts on at least two of Shakespeare's plays. At the outdoor Glen, audience members are encouraged to bring a picnic; this can make for a romantic date or a fun outing for the whole family.

Live music, performing artists, lectures, movie nights, comic acts, and youth performances grace the stage on the weekend at **The Rio Theatre for the Performing Arts** (1205 Soquel Ave., 831/423-8209, www.riotheatre.com); check the website for upcoming events. Built from Davenport-area cement and Hebbron-Nigh lumber, the theater dates to 1949.

CINEMA

Local resident Jim Schwenterley provides a classic moviegoing experience at the cozy, beautifully restored **Del Mar Theater** (1124 Pacific Ave., 831/469-3220, www.thenick.com). Screenings include foreign, older, art house, and independent films. Check the website for showtimes and advance tickets.

Also owned and operated by Schwenterley is the Gothic 1970s **Nickelodeon Theaters** (210 Lincoln St., 831/426-7500, www.thenick.com), with indie, art house, and foreign films along with some mainstream movies that don't overlap with what the Del Mar is showing. Check the movie listings online.

There are two Regal Cinemas in Santa Cruz, **Regal Cinema 9 Santa Cruz** (1405 Pacific Ave., 831/457-3505) and **Regal Cinemas Riverfront Stadium Twin** (155 South River St., 831/429-7250), to catch the latest wide releases. The theaters are slightly outdated, but that is part of the Santa Cruz charm.

FESTIVALS AND EVENTS

Throughout the year, Santa Cruz hosts a diverse range of festivals and events, gatherings at local state parks to Santa surfing into Capitola with his reindeer.

Spring

Celebrate Mother Nature at **Earth Day Santa Cruz** (San Lorenzo Park, 809 Center St., and San Lorenzo River Park Benchlands, 701 Ocean St., behind the county building, 831/477-3988, www.ecocruz.org) in mid-April.

SANTA CRUZ ANNUAL PRIDE PARADE AND FESTIVAL

The rainbow flags fly high as summer heats up in liberal-minded Santa Cruz. The annual full-day **Pride Santa Cruz LGBT Parade,** sponsored by the Diversity Center of Santa Cruz (1117 Soquel Ave., 831/425-5422, www.diversitycenter.org), has been held in early June for nearly two decades. People from all over gather to celebrate lesbian, gay, bisexual, and transgender pride. The morning begins with a parade, traditionally led by the Dykes on Bikes motorcycle club, down Pacific Avenue and Cathcart Street; the parade usually draws more than 5,000 participants.

The festival ($5) kicks off immediately after the parade at San Lorenzo Park (137 Dakota St.), which fills with great food, vendors, and live performances. There is a dance tent and a children's area, so there's fun for the whole family.

Earth-oriented festivities include activities for kids, live music, and information on environmental awareness and greener business.

Spring break is almost a religious event for high school and college students at **Spring Break at the Santa Cruz Beach Boardwalk** (400 Beach St., 831/423-5590, www.beachboardwalk.com) on a weekend in late April. Youths and popular cable networks gather for interactive games, beach competitions, live music, and talented guest appearances.

If you're an indie-film fan, the **Santa Cruz Film Festival** (831/359-4888, www.santacruzfilmfestival.org) in early-mid-May is a mustsee if you're in the area. Since 2002 the festival has showcased local filmmakers and screened independent films during a two-week period.

Feel the chord progressions at the **Santa Cruz Blues Festival** (Aptos Village Park, 305 Village Creek Rd., Aptos, 831/479-9814, www. santacruzbluesfestival.com) in late May. For the last 20 years or so this annual musical event has been a fun weekend with food, beer, and wine.

Summer

Kick off the summer in late June like the Beach Boys would have with **Surf City Classic: Woodies on the Wharf** (Municipal Wharf, 831/420-5273, www.santacruzwharf.com). The 20-year-old annual family-friendly event is all about classic cars and the surf spirit.

Celebrate an **Old-fashioned Independence Day** (Wilder Ranch State Park, Hwy. 1, 2 miles north of Santa Cruz, 831/426-0505, www.santacruzstateparks.org, July 4 11 A.M.-4 P.M.) ranch-style with the California State Parks. The parade and flag-raising start at noon; the crafts, games, live old-time music, and ice cream making are a whole lot of family fun.

Early August is the time to celebrate the famous strawberries of the Central Coast region at the **Watsonville Strawberry Festival at Monterey Bay** (downtown Watsonville, 831/768-3240, www.celebratestrawberries.com). Everybody will love the menu of strawberry treats, all-day entertainment, and plenty of contests; you may even get your fill of strawberry treats at this two-day event.

The annual two-day outdoor **Cabrillo Music, Art & Wine Festival** (307 Church St., in front of the Civic Auditorium, downtown Santa Cruz, 831/426-6966, www.cabrillomusic.org) in early August has over 50 art and craft vendors, world dancing and music, and free art and music workshops for children.

For over 20 years in early August the annual **Santa Cruz Amateur Golf Championship** (DeLaveaga Golf Course, 401 Upper Park Rd., 831/423-7214, www.delaveagagolf.com) has given amateurs the chance to golf alongside some of Northern California best golfers. The event is two full day of hilly competition overlooking Santa Cruz.

Fall

For over 100 years, the **Santa Cruz County**

© KRISTIN LEAL

Watsonville, home of August's strawberry festival, produces more than 8.75 million trays of strawberries annually.

Fair (Santa Cruz County Fairgrounds, 2601 E. Lake Ave., Watsonville, off Hwy. 152, 831//24-5671, www.santacruzcountyfair.com) in mid-September has been a great way to celebrate the fall with six days of carnival games, rides for children of all ages, arts and crafts, and old fashioned carnival eats.

The elegant sounds of the **Santa Cruz County Symphony** (Civic Auditorium, 307 Church St.; and Henry J. Mello Center, 250 E. Beach St., Watsonville, 831/420-5260, www.santacruzsymphony.org) start in late September. Founded in 1955, the symphony has grown to be one of the finest orchestras of its size in the state. The regular season (Oct.-May) has 10 classical concerts; visit the website for an up-to-date list of performances.

For car lovers, **Hot Rods at the Beach** (River parking lot, end of Beach St., 831/423-3720, www.hotrodssatthebeach.com) in early October brings over 500 classic cars and street hot rods in a display of shiny eye candy and

roaring engines. There is food, local vendors, raffles, music, and scores of displays.

Where else could you catch a glimpse of **Surfing Santa** (Capitola City Beach, San Jose Ave. and Esplanade, Capitola, 831/475-6522, www.capitolasoquelchamber.com) besides Surf City USA? Celebrate the holiday season in late November as Santa and his reindeer ride the waves onto the shores of Capitola. Santa arrives by surfboard, and the reindeer come in on an outrigger canoe. The whole family can enjoy this event, with plenty of candy canes to go around; don't forget to tell the old guy just what you want for Christmas.

Winter

Come one, come all, and feel the holiday spirit in early December as the **Downtown Santa Cruz Holiday Parade** (Pacific Ave., 831/429-8433, www.downtownsantacruz.com) sees decked-out floats, marching bands playing holiday songs, brightly lit fire trucks, horses, classic cars; of course, Santa will be there too.

SANTA CRUZ

Shopping

⚹ PACIFIC AVENUE

There's no shopping area in California quite like the **Pacific Garden Mall** (Pacific Ave., 831/429-8433, www.downtownsantacruz. com). Hanging out "on the Mall," as locals say, is a pastime for both teens and adults. The Mall is along Pacific Avenue and its side streets, which are usually open to (very slow) auto traffic. Park in one of the structures a block or two off the Mall and walk. At the north end, shoppers peruse antiques, boutique clothing, and kitchen wares; at the seedier south end, you can get shiny body jewelry or a new tattoo. Near the middle of the Mall are independent eateries, coffee shops, and cocktail lounges. The Mall has just a few chain stores, as they are reviled by many fiercely anticorporate Santa Cruz residents. The Mall provides a sampling of the people of Santa Cruz, and you can get a good feel for the local culture and a glimpse into local politics.

A proudly independent local bookseller since 1966 is **Bookshop Santa Cruz** (1520 Pacific Ave., 831/423-0900, www.bookshopsanta-cruz.com, Sun.-Thurs. 9 A.M.-10 P.M., Fri.-Sat. 9 A.M.-11 P.M.). New and used books fill 20,000 square feet, and there is an extensive magazine section, a special children's section, small gifts, and cards. Scheduled events include an ongoing authors series; check the website for upcoming events.

Streetlight Records (939 Pacific Ave., 831/421-9200, www.streetlightrecords.com, Mon.-Sat. 10 A.M.-10 P.M., Sun. noon-8 P.M.) is a large store filled with hard-to-find vinyl, CDs, DVDs, cassettes, LPs, 45s, and videodiscs. They buy, trade, and sell every genre of music.

Down toward the divide between the "good side" and the "less good side" of the Mall is **Camouflage** (1329 Pacific Ave., 888/309-2266, http://experiencethefantasy.com, Mon.-Thurs.

10 A.M.-8 P.M., Fri.-Sat. 10 A.M.-10 P.M., Sun. 11 A.M.-7 P.M.), an independent women-operated, women-friendly adult store. The front room contains mostly lingerie, and through the narrow black-curtained passage is the *other* room, with adult toys for every proclivity. Women won't feel uncomfortable shopping here, as the clientele includes as many women as men.

For glass smoking accessories, **Graffix Pleasure** (809 Pacific Ave., 831/423-2940, daily 11 A.M.-9 P.M.) has a back room with a full line of smoking products, much of it handblown by local and visiting artists. There is also a large jewelry case, T-shirts, bumper stickers, patches, and other accessories.

A small antiques shop, **Miss Jessie May's** (1533 Pacific Ave., 831/458-9131, daily 11 A.M.-5:30 P.M.) has good deals on items such as earrings and wall paintings. There is a cool $5 basket with all kinds of scarves and other treasures. There isn't a lot of furniture; the inventory is rather mostly small unique items and jewelry.

Santa Cruz has plenty of secondhand clothing stores, and one of the largest is a block from Pacific Avenue, the aptly if redundantly named **Thrift Center Thrift Store** (504 Front St., 831/429-6975). This large and somewhat dirty retail space has a wide array of cheap secondhand clothes. You'll have to hunt a bit to find that perfect vintage item, but isn't that the fun of thrift-store shopping?

It is all about the '50s, '60s, '70s, and '80s at **Retro Paradise** (1010 Pacific Ave., 831/460-9960, www.retroparadiseclothing.com, Sun.-Thurs. 11 A.M.-7 P.M., Fri.-Sat. 11 A.M.-8 P.M.), with groovy clothing for both men and women, including a burlesque section.

ANTIQUES SHOPPING

The main shopping opportunity in the Santa Cruz Mountains is antiquing, with several antiques shops in small towns such as Felton, Scotts Valley, and Boulder Creek. They are always right on the main drag, so they are hard to miss. Stop by on your way through, or make a day of antiques shopping. The drive north along Highway 9 is beautiful, and nature burns bright during the fall months when the foliage changes colors.

There are two shops you won't want to miss in Soquel. Discover a mix of Old World pieces and early American furnishings at **Center Street Antiques** (3010 Center St., Soquel, 831/477-9211, www.centerstreetantiques.com, Mon.-Sat. 11 A.M.-5 P.M., Sun. 11 A.M.-5 P.M.), with 23 creative dealers in 5,000 square feet. You'll find chandeliers, silver, architectural treasures, vintage art, home embellishments, and garden objects.

Shop for your home and garden at **Wisteria Antiques and Design** (5870 Soquel Dr., Soquel, 831/462-2900, www.wisteriaantiques.

net, daily 11 A.M.-5 P.M.). Here you will find an expansive garden crawling with English roses, brilliant hydrangeas, outdoor accents, iron items, and dozens of other plants. In the many rooms throughout the grounds are large antique furniture pieces, chandeliers, mirrors, pillows, quilts, vintage art, and more. Most of the spaces display an array of household bits and pieces in the French country style.

BEACH BOARDWALK

For all your Santa Cruz Beach Boardwalk (400 Beach St., 831/423-5590, www.beachboardwalk.com) and Santa Cruz souvenirs, sunglasses, affordable body boards, skim boards, sweet treats, and an O'Neill surf shop, the cluster of shops between the Boardwalk and Neptune Kingdom is a generic stop if you forgot the sunscreen or want to try body boarding. Most of the shops are run by the Santa Cruz Beach Boardwalk, but **Marini's Boardwalk**

Stop into Wisteria Antiques and Design for old-fashioned treasures.

© KRISTIN LEAL

SANTA CRUZ

(400 Beach St., 831/423-5590, www.marinis-candies.com, daily 11 A.M.-11 P.M.) is independent. The Marini family has been pulling saltwater taffy on the beach and specializing in caramel apples since 1915.

O'Neill at the Boardwalk (400 Beach St., 831/459-9230, www.oneill.com, Mon.-Fri. 10 A.M.-5 P.M., Sat.-Sun. 10 A.M.-8 P.M.) is one of chain's smaller stores, carrying a limited selection of surfboards, wetsuits, skateboards, accessories like the board wax you left at home,

and brand-name clothing. In the off-season, this is a good shop for large year-end discounts.

CAPITOLA MALL
Capitola Mall (1855 41st Ave., 831/465-0773, www.shopcapitolamall.com, Mon.-Fri. 10 A.M.-8 P.M., Sat. 10 A.M.-8 P.M., Sun. 11 A.M.-7 P.M.) has modest flair with over 80 stores. Several shops specialize in skate and surf apparel, and you will find department stores like Sears and Macy's.

Accommodations

CAMPING
The Santa Cruz region has rich camping possibilities in wilderness areas and small towns. Camp beside the beach or wake up next to a strawberry field.

In summer, make camping reservations far in advanced. For any of the state parks, you can check availability and reserve sites through **Reserve America** (800/444-7275, www.reserveamerica.com).

For lakeside camping, head to **Pinto Lake City Park** (451 Green Valley Rd., Watsonville, 831/722-8129, www.pintolake.com, $28) in Watsonville. The city park has load of RV sites with full hookups and plenty of activities, including horseshoes, a softball diamond, volleyball, a playground, and paddleboats. The local Little League use the diamond regularly, but most of the time it is available for play.

Next door at **Pinto Lake County Park** (757 Green Valley Rd., Watsonville, 831/454-7956, www.scparks.com) is a nice paved trail through the oaks, willows, and eucalyptus as well as lovely covered barbecue pavilions, available by reservation at the Simpkins Family Swim Center (979 17th Ave., Santa Cruz). Both parks allow leashed dogs, and the lake has a fishing pier.

Get a little rugged and do some backpacking in 10,000-acre **The Forest of Nisene Marks**

(Aptos Creek Rd. and Soquel Dr., Aptos, 831/763-7064, www.parks.ca.gov, $5 per person). The campground is on a trail six miles from the parking lot; it's an easy day's hike in. The sites are first come, first served and must be arranged through the ranger station. Be prepared for changeable weather with limited resources; fires are not allowed, and there is no running water at the campground. Note that poison oak grows throughout the park, so beware of it encroaching on trails.

Find secluded camping with beach access year-round at **C Sunset State Beach** (San Andreas Rd., Watsonville, 16 miles south of Santa Cruz, 831/763-7062, www.parks.ca.gov, daily 8 A.M.till 30 minutes after sunset, $35). The three large campgrounds have 90 family sights along with a separate group camp. One campground is beside strawberry fields in an oak forest; one campground is sheltered by an oak grove just above a long stretch of beach; and the third, my favorite, has ocean views. RVs and tents are welcome with some length limitations. The showers take quarters, the toilets flush, firewood is sold, and beach bonfires are allowed.

Once known as a Chinese fishing village, **New Brighton State Beach** (1500 Park Ave., Capitola, 831/464-6330, www.parks.ca.gov,

© KRISTIN LEAL

Camp alongside the beach at Seacliff State Beach.

daily 8 A.M. till 30 minutes after sunset, $35) is a first come, first served campground containing with over 100 sites on a bluff overlooking Monterey Bay. The park has hiking, swimming, and fishing possibilities year-round, and wildlife can be seen on the two miles of trails and the sandy beach; pelicans, playful harbor seals, sea otters, dolphins, and whales are all local to the area.

Beach-side RV and trailer camping can be found at **C** **Seacliff State Beach** (west end of State Park Dr., 831/685-6442, www.parks. ca.gov, daily 8 A.M.-sunset, $55). Sites are along the beach, and many have water and electrical hookups. The sandy beaches are great for swimming and extend more than one mile north to the wooded bluffs of New Brighton State Beach. There is a snack shack along with a visitors center, and the park is known for its long fishing pier and a shipwreck at the end of the pier: The ship, made of cement, was originally built for use in World War I, but it was never used. It was intentionally sunk as a fishing attraction in 1929.

Surf in, surf out accommodations can be found at **Manresa State Beach** (400 San Andreas Rd., 831/761-1795, www.parks.ca.gov, daily 8 A.M.-sunset, campground May 16-Oct. 31, $35), beach camping with 64 walk-in tent campsites, hot showers (bring quarters), flush toilets, great surf, plenty of fish to catch, and a wide sandy beach.

A little-known RV park is the **Santa Cruz Harbor RV Park** (Santa Cruz North Harbor, 7th Ave. and Brommer St., 831/475-3279, www. santacruzharbor.org, $40), with 12 full-hookup sites and an on-site dump station. Views of the north harbor are beautiful, and you are close to restaurants and kayak rentals, and not a far by car from downtown and the Boardwalk. Reservations are advised as space is limited.

For a base 0.5 miles from the beach that will keep the whole family entertained, **Santa Cruz KOA Kampground** (1186 San Andres Rd.,

SANTA CRUZ

831/722-0551 or 831/722-8051, www.santacruzkoa.com, $55-70) is a little like home, with a pool and a hot tub on-site, camping cabins, camping lodges, Airstream trailer rentals, the KOA fun train, an outdoor cinema, a climbing wall, miniature golf, banana bikes, a game room, an espresso bar, a pet play area, and planned recreation everyone can take part in.

HOSTELS

Staying at a hostel in this bohemian backpacker-friendly town feels about right. The **Santa Cruz Youth Hostel Carmelita Cottages** (321 Main St., 831/423-8304, www.hi-santacruz.org, dorm $25, private rooms $60, cottage $160) offers great local atmosphere. For the cottage, advance reservations are required, and there is an extra cleaning fee; you can email manager@hi-santacruz.org. Like most Santa Cruz buildings, it doesn't look like much from the outside, and the interior certainly doesn't have new furniture or paint, but it's clean, cheap, friendly, and close to the beach.

You can store your surfboard or bike for free, and parking is $1 per day. The big homey kitchen is open for guest use, and you might even score some forgotten food in its cupboards. Expect hostel-style amenities, a nice garden out back, free linens, laundry facilities, and a free Internet kiosk.

Twenty minutes north of Santa Cruz are oceanfront accommodations at ◖ **Pigeon Point Lighthouse** (Pigeon Point Rd., Pescadero, 650/879-2120, reservations 650/879-0633, www.norcalhostels.org, dorm $24-26, private rooms $72-156). It is a great overnight getaway and operates year-round as a hostel. The secluded location has glorious ocean views and plenty of outdoors to discover, with Año Nuevo State Park just south. There is even a hot tub on-site.

Beside the lighthouse is a protected beach, perfect for exploring tide pools. A wooden deck winds around the lighthouse, making it easy to see the local sealife. Migrating whales frequent these waters; look for their spouts of water shooting up into the air in the distance. The majestic beasts usually travel in pods, so you may see many of them spouting in a cluster. California harbor seals and sea otters like to hang out near the back of the lighthouse, and rabbits hop around the property.

UNDER $150

Santa Cruz's budget digs are great for family getaways with a hot shower and a bed. Some are within walking distance of the beach and the Boardwalk.

Just across from the inviting beach and Boardwalk is the **Aqua Breeze Inn** (204 2nd St., 831/426-7878, www.santacruzaquabreezeinn.com, $50-69), with 50 clean and well-equipped guest rooms with mini fridges, microwaves, coffeemakers, sundecks, Internet access, and HBO on TV. There is an outdoor heated pool, and pets are welcome.

You can look forward to newly remodeled guest rooms and an affordable stay at the **Budget Inn** (110 San Lorenzo Blvd., 831/426-2828, $45-75). Amenities are just the basics: coffee, HBO on TV, and a bath. It is a short one-mile walk or a quick drive to the Boardwalk and Wharf.

Centrally located near the Boardwalk and the beach, and three blocks from downtown, is the **Continental Inn** (414 Ocean St., 831/429-1221 or 831/343-6941, www.continentalsantacruz.com, $75-95). Guest rooms are modern and have microwaves, mini fridges, free Wi-Fi, and jetted tubs; kids will like the pool while the adults relax in the hot tub.

Resting halfway between Santa Cruz and Monterey is the **Best Western Rose Garden** (7040 Freedom Blvd., Watsonville, 831/724-3367 or 800/685-5760, www.bestwesternwatsonville.com, $89-119), a good location from which to explore the region. There are 46 spacious guest rooms that have mini fridges, microwaves, fireplaces, jetted tubs, and TV with

HBO and ESPN. You can also find a pool, a hot tub, a fitness center, free high-speed Internet, and continental breakfast. Pets are welcome.

The four-room **Adobe on Green Street** (103 Green St., 831/469-9866, www.adobeongreen. com, $119-199) offers lovely bed-and-breakfast accommodations close to the heart of downtown Santa Cruz and within walking distance of the Pacific Garden Mall. Decor is minimalist Spanish mission style befitting Santa Cruz's history. Each guest room has a queen bed, a private bath (most with tubs), a small TV with a DVD player, and lots of other amenities. An expanded continental spread is set out in the dining room each morning 8-11 A.M.; expect yummy local pastries, organic and soy yogurts, and multicolored eggs laid by a neighbor's flock of chickens. In keeping with the Santa Cruz environmentalist ethos, the B&B runs on solar power.

Just steps away from the ticket booth of the Santa Cruz Beach Boardwalk is the **[Carousel Motel** (110 Riverside Ave., 831/425-7090 or 800/214-7400, www.santacruzmotels.com, $59-209). It is nothing flashy but has the basics, including Internet access, coffeemakers, continental breakfast, cable TV, and private balconies. Guest rooms have space for you, the kids, and all the gear.

The Spanish-style **Mission Inn** (2250 Mission St., 831/425-5455 or 800/895-5455, www.mission-inn.com, $80-125) is near Highways 1 and 9 for easy access to the mountains; the beach is five minutes' drive. The inn has 53 nonsmoking guest rooms modestly equipped with coffeemakers, Wi-Fi, cable TV, and whirlpool tubs. Continental breakfast is included.

Beachview Inn (50 Front St., 831/426-3575, www.beach-viewinn.com, $50-240) has ocean views just half a block from the beach, the Boardwalk, and the Wharf. Guest rooms are a bit small but are perfect if you don't intend to spend a lot of time in your room.

All 28 queen and king rooms and suites are nonsmoking at **Best Western Inn-Santa Cruz**

(126 Plymouth St., 831/425-4717, www.bestwestern.com, $89-250). Amenities in the clean, simple guest rooms include Internet access, jetted tubs, and the other basics. The property has a fitness center, a pool, and a hot tub.

For larger guest rooms and spacious suites just a few minutes from several state beaches, **Best Western Inn-Seacliff** (7500 Old Dominion Court, 831/688-7300 or 800/367-2003, www.seacliffinn.com, $119-329) is a six-acre property in Best Western's "Plus" category, with slightly better amenities than most. The pool is inviting, guest rooms are recently renovated and roomy, and there is a fitness center.

The **Inn at Pasatiempo** (555 Hwy. 17, 831/423-5000, www.innatpasatiempo.com, $75-195), next door to the Pasatiempo Golf Club, makes it easy to get in a round of golf. Guest rooms are decorated country-style with fireplaces and sitting areas; There is an outdoor pool and a decent American restaurant on-site.

$150-250

Sea & Sand Inn (201 W. Cliff Dr., 831/427-3400, www.santacruzmotels.com/sea_and_sand.html, $189-229) has an unbeatable location on the ocean side of West Cliff Drive at Bay Street; the neighborhood is mostly residential and quiet. Every guest room overlooks the sea, which explains the higher rates for the pretty basic accommodations. Amenities include private baths and Internet access included in the room rates.

Despite its bohemian reputation, there is plenty of money in Santa Cruz. For plush accommodations, consider the **Pleasure Point Inn** (23665 E. Cliff Dr., 831/475-4657, www. pleasurepointinn.com, $225-295), a small exclusive property with a rooftop deck and a hot tub and an expansive common living room with views of the ocean. The four luxurious guest rooms, each with views of the surfers at Pleasant Point, wood floors, a gas fireplace, a private deck or patio, private bath, also have

© CHAMINADE RESORT & SPA

Tucked away within the rolling hills of Santa Cruz is the Chaminade Resort and Spa.

TVs, phones, and Internet access. A continental breakfast is laid out each morning, and you can set up a surfing lesson through the inn and Club Ed when you reserve your room.

High on a bluff with breathtaking views of Monterey Bay and the Santa Cruz Mountains is the **(Chaminade Resort and Spa** (1 Chaminade Lane, 831/475-5600 or 800/283-6569, www.chaminade.com, $159-399), with a fitness center, tennis courts, a pool, a hot tub, and an all-inclusive spa. Guest rooms are open and elegant, with modern decor and outdoor patios. This is a nice stay if you're on a wine tour or romantic getaway.

The **(Santa Cruz Dream Inn** (175 W. Cliff Dr., 831/426-4330 or 831/460-5007, www.dreaminnsantacruz.com, $189-409), right on the beach and just steps from the Wharf and the Boardwalk, has an outdoor pool and a hot tub. Guest rooms all have private balconies and ocean views.

Off the beaten path but nestled quietly right on the beach in Aptos, **Seascape Beach Resort-Monterey Bay** (1 Seascape Resort Dr., Aptos, 831/688-6800 or 800/929-7727, www.seascaperesort.com, $229-774) is a luxury resort that feels like a beach house. Views of the bay are dramatic. Take advantage of in-room massages and special packages that include Girls Gone to the Beach and Super Seniors. Guest rooms are like private villas with all the necessities and services at your fingertips.

Food

SANTA CRUZ

AMERICAN

At **Cafe Cruz** (2621 41st Ave., Soquel, 831/476-3801, www.cafecruz.com, lunch Mon.-Sat. 11:30 A.M.-2:30 P.M., dinner daily 5:30 P.M.-close, $16till 30), the menu is homey American favorites with a California twist: ribs, rotisserie chicken, bowls of pasta, and fresh crunchy salads. Cafe Cruz purchases fresh local produce, meat, and seafood. Have locally caught fish with goat cheese from Half Moon Bay along with an organic soda from Monterey. The attractive white-tablecloth dining room welcomes casual and elegant diners alike, and if you choose wisely, you can get an upscale meal at medium-scale prices.

It's all about fine organic cuisine and notable wines at the **(Bonny Doon Vineyard's Cellar Door** (328 Ingalls St., 831/425-6737, www.bonnydoonvineyard.com, lunch Sat.-Sun. noon-3 P.M., dinner Wed.-Sun. 5:30 P.M.-close, $40-50). The menu changes daily according to what is fresh in the garden. The chef has a continual focus with local ingredients sourced from small growers in Santa Cruz and Monterey Counties. The prix fixe menu is beautifully paired with two-ounce pours of three wines through the meal.

Fine dining seaside is at the Dream Inn's **Aquarius** (173 W. Cliff Dr., 831/460-5012, www.aquariussantacruz.com, daily 7 A.M.-10:30 P.M., $20till 30). Large windows offer an expansive view of magical sunsets over the bay. Aquarius is a modern American bistro featuring sustainable seafood, local organic produce, and local vineyards.

ASIAN

Local sushi lovers go to **Shogun Sushi** (1123 Pacific Ave., 831/469-4477, Mon.-Wed. 5-9 P.M., Thurs.-Fri. 5-10 P.M., Sat. 3-10 P.M., $12-25) on the Pacific Garden Mall. The *nigiri* comes in big fresh slabs, and there is an interesting collection of *maki* (rolls). Meats and other dishes are available. Although service can be spotty, it is usually efficient. Prices may seem high but are quite reasonable for the quality of the food. There's often a wait for a table in the evening, especially on weekends.

Ocean City Buffet (431 Front St., 831/426-8168, daily 10:30 A.M.-10 P.M., $11till 30) is affordable Chinese with friendly service right downtown. There is a vast made-to-order sushi bar as well as a buffet of traditional Chinese favorites such as kung pao chicken, Singapore noodles, sweet-and-sour chicken, broccoli beef, grilled chicken legs, and pot stickers. The cold section of the buffet always has peel-and-eat shrimp, salads, and fresh fruit.

For an authentic Thai experience, try **[Bangkok West** (2508 Cabrillo College Dr., Aptos, 831/479-8297, lunch buffet Mon.-Fri. 11 A.M.-2:30 P.M., dinner daily 5-9:30 P.M., $10-20). The outdoor garden evokes Thailand; ask to sit in the little house (table 9) for a truly traditional encounter. The curries are mouthwatering and addicting, and the lunch buffet has a bit of everything, including to-die-for fresh spring rolls.

BEACH FOOD

Classic beach fare is available at the **Santa Cruz Beach Boardwalk** (400 Beach St., 831/423-5590, www.beachboardwalk.com, $8-15). From Neptune's Kingdom to the farthest reaches of the children's area, the aroma of junk food permeates the Boardwalk; vendors sell corn dogs, fried Twinkies, cotton candy, Dippen Dots, cheeseburgers, french fries, fish-and-chips, fried calamari, and even some Pizza Hut personal pies. And really, a trip to Santa Cruz wouldn't be complete without a stop at the Boardwalk for some entertainment and a bite to eat.

You can also grab some quick beach grub at the far end of the Wharf with two takeout windows competing for your business. Their menus mirror each other, with fried delights such as clams, shrimp, calamari, corn dogs, and french fries. Order up a cheeseburger or a beach classic, clam chowder in a bread bowl. Breakfast can be a light bagel or something hot and more substantial. The first window is run by the **[Dolphin Restaurant** (71-A Municipal Wharf, 831/426-5830, daily 8 A.M.-9 P.M., $5-10). Based on the name, you wouldn't think that the second place, **Andy's Bait & Tackle Shop** (71-B Municipal Wharf, 831/429-1925, daily 9 A.M.-9 P.M., $5-8), served hot food, but they do.

Harking back to the 1950s origins of fast food, **[Snow White Drive Inn** (223 State Park Dr., 831/688-4747, winter daily 6 A.M.-8:30 P.M., summer daily 6 A.M.-9:30 P.M., $8-12) doesn't have carhops skating to your car, but the atmosphere is retro. It should be a required stop on the way to Seacliff State Beach for dipped cones, corn dogs, chili fries, cheeseburgers, chicken sandwiches, fried calamari, onion rings, and chicken tenders. And, hello, they serve hot breakfasts too.

BREAKFAST

For a casual sandwich or pastry, head for **Kelly's French Bakery** (402 Ingalls St.,

831/423-9059, www.kellysfrenchbakery.com, Sat.-Thurs. 7 A.M.-7 P.M., Fri. 7 A.M.-8 P.M., $12). This popular bakery is in an old industrial warehouse space, and its dome shape, built of corrugated metal, looks like anything but a restaurant. Full breakfasts and luncheon sandwiches are served at both indoor and outdoor seating, and you can order to go. Pick up a pastry, bread, or cake while you're here.

Do as the locals do and stop in at **Emily's Good Things to Eat** (1129 Mission St., 831/429-9866, www.emilysbakery.com, daily 7 A.M.-3 P.M., $8) for a cup of joe and mouthwatering savory or sweet pastries. Get it to go, or stay for a while. A laid-back vibe sometimes includes local musicians jamming in the corner. The rear deck beckons for longer stays, especially on sunny days, and the inside seating is cozy.

For a traditional breakfast with a Mexican twist, **Walnut Avenue Café** (106 Walnut Ave., 831/457-2307, www.walnutavenuecafe.com, Mon.-Fri. 7 A.M.-3 P.M., Sat.-Sun. 8 A.M.-4 P.M., $10) does large three-egg omelets, eggs Benedict with a shrimp and tomato spin, griddle classics, huevos Mexicanos, and *chilaquiles*. They also do a weekend brunch that will surely satisfy even the hungriest.

For a cheap breakfast that is hot off the griddle, **Windmill Café** (21231 E. Cliff Dr., 831/464-4698, www.windmillcafesantacruz.com, Mon.-Sun. 7 A.M.-3 P.M., $5-8) does a little of everything, including scrambles, specialty bagels, vegetarian or carnivore breakfast burritos, and a daily waffle. The vegetables are fresh and organically grown in Windmill's own garden.

CALIFORNIA

The Santa Cruz region boasts one seriously upscale eatery, the **Shadowbrook** (1750 Wharf Rd., Capitola, 800/975-1511, www.shadowbrook-capitola.com, Mon.-Fri. 5-8:45 P.M., Sat. 4:30-9:30 P.M., Sun. 4:30-8:45 P.M., $25), on a cliff with an actual brook flowing through the dining room. It has perhaps the most impressive views and atmosphere of any restaurant in the region. The Shadowbrook is perfect for a romantic date, complete with roses, candlelight, and fine chocolate desserts.

Soak in the views of the harbor at **Johnny's Harborside** (493 Lake Ave., 831/479-3430, www.johnnysharborside.com, Mon.-Fri. 11:30 A.M.-10 P.M., Sat.-Sun. 10 A.M.-9 P.M., $15 till 30). In true Central Coast style, up to eight different choices of fresh fish are served daily, along with pastas, steaks, salads, and sandwiches. Only the freshest seasonal ingredients from local growers are used to tantalize your palate, and there is a gluten-free menu.

Carnivores, prepare for juicy bites at the **Hindquarters Bar and Grill** (303 Soquel Ave., 831/426-7770 or 831/426-7773, www.thehindquarter.com, Mon.-Sat. 11:30 A.M.-2:30 P.M. and 5:30-9:30 P.M., Sun. 10:30 A.M.-2:30 P.M. and 5:30-9:30 P.M., $20-37), serving numerous cuts of steak grilled any way you like it. Vegetarians can find menu options as well.

Overlooking the water in Capitola is the **Paradise Beach Grill** (215 Esplanade, 831/476-4900, www.paradisebeachgrill.com, daily 11 A.M.-close, $18-32), with a mix of fun, fine food, and good service. Weekly specials are inspired fresh seasonal products, often in Californian-Hawaiian combinations. Every Tuesday 6-9 P.M., catch a jazz and blues session with your meal.

FRENCH

In Aptos, **Cafe Sparrow** (8042 Soquel Dr., Aptos, 831/688-6238, www.cafesparrow.com, Mon.-Sat. lunch 11:30 A.M.-2 P.M., Sun. 9:30 A.M.-2 P.M., dinner daily 5:30 P.M.-close, $20) serves consistently tasty country French cuisine. The seafood is noteworthy, especially the Friday-night bouillabaisse, as are the steaks. Cafe Sparrow uses all fresh ingredients, and the chef, who can sometimes be seen out in the dining room checking on customer satisfaction, thinks up innovative preparations and creates tasty sauces. He's also willing to accommodate special requests and dietary restrictions without attitude. The best deal is the daily prix-fixe menu; for dessert, try the profiteroles, which can be created with either ice cream or pastry cream.

SEAFOOD

The most famous place for seafood in Santa Cruz is **❰ Stagnaro Bros. Restaurant** (Municipal Wharf, 831/423-2180, www.stagnarobros.com, daily 11 A.M.-close, $20), with over 20 differing seafood dishes daily. They pride themselves on serving the freshest seafood possible. The upper deck of seating has a nautical feel, and the lower deck feels more traditional and intimate. The full menu is offered on both decks, and there are two bars.

The **Crow's Nest** (2218 E. Cliff Dr., 831/476-4560, www.crowsnest-santacruz.com, Mon.-Sat. 11:30 A.M.-close, Sun. 11 A.M.-close, $17till 30) has a casual atmosphere upstairs with a full bar and cheap eats, while downstairs is a little more formal, serving up steaks, local seafood, and specialty seafood salads.

A fantastic Mexican place with a menu of fresh seafood from local fisheries is **❰ El Palomar Restaurant** (1336 Pacific Ave., 831/425-7575, www.elpalomarcilantros.com, daily 11 A.M.-10:30 P.M., $11-27), in the heart of downtown in the Palomar Inn. Inspired by the cuisine of southern Mexico's Michoacán state, El Palomar delights the taste buds with local produce and seafood from Monterey Bay. A local favorite since the early 1980s, El Palomar creates fresh house salsas, award-winning margaritas (voted Best Margarita by the local *Good Times* newspaper in 2008), and handmade corn tortillas.

Casablanca Restaurant (101 Main St. at Beach St., 831/426-9063, www.casablanca-santacruz.com, daily 5 P.M.-close, $10-27) has ocean views from every table, exquisite food, and a massive selection of wine. The beachside atmosphere is relaxed and graceful, and dishes include prime-cut steaks, tender chicken, pastas, and, of course, fine seafood. The chef is experienced and creative.

SOUTH AMERICAN

Painted rainforest green with bright yellow and blue trim, it's hard to miss **Cafe Brasil** (1410 Mission St., 831/429-1855, www.cafebrasil.us, daily 8 A.M.-3 P.M., $15-25), a very Santa Cruz breakfast and lunch joint. Morning has omelets and Brazilian specialties, and lunch includes pressed sandwiches as well as meat and tofu dishes. The juice bar provides rich but healthy meal accompaniments that can be light meals on their own. For something different, get an açaí bowl—açaí is a South American fruit—or an Amazon cherry juice and orange juice blend.

FARMERS MARKETS

Established in 1990, the **Santa Cruz Community Market** (831/454-0566, www.santacruzfarmersmarket.org) hosts five markets in the area with three right in Santa Cruz. All the markets place special emphasis on sustainability and do-it-yourself artistry.

One of the larger markets, filling an entire parking lot, is the **Downtown Market** (Cedar St. and Lincoln St., summer Wed. 1:30-6:30 P.M., winter Wed. 1:30-5:30 P.M.), held year-round regardless of the weather. On display are local organic produce, nuts, dried fruit, dates, honey, nursery starters, potted plants, avocados, Central Valley fruit, pasture-raised meat and eggs, freshly cut flowers, bakeries, and a mini food court.

For a fresh snack, head to the **Westside Market** (2801 Mission St., year-round Sat.-Sun. 9 A.M.-1 P.M.), with over 25 food vendors and farms consistently participating.

On the other side of town is the **Live Oak-Eastside-Pleasure Point Market** (East Cliff Shopping Center, E. Cliff Dr. at 15th Ave., year-round Sun. 9 A.M.-1 P.M.), for delicious breakfast fare, live music, and local farm products.

The **Aptos Farmers Market** (Cabrillo College Campus, 6500 Soquel Dr., 831/728-5060, www.montereybayfarmers.org, 8 A.M.-noon year-round) is home to over 80 vendors with fresh flowers, locally grown produce, artisanal products, and live bluegrass music. Celebrate local farms and the people who bring produce to our tables.

Information and Services

VISITOR INFORMATION

While it can be fun to explore Santa Cruz following your instincts and sense of the bizarre, those who want a bit more structure can visit the **Santa Cruz Visitors Center** (1211 Ocean Ave., 800/833-3494, www.santacruzca.org, Mon.-Fri. 9 A.M.-4 P.M. Sat.-Sun. 11 A.M.-3 P.M.) for maps, advice, and information.

MEDIA AND COMMUNICATIONS

Santa Cruz has its own daily newspaper, the *Santa Cruz Sentinel* (www.santacruzsentinel. com), with a dose of national wire-service news and current events, local news, and some good stuff for visitors. The *Sentinel* has a Food section, a Sunday Travel section, and plenty of up-to-date entertainment information.

Santa Cruz is, like, totally wired. You can access the Internet in a variety of cafés and hotels. Starbucks locations sell access, and the many indie cafés have sometimes-free Wi-Fi.

The **post office** (850 Front St., 831/426-0144) is near the Pacific Garden Mall. Santa Cruz has plenty of banks and ATMs, including ATMs on the arcade at the Boardwalk. Bank branches are clustered downtown near the Mall. The west side is mostly residential, but you'll find a few ATMs in supermarkets and gas stations.

MEDICAL SERVICES

Despite its rep as a funky bohemian beach town, Santa Cruz's dense population dictates that it has at least one full-fledged hospital; get medical treatment and care at **Dominican Hospital** (1555 Soquel Ave., 831/426-7700, www.dominicanhospital.org).

Getting There and Around

GETTING THERE

If you're driving to Santa Cruz from Silicon Valley, there two choices. Most drivers take fast (50 mph) and more dangerous Highway 17, a narrow road that doesn't have any switchbacks and is the main truck route "over the hill." Most locals drive this road faster than they should, and several people die in crashes every year. I once crashed my vehicle into an overturned pickup on Big Moody curve. If you're new to the road, keep to the right and take it slow, regardless of what the traffic on the left is doing. Check traffic reports before you head out; Highway 17 is one of the most congested commuting roads in the Bay Area, and the weekend beach traffic in the summer backs up fast in both directions.

For a more leisurely drive from Silicon Valley, you can opt for two-lane Highway 9. The tight curves and endless switchbacks keep cars at a reasonable speed; use the turnouts to let faster drivers past. On Highway 9, the biggest obstacles tend to be groups of bicyclists and motorcyclists, both of whom adore the slopes and curves of this technical drive. The good news is that you'll get an up-close view of the

© KRISTIN LEAL

the northern reaches of Santa Cruz County

forested Santa Cruz Mountains, complete with views of the valley to the north and ocean vistas to the south.

To reach Santa Cruz from San Francisco (75 miles, 90 minutes), first take U.S. 101 south to I-280 south. You then meet Highway 17 south, which leads into the heart of Santa Cruz. From Los Angles (350 miles, 6 hours), the easiest route is U.S. 101 north to Highway 183 in Salinas, and then Highway 1 north into Santa Cruz.

GETTING AROUND

Before you drive or bike around Santa Cruz, get a good map, either before you arrive or at the visitors center (1211 Ocean Ave., 800/833-3494, www.santacruzca.org). Navigating the winding, occasionally noncontinuous streets of this oddly shaped town isn't for the faint of heart. Highway 1, which becomes Mission Street on the west side, acts as the main artery through Santa Cruz and Capitola, Soquel, Aptos, and coastal points farther south. Near

the interchange with Highway 17, Highway 1, sometimes for several miles, is heavily congested most of the time. No, it's probably not a major collision or a special event; it's just congested all the time.

Parking

Parking in Santa Cruz can be its own special kind of horror. If you're driving into downtown, head straight for the parking structures one block from Pacific Avenue on either side. They're much easier to deal with than trying to find street parking.

The same goes for the beach and Boardwalk areas: At the Boardwalk, just pay the fee to park in the big parking lot adjacent to the attractions. You'll save an hour of driving around trying to find street parking and possibly a break-in or theft in the sketchy neighborhoods that surround the Boardwalk.

By Bus

In town, transit buses are run by **Santa Cruz**

SANTA CRUZ

METRO (831/425-8600, www.scmtd.com, $1.50 per ride adults, passes available). With 42 routes in Santa Cruz County, you can probably find a way to get nearly anywhere you'd want to go.

Santa Cruz Mountains

Deep in the Santa Cruz Mountains, easily accessible diversions include the great outdoors of Henry Cowell Redwoods State Park and Big Basin Redwoods State Park, the tantalizing flavors of wine country, and antiquing in small mountain towns.

SIGHTS
Mount Hermon Zip-Line Tour
Get ready to feed your need for speed at Mount Hermon Zip-Line Tours (17 Conference Dr., Mount Hermon, 831/430-4357, http://mounthermon.org, year-round daily), with high-flying action through a redwood forest on zip lines and rope bridges. Ride from tree to tree while gaining a new perspective on the wilderness below. This is the original redwood-forest canopy tour and still one of a kind. The two-hour guided tour ($80 pp) includes six zip-line runs and two rope bridges. Bring a group of eight and one person flies for free.

◖ Roaring Camp Railroads
All aboard for an antique steam train ride through the redwood forest or to the beach. Roaring Camp Railroads (5355 Graham Hill Rd., Felton, 831/335-4484, www.roaringcamp.com, year-round daily, check website for hours, $24-26 adults, $17-20 children, free under age 3) is Wild West fun for the whole family deep in the Santa Cruz Mountains. Hop aboard an antique train, explore the Wild West Main Street, or rent a picnic area. This is a dog-friendly place-dogs are even allowed on the train.

The train winds through the redwoods up Bear Mountain on a one-hour route; other trips include a beach route, a seasonal haunted Halloween ride, and a holiday trip with Santa. Don't forget your camera.

Roaring Camp Railroads is fun for the whole family any time of the year.

There are playing fields on the Roaring Camp grounds that include a baseball field, a volleyball court, tetherball, and horseshoe pits. Lunch options include a birthday caboose, chuck wagon barbecue, and a food stand near the General Store.

Bigfoot Discovery Museum
Located deep in the Santa Cruz Mountains among the towering redwoods is the Bigfoot Discovery Museum (5497 Hwy. 9, Felton, 831/335-4478, www.bigfootdiscoveryproject.com, summer Wed.-Mon. 11 A.M.-6 P.M., fall Wed.-Fri. 1-6 P.M., donation $3-5), which contains a full collection of local history tied to

the creature, including actual evidence that the Sasquatch roams the Santa Cruz Mountains. There is a video presentation, and you can examine plaster casts of both the feet and hands of the formidable beast.

🜨 Boulder Creek

A small community filled with charming antiques shops, Boulder Creek (Hwy. 9, www.boulder-creek.com) also has a local brewery, a few winemakers, state parks, and a majestic golf course surrounded by redwoods. It is just under an hour from Santa Cruz but is much less visited.

Boulder Creek began as a rough Western town of saloons, cathouses, gambling dens, and hotels, a hint of which remains today. Devote at least a day to exploring this area's wineries and restaurants. Cozy riverside cabins and camping allow for overnight stays, and the Skyline-to-the-Sea backpacking trail runs through Big Basin Redwoods State Park.

SPORTS AND RECREATION

Big trees, freshwater access, and a plethora of hiking opportunities in the Santa Cruz Mountains come in a range of difficulty levels.

Henry Cowell Redwoods State Park

The northern redwood forest of Henry Cowell Redwoods State Park (101 N. Big Tree Rd., Felton, 831/335-4598 or 831/438-2396, www.parks.ca.gov, $10) offers a vast variety of outdoor activities. The 4,600-acre park has camping, biking, hiking, guided nature walks, swimming, picnicking, and horseback-riding trails.

The large **Nature Center** has interactive and educational kid-friendly exhibits. There are sections dedicated to each of the four habitats of the park. Every year, local schoolchildren come to the park to release fish back into the river, described here in an exhibit and video.

The main park has 15 miles of **hiking and dirt-biking trails** that weave about old-growth forest, where the trees are 1,400-1,800 years

old. Dogs are allowed on the Pipeline Road, Graham Hill Trail, and Meadow Trail. The River Trail follows the San Lorenzo River, where there is swimming access.

The northern part of the park, known as **Fall Creek,** has 20 miles of hiking trails deep into the wooded mountains, where giant trees abound. The Fall Creek Trail has a 3.2-mile loop with a 200-foot elevation gain; the longer option on this trail is a seven-mile round-trip route around Ben Lomond Mountain that gains 900 vertical feet.

Several dirt roads allow bicycle riders to explore the park. Bikes are allowed on the Pipeline Road, Rincon Fire Road, Ridge Fire Road, and Powder Mill Fire Road. Helmets are required for riders under age 18.

Horses and riders can travel many of the trails, except Redwood Grove Trail, Meadow Trail, Ox Trail, and Pipeline Rode south of the Rincon Fire Road. At the Powder Mill Trailhead is a parking lot where horses can be staged and trailers parked. The lot is in the southeast corner of the park on Graham Hill Road near the campgrounds.

Loch Lomond Recreation Area

A dog-friendly retreat into a freshwater zone is 175-acre Loch Lomond Recreation Area (100 Loch Lomond Way, Felton, 831/335-7424, www.cityofsantacruz.com, mid-Mar.-Oct. daily 7 A.M.-dark, $10), a large reservoir in a canyon. The reservoir has plenty of shady coves to fish for trout, largemouth bass, and bluegills. can all be found within these waters. Fishing is only permitted during park hours, and the park store has bait, tackle, and fishing licenses.

The recreation area as seven established picnic areas with tables, barbecues, running water, and restroom facilities. The Glen Corrie Picnic Area is a trailhead for several hikes. Accessible by boat, Clar Innis is a small island with picnic tables.

Loch Lomond has 10 miles of established trails that meander through coastal redwoods, Douglas

© KRISTIN LEAL

Discover the big trees of Big Basin Redwoods State Park.

firs, tanbark oak, ferns, wild blackberries, and the scent of wild lilacs where the sun is plentiful. Guided nature walks with rangers are available.

The park store has a 40-boat fleet of pedal boats, rowboats, and electric-assist rowboats for rent. Pedal boats are easy for kids to control, and the electric-assist rowboats allow for exploration of the many coves. No private boats are allowed here.

Castle Rock State Park

For panoramic views along the crest of the Santa Cruz Mountains, Castle Rock State Park (15000 Skyline Blvd./Hwy. 35, 2.5 miles south of Hwy. 9, 408/867-2952, www.parks.ca.gov, $10) is home to noble redwoods in a lush mossy forest in steep canyons. Its many unusual rock formations are popular with rock climbers. The trail system is expansive, with over 32 miles to discover on horseback or on foot. These trails connect to those in Big Basin Redwoods State

Park and continue as far as the coast and the Santa Clara and San Lorenzo Valleys.

◖ Big Basin Redwoods State Park

Massive 18,000-acre Big Basin Redwoods State Park (Hwy. 236, Boulder Creek, 831/338-8600, www.parks.ca.gov, daily 8 A.M.-sunset, $10) is 25 miles northwest of Santa Cruz Deep in the shade of towering old-growth redwoods. Established in 1902, it is California's oldest State Park. Along the park's 80 miles of trails and roadways are some of the tallest redwoods in the world as well as gushing waterfalls, freshwater streams, and steep mountain inclines. Hiking routes include the 29.5-mile Skyline-to-the-Sea Trail, along which you can backcountry camp.

Big Basin is an old-growth forest with a variety of trees at all stages of their life cycles. Some redwoods are up to 2,000 years old, their massive trunks dwarfing the surrounding foliage and their tops reaching into the clouds. The tallest redwood in the park is the 329-foot-tall "Mother of the Forest," on the Redwood Trail near the general store.

Año Nuevo State Reserve

Just about any time of the year is a good time to visit Año Nuevo State Reserve (New Year's Creek Rd., off Hwy 1, 605/879-0227 or 605/879-2025, www.parks.ca.gov, sunrise until a half hour after sunset, year-round with a small closure in late Nov.-early Dec., $10 parking, $7 per person for visitors permit, permits must be purchased by 3:30 P.M.). The reserve voices a constant echo of snarls and snorts from the many elephant seals who make this their home. Peak season to view the giant elephant seals is December through March when the seals are breeding and giving birth to their pups. The reserve is home to the largest mainland breeding colony in the world for the northern elephant seal. Young teenaged males arrive along the tumultuous shoreline to molt during the summer months. They shed their outer layer of skin and fur, which can take four to six weeks. Young males are there May-June, with the older males arriving in July and staying through August.

You can encounter these massive creatures along the Año Nuevo Point Trail. A local volunteer will lead the way into the dunes to the viewing points. Make sure to stay close to the group and do not wander off as you are likely to wander right into a molting seal; as they wander further inland than you may expect. A 3- to 4-mile hiking trail winds through the bluffs of the steep shoreline through a grassy field and into the sand dunes. Beyond the rolling dunes there is access to the viewing points where the enormous animals can be observed.

The North Point examination area usually has the most seals and is another 0.5 miles form the South Point, which is the first look-out on the edge of the dunes. You can expect to spend at least 2-3 hours touring the park, and you may stay longer if you decide to picnic and peruse the visitors center.

SHOPPING

As you climb into the coastal mountains, visit **Ivy's Porch** (5311 Scotts Valley Dr., Scotts Valley, 831/438-1228, www.ivysporch.com, Mon.-Sat. 10 A.M.-5 P.M., Sun. 11 A.M.-4 P.M.) to discover collectables, antiques, outdoor pieces, and garden goodies. A cottage-style collective, Ivy's is in a beautiful one-acre garden. Outside are magnificent arbors, birdbaths, gazebos, iron items, and fountains. Among the things inside are French antiques and early American furniture.

Hunt for treasure throughout the 10,000-square-foot **Lacey Days Antiques** (9280 Hwy. 9, Ben Lomond, 831/336-2686, daily 11 A.M.-5 P.M.), which operates primarily as a furniture store and carries many larger pieces, such as kitchen tables, china cabinets, chairs, nightstands, chests, and bookcases. The furniture inside is mid-century to contemporary, some antiques but many not. Prices are reasonable, and there are occasional sales throughout the year.

Towne & Country Antiques (9280 Hwy. 9, Suite 22, Ben Lomond, 831/336-5993, daily 11 A.M.-5 P.M.) is a rustic country shop with treasures big and small and a constant influx of new items. The selection includes glassware, garden accents, jewelry, wall hangings, art, books, and kitchenware.

The largest antiques shop in the Santa Cruz Mountains is **Boulder Creek Antiques** (13164 Hwy. 9, Boulder Creek, 831/338-0600, www.bouldercreekantiques.blogspot.com, daily 11 A.M.-5:30 P.M.). The place seems to go on forever, a beautiful maze indoors and out. Several sections are targeted specifically at men, and there are jewelry cases, a garden section, laces, linens, furniture, small items in cases, antique radios, toy cars, and kitchenware.

ACCOMMODATIONS
Camping
Henry Cowell Redwoods State Park (101 North Big Tree Rd., Felton, 831/335-4598 or 831/438-2396, www.parks.ca.gov, $35) has over 100 campsites deep in the redwood forest with freshwater streams nearby; there are also a number of group camps. The Junior Ranger and Campfire Programs are great for children, and the Little Ones Nature Club meets on Friday-Sunday. Each year a troupe of veteran Santa Cruz actors comes for *Reader's Theater—Tales with a Twist* (July 23, 8 P.M.) at the Campfire Center. The Nature Center in the Park is also great for some hands-on discovery, and recreational opportunities abound in the park.

Big Basin Redwoods State Park (Hwy. 236, Boulder Creek, 831/338-8600, www.parks.ca.gov, daily 8 A.M.-sunset, $35) has RV and tent sites as well as tent cabins for rent. There are 146 campsites at four different campgrounds alongside creeks and meadows and in the shade of the forest. Each campground has trail access, and you may see black-tailed deer, gray squirrels, chipmunks, raccoons, foxes, coyotes, bobcats, and opossums.

For backpacking and primitive camping off the grid, **Castle Rock State Park** (15000 Skyline Blvd./Hwy. 35, 2.5 miles south of Hwy. 9, 408/867-2952, www.parks.ca.gov) is deep in the coastal range. Camping must be arranged with park officials and permits are issued on a first-come, first-served basis. You can even horseback ride into the wilderness to camp like the pioneers.

Under $150

Escape into the majestic redwood forest at **Fern River Resort Motel** (5250 Hwy. 9, Felton, 831/335-4412, www.fernriver.com, $69-233), with snug private cottages equipped with fireplaces, small kitchens, and outdoor decks with barbecues. The river is close by, and a private beach has great swimming, especially in the heat of the summer.

Jaye's Timberlane Resort (8705 Hwy. 9, Ben Lomond, 831/336-5479, www.jayestimberlane.com, $85-175) has 10 cabins on seven attractive acres among towering redwoods. The property has a solar-heated pool, horseshoe pits, and tennis courts; it's great for a family stay as kids are welcome.

Overlooking the San Lorenzo River is the **Quality Inn & Suites Santa Cruz Mountains** (9733 Hwy. 9, Ben Lomond, 831/336-2292, www.qualityinn.com, $69-299), newly remodeled with 25 guest rooms, continental breakfast, an outdoor heated pool, free Wi-Fi, and fax services. The standard rooms are a bit small and are equipped with coffeemakers, irons and ironing boards, and hair dryers. The suites are better for families as the extra sitting room provides more space.

$150-250

Some travelers prefer to stay in the woods rather than downtown or out by the busy Boardwalk. Northwest of Santa Cruz, **Redwood Croft Bed & Breakfast** (275 Northwest Dr., Bonny Doon, 831/458-1939, www.redwoodcroft.com, $155-275) is a funky two-room B&B set back in a redwood forest. The inn itself takes the woodsy theme indoors, using natural wood on the walls and furniture to create a serene retreat feeling. Both guest rooms have beautiful appointments, lovely stone baths, and views into the forest.

FOOD
American

One of the last American roadhouses, **Henflings Tavern** (9450 Hwy. 9, Ben Lomond, 831/336-9318, www.henflings.net, daily 11 A.M.-2 A.M., $15) serves traditional pub fare and has a full bar. In the evening, expect live music or a little karaoke. The outdoor seating is nice, and the atmosphere is about as casual as it gets.

Since 1989 the **Boulder Creek Brewery & Café** (13040 Hwy. 9, 831/338-7882, www.bouldercreekbrewery.net, Mon.-Thurs. 11:30 A.M.-10 P.M., Fri.-Sat. 11:30 A.M.-10:30 P.M., $8-15) has served handcrafted beers and juicy burgers, all-American classics, soups, salads, espresso, and desserts. Bring the whole family and sit by the fire on a cool fall night or a rainy winter day. Boulder Creek Brewery has owned Santa Cruz Brewery since 2003 and uses its refurbished brew house and tanks at this location. It features a full bar; happy hour is Monday-Friday 4-6 P.M. and Saturday 9-10 P.M.

Asian

For a taste of Thailand in the Santa Cruz Mountains, **Kao Sook** (245 Mt. Hermon Rd., Scotts Valley, 831/439-9520, Mon.-Fri. 11 A.M.-9 P.M., Sat.-Sun. noon-9 P.M., $8-12) has addicting curries, noodle dishes, and salads.

Breakfast

Have a cup of coffee and a bite at the **Coffee Cat** (255 Mt. Hermon Rd., Scotts Valley, Mon.-Thurs. 6 A.M.-10 P.M., Fri.-Sat. 6 A.M.-11 P.M., $3-8). If you're camping, this comfortable lounge is a good space to catch up Internet use. The coffee is roasted in-house and served any way you like it along with a full menu of homemade savory and sweet goodies.

For a hearty mountain breakfast that won't break the bank, **Rocky's Café** (6560 Hwy. 9, Felton, 831/335-4637, Mon.-Sun. 7:30 A.M.-2:30 P.M., $8-10) serves typical breakfast fare that includes oatmeal and banana pancakes, and the portions are large enough to hold you over until lunch and maybe even dinner. Inside is a rustic log-cabin atmosphere.

Cheap Eats

For picnic supplies, head to one of the two locally owned **New Leaf Community Markets** (6240 Hwy. 9, Felton, 831/334-7322, www.newleaf.com, daily 9 A.M.-9 P.M.; 13159 Hwy. 9, Boulder Creek, daily 9 A.M.-9 P.M.). For nearly 20 years, owners Scott and Rex have been providing their customers with fresh local organic goods. The deli can provide lunch goodies, the cracker isle is a must, and the beverage selection sprawls with specialty drinks and local brews.

German

For a warm fire in a comfy chalet, head to the **Tyrolean Inn** (9600 Hwy. 9, Ben Lomond, 831/336-5188, www.tyroleaninn.com, Tues.-Thurs. 5-9 P.M., Fri.-Sat. 4-10 P.M., Sun. noon-9 P.M., $18) and enjoy authentic Bavarian cuisine. German favorites are on the menu, including sausage, *zigeuner schnitzel, rindsrouladen,* and *zwiebelrostbraten.* The service is always friendly, the German beers are large, and the food is comforting. On weekends enjoy live Bavarian folk music, and you can sit in the sunroom or, on warm nights, outside.

Italian

Mama Mia's Ristorante Italiano (6231 Graham Hill Rd., Felton, 831/335-4414, www.mamamias.com, daily 4-9 P.M., $18-32) has pizzas for the whole family and offers a full menu of pastas, Italian specialties, chicken dishes, and steaks.

Mexican

Don Quixote's International Music Hall (6275 Hwy. 9, Felton, 831/603-2294, www.donquiotesmusic.com, daily 11 A.M.-2 A.M., $10-26) is more about music than food, but they serve up Southern fried chicken, several seafood entrées, burritos, and other Mexican dishes. Families are welcome, with a kids menu to satisfy the little ones.

Farmers Markets

The **Santa Cruz Community Market** (831/454-0566, manager@santacruzfarmersmarket.org, www.santacruzfarmersmarket.org, music series sccfmmusic@gmail.com) brings two abundant farmers market to the mountain communities. The **Scotts Valley Farmers Market** (Scotts Valley Community Center, 360 Kings Village Dr., Scotts Valley, Sat. 9 A.M.-1 P.M.) happens year-round, rain or shine. There can be up to 25 vendors providing organically grown fruits and vegetables along with freshly made organic foods. Vendors change as the harvest changes with the seasons.

The **Felton Farmers' Market** (Hwy. 9 and Russell Ave., Felton, year-round Tues. 2:30-6:30 P.M.) has at least 15 farms and 10 food vendors. Bring your dull knives to be sharpened while you shop; offerings include fresh organic ice cream, hand-tossed pizza, fresh fish, and fruits and vegetables.

INFORMATION AND SERVICES
Media and Communications

Santa Cruz has its own daily newspaper, the *Santa Cruz Sentinel* (www.santacruzsentinel.com), with a daily dose of national wire-service news and current events, local news, plus some good stuff for visitors. The *Sentinel* has a Food section, a Sunday Travel section, and plenty of up-to-date entertainment information.

Medical Services

Despite its rep as a funky bohemian beach

town, Santa Cruz's dense population dictates that it has at least one full-fledged hospital; get medical treatment and care at **Dominican Hospital** (1555 Soquel Ave., 831/426-7700, www.dominicanhospital.org).

GETTING THERE AND AROUND
By Car

There are a few ways to reach the Santa Cruz Mountains. Highway 9 from Santa Cruz runs north to Felton, Ben Lomond, and Boulder Creek. You can also take Highway 17 north of Santa Cruz and take the exit for Mount Herman Road, which leads to Grahamhill Road and then Highway 9. Big Basin Redwoods State Park is on Highway 236 west of Highway 9. You can also approach it from Highway 1 and Bonny Dune Road.

By Bus

Throughout the Santa Cruz Mountains, transit buses are run by **Santa Cruz METRO** (831/425-8600, www.scmtd.com, $1.50 per ride adults, passes available). With 42 routes in Santa Cruz County, you can probably find a way to get nearly anywhere you'd want to go.

BIG SUR

Soaring cliffs dropping to white-sand beaches exemplify the California coast made legendary in film and literature. From north to south, the Pacific Ocean changes from slate gray to a gentler blue, and the endless crash of the breakers on the shore is a constant lullaby in Big Sur's coastal towns.

Big Sur is both the name of a town and the semiofficial name of the coastal region south of Carmel and north of San Simeon. The region is explored via Highway 1, also called the Pacific Coast Highway, a road that hugs sheer cliffs and passes several state parks, resorts, and restaurants like Nepenthe, seemingly perched on the edge of the world. Once you get off the well-traveled highway, there are surf spots, secluded waterfalls, kayaking, and horseback riding. A

popular side trip is the rough drive on the Old Coast Road to Andrew Molera State Park, with spectacular ocean views. The town of Lucia is a must-see, with the Lucia Lodge perched on coastal cliffs, beaches that are known for jade hunting, and Limekiln State Park.

Big Sur attracts many types of visitors. Nature lovers come to camp and hike in pristine wilderness areas, throw on thick wetsuits and surf the sometimes deserted beaches, and even hunt for jade in rocky coves. Some come for retreats at the Esalen Institute. Some of the world's wealthiest people luxuriate at unbelievably plush hotels and spas.

Part of the charm of Big Sur is being peacefully separate from the Information Age—yes,

© KRISTIN LEAL

HIGHLIGHTS

0   10 mi

0   10 km

© AVALON TRAVEL

LOOK FOR ◖ TO FIND RECOMMENDED SIGHTS, ACTIVITIES, DINING, AND LODGING.

◖ **Big Sur Coast Highway:** This twisting coastal drive along Highway 1 is iconic Big Sur, with jutting cliffs, crashing surf, and glorious views all the way (page 182).

◖ **Bixby Bridge:** The picturesque single-span arch bridge along Highway 1 reaches across the crashing ocean and dramatic cliffs. It's a structural piece of art and one of the most popular photo ops along the coast (page 183).

◖ **Bottchers Gap:** This is one of the best locations in Big Sur to enter the wilderness of the Los Padres National Forest, with hiking trails through rolling mountains (page 183).

◖ **Henry Miller Memorial Library:** Browse the collection of literature, enjoy local performances, and have a cup of coffee at Henry Miller's library, museum, and gathering place (page 184).

◖ **Point Sur Light Station:** One of the grandest lighthouses along California's coast sits against a backdrop of the wide blue ocean (page 186).

◖ **McWay Falls:** A river falls off a sheer cliff onto a beach hundreds of feet below. A hiking trail winds high above the cove for dramatic views of the waterfall (page 187).

◖ **Pfeiffer Beach:** Rock islands are scattered in the foam of the surf, and small caves and windows are visible in these rock formations (page 189).

◖ **Andrew Molera State Park:** With over 20 miles of hiking trails, beach access, hike-in camping, bike riding, and horseback riding, this park has much to explore (page 191).

◖ **Pfeiffer Big Sur State Park:** The largest and most developed park in Big Sur offers Big Sur Lodge, a restaurant and café, a shop, an amphitheater, plenty of hiking-only trails, and lovely redwood-shaded campsites (page 191).

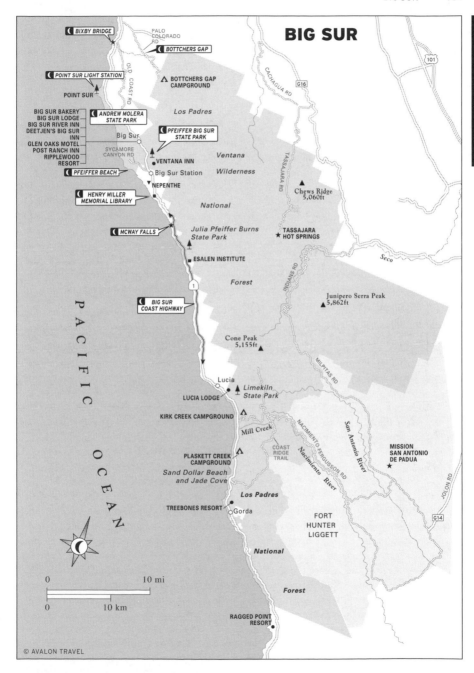

BIG SUR

BIG SUR

◖ BIXBY BRIDGE

PALO COLORADO RD

◖ BOTTCHERS GAP

◖ POINT SUR LIGHT STATION

POINT SUR

BOTTCHERS GAP CAMPGROUND

CACHAGUA RD

G16

101

OLD COAST RD

Los Padres

BIG SUR BAKERY
BIG SUR LODGE
BIG SUR RIVER INN
DEETJEN'S BIG SUR INN
GLEN OAKS MOTEL
POST RANCH INN
RIPPLEWOOD RESORT

◖ ANDREW MOLERA STATE PARK

◖ PFEIFFER BIG SUR STATE PARK

Big Sur

SYCAMORE CANYON RD

VENTANA INN

Ventana

TASSAJARA RD

◖ PFEIFFER BEACH

Big Sur Station

Wilderness

Chews Ridge
5,060ft

NEPENTHE

◖ HENRY MILLER MEMORIAL LIBRARY

National

◖ MCWAY FALLS

Julia Pfeiffer Burns State Park

TASSAJARA HOT SPRINGS

ESALEN INSTITUTE

INDIANS RD

Seco

1

Forest

Junipero Serra Peak
5,862ft

◖ BIG SUR COAST HIGHWAY

Cone Peak
5,155ft

P A C I F I C

MILPITAS RD

Lucia

Limekiln State Park

LUCIA LODGE

KIRK CREEK CAMPGROUND

NACIMIENTO-FERGUSSON RD

San Antonio River

MISSION SAN ANTONIO DE PADUA

Mill Creek

COAST RIDGE TRAIL

Nacimiento River

PLASKETT CREEK CAMPGROUND

O C E A N

Sand Dollar Beach and Jade Cove

Los Padres

TREEBONES RESORT

Gorda

FORT HUNTER LIGGETT

JOLON RD

G14

National

Forest

0   10 mi

0   10 km

RAGGED POINT RESORT

© AVALON TRAVEL

this means that your cell phone won't work in many parts of region. The farther south you go, the more you get off the grid.

PLANNING YOUR TIME

Whether you are coming for a day or a longer stay, it is a good idea to have a general plan; the Big Sur region is vast and has sparse services. The 25-mile drive south from Carmel to the village of Big Sur generally takes 40 minutes. It is about 95 miles from Carmel to San Simeon and takes over two hours.

The drive can take a while, partly from negotiating the difficult twisting road and partly from using the many convenient turnouts to take photos of the spectacular scenery. Most of the major parks in the Big Sur region are right along Highway 1, making it easy to spend a few days traveling this road, stopping at Julia Pfeiffer or Andrew Molera to hike for a few

hours or have a picnic on the beach. A day trip can involve a leisurely drive or an all-out hiking adventure. There are many short hikes right near the highway that are nice to stretch your legs along the way.

To access the backcountry or long-distance hikes, head to one of the state parks. Bottchers Gap and Salmon Creek Waterfall have no services but are good entry points into the backcountry of the Los Padres National Forest for primitive camping.

If you are planning to stay over in Big Sur, spend a couple of nights. It is important to make reservations, especially in the summer months when accommodations book up fast ahead of time. Accommodations options are much more expansive than you'd expect in a rugged wilderness area; Options range from luxurious tree houses to pitching a tent in the backcountry.

Carmel to Lucia

Sprawling state parks with ragged cliffs and towering redwoods, high-end restaurants, and laid-back lodging line the coast of the northern part of the Big Sur region. This is the most populated portion of the 90-mile route.

SIGHTS
◖ Big Sur Coast Highway

Even if you're not up to tackling the hiking trails and backcountry, you can still get a good sense of the glory of the Big Sur region just by driving through it. The Big Sur Coast Highway, a 90-mile stretch of Highway 1, runs atop jagged cliffs and along rocky beaches, through dense redwood forest, over historic scenic bridges, and past several parks. Construction on this stretch of road was completed in the 1930s to connect Cambria to Carmel. You can start out at either end and spend a whole day making your way along this road. There are

plenty of wide turnouts on picturesque cliffs, which makes it easy to stop to admire the glittering ocean and stunning wooded cliffs. Don't forget the camera.

Old Coast Road

Easily found on the left side of Highway 1, about 13 miles south of Carmel and just before Bixby Bridge, the unsurfaced Old Coast Road cuts high into the coastal range of Big Sur through a variety of landscapes that will challenge the driver while providing spectacular views. There are steep grades with areas of chunky quartz, slick muddy sections, tight turns through the redwoods, and narrow ledges.

It is a little more than 10 miles to the end of the road and Andrew Molera State Park. The road is passable in dry weather, but in wet weather there are many flood-prone sections in the forest and steep loose grades. Most vehicles

scenic Highway 1

can handle the drive when it's dry; I've seen small city cars, a few trucks, and even convertibles take the journey. The road has a handful of drainage pipes that are somewhat bumpy; like large speed bumps, low-clearance vehicles should traverse these with caution.

◖ Bixby Bridge

You'll probably recognize the Bixby Bridge when you come to it on Highway 1, about 18 miles south of Carmel. Among the world's highest, Bixby Bridge is over 260 feet high and more than 700 feet long. The cement open-spandrel arched bridge is one of the most photographed bridges in the nation, and it has been used in countless car commercials over the years. The bridge was built in the early 1930s as part of the massive New Deal government works project to complete Highway 1 and connect Northern California to the south along the coast. Today, you can pull out at either end of the bridge to take photos or just to view the

attractive span and Bixby Creek flowing into the Pacific far below.

Are there two Bixby Bridges? No; the Rocky Creek Bridge (Hwy. 1, north of Bixby Bridge) is similar in design but not quite as grand and picturesque.

◖ Bottchers Gap

Where the shaded redwood groves meet the steep canyons, the Ventana Wilderness of the Los Padres National Forest is accessed at Bottchers Gap (end of Polo Colorado Canyon Rd., 805/968-6640, day-use $5). Palo Colorado Road runs eight miles from Highway 1 to the small Bottchers Gap campground. This is one of the best locations in Big Sur to enter the savage terrain of the Los Padres National Forest, nearly two million acres of coastal mountain environment that stretches 220 miles from Monterey County to Los Angeles County. Joe's Landing, at the mouth of Palo Colorado Canyon, was one of many villages that shipped bark and redwood logs from here between 1898 and 1907. Fully paved Palo Colorado Road twists and turns through the shaded forest, allowing year-round access.

There are 12 campsites at Bottchers Gap, and it's possible to camp at 55 designated primitive camping sites in the backcountry with a free wilderness and fire permit from the Los Padres National Forest District Office (805/385-5434, www.campone.com). Several well-traveled trails and some more challenging trails start from here, including the Skinner Ridge Trail and Pico Blanco Boy Scouts of America Road Trail, which lead in opposite directions into the backcountry to waterfalls, the Little Sur River, and Devils Peak, the highest point in this part of the forest.

One of the popular hikes off the Pico Blanco Trail is the Little Sur Trail, which picks up at the bottom of the Boy Scouts' private property line. The Skinner Ridge Trail has plenty of rugged camps and tricky terrain with primitive camping along the way.

Old Coast Road

Big Sur Station

If you haven't stopped at one of the large state park visitors centers, pull in at Big Sur Station (Hwy. 1, south of Pfeiffer Big Sur, 831/667-2315, daily 8 A.M.-4:30 P.M.). This ranger station offers maps and brochures for all the major parks and trails of Big Sur, plus a small bookshop. The visitors center and services at Pfeiffer Big Sur State Park have the same or more information, so if you're planning to visit that park, skip this stop. Several of the smaller parks and beaches (Limekiln, Garrapata, and Sand Dollar) have no visitor services, so Big Sur Station serves visitors who only plan to go to one of those less-traveled spots. You can also get a backcountry permit for the Ventana Wilderness here.

◀ Henry Miller Memorial Library

A number of authors and writers have spent time in Big Sur, soaking in the remote wilderness and sea air to gather inspiration for their work. Henry Miller lived and wrote in Big Sur for 18 years. He began to cultivate this region as an artists colony in 1944, and his utopian 1957 novel *Big Sur and the Oranges of Hieronymus Bosch* put his Big Sur dream on the map. Today, the Henry Miller Memorial Library (Hwy. 1, 0.25 miles north of Deetjens, 831/667-2574, www.henrymiller.org, Wed.-Mon. 11 A.M.-6 P.M.) celebrates the life and work of Miller and his peers in this quirky community center, museum, coffee shop, and gathering place. You can flip through the collection of literature, be entertained by local performances, attend short film festivals, and more.

The library is easy to find on Highway 1— look for the hand-painted sign and funky fence decorations. What you won't find is a typical lending library, bookshop, or slick museum. Instead, you can wander the lovely sun-dappled meadow soaking in the essence of Miller's life here, come inside and talk to the docents about the racy novels Miller wrote, and maybe

BIG SUR

HISTORY OF THE EL SUR RANCH

© KRISTIN LEAL

Today the El Sur Ranch raises cattle.

In 1834, when California was under Spanish-Mexican rule, the El Sur Ranch was set up for Juan Bautista Alvarado, one of several hundred ranchos set up by Governor José Figueroa. The ranch was managed and then taken over by Alvarado's uncle, Captain John Rogers Cooper. The property was leased to others several times, and mules, dairy cows, and beef cattle would roam the region throughout the 19th century.

By the 1920s, Cooper and his family were some of the largest landowners in Monterey County. Besides cattle they also began to plant coastal crops such as artichokes and peas. Harry Hunt bought the ranch in the late 1920s and planted alfalfa, barley, corn, potatoes, and car-

rots. To keep up with ranch growth, Hunt installed the first centrifugal pump-wells for irrigation.

Around the time electricity reached Big Sur, in 1948, the ranch returned to pasture. Hunt sold it in 1955 to Cortlandt Hill, whose family still retains the property. They manage the land to preserve its historic pastoral splendor.

The El Sur Ranch can be seen as you travel to Big Sur from the Carmel Highlands. You can see sections of the El Sur land along Highway 1 and Old Coast Road. Even the lush hillsides and land around the Point Sur Lighthouse are part of the El Sur Ranch. You can often see their cattle grazing along the bluffs near Point Sur and on Old Coast Road (near the Andrew Molera park entrance).

© KRISTIN LEAL

The Bixby Bridge is known as the gateway to Big Sur.

sit back with a cup of coffee to meditate on life, art, and the gorgeous scenery. The library offers a glimpse into the facet of Big Sur as a dispersed art colony that has inspired countless works.

◖ Point Sur Light Station

Sitting alone and isolated out on its cliff, the Point Sur Light Station (Hwy. 1, 0.25 miles north of Point Sur Naval Facility, 831/625-4419, tours Nov.-Mar. Sat.-Sun. 10 A.M. and 2 P.M., Apr.-June and Sept.-Oct. Wed. and Sat.-Sun. 10 A.M. and 2 P.M., July-Aug. Wed. and Sat.-Sun. 10 A.M. and 2 P.M., Thurs. 10 A.M., $10 adults, $5 children, call for times of moonlight tours, $15 adults, $10 children) keeps watch over ships navigating the rocky waters of Big Sur. It's the only complete 19th-century light station in California that you can visit, and even so, access is severely limited; you can only visit on a tour. First lit in 1889, this now fully automated light station still provides navigational aid; keepers stopped living and

working in the tiny stone-built compound in 1974. But is the lighthouse truly uninhabited? Take one of the moonlight tours (call for details) to learn about the haunted history of the light station buildings.

You can't make a reservation for a Point Sur tour, so you should just show up early and park off Highway 1 on the west side by the farm gate. Your guide will meet you there and lead you up the paved road 0.5 miles to the light station. Once there, you'll climb the stairs up to the light, explore the restored keepers' homes and service buildings, and walk out to the cliff's edge. Expect to see a variety of flora and fauna, from brilliant wildflowers in the spring to gray whales in the winter and flocks of pelicans flying in formation at any time of year. Be sure to dress in layers; winter or summer it can be sunny and hot or foggy and cold, and sometimes both on the same tour. Tours last three hours and require more than one mile of walking, with a bit of incline and more than 100 stairs.

The farm gate is locked, and there's no access

Sailors relied on the light of Point Sur Light Station to guide them away from the rugged coastline of Big Sur.

to the light station without a tour group. Tour schedules can vary from year to year and season to season; it's a good idea to call ahead before showing up. If you need special assistance for your tour or have questions about accessibility, call 831/667-0528 as far ahead as possible to make arrangements. No strollers, food, pets, or smoking are allowed on the property.

Big Sur Spirit Garden

A favorite among local art lovers, the Big Sur Spirit Garden (47504 Hwy. 1, Loma Vista, 831/238-1056, www.bigsurspiritgarden.com, daily 9 A.M.-6 P.M.) changes a little almost every day. The "garden" part includes a variety of plantlife, while the "spirit" part is modern and postmodern fair-trade art nearby and as far away as India. The artwork tends toward brightly colored small sculptures done in exuberant native style. The Spirit Garden offers educational programs, community celebrations, musical events, and more. Call ahead for information on upcoming events.

◖ McWay Falls

A popular photo spot in Big Sur is the breathtaking McWay Falls at Julia Pfeiffer Burns State Park (40 miles south of Carmel, 831/667-2315, www.parks.ca.gov, 30 minutes before sunrise-30 minutes after sunset, $10). A ribbonlike stream spews out of Anderson Canyon and falls some 200 feet to the pale beach below. The stream flows year-round, with heavier volume in winter and early spring. The walk to the waterfall is windy, but it is worth the trek as the falls will always impress.

The trail begins at Julia Pfeiffer Burns State Park, where the rolling hills drop dramatically to the sea and redwood forests protect the inland reaches. The hike to view the stunning McWay Falls is less than one mile and offers stunning views of the Big Sur coastline. The

GHOSTS AT POINT SUR LIGHT STATION

The moonlight tours at the Point Sur Light Station are a spooky treat.

For a chance to see a ghost and hear a ghost story or two, make your way to the Point Sur Light Station in Big Sur. The creepy annual Halloween Ghost Tour (www.pointsur.org, $60) happens by the light of a full moon. Docents lead guests on a 0.5-mile walk up to the Light Station where they share its history and a few ghostly encounters along the way. The tour begins just before sunset, and the views are unmatched. There are beverages, a light buffet, and ghost stories told by a local professional actor at the barn after a look at the actual lighthouse.

The tours typically run in mid-late October, depending on the moon's schedule. Check the website for tour times and dates. You must reserve the tour in advance (831/649-7139, cclk@pointsur.org), and they tend to fill up fast. Tours are limited to 40 people, and it is not recommended for small children. Wear warm clothing as it gets cold and windy here.

trail ends at the ruins of the McWay Waterfall House, during the 1920s the home of Lathrop and Helen Hopper Brown. Today, a decaying foundation of the terrace is all that remains. Helen Hopper Brown eventually donated the property to the state in memory of her dear friend Julia Pfeiffer Burns.

Also at Julia Pfeiffer Burns State Park, you can head inland on the east end of the park near the parking area and find more hiking trails and picnic tables. You can park along the ocean side of Highway 1 and not pay the entrance fee, but be careful, as this is a busy highway and the roadsides are often full. You can also find another small pullout on the inland side, just slightly south of the other pull out. Beyond the park gates are the paved parking area and restrooms.

© KRISTIN LEAL

the stunning McWay Falls at Julia Pfeiffer Burns State Park

Pfeiffer Beach

Secluded at the end of a winding road through the damp forest, just across from the entrance to Big Sur Station, is Pfeiffer Beach (Sycamore Canyon Rd., off Hwy. 1, 26 miles south of Carmel, 805/434-1996, www.campone.com, daily 9 A.M.-8 P.M., $5). The beach is easily accessed on a short sandy trail. Rocky islets rise beyond the foam of the surf with small caves and windows visible. The grainy white sand is marbled with red and black silt, creating unique textures and colors. Sunsets in the cove ignite the horizon with a surge of orange that blends into sheets of pink across the fading blue sky. Anglers are known to visit the beaches in the early morning, and surfers frequent the waves.

Esalen Institute

The Esalen Institute (55000 Hwy. 1, 831/667-3000, fax 831/667-2724, www.esalen.org, year-round by reservation only) is known as the home of the California massage technique, a forerunner and cutting-edge player in ecologi cal living, and a space to retreat from the world and build a new and better sense of self. People come from all over to this haven, sometimes called "the New Age Harvard," for lengthy courses and classes, but massages and use of the bathhouse are available to travelers.

Esalen isn't a day spa. You have to make an appointment for a massage (75 minutes, $150), which grants you access to the hot tubs for an hour before and an hour after your session. If you just want to sit in the bathhouse's hot tubs, you have to stay up late-very late. Inexpensive open access to the Esalen tubs (831/667-3047, $20) is by reservation and only from 1 A.M. to 3 A.M. Many locals consider the sleep deprivation worth it to get the chance to enjoy the healing mineral waters and the stunning night sky.

The bathhouse, down a rocky path on the edge of the cliffs overlooking the ocean, a motley collection of mineral-fed hot tubs with ocean views. You can choose the Quiet Side or

© KRISTIN LEAL

Find beach access at Garrapata State Park.

the Silent Side to sink into the water and contemplate the Pacific, meditate on the sunset, or (on the Quiet Side) get to know your fellow bathers. Esalen's bathhouse area is clothing-optional in a philosophy that puts the essence of nature above the sovereignty of people and encourages openness and sharing among its guests. You'll also find a distinct absence of staff to help you find your way around. Once you've parked and been given directions, it's up to you to find your way down to the cliffs. You'll have to find your own towel, ferret out a cubby for your clothes in the changing rooms, grab a shower, and then wander out to find a hot tub. Be sure to go all the way outside past the individual claw-foot tubs to the glorious shallow cement tubs right out on the edge of the cliff with the surf crashing just below.

If you're not comfortable with nudity or silence, Esalen is not for you. But if it sounds like a fabulous California experience, reserve by fax or phone; check the website for more information.

HIKING

The main reason to come to Big Sur is to hike, visit the beaches, and marvel at its magnificent forests. Along Highway 1, the parks offer everything from day use to an overnight stays. Take your pick or visit them all; each is unique and offers different perspectives on the Big Sur region.

Garrapata State Park

The hike around Garrapata State Park (Hwy. 1, 6.7 miles south of Rio Rd., 831/624-4909, www.parks.ca.gov, free) is inspirational. Coastal cliffs drop dramatically to sandy beaches, and mountains of the Santa Lucia Range rise above. There are several access gates, but the main parking area is along the strip of cypress trees.

The **Soberanes Point Trail** is two miles of paths among the wildflowers overlooking the ocean, and the **Rocky Ridge Trail** is a strenuous 4.5-mile hike and climb. The one-mile **North Fork Trail** and 1.5-mile **Peak Trail** branch off to add more distance. The variety of microclimates along the **Sorberanes Canyon Trail,** part of the Rocky Ridge Trail, is amazing. It runs through landscape open to a hillside covered in cacti with willows lining the creek below. Thick patches of sage grow among the coastal flowers that shoot yellows, oranges, and reds into the semiarid scenery. The trail eventually leads to the trickling sound of a creek and a valley of poppies, then into lush forest and up a peak with inspiring ocean vistas.

For a less strenuous hike, the trails on the ocean side of the park are stunning. They meander along the coast at the tops of the cliffs. The trails form a loop with a short spur leading up to Whale Peak. This is a great place to bring binoculars to search for the migrating gray, blue, and humpback whales that frequent Monterey Bay year-round. Look for the spouts of water that shoot up one after another. They travel close to shore and farther off near the horizon. Some trails lead down to the beach, but be cautious, as the tide comes in quickly and large waves often hit these beaches. For your own safety, always obey the state park signs and beach closures. Within the park, Garrapata Beach allows dogs.

Expect few to no facilities; you park in a wide spot on Highway 1, and at most you might find a pit toilet.

◖ Andrew Molera State Park

The first park you encounter driving south from Carmel into the Big Sur region is Andrew Molera State Park (Hwy. 1, 22 miles south of Carmel, 831/667-2315, www.parks.ca.gov, day use $10). Once home to small camps of Native Americans Esselen people, and later a Spanish land grant, this chunk of Big Sur eventually became the Molera ranch, used to grow crops and ranch animals as well as a hunting and fishing retreat for family and friends. In 1965, Frances Molera sold the land to the Nature Conservancy, and when she died three years later the ranch was sold to the California State

Park system as per her will. Today, the **Molera Ranch House Museum** (831/620-0541, bshs@ mbay.net, Sat.-Sun. 11 A.M.-3 P.M.) displays stories of the life and times of Big Sur's pioneers and artists as well as the wildlife and plants of the region. Take the road toward the horse tours to get to the ranch house.

The park has numerous hiking trails that run down to the beach and up into the forest along the river, and many allow biking and horseback riding as well. Most of the park trails are west of the highway. The beach is a one-mile walk down the easy multiuse **Trail Camp Beach Trail.** From there, climb back out on the **Headlands Trail,** a 0.25-mile loop, for a beautiful view from the headlands. If you want a better look at the Big Sur River, take the flat, moderate **Bobcat Trail** (5.5 miles round-trip) and perhaps a few of its ancillary loops. The trail leads right along the riverbank and its microhabitats. Watch out for bicycles and the occasional horse and rider. For an even longer and more difficult trek up the mountains and down to the beach, take the eight-mile **Ridge Bluff Loop.** It starts at the parking lot on the Creamery Meadow Beach Trail, then makes a left onto the long and fairly steep Ridge Trail. Turn left again onto the Panorama Trail, which runs down to the coastal scrublands, and finally out to the Bluffs Trail, which takes you back to Creamery Meadow.

At the park entrance are restrooms but no drinkable water and no food concessions. If you're camping here, bring plenty of your own water for washing as well as drinking. If you're hiking for the day, pack in bottled water and snacks.

◖ Pfeiffer Big Sur State Park

The biggest and most developed park in Big Sur is Pfeiffer Big Sur State Park (47225 Hwy. 1, 831/667-2315, www.parks.ca.gov, day-use $10). It has the Big Sur Lodge, a restaurant and café, a shop, an amphitheater, a somewhat incongruous softball field, plenty of hiking-only

BIG SUR'S SECRET SEA OTTERS

© KRISTIN LEAL

These otters are the direct descendants from the Big Sur colony that saved the species.

The Spanish became known as the first sea otter hunters in the late 18th century as they began to establish settlements along the California coast. They were after the pelts, a sign of wealth and high fashion in Europe and Asia, especially in Russia and Britain. During this period, the pelts could easily be sold overseas. Sea otters were hunted all along the northern shores of California, and thousands of sea otter pelts were exported every year. By the early 19th century the mammals were nearly hunted to extinction, and by the 1840s commercial sea otter hunting had collapsed.

At one time it was believed that the species was extinct. It wasn't until 1915 that a small group was discovered in the remote reaches of Big Sur. Protected in a hidden cove, local people kept them secret until 1938, when Highway 1 was constructed and they could be seen from the road above. Today, all California sea otters are direct descendants of the Big Sur colony and have been protected by law as a threatened species under the 1972 Endangered Species Act.

trails, and lovely redwood-shaded campsites. This park isn't near the beach but rather up in the coastal redwood forest, with a network of roads that can be driven or biked into the trees and along the Big Sur River.

Pfeiffer Big Sur has the tiny **Ernest Ewoldsen Memorial Nature Center,** which features

stuffed examples of local wildlife. It's open seasonally; call the park for operating hours. Another historic exhibit is the **Homestead Cabin,** once the home of part of the Pfeiffer family-the first European immigrants to settle in Big Sur. Day-trippers and overnight visitors can take a stroll through the cabins of the Big

© KRISTIN LEAL

Driftwood at Andrew Molera State Park is perfect for building forts.

Sur Lodge, built by the Civilian Conservation Corps during the Great Depression.

No bicycles or horses are allowed on trails in this park, which makes it quite peaceful for hikers. For a starter walk, take the easy 0.7-mile **Nature Trail,** a loop from Day Use Parking Lot 2. Grab a brochure at the lodge to learn about the park's plantlife as you walk the trail. For a longer stroll, head out on the popular **Pfeiffer Falls Trail** (1.5 miles round-trip). You'll find stairs on the steep sections and footbridges across the creek, then a lovely platform at the base of the 60-foot waterfall, where you can rest and relax halfway through the hike. For a longer, more difficult, and interesting hike deeper into the Big Sur wilderness, start at the Homestead Cabin and head to the difficult **Mount Manuel Trail** (10 miles round-trip). From the Y intersection with the Oak Grove Trail, it's four miles of strenuous hiking to Mount Manuel, one of the most spectacular peaks in the area.

Need to cool off after hiking? Scramble out to the entirely undeveloped Big Sur River Gorge, where the river slows and creates pools that are great for swimming. Relax and enjoy the water, but don't try to dive in.

This is one of the few Big Sur parks to offer a full array of services. Before you head out into the woods, stop at the Big Sur Lodge restaurant and store complex to get a meal and some water and to load up on snacks and sweatshirts. Between the towering trees and the summer fog, it can get quite chilly and somewhat damp on the trails.

Julia Pfeiffer Burns State Park

One of the best-known and easiest hikes in the Big Sur region is in Julia Pfeiffer Burns State Park (Hwy. 1, 12 miles south of Pfeiffer Big Sur State Park, 831/667-2315, www.parks.ca.gov, $10). The **Overlook Trail** (0.7 miles round-trip) is along a level wheelchair-friendly boardwalk. Stroll under Highway 1, past the Pelton wheelhouse, and out to the observation deck for a stunning view of McWay Falls.

The medium-size waterfall cascades year-round from a cliff onto the beach of a remote cove, where the water wets the sand and trickles into the sea. The cove gleams bright blue against the off-white sand—it looks more like the South Pacific than Northern California. Anyone with an ounce of love for the ocean would want to build a hut right there beside the waterfall, but the reason the beach is pristine and empty is that there's no way down to the cove that's even remotely safe.

The tiny Pelton wheel exhibit off the Overlook Trail isn't much unless you're a fan of hydraulic engineering history. It does have an interpretive exhibit, including the old Pelton wheel itself, describing what a Pelton wheel is and what it does. This is the only museum at the park, although there's a small visitors center adjacent to the parking lot.

If you're up for a longer hike after taking in the falls, go back the other direction to the **Ewoldsen Trail** (moderate-difficult, 4.5 miles round-trip). This trek takes you through McWay Canyon, and you'll see the creek and surrounding lush greenery on the walk. The trail then loops away from the water and climbs into the hills. Be sure to bring drinking water, as this hike can take several hours.

If you want to spend the day at Julia Pfeiffer Burns State Park, drive north from the park entrance to the Partington Cove pullout and park along the side of Highway 1. On the east side of the highway, start out along the **Tanbark Trail** (difficult, 6.4 miles round-trip). You'll walk through redwood groves and up steep switchbacks to the top of the coastal ridge. Bring your camera to record the stunning views before you head back down the fire road to your car.

The Ventana Backcountry

Some savage terrain can be found in the remote wilderness of the Los Padres National Forest

Ventana Backcountry (831/385-5434, www.fs.usda.gov). There are several entry points, but some of the more common trailheads are at Bottchers Gap, Big Sur Station, and Plaskett Creek Campground. If you are a first-timer, start at Big Sur Station; the visitors center can provide a map and information about the region before you venture into the wild.

The 167,323 acres of wilderness has steep hillsides, sharp ridges, and deep V-shaped valleys with thermal springs, waterfalls, and deep pools. The climate is mild except in the winter months, when heavy storms drop massive amounts of water and make the area unpredictably rugged.

Hiking here is not to be undertaken casually, as the elevation gains range 600-5,750 feet. Expect solitude in the thick redwood forest, chaparral meadows, rocky river banks, and deep canyons. There are 273 miles of trails with access to 55 designated primitive camping sites.

Sykes Hot Springs

In the backcountry of Big Sur and the Ventana Wilderness is popular Sykes Hot Springs, a 20-mile round-trip hike on the Sykes Trail that requires at least an overnight stay at Sykes Campground. The best way to access the trail is at **Big Sur Station No. 1** (47555 Hwy. 1, 831/667-2315, www.parks.ca.gov, parking $5 per night), where you can pick up a detailed map.

The hike, through grand redwood groves and rolling chaparral, is breathtaking. The terrain is challenging in places, even for avid hikers, with steep inclines in both directions. At the end of the trail, the reward is nature's soothing riches—the Big Sur River and Sykes Hot Springs.

The natural hot-spring pools are terraced above the Big Sur River. The largest is about 10 feet across and bubbles at an average temperature of 100°F; it can accommodate about six adults. Depending on the flow of the springs, you are likely to find other smaller pools marked by past visitors with cairns. This is a popular destination in peak months (Apr.-Sept.) but quieter midweek and in the off-season (Nov.-Mar.).

HORSEBACK RIDING

You can take a guided horseback ride into the forest or onto the beaches of Andrew Molera State Park with **Molera Horseback Tours** (831/625-5486, http://molerahorsebacktours. com, $25-60). In spring and summer, tours of 1-2.5 hours depart daily at 9 A.M.—call ahead to guarantee a spot, or take a chance and just show up at the stables 15 minutes ahead of time. Call ahead if you want to ride in fall or winter. You can also call to book a private guided ride. Each ride takes you from the modest corral area along multiuse trails through forests and meadows or along the Big Sur River and down to Molera Beach.

Molera Horseback Tours are suitable for children over age six and riders of all ability levels; you'll be paired with the right horse. All rides go down to the beach. Guides share their knowledge of the Big Sur region and wildlife, and they welcome questions about the plantlife. Early morning and sunset rides tend to be the prettiest and most popular.

FISHING

There are no harbors around Big Sur for ocean-going charters, but shore and river fishing is possible with a rod and reel. Steelhead run up the Big Sur River to spawn each year, and a limited fishing season follows them up the river into **Pfeiffer Big Sur State Park** and other accessible areas. Steelhead season runs roughly form December 1 to March 7 but is subject to change depending on inland river flow. You can call the local **Steelhead and Trout Fishing Hotline** at 831/649-2886 for up to date river fishing information. Check with Fernwood Resort (831/667-2422, www.fernwoodbigsur. com) and other lodges around Highway 1 for the best fishing spots.

the Big Sur River

The numerous creeks that feed the Big Sur River are also home to fish. Cast for trout in the creeks of Pfeiffer Big Sur and other clear-water streams in the area. The California Department of Fish and Game (www.dfg.ca.gov) can give you specific locations and dates to fish legally, along with the regulations.

To fish in the ocean, you can cast from several beaches for the rockfish that inhabit near-shore reefs. **Garrapata State Beach** has a good fishing area.

SCUBA DIVING

Big Sur has no services for beginning divers or diver training, but experienced divers can expect cold water-temperatures are in the mid-50s in the shallows and into the 40s as you dive deeper. Visibility is 20-30 feet, although rough sea conditions can diminish it significantly; the best season for clear water is September-November.

The biggest and most interesting dive locale is the **Julia Pfeiffer Burns State Park**

© KRISTIN LEAL

(Hwy. 1, 12 miles south of Pfeiffer Big Sur, 831/667-2315, www.parks.ca.gov, daily sunrise-sunset). You have to prove your diving experience and get a special permit at Big Sur Station to dive at this protected underwater park, part of Monterey Bay National Marine Sanctuary along with the rest of the Big Sur coast. You can enter the water from the shore only, which gives you the chance to see the various ecosystems before heading out to the rocky reefs and the kelp forests.

Divers at access-hostile **Jade Cove** (Hwy. 1, 2 miles south of Sand Dollar State Beach) aren't usually interested in cute colorful nudibranchs or even majestic gray whales. Jade Cove divers stalk wily semiprecious jade pebbles and rocks. Jade striates the coastline here, and storms tear clumps of it out of the cliffs and into the sea. It settles just offshore of the tiny cove, and divers hunt jewelry—quality stones to sell for profit.

If you're looking for a guided scuba tour of the Big Sur region, contact **Adventure Sports Unlimited** (303 Potrero St., Suite 15, Santa Cruz, 831/458-3648, www.asudoit.com), or the **Under Water Company** (831/915-6600) in Monterey for deep-water trips and technical expeditions with Phil Sammet.

BIRD-WATCHING

Many visitors come to Big Sur just to see the birds. The coast is home to numerous species, from tiny bush tits to pelicans. The most famous avian residents of this area are no doubt the rare and endangered California condors. By the 1980s condors were all but extinct, with only a few left alive in captivity, and conservationists struggling to help them breed. Today, more than 30 birds soar above the trails and beaches of Big Sur. You might even see one swooping low over your car on Highway 1. You'll definitely know it if this happens: A condor's wingspan can exceed nine feet. Check with the park rangers for the best times and places to see condors.

The **Ventana Wilderness Society** (VWS, www.ventanaws.org) watches over many of the endangered and protected avian species in Big Sur. As part of their mission to raise awareness of the condors and many other birds, the VWS offers bird-watching expeditions; these can be simple two-hour tours or overnight wilderness camping trips, depending on your level of interest. Check their website for schedules and rates. One of the hot spots of VWS conservation efforts and tours is Andrew Molera State Park, where you can also head out on your own to look for some of the most interesting species in the Big Sur area.

EVENTS AND ENTERTAINMENT

The primary entertainment in Big Sur involves outdoor activities, but if you need a bit more, there are a few events and entertainment options.

Each year in October, Pacific Valley School hosts the fund-raising **Big Sur Jade Festival** (www.bigsurjadeco.com/festival.html). Come to the school, located across Highway 1 from Sand Dollar State Beach, to see the artists, craftspeople, jewelry makers, and rock hunters displaying their wares. Munch on snacks and enjoy live music. Check the website for more details.

Every year on October 31, Nepenthe in Big Sur is known to throw a freaky Halloween bash, the **Halloween Ball Masque** (831/667-2345, www.nepenthebigsur.com). Things get psychedelic with everyone dressed in trippy costumes.

Celebrate the harvest at **Big Sur Food and Wine** (831/667-0800, www.bigsurfoodandwine.org) in November. Taste the wealth of the Big Sur region with the creative culinary artistry and hospitality of local chefs.

The best marathon in Northern California is widely said to be the **Big Sur International Marathon** (831/625-6226, www.bsim.org) in late April-early May. It has a breathtaking course along majestic Highway 1. For nearly 30 years the annual event has included a marathon; a marathon relay; walking or running races of 21, 10.6, and 9 miles; a 5K; and a children's 3K fun run.

Live Music

It probably won't be a surprise to learn that Big Sur is not a hotbed of cutting-edge clubs and bars. Most visitors spend their days outside engaged in vigorous activity and thus go to bed early. If you just can't bear to hit the sack before 10 P.M., you can find some fun at the **Fernwood Tavern** (Hwy. 1, 831/667-2422, Sun.-Thurs. noon-midnight, Fri.-Sat. noon-1 A.M.). Live music entertain locals and visitors alike, and you might hear country, folk, or even indie rock from the small stage. Most live music happens on the weekend, especially Saturday night, starting at 9 P.M. Even without the music, the tavern can get lively in the evening (it's good to be the only game in town), with locals drinking at the full bar, eating, and holding parties in the meandering dim rooms.

Spas

The **Spa at Ventana** (831/667-4222, www.ventanainn.com, fall-spring daily 9 A.M.-7 P.M., summer daily 9 A.M.-8 P.M., 50-minute massage $120) offers a large menu of spa treatments for guests and nonguests. You'll love the serene atmosphere of the treatment and waiting areas. Greenery and weathered wood create a unique relaxing atmosphere. Indulge in a soothing massage, purifying body treatment, or rejuvenating or beautifying facial. Take your spa experience a step further in true Big Sur fashion with a Reiki or craniosacral treatment, or go for a private New Age reading, a personal yoga or meditation session, or a private guided hike. If you're a guest of the hotel, you can have your spa treatment in your room or on your own private deck.

Just across the highway from the Ventana, the **Post Ranch Inn and Spa** (Hwy. 1, 831/667-2200, 1-hour massage $140) is another ultra-high-end resort spa. Massage, body, and facial work focuses on organics as well as gem and crystal therapies.

You can also indulge in private sessions, including shamanic meetings that focus on indigenous techniques that are said to enhance life.

CAMPING

Many visitors to Big Sur want to experience the unspoiled beauty of the landscape. Many of the parks and lodges in the area have overnight campgrounds, from full-service RV-accessible areas to environmental tent campsites and wilderness backpacking. You can camp in a state park or out behind one of the small resort motels near a restaurant and a store and even by the cool refreshing Big Sur River.

Andrew Molera State Park

Andrew Molera State Park (Hwy. 1, 22 miles south of Carmel, 831/667-2315, www.parks.ca.gov, $35) offers 24 walk-in, tent-only campsites located 0.25-0.5 miles from the parking lot via a level well-maintained trail. You pitch your tent in a pretty meadow near the Big Sur River at sites that include picnic tables and a fire rings. No reservations are taken, so come early in summer to get one of the prime spots under a tree. While you're camping, look for bobcats, foxes, deer, raccoons (stow your food securely), and a wide variety of bird species.

As of 2007, no potable water was available at Andrew Molera. Toilets are a short walk from the camping area, but showers are not available.

Fernwood Resort

The Fernwood Resort (Hwy. 1, 831/667-2422, www.fernwoodbigsur.com, $45-75 camping, $108 adventure tent, $195 cabins) maintains a large campground area on both sides of the Big Sur River. You can pitch your own tent, pull in an RV, or rent a tent cabin. The resort has easy access to the river, where you can swim, inner tube, and hike. You'll also have access to the restaurant, store, and tavern.

Tent cabins are canvas spaces with room for four people in a double bed and two twins. You can pull your car right up to the back of your cabin. Bring your own linens or sleeping bags, pillows, and towels. Hot showers and restrooms are a short walk away. Tent campsites are scattered in great places—tucked in by the river or under shady redwood trees. You can even park your RV under a tree at sites with water and electric hookups.

Pfeiffer Big Sur State Park

The biggest and most developed campground in Big Sur is Pfeiffer Big Sur State Park (Hwy. 1, 800/444-7275, www.parks.ca.gov, $35, river view $50), with 212 individual sites, each of which can take two vehicles and eight people, RVs up to 32 feet, or trailers up to 27 feet. There is a dump station on-site. During the summer, a grocery store and laundry facilities operate in the campground, and plenty of flush toilets and hot showers are scattered throughout. In the evening, walk down to the

© KRISTIN LEAL

the Ventana backcountry

Campfire Center for entertaining and educational programs. If you prefer a quieter and less asphalt-oriented camping experience, check out the hike-in and bike-in campgrounds that make up part of the Pfeiffer Big Sur complex.

Pfeiffer Big Sur fills up fast in the summer, especially on weekends. Advance reservations (800/444-7275, www.reserveamerica.com) are strongly recommended.

Primitive Camping

The wilderness area of the Big Sur region is the **Los Padres National Forest,** with good primitive camping at 55 designated sites in the backcountry. Get a free wilderness and fire permit from the Los Padres National Forest District Office (805/385-5434, www.campone.com). Good trailheads with backcountry access are Bottchers Gap and Big Sur Station.

Palo Colorado Road, off Highway 1, runs eight miles to **Bottchers Gap** (805/968-6640). Two major trails start here and lead in opposite directions into the wilderness. There are three primitive sites in the redwood forest at **Jackson Camp,** five miles in from Bottchers Gap; **Pico Blanco Camp** is seven miles in. Up the Skinner Ridge Trail are plenty of rugged campsites and difficult terrain to explore. **Apple Tree Camp** is a little over three miles in, and **Turner Creek Camp** is five miles in. Devils Peak has nice campsites just one mile beyond **Cummings Camp.** For a good look at the Carmel watershed drainage, check out Pine Creek, 6.5 miles in, and Pat Springs, eight miles in. There is also the extreme 60-mile Big Sur loop for the adventurous; it has primitive camping all along the way.

Entering the Ventana Backcountry from the **Big Sur Station** can lead in several directions into the heart of the backwoods. Stop in at the visitors center for a detailed map of the area before you head out. From this entrance, **Ventana Camp** can easily be reached in a day, **Barlow Flat Camp** is deep in the backcountry, and **Tassajara**

Camp, near the Tassajara Hot Springs, is a well-known spot for a seriously relaxing soak at the Tassajara Zen Mountain Center.

ACCOMMODATIONS
Under $150

When locals speak of Deetjens, they could be referring to the inn, the restaurant, or the family that created both. But they do speak of Deetjens, which operates as a nonprofit organization dedicated to offering visitors to the Big Sur region great hospitality for reasonable rates. To stay at **Deetjens Big Sur Inn** (48865 Hwy. 1, 831/667-2377, www.deetjens.com, $80-250) is to enjoy a small part of Big Sur history and culture. It may not look like a spot where legions of famous writers, artists, and Hollywood stars have slept, but Deetjens can indeed boast a guest list that many hostelries in Beverly Hills would kill for. And yet the motley collection of buildings has also welcomed transient artists, San Francisco bohemians, and the occasional criminal looking for a spot to sleep as they traveled the coast by bicycle or even on foot. Your guest room will be unique, decorated with the art and collectibles chosen and arranged by Grandpa Deetjen many moons ago. The inn prides itself on its rustic historic construction—expect thin weathered walls, funky cabin construction, no outdoor locks on the doors, and an altogether unique experience. Many guest rooms have shared baths, but you can request a room with a private bath when you make reservations. Deetjens prefers to offer a serene environment, and to that end does not permit children under 12 unless you rent both rooms in a two-room building. Deetjens has no TVs or stereos, no phones in the guest rooms, and no cell phone service. Two pay phones are available for emergencies, but other than that, you're cut off from the outside world. Decide for yourself whether this sounds terrifying or wonderful.

For a rustic cabin experience, check into the **Ripplewood Resort** (47020 Hwy. 1, 831/667-2242 or 800/575-1735, www.ripplewoodresort.com, $95-175). It is like stepping back in time as the cabins are simple redwood structures, the smaller ones only a few steps up from tent camping. The 17 cabins, most with kitchens, are along the Big Sur River deep in the redwoods and are suitable for young couples and small families. With limited space, you have to book ahead; for summer you may have to book a year ahead.

For more rustic cabins, try **Riverside Campgrounds and Cabins** (40720 Hwy. 1, 831/667-2414, www.riversidecampground.com, $95-180), with 11 cabins that can accommodate up to four people; some allow dogs. Within the beautiful natural wood interiors are queen and double beds. Many of the cabins have decks and outdoor fireplaces. The river is nearby, making an afternoon float in an inner tube a must.

Along Highway 1 in the village of Big Sur are a couple of small motels, including **Fernwood Resort** (Hwy. 1, 831/667-2422, www.fernwoodbigsur.com, $95-200). The low-slung sprawling buildings have a 12-room motel, a small grocery and convenience store, a restaurant, and a tavern that passes for the local nighttime hot spot. Farther down the small road is the campground, with tent cabins as well as tent and RV sites. If all this a "resort" makes, so be it. Motel rooms are modest spaces in a blocky, one-level building beside the main store and restaurant buildings. Not much sunlight gets into the guest rooms, but the decor is light-colored and reasonably attractive. Guest rooms have queen beds and attached private baths but no TVs. If you tend to get chilly in the winter or in the summer fog, ask for a room with a gas stove. One room has a two-person hot tub just outside on the back deck. In the summer months, book in advance to be sure of getting a room, especially on weekends.

Another lodge-style motel set in a redwood forest, the **Big Sur River Inn** (Hwy. 1 at Pheneger Creek, 800/548-3610, www.

bigsurriverinn.com, $125-150) is in one of the "populated" parts of Big Sur. First opened in the 1930s by a member of the locally famous Pfeiffer family, the inn has been in continuous operation ever since. Today, it boasts 20 motel rooms, a restaurant, and a gift shop. Guest rooms are small but comfortable, with chain-motel comforters and curtains juxtaposed with rustic lodge-style wooden interior paneling. Budget-conscious guest rooms have one queen bed. Families and small groups can choose between standard rooms with two queen beds and two-room suites with multiple beds and attractive back decks that look out over the Big Sur River. All guests can enjoy the attractively landscaped outdoor pool with its surrounding lawn leading down to the river. The attached restaurant serves three meals a day. Be sure to make reservations in advance, especially for summertime weekends.

$150-250

If you want to stay inside one of the parks but tents just aren't your style, book a cabin at the **Big Sur Lodge** (47225 Hwy. 1, 800/424-4787, www.bigsurlodge.com, $159-369) in Pfeiffer Big Sur State Park. The lodge was built in the 1930s as a New Deal government works project to create jobs for people suffering through the Great Depression—by then Big Sur's astounding beauty and peace had been recognized by both federal and state governments, and much of the land was protected as parks. Although the amenities have been updated, the cabins of Big Sur Lodge still evoke the classic woodsy vacation cabin. Set in a redwood forest with an array of paths and small roads, the cabins feature patchwork quilts, rustic furniture, understated decor, and simple but clean baths. Many cabins have lots of beds—perfect for larger families or groups of adults traveling together. The largest cabins have fireplaces and kitchens. You can stock your kitchen at the on-site grocery store, or just get a meal at the lodge's

restaurant or café. The lodge has a swimming pool for those rare sunny summer days, but the real attraction is access to the Pfeiffer Big Sur trails right outside your door. Leave your car outside your room and hike all day in the park. Or take a short drive to one of the other state parks and enjoy their charms for free with proof of occupancy at Big Sur Lodge. Note that staying at the state park grants you access to all state parks for your stay; simply display your lodging tag on your car windshield.

One of the most romantic and affordable digs is at ◖ **Glen Oaks Big Sur** (Hwy. 1, 831/667-2105, www.glenoaksbigsur.com, $155-300). You can stay at the lodge, a cozy cabin, or the Oak Tree Cottage. The guest rooms in the lodge are modern and spacious, while the cabins are fully functional with full kitchens, outdoor decks, and plenty of space to spread out. There are cabins with river views and forest views.

Over $250

If money is no object, you cannot beat the lodgings at the ◖ **Ventana Inn** (48123 Hwy. 1, 800/628-6500, www.ventanainn.com, $600-1,350), a place where the panoramic ocean views begin in the parking lot. This might well be the best hotel in the state. Picture home-baked pastries, fresh yogurt, in-season fruit, and organic coffee delivered to your guest room in the morning, then enjoying that sumptuous breakfast outdoors on your own private patio overlooking a wildflower-strewn meadow that sweeps out toward the blue-gray waters of the ocean. And that's just the beginning of an unbelievable day at the Ventana. Next, don your plush spa robe and rubber slippers (that's all you are required to wear on the grounds of the hotel and spa) and head for the Japanese bathhouse. Choose from two bathhouses, one at each end of the property. Both are clothing-optional and gender segregated, and the upper house has glass and open-air windows that let you look out to the ocean. Two swimming pools offer a cooler respite; the lower pool is clothing-optional, and the upper pool perches on a high spot for enthralling views. Almost every other amenity imaginable, including daily complimentary yoga classes, are available. Guest rooms range from "modest" standard rooms with king beds, tasteful exposed cedar walls and ceilings, and attractive green and earth-tone appointments to gorgeous spacious suites and full-size multiple-bedroom houses. If you have the resources, the Vista Suites boast the most beautiful hotel accommodations imaginable. You reach the guest rooms by walking along paved paths crowded by lush landscaping, primarily California native plants that complement the wilds of the trails behind the main hotel buildings. You can also take an evening stroll down to the Cielo dining room—the only spot on the property where you have to wear more than your robe and flip-flops. If you're headed to the Allegria Spa for a treatment, you can go comfy and casual.

Post Ranch (47900 Hwy. 1, 800/527-2200, www.postranchinn.com, $550-2,285) is another exclusive luxury resort perched on the cliffs of Big Sur. Spa, yoga, and a unique yet rustic atmosphere are just a few of its amenities. The outdoors is highlighted throughout the handcrafted tree houses, guest rooms, and private houses with ocean and forest views. Guest rooms are far from modest but still have the rustic flair of Big Sur. Make sure to check out the resort activities, which include locally guided hikes. In the evening, enjoy the custom-built furniture by the fire and watch the sunset over the ocean from your glass-walled private suite.

FOOD

As you travel the famed Highway 1 through Big Sur, you'll quickly realize that a ready meal isn't something to take for granted. You'll see no McDonald's, Starbucks, 7-Elevens, or Safeways lining the road. While you can find groceries, they tend to appear in small markets attached to motels. The motels and resorts usually have restaurants attached as well, but they're not all meals all-day or 24-hour places. Plan in advance to make it for meals during standard hours, and expect to have dinner fairly early. Pick up staple supplies before you enter the area if you don't plan to leave again for a few days to avoid paying a premium at the minimarts.

Casual Dining

Serving three meals each day to lodge guests and other travelers, the **Big Sur Lodge Café and Restaurant** (47225 Hwy. 1, 800/242-4787, www.bigsurlodge.com, daily 7 A.M.-9 P.M., $25) has a dining room as well as a cute espresso and ice cream bar out front. The dining room dishes up a full menu of American classics for every meal, and you can grab a quick sandwich to go from the espresso bar.

Grab a burger and get your feet wet at the **◖ River Inn** (46840 Hwy. 1, at Pheneger Creek, 831/667-2700 or 800/548-3610, www.bigsurriverinn.com, $15-37). When the locals want to cool off in Big Sur, they grab a drink from this full bar and sit in the river. Outside you will find that there are a few scattered wooden chairs sitting right in the water.

The **Redwood Grill** (Hwy. 1, 831/667-2129, www.fernwoodbigsur.com, daily 11:30 A.M.-9 P.M., $25) at Fernwood Resort looks and feels like a grill in the woods ought to. Even in the middle of the afternoon, the aging wood-paneled interior is dimly lit and strewn with slightly saggy couches and casual tables and chairs. Walk up to the counter to order somewhat overpriced burgers and sandwiches, then on to the bar to grab a soda or a beer.

The northernmost dining option on the Big Sur coast, **Rocky Point Restaurant** (36700 Hwy. 1, 831/624-2933, www.rocky-point.com, daily 9 A.M.-3 P.M. and 5 P.M.-close, $40) offers decent food and great views. Enjoy the smell of mesquite from the grill as you wait for your steak or fish. Meat eaters will find solid dishes for breakfast, lunch, and dinner, but vegetarian options are limited.

The ◖ **Big Sur Bakery** (47540 Hwy. 1, 831/667-0520, www.bigsurbakery.com, lunch Tues.-Fri. 11 A.M.-2:30 P.M., Sat.-Sun. 10:30 A.M.-2:30 P.M., dinner Tues.-Sun. 5:30 P.M.-close, $45) might sound like a casual walk-up eating establishment, and the bakery part of it is. You can stop in from 8 A.M. every day to grab a freshly baked scone, homemade jelly doughnut, or a flaky croissant sandwich for lunch later on. But on the dining-room side, an elegant surprise awaits diners who've spent the day hiking the redwoods and strolling the beaches. Be sure to make reservations, or you're unlikely to get a table. This organic gourmet restaurant features ingredients grown in the Big Sur region, and there's even a garden on-site. For your meal, sit outside beneath a redwood canopy or inside the warm cabin—both are majestic. Don't forget to grab some local Big Sur honey to go.

According to Big Sur locals, the best breakfast in the area is at **Deetjens** (48865 Hwy. 1, 831/667-2377, www.deetjens.com, breakfast and dinner daily, $20-35). The funky dining room, with its mismatched tables, dark wooden chairs, and cluttered wall decor, belies the high quality of the cuisine served. Enjoy delectable dishes created from the freshest local ingredients for breakfast and then again at dinnertime.

Fine Dining

You don't need to be a guest at the gorgeous Ventana to enjoy a fine gourmet dinner at ◖ **The Restaurant at Ventana** (Hwy. 1, 831/667-4242, www.ventanainn.com, daily noon-3:30 P.M. and 6-9 P.M., $30-40). The spacious dining room has a warm wood fire, an open kitchen, and comfortable banquettes with throw pillows. On a sunny day, get a table outside to enjoy the stunning views. The dining room inside has great views from the bay windows too, along with white tablecloths and pretty light wood furniture. The chef offers California cuisine made with organic produce and local meats as well as some seafood offerings. If you're vegetarian or have dietary restrictions, the chefs can whip up something special for you. The best value is the prix fixe menu, with a choice of several courses, and be sure to save room for dessert.

When you dine at ◖**Nepenthe** (48510 Hwy. 1, 831/667-2345, www.nepenthebigsur.com, daily 11:30 A.M.-10 P.M., $35), be sure to ask for a table outdoors even on a partly sunny day. The restaurant offers a short but tasty menu of meat, fish, and plenty of vegetarian dishes.

On an outdoor patio, the seasonal **Café Kevah** at Nepenthe (Mar.-Jan. daily breakfast and lunch, $15-18) offers a similar sampling of breakfast items and sandwiches at slightly lower prices.

The **Sierra Mar** (47900 Hwy. 1, 831/667-2800, www.postranchinn.com, daily 8-10:30 A.M., noon-3 P.M., and 3-9 P.M., $110) restaurant at the Post Ranch Inn offers a decadent four-course prix fixe dinner menu in a stunning ocean-view setting. Casual lunch and snacks are served through the afternoon, but expect to dress up for a formal white-tablecloth dinner experience at this very upscale restaurant.

Markets

With no supermarkets or chain minimarts anywhere in the Big Sur region, the local markets do a booming business. You can stock up on staples such as bread, lunch meat, eggs, milk, marshmallows, and graham crackers at various local stores. In town, the full-service **Fernwood Resort** (Hwy. 1, 831/667-2422, www.fernwoodbigsur.com) has a market. You'll also find a seasonal market in the campground at Pfeiffer Big Sur State Park.

Lucia to San Simeon

Beyond the coastal village of Big Sur are several small unincorporated villages with small populations. Driving south along Highway 1 you'll pass through Lucia, Gorda, and Ragged Point. As you travel this stretch of highway you will find many state and federal recreation areas that provide four-by-four driving opportunities, camping, hiking, fishing, beaches, accommodations, and a few stops to grab a bite to eat.

BEACHES
Jade Beach Reserve
Several beaches in the southern part of the Big Sur region are known for jade, including Jade Beach Reserve (Hwy. 1, 9.7 miles south of Lucia, www.campone.com, daily 30 minutes before sunrise-30 minutes after sunset), a U.S. Forest Service reserve marked by a road sign but not much else. You can park in the dirt-and-gravel strip along the road and walk past the fence into the park. Read the unusual signs along the narrow path that seems to lead to the edge of a cliff explaining that you cannot bring in mining equipment or take away rocks or minerals obtained from above the high-tide line. You can, however, hang-glide off the cliffs here.

From the top of the cliff, the short trail becomes rough. It's only 0.25 miles, but it's almost straight down a rocky, slippery cliff face. Don't climb down if you're not in reasonably good physical condition, and even if you are, use your hands to steady yourself. At the bottom, you'll find huge boulders and smaller rocks but very little sand. You may also see a small herd of people dressed in wetsuits and scuba gear hunting for jade. But most of all, you'll find amazing minerals in the boulders and rocks. Reach out and touch a multiple-ton boulder shot through with jade, and search the smaller rocks beneath your feet for chunks of sea-polished jade. If you're a hard-core rock hound, you can join the locals scuba diving for jewelry-quality jade. As long as you find it in the water or below the high-tide line, it's legal to take whatever you find.

Willow Creek
Another location to find pieces of jade is Willow Creek (Hwy. 1, 62 miles south of Carmel, 831/385-5434, www.campone.com, daily 30 minutes before sunrise-30 minutes after sunset), tucked away under one of the many Highway 1 bridges where freshwater cuts through a dark pebbly beach and spills into the foam of the ocean. The combination of strong tides and a decaying hillside rich with natural deposits of jade makes it an ideal spot for digging. Willow Creek has parking practically on the sand, and dogs are allowed.

Mill Creek
If you are looking for an easy-access launch spot for your kayak along the Big Sur coast, Mill Creek (53 miles south of Carmel, 805/434-1996, www.campone.com, daily 30 minutes before sunrise-30 minutes after sunset) is the spot. The parking is just a few steps from the water near the put-in spot, but be careful as the path to the water is a bit rough with a cluster of rocks to walk over. Locals frequent this location to fish from the bluffs and rocks. There are no amenities besides pit toilets and the paved parking lot.

Sand Dollar State Beach
An impressive spot for surfing and lounging is Sand Dollar State Beach (60 miles south of Carmel, www.campone.com, daily 30 minutes before sunrise-30 minutes after sunset, 805/434-1996). The breakers are far enough off shore to provide a pleasant ride. Sunbathers will find plenty of secluded spots on the longest beach in the region. At low tide, there is

© KRISTIN LEAL

Take a walk along Sand Dollar State Beach and explore a sea cave during low tide.

an interesting cave to explore, but keep an eye out for the incoming tide, as it floods the cave.

PARKS
Limekiln State Park

There is plenty of outdoor action and good camping at 717-acre Limekiln State Park (52 miles south of Carmel, 831/667-2403, www.parks. ca.gov, $8). Besides the historical limekilns, there are deep-woods hiking trails and beach kayaking, fishing, and swimming. Squirrels, deer, foxes, and raccoons are often seen, attracted by the two creeks in the park. Mountain lions, bobcats, and ring-tailed cats are much more elusive but are known to roam the area.

In the thick redwoods and along a sheltered cove are 33 campsites (summer by reservation, winter first-come, first-served, $35) that can accommodate RVs up to 24 feet. The three sections of the campground are the Beach, Lower Creek, and Redwood Campgrounds.

The day-use parking is limited to 12 spots, but you can park in the pullouts along Highway 1 just above the park. Day-use activities include picnicking, good shore fishing, and kayaking from the beach. Three hiking trails start just beyond the Redwood Campground. The Limekiln Trail is a 0.5-mile hike to the cluster of historic lime kilns. The Falls Trail branches off the Limekiln Trail and leads to a 100-foot waterfall; be prepared to get your feet wet. The Hare Creek Trail is an easy hike through the majestic redwood forest alongside the rushing water.

OFF-ROADING

South past the village of Lucia are three good dusty off-road routes in the Los Padres National Forest (831/386-2513). **Nacimiento-Fergusson Road** is just across Highway 1 from Kirk Creek Campground. The paved road meanders for 19 miles with off-road spurs all along the way. **Plaskett Ridge Road** is a five-mile ride with challenging ruts. It is a nice beginner venture with wide turnarounds and mild inclines that connect up with the outlets along Nacimiento-Fergusson Road, and it has many places to pull off for a picnic. It starts just beyond Sand Dollar State Beach, at the back side of Plaskett Creek Campground. The third route, **Willow Creek Road,** runs eight miles to **South Coast Road,** a 24-mile intermediate-level venture into the San Lucia Range for skilled drivers; it has steep grades, tight turns, rough ruts, rock crawls, washed-out sections, and no outlet. It becomes an expert course after wet weather.

FISHING
Cast off from several beaches, including Sand Dollar State Beach, for the rockfish that scurry around the near-shore reefs. Other good spots are Mill Creek and Limekiln State Park.

CAMPING
Limekiln State Park
The small but pretty campground at Limekiln State Park (Hwy. 1, 2 miles south of Lucia, 831/667-2403, www.parks.ca.gov, $5) has 33 campsites with hot showers and flush toilets out an attractive creek that runs toward the nearby ocean. RVs and trailers up to 24 feet are welcome, but hookups and dump stations aren't available. In the summer, make reservations early. In the winter, no reservations are taken, and many sites are closed; call ahead in winter.

Kirk Creek Campground
On bluffs overlooking the ocean, Kirk Creek Campground (55 miles south of Carmel, 805/434-1996, 877/444-6777, www.campone.com, reservations www.recreation.gov, $22) has 34 campsites with full panoramic view of the ocean. Reservations are a must to stay at this jewel of Big Sur.

Hikers can access the Los Padres National Forest's Ventana Wilderness from the Nacimiento-Fergusson Road, just across the highway. The backcountry has secluded

waterfalls, shaded streams, and sun-drenched canyons to discover.

Plaskett Creek Campground
Tucked in the shade of Monterey pines and cypress trees, Plaskett Creek Campground (60 miles south of Carmel, 877/444-6777, www.campone.com, reservations www.recreation.gov, $22) welcomes tents and RVs, with 44 sites, restrooms, fire rings, and pedestal grills.

Outdoors enthusiasts will find abundant recreation opportunities in the Los Padres National Forest's Ventana Wilderness. The largest stretch of sandy beach in Big Sur is just across the highway, the surfing is consistently good, and you can fish from shore or sunbathe.

Primitive Camping
There are many primitive campsites off the Nacimiento-Ferguson Road. About 11 miles in, the small **Nacimiento Campground** is alongside a mountain trout stream. Keep heading east for the **Ponderosa Campground,** with 23 sites with fire rings, picnic tables, and pedestal grills. Farther east along the road are several more primitive campsites.

Some great primitive camping is along four-by-four-only Willow Creek Road. Take the road east and follow signs for **Lion's Den Camp** and **Alder Creek Campground.** Here you can experience camping as it should be.

ACCOMMODATIONS
Under $150
Despite the forbidding name, **Ragged Point Inn** (19019 Hwy. 1, 805/927-4502, http://raggedpointinn.net, $99-309) takes advantage of its location to create an anything-but-ragged hotel experience perched on one of Big Sur's famous cliffs and offering stellar views from the purpose-built glass walls and private balconies or patios of almost every guest room. Budget-friendly guest rooms still have plenty of space, a comfy king or two double beds, and

ocean views. If you've got a bit more cash, go for a luxury room, with optimal views, soaring interior spaces, plush amenities, and romantic two-person spa bathtubs. Enjoy a meal in the full-service restaurant or get picnic supplies from the snack bar or the minimart, fill up for a day trip at the on-site gas station, or peruse the works of local artists in the gift shop or jewelry gallery. A special treat is the hotel's own hiking trail, which drops 400 feet past a waterfall to Ragged Point's beach.

$150-250

Where the Santa Lucia Mountains meet the sea is where the **Lucia Lodge** (62400 Hwy. 1, 831/677-2391, www.lucialodge.com, $150-275) is, midway between Carmel and San Simeon. There are 10 updated shabby-chic cabins and guest rooms. The guest rooms are tucked into the cliff side for stunning views. The cabins are more spacious and farther from the cliffs.

A high-end California green lodging-cum-camping experience is a yurt (a circular structure made with a wood frame covered by cloth) at the **Treebones Resort** (71895 Hwy. 1, 877/424-4787, www.treebonesresort.com, $155-280). The resort got its name from local descriptions of this bit of land, once a wood recycling plant with sun-bleached logs or "tree bones" lying around. Yurts at Treebones tend to be spacious and charming, with polished wood floors, queen beds, seating areas, and outdoor decks for lounging. There are also five walk-in campsites ($65 for 2 people). In the central lodge are hot showers and usually clean restrooms. Treebones offers a somewhat pricey casual dinner each night as well as basic linens. If you like extra pillows and towels, you'll have to bring your own. Check the website for a list of items to bring and more information on the resort's facilities. To maintain the quiet

atmosphere at the resort, Treebones welcomes children only if they are over age 6.

FOOD

Stop at the **Lucia Lodge Restaurant** (62400 Hwy. 1, 831/688-4884 or 866/424-4787, www.lucialodge.com, daily 11 A.M.-4:30 P.M. and 5-9 P.M., $19-35) for a great view and a tasty meal. The menu is quite extensive, considering the isolated location, with dinner delights that include bacon-wrapped filet mignon, award-winning fish-and-chips, and homemade chicken cordon bleu. For lunch you can order a hearty salad, burger, sandwich, or choose a few appetizers to go around. The views are spectacular, and on warm days, take a table outside and sit cliff-side.

At the Treebones Resort is the **Wild Coast Restaurant & Sushi Bar** (71895 Hwy. 1, 877/424-4787, www.treebonesresort.com, dinner daily 6-8:30 P.M., sushi bar Tues.-Sun. 5:30-8:30 P.M., $12-33). Globally inspired dishes created from ingredients grown in Wild Coast's own garden will tantalize your taste buds. You can get everything from fresh sushi to tender cuts of beef, roast chicken, and Japanese-inspired dishes like sesame tuna *tataki*.

For southbound drivers, the last dining stop atop the majestic jagged cliffs is at the **Ragged Point Resort Restaurant and Snack Bar** (19019 Hwy. 1, 805/927-4502, www.ragged-pointinn.net, restaurant daily 8 A.M.-8 P.M., snack bar daily 8 A.M.-5 P.M., restaurant $15-60, snack bar $5-20). You can grab a quick bite at the snack bar or stay to dine at the restaurant. The restaurant menu consists of a semi-traditional California coastal cuisine. The fried potatoes at breakfast are addicting, and the local wine choices in the evening are delightful. The snack bar is like a small café serving espressos, sandwiches, and wine. There is seating inside and many picnic spots outside around the expansive property, including a romantic secluded beach.

Information and Services

VISITOR INFORMATION

There are two comprehensive visitors centers in Big Sur; one is at **Pfeiffer Big Sur State Park** (47225 Hwy. 1, 831/667-2315, www.parks. ca.gov), where you'll find the visitors center with the Big Sur Lodge Restaurant, the hotel check-in, and a small store. A tiny nature museum is 0.25 miles or so up the park's main road. This visitors center is a good spot to get maps and information for hiking here and at other Big Sur parks that don't have visitors centers. This large park also offers laundry facilities, some basic staples at the store, and food all day at the restaurant and attached espresso bar.

Farther south at **Julia Pfeiffer Burns State Park** (Hwy. 1, 12 miles south of Pfeiffer Big Sur, 831/667-2315, www.parks.ca.gov), the visitors center is easily accessible from the main parking lot. Rangers can advise you about hiking and activities both in their park and at other parks in the region. You'll find fewer services here than at Pfeiffer Big Sur—if you need to shop, do laundry, or gas up, head north.

For current information about the trails throughout the Los Padres National Forest, contact the **King City District Forest Service** (831/385-5434). For the status of off-road and four-by-four trails call 831/386-2513. For trail maps, permits, and general information, head to the **Big Sur Station** (just south of Pfeiffer Big Sur State Park, 831/667-2315, daily 8 A.M.-4:30 P.M.).

The **Big Sur Volunteer Fire Brigade** (831/667-2113, www.bigsurfire.org) has three stations in the Big Sur area. One is on the property of Post Ranch Inn, another near Esalen Institute, and one near the south end of the Willow Springs Caltrans yard. The brigade also has a county-sponsored ambulance and a 24-hour paramedic team.

MEDIA AND COMMUNICATIONS

Be aware that your cell phone may not work in the Big Sur region, especially in the undeveloped reaches of forest and on Highway 1 away from the villages of Big Sur and the Post Ranch. Emergency call boxes are placed at regular intervals along the highway.

MEDICAL SERVICES

For health matters, the **Big Sur Health Center** (46896 Hwy. 1, Big Sur, 831/667-2580, Mon.-Fri. 10 A.M.-5 P.M.) can take care of minor medical needs and provides an ambulance service and limited emergency care. The nearest full-service hospital is the **Community Hospital of the Monterey Peninsula** (23625 Holman Hwy., Monterey, 831/624-5311).

Getting There and Around

BY CAR

"Highway 1" might sound like a major artery, but through the Big Sur region Highway 1 is a narrow, twisting, cliff-carved track that's breathtaking both because of its beauty and because of its dangers. Once you get five miles or so south of Carmel, expect to slow down—in many spots you'll be driving no more than 20 mph around hairpin turns carved into vertical cliffs. If you're coming up from the south, Highway 1 is fairly wide and friendly through Cambria, only narrowing into its more hazardous form as the cliffs get higher and the woods thicker north of San Simeon. Be aware that fog often comes in on the Big Sur coast at sunset, making the drive even more hazardous (and much less attractive). If you must drive at night, take it slow.

To Big Sur from San Francisco (2 hours and 45 minutes, 141 miles), take U.S. 101 south to Highway 85 south, where you merge onto Highway 17 south, and then onto Highway 1 south. From Los Angeles (5 hours and 40 minutes, 297 miles), take U.S. 101 north to the Morro Bay/Hearst Castle exit onto Highway 1, and continue north to Big Sur. If you are coming from Monterey (40 minutes, 28 miles) drive south on Highway 1. From Carmel (about 36 minutes, 26 miles) as well, head south on Highway 1.

BY BUS

You can get as far south as Nepenthe from Monterey, Carmel, or Salinas on **Monterey-Salinas Transit** (831/899-2555, www.mst.org, $1.50-3.50, exact change required) a few times a day. The bus route starts in downtown Monterey at the Transit Plaza (end of Alvarado St.) and runs through Carmel. Get a full schedule of routes and fares on the website.

SAN SIMEON, CAMBRIA, AND MORRO BAY

Just south of Monterey County, time begins to slow, and you know you're entering San Louis Obispo County. Locals lovingly refer to this area as "SLO," and just like it sounds, life moves a little slower here. The laid-back vibe can be felt all along the casual coast. Locals are friendly, the food is good, and seaside accommodations come by the dozens. There is much to discover in this craggy windswept coastal landscape.

Load up the car, grab the surfboards, toss in the fishing poles, and don't leave the kids behind. San Simeon, Cambria, and Morro Bay offer entertainment for the whole family or a romantic escape for a couple's getaway. Beaches curve and stretch along the cliffs for miles, the ocean warms up the farther south you go, and the state park system grants access to an incredible coastline with diverse sealife and swelling waves. Charming towns cluster along the seaside, each with its own flavor. Hearst Castle is an opulent attraction, while more subdued gems like San Simeon, Cambria, and Cayucos offer opportunities for viewing elephant seals, wine tasting, and antiques shopping.

PLANNNING YOUR TIME

The coastal towns of San Simeon, Cambria, Cayucos, and Morro Bay offer a good number of distractions. Each town is quite different from the other, and to really hit all the must-see sights, you will want to spend at least two to three days exploring the area. If you really want

HIGHLIGHTS

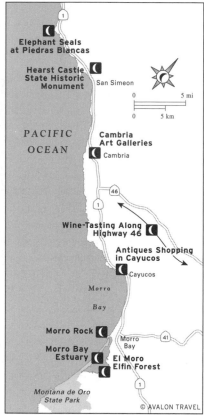

LOOK FOR ◖ TO FIND RECOMMENDED SIGHTS, ACTIVITIES, DINING, AND LODGING.

◖ **Hearst Castle State Historic Monument:** High above the sea along California's central coast is this dazzling castle, built by newspaper mogul William Randolph Hearst (page 212).

◖ **Elephant Seals at Piedras Blancas:** Seven miles north of San Simeon is the Northern Elephant Seal Rookery, home to roughly 15,000 northern elephant seals (page 213).

◖ **Cambria Art Galleries:** This small beach town is home to many charming art galleries (page 218).

◖ **Wine-Tasting Along Highway 46:** If you are a wine enthusiast or just beginning to discover vibrant California wines, you won't be disappointed with the local vintages readily available on the route from Paso Robles to Cambria (page 219).

◖ **Antiques Shopping in Cayucos:** The tiny town of Cayucos is crammed with diverse antiques shops (page 230).

◖ **Morro Rock:** At 581 feet high and more than 20 million years old, this magnificent landmark is hard to miss (page 234).

◖ **Morro Bay Estuary:** The estuary grants access to playful sea otters, dive-bombing pelicans, elegant white egrets, and handsome great blue herons (page 234).

◖ **El Moro Elfin Forest:** Named after the pygmy oak trees found along this stretch of the coast, the forest offers a self-guided tour along a mile-long boardwalk (page 234).

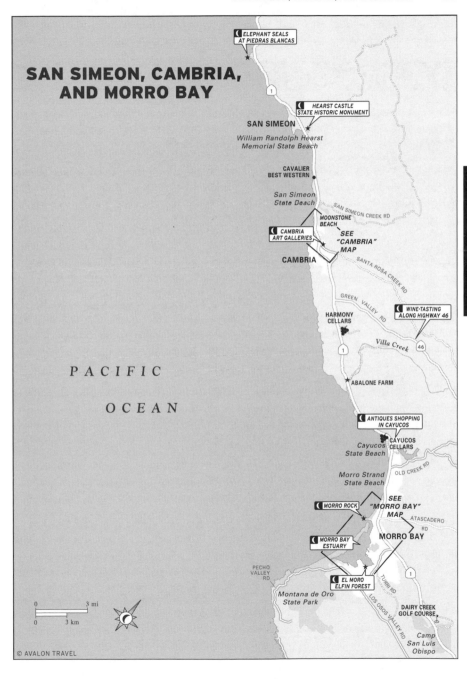

SAN SIMEON, CAMBRIA, AND MORRO BAY

ELEPHANT SEALS AT PIEDRAS BLANCAS

HEARST CASTLE STATE HISTORIC MONUMENT

SAN SIMEON

William Randolph Hearst Memorial State Beach

CAVALIER BEST WESTERN

San Simeon State Beach

SAN SIMEON CREEK RD

MOONSTONE BEACH

CAMBRIA ART GALLERIES

SEE "CAMBRIA" MAP

CAMBRIA

SANTA ROSA CREEK RD

GREEN VALLEY RD

HARMONY CELLARS

WINE-TASTING ALONG HIGHWAY 46

Villa Creek

ABALONE FARM

PACIFIC

OCEAN

ANTIQUES SHOPPING IN CAYUCOS

CAYUCOS CELLARS

Cayucos State Beach

OLD CREEK RD

Morro Strand State Beach

SEE "MORRO BAY" MAP

ATASCADERO RD

MORRO ROCK

MORRO BAY

MORRO BAY ESTUARY

PECHO VALLEY RD

EL MORO ELFIN FOREST

TURRI RD

Montana de Oro State Park

LOS OSOS VALLEY RD

DAIRY CREEK GOLF COURSE

Camp San Luis Obispo

0   3 mi
0   3 km

© AVALON TRAVEL

SAN SIMEON

to experience the laidback nature of life along this stretch of coast, four to five days will give you time for picnics on the beach, hiking in the state parks, antiques shopping, and wine-tasting.

San Simeon

San Simeon is rich with beauty as the beaches begin to widen and expose turquoise coves. The coastal range rolls back away from the sea, and cattle roam the grassland. A wooden pier stretches out from the shore.

The San Simeon area was made famous by William Randolph Hearst and his early-20th-century castle on the hill. Today, it remains much as it was back then, minus the celebrity guest list. The town of San Simeon is small and appropriate for an overnight or weekend stay, with a handful of camping, lodging, and dining options.

SIGHTS
◖ Hearst Castle State Historic Monument

There's nothing quite like the regal Hearst Castle (Hearst Castle Rd., off Hwy. 1, 800/444-4445, www.hearstcastle.org, tours daily 9 A.M.-3:20 P.M., $25 adults, $12 children, evening tours $36 adults, $18 children). Newspaper magnate William Randolph Hearst conceived the grand Mediterranean-style mansion on ranchland his parents owned along the California coast. Memories of camping in the hills above the Pacific as a child led him to choose the site where the castle now stands.

Hearst hired Julia Morgan, the first woman to graduate from the University of California, Berkeley, in civil engineering, to design and build the castle. She did a brilliant job with every detail, despite the ever-changing ideas of her employer. For decoration, Hearst relocated hundreds of medieval and Renaissance antiquities from Europe, from tiny tchotchkes to entire gilded ceilings. He also adored exotic animals and created one of the largest private zoos in the nation on his thousands of Central

Coast acres. Although most of the zoo is gone, you can still see the occasional zebra grazing peacefully along Highway 1, a sign of the exotic castle that lies ahead.

At the foot of the hill, the **Hearst Castle visitors center** is an extensive structure that houses a gift shop, a restaurant, a café, the ticket booth, and a movie theater, where you can watch *Hearst Castle—Building the Dream,* which provides an overview of the construction and history of the marvelous buildings and of Hearst's empire. After buying your ticket, a shuttle bus takes you up the hill to begin the tour. No private cars are allowed on the roads up to the castle. There are four tours available, each focusing on different spaces and aspects of the castle. You're welcome to sign up for more than one tour over the course of a day. The Grand Rooms Museum Tour is recommended for first-time visitors; the Evening Tour is a seasonal tour with volunteers dressed in 1930s fashion who welcome guests as if to one of Hearst's legendary parties. Other tours include the Upstairs Suites Museum Tour and the Cottages and Kitchen Tour. For visitors with limited mobility, special wheelchair-accessible tours are available. Strollers are not permitted. All tours provide access to the outdoor Greco-Roman style Neptune Pool, the indoor Roman Pool with blue Venetian glass and gold tiles, and the extensive gardens you can explore on your own.

On any of the tours (except the accessible tour) expect to walk for 45-60 minutes and to climb up and down many stairs. Even the most jaded traveler can't help but be amazed by the beauty and opulence of every room in the complex. Admirers of European art and antiques will want to linger. The two swimming

SAN SIMEON

© CA STATE PARKS

The gardens at Hearst Castle are a must-see.

pools, one indoor and one outdoor, sparkle with grandeur, all marble, glass tile, and a mix of antiques and custom-created statuary and fixtures. The sheer size and attention to detail is marveling throughout the estate, from the rooftops to the gardens.

It is recommended that visitors reserve tour tickets at least a few days in advance, and even farther ahead for the Evening Tour and tours on summer weekends. The restrooms and food concessions are all located in the visitors center, but no food, drink, or chewing gum is allowed on any tour.

Historic San Simeon

The tiny village of San Simeon was established primarily to support the construction efforts up the hill at Hearst Castle. The village dock provided a place for ships to unload tons of marble, piles of antiques, and dozens of workers. The general store and post office acted as a central gathering place for the community. You can still walk up the weathered wooden steps

to shop at the store. Around the corner, at the building's second door, you can buy a book of stamps or mail a letter at the tiny but operational post office.

William Randolph Hearst Memorial State Beach (750 Hearst Castle Rd., 805/927-2020, www.parks.ca.gov, daily dawn-dusk, $10) includes San Simeon's cute little cove and encompasses the remaining structure of the old pier. You can lie on the beach or have a picnic on the lawn above the sand.

◖ Elephant Seals at Piedras Blancas

On at the vista point with a parking lot just beyond the Piedras Lighthouse is a famous location to view elephant seals at the **Northern Elephant Seal Rookery** (Hwy. 1, 7 miles north of San Simeon, www.elephantseal.org, 805/924-1628, daily sunrise-sunset, free). Home to roughly 15,000 giant northern elephant seals year-round, you can witness them molt, breed, give birth, and—their favorite

SAN SIMEON

© CA STATE PARKS

the Neptune Pool at Hearst Castle

pastime—rest. During the summer the young males rest along the beach to soak up the sun while they experience the summer molt. Much of the time the elephant seals are quite calm, but occasional sparring matches provide the best action and deep guttural growling. Be careful not to get too close to these creatures; remember they are wild animals and can therefore be unpredictable and dangerous.

A large parking area just off Highway 1 sits alongside the beach, where you can view these impressive animals.

Piedras Blancas Lighthouse

Six miles north of San Simeon is the Piedras Blancas Lighthouse (15950 Hwy. 1, 805/927-7361, www.piedrasblancas.org, tours Tues., Thurs., and Sat. 9:45 A.M., $10 adults, $5 children, free under age 5), named after the white rock outcropping just off the point. It was completed in 1875, with the original tower 110 feet tall. The beach around the lighthouse is

a favorite resting spot for elephant seals. If you plan to take the tour, you may want to arrive early to ensure a spot, as space is limited. Tours meet at the old Piedras Blancas Motel, 1.5 miles north of the lighthouse.

SPORTS AND RECREATION

San Simeon's outdoor pursuits include fishing from the pier, hiking through the chaparral hills, and surfing, sunbathing, and evening strolls on the beach.

William Randolph Hearst Memorial State Beach

Directly across Highway 1 from Hearst Castle is William Randolph Hearst Memorial State Beach (750 Hearst Castle Rd., 805/927-2020, www.parks.ca.gov, daily dawn-dusk, $10). Access to the beach is from a 150-space parking lot steps away. The wide beach is appealing for sunbathers, as the winds are mild and the sand gets warm. There are 24 picnic sites with

© KRISTIN LEAL

Elephant seals snooze just seven miles north of Hearst Castle.

pedestal grills as well as public restrooms and water spigots. The shade of a fragrant eucalyptus grove offers sunbathers relief on the warmest summer days.

The protected cove has mild waves for beginning surfers or body boarders, although the water temperature averages only 55-60°F. During the summer months, the chilly water seems inviting as air temperatures can reach the low 90s. Kayaks and body boards are available for rent.

Fishing from the pier doesn't require a fishing license, although fishing limits are strictly enforced. It doesn't take much skill to hook something along this stretch of coast.

A walk along the **San Simeon Bay Trail** to **Simeon Point** is a beautiful way to take in the bay. The trail begins just north of the fishing pier; after you pass through the picnic area and reach the beach, head north. As the beach arcs west toward the sea, follow the narrow dirt road that leads to the wooded bluffs, where the views are inspiring. The two-mile round-trip trek

offers coastal vistas and views of Hearst Castle on the hill. Note that the state park property ends at San Simeon Creek; obey the private property signs.

Kite Surfing and Windsurfing

As you head south along Highway 1 from Piedras Blancas Lighthouse to the village of San Simeon, you will see countless pullouts with beach access. Winds are consistently high along this stretch of coast, which attracts both kite surfers and windsurfers year-round. Whether you are an avid boarder or just a spectator, look for the clusters of cars lining the roadway and the large half-moon kites sailing over the water.

SHOPPING

You're not likely to find a whole lot of shopping in tiny San Simeon, but there are a few locations to pick up a souvenir or two. The most visited souvenir shop is at **Hearst Castle visitors center** (Hearst Castle Rd., off Hwy. 1,

SAN SIMEON

© KRISTIN LEAL

pier fishing in San Simeon

800/927-2035 or 800/777-0369, www.hearst-castle.org, daily 8 A.M.-4:30 P.M.), with typical tacky tourist treasures like mugs, shot glasses, T-shirts, key chains, hats, posters, postcards, books, and bookmarks. The shop is operated by an independent company, and a percentage of sales goes directly to upkeep of the historic monument.

Just across Highway 1 from Hearst Castle is **Sebastian's Store** (442 Slo San Simeon Rd., 805/927-3307, Wed.-Sun. 11 A.M.-4 P.M.), an old-fashioned mom-and-pop shop with a variety of gifts, local art, and bits of history. Everyone working here is knowledgeable about the area and ready to share local lore or offer directions.

Another fun stop is the **Wampum Trading Post** (9190 Castillo Dr., 805/927-1866, daily 10 A.M.-4 P.M.), where you will find an assortment of authentic Native American treasures that include moonstone bracelets, necklaces, rings, and earrings. If you are visiting during

the off-season, be sure to call ahead, as the store sometimes closes during slow periods.

ACCOMMODATIONS

The Morgan San Simeon (9135 Hearst Dr., 805/927-3878 or 800/451-9900, www.hotel-morgan.com, $79-199) is named after celebrated Hearst Castle architect Julia Morgan, the ambiance is modern with contemporary design and a touch of elegance. Guest rooms are sizable, and the Morgan Suite has an extra room for lounging and entertaining. This is a full-service hotel, and guests are welcome to visit the on-site spa and dine at the El Chorlito Mexican Restaurant.

The beach-inspired **San Simeon Lodge** (9520 Castillo Dr., 805/927-4601, www.san-simeonbeachresort.net, $49-250) is located in the center of San Simeon, near Hearst Castle and only a block from William Randolph Hearst Memorial State Beach. Vibrant gardens surround the resort, with rooms decorated in blond wood furniture, light blue, and room to move around. There is an outdoor pool and an on-site fitness center.

Stay alongside the ocean at the **Best Western Cavalier Resort** (9415 Hearst Dr., 805/927-4688, www.cavalierresort.com, $99-319). This oceanfront venue is known for its comfort and service, offering everything from family-size guest rooms to romantic escapes. Guest rooms have coffeemakers, minibars, DVD players, full baths, fridges, and hair dryers; many have ocean views and some feature fireplaces and outdoor patios. The Cavalier Restaurant is on-site.

FOOD

There are a handful of dining options in this little coastal village. Dine at your hotel or see what other lodgings have to offer.

Casual Dining

For beachside dining indoors or out, the **San Simeon Beach Bar & Grill** (9520 Castillo Dr., 805/927-4604, www.sansimeonrestaurant.com, daily 7:30 A.M.-9:30 P.M., bar Fri.-Sat. until 2 A.M., $18-24) is casual and laid-back, with everything from early morning breakfast to late-night cocktails, salads, pastas, and pizzas. Karaoke happens Saturday-Sunday 9 P.M.-1 A.M., and happy hour is daily 4-6 P.M.

With a great ocean view, **El Chorlito Mexican Restaurant** (9135 Hearst Dr., 805/927-3878 or 800/451-9900, www.elchorlito.com, $9-28) offers traditional dishes like burritos, tacos, *carnitas,* tostada, fajitas, and enchiladas. House specialties include lamb shanks in a mild tomato sauce as well as seafood dishes.

Reasonably priced American food is on offer at **The Cavalier Restaurant** (9415 Hearst Dr., 805/927-4688, www.cavalierresort.com, winter daily 7 A.M.-9 P.M., summer daily 7 A.M.-10 P.M., $5-19). Breakfast is strictly traditional with a few specialties like eggs benedict and eggs florentine served all day. The lunch and

dinner menus focus on comfort foods like pot pies and chicken-fried steak, seafood, pasta, soup, and salad.

Take in the grand ocean views at the **Ragged Point Restaurant** (9019 Hwy. 1, 805/927-4502, www.raggedpointinn.com, daily 8 A.M.-9 P.M., $10-29), where the windows stretch floor to ceiling. The menu has fresh California-style cuisine with a focus on regional ingredients and local wines. You can linger over a meal in the dining room or grab something quick at the Wine Bar, Espresso Bar, and Sandwich Stand. The daily chalkboard menu features seasonal entrées of local fisheries and farm fare that are cooked with fresh herbs from Ragged Point's garden.

Cheap Eats

At **Sebastian's Café** (442 Slo San Simeon Rd., 805/927-3307, Wed.-Sun. 11 A.M.-4 P.M., $3-10), grab a sandwich to go, a cup of coffee for breakfast, or order a burger and eat in the shade of the eucalyptus trees at one of the picnic tables. A recent addition to the store-café is the wine-tasting room, with local vintages that include Hearst Ranch Vineyard.

If you are headed to Hearst Castle, you can save time by eating at **Hearst Castle café** (Hearst Castle Rd., off Hwy. 1, 800/927-2035 or 800/777-0369, www.hearstcastle.org, daily 8 A.M.-4:30 P.M., $5-10), serving Hearst Ranch beef in chili or hamburgers as well as chicken sandwiches, hot dogs, and stir-fried meat and vegetables.

INFORMATION AND SERVICES

If your primary interest is Hearst Castle, the huge **visitors center** is at the parking lot below the castle and where all tours start. Inside, pick up your tour tickets, grab a coffee or a meal, and peruse the extensive bookshop, which includes many books about the Hearst family, the castle, and the town of San Simeon.

For a general overview of the area, visit the **San Simeon Chamber of Commerce** (250

San Simeon Ave., Suite 3A, 805/927-3500 or 805/927-0640, www.sansimeonchamber.org, daily 10 A.M.-4 P.M.). Local volunteers run the office and have information on local lodging, food, entertainment, recreation, and many other attractions in the area.

For the closest emergency services, the town of Templeton has **Twin Cities Hospital** (1100 Las Tablas Rd., Templeton, 805/434-3500, www.twincitieshospital.com), about 25 miles east of San Simeon; take Highway 41 or Highway 46 near Paso Robles to U.S. 101.

GETTING THERE AND AROUND

The village of San Simeon is along Highway 1; take U.S. 101 to either Highway 41 or Highway 46, which lead to Highway 1. The village is halfway between San Francisco and Los Angeles, each about 240 miles away.

The regional bus system **San Luis Obispo RTA** (805/781-4427, bus info 805/541-2228, www.slorta.org, $1.30-3, day pass $5) will get you around the southern part of Central California; Route 12/15 accesses Hearst Castle from Morro Bay on three daily round-trips.

Cambria

Nearby Cambria began as an artists colony. The windswept hills and sparkling ocean have always provided inspiration for painters, writers, sculptors, glassblowers, and other creative minds. The seaside town is a tight cluster of art galleries, antiques malls, shops, ocean-side accommodations, and restaurants. Downtown has most of Cambria's amenities within walking distance. The main part of town flanks Moonstone Beach, and wineries dotting the hillsides provide places to sample the local vintages.

SIGHTS
Cambria Cemetery
Artsy isn't a word usually associated with graveyards, but in Cambria it seems to fit. The Cambria Cemetery (6005 Bridge St., 805/927-5158, www.cambriacemetery.com) reflects the artistic bent of the town's residents in its tombstone decor. Family and friends of the deceased are allowed to place all manner of personal objects at the graves. You'll see painted tombstones, beautiful panes of stained glass, unusual wind chimes, and many other unique expressions of love, devotion, and art as you wander the 12 wooded acres.

Nitt Witt Ridge
While William Randolph Hearst built one

of the most expensive homes California has ever known, local eccentric Arthur Harold Beal (a.k.a. "Captain Nitt Witt" or "Der Tinkerpaw") got busy building the cheapest "castle" he could. Nitt Witt Ridge (881 Hillcrest Dr., 805/927-2690, tours by appointment, free) is the result of five decades of scavenging trash and using it as building supplies to create a multistory home like no other. Today, you can make an appointment with owners Michael and Stacey O'Malley to take a tour of the property (but don't just drop in). It's weird, it's funky, and it's fun—an oddly iconic experience of the Central Coast.

◖ Art Galleries
Cambria is known as an artistic community, so it is no surprise that art galleries are plentiful in town. Each gallery is unique and features both local and widely known artists. Find art in a variety of mediums, and marvel at everything from colorful twisting handblown glass to textured paintings. There are at least 15 galleries in town, many on Main Street, with glass art, Western art, wall art, paintings, fine art, decorative art, American art, and works by Central Coast artists.

The Vault Gallery (2289 Main St., 805/927-0300, www.vaultgallery.com, daily

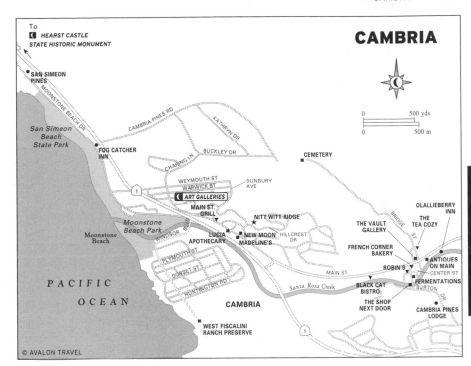

To
HEARST CASTLE STATE HISTORIC MONUMENT

CAMBRIA

SAN SIMEON PINES

San Simeon Beach State Park

MOONSTONE BEACH DR

CAMBRIA PINES RD

KATHRYN DR

BUCKLEY DR

CHARING LN

FOG CATCHER INN

CEMETERY

0   500 yds
0   500 m

WEYMOUTH ST
WARWICK ST
SUNBURY AVE
ART GALLERIES

MAIN ST. GRILL

NITT WITT RIDGE

OLALLIEBERRY INN

THE VAULT GALLERY

THE TEA COZY

Moonstone Beach Park

Moonstone Beach

WINDSOR

LUCIA APOTHECARY

NEW MOON
MADELINE'S

HILLCREST DR

FRENCH CORNER BAKERY

PLYMOUTH ST

PACIFIC

DORSET ST

HUNTINGTON RD

Santa Rosa Creek

MAIN ST

ROBIN'S

ANTIQUES ON MAIN
CENTER ST

FERMENTATIONS
BURTON DR

OCEAN

CAMBRIA

BLACK CAT BISTRO

THE SHOP NEXT DOOR

CAMBRIA PINES LODGE

WEST FISCALINI RANCH PRESERVE

© AVALON TRAVEL

SAN SIMEON

10:30 A.M.-5:30 or 6 P.M.) opened in 1990 to showcase fine art produced by local artists. You will not find any mainstream or commercial art here.

Come to the place where American imagination takes shape at **The Art of America Moonstones Gallery** (4070 Burton Dr., 805/927-3447 or 800/424-3827, www.moonstones.com, daily 10 A.M.-10 P.M.), with a bit of everything and always something new in a variety of mediums. Become hypnotized by the liquid-like handblown glass pieces, and get lost in the detail of the wood carvings.

Most afternoons you can visit the **Patricia Griffin Studio & Gallery** (880 Main St., 805/924-1050 or 805/927-1871, www.patriciagriffinstudio.com, daily from noon) and take a peek at Patricia up to her elbows in mud. Within the walls of a 100-year-old schoolhouse, she creates contemporary pottery that is almost organic. The beauty of nature is reflected in many of her pieces in a combination of earthy tones. Call to make sure the studio doors are open.

Wine-Tasting Along Highway 46

As you leave U.S. 101 onto Highway 46 west in Paso Robles on the way to Cambria, you will find a trail of vineyards all the way to the sea. Many vineyards and tasting rooms are on Highway 46 or just off the highway on country roads. Beyond wine tasting, the drive itself is beautiful, through vibrant vineyards and the lush Santa Lucia Mountain Range, with views of Morro Rock and Estero Bay.

The gothic style of **Eagle Castle** (3090 Anderson Rd., Paso Robles, 805/227-1428, www.eaglecastlewinery.com, daily 10 A.M.-5:30 P.M., tasting $5, waived with wine purchase or wine-club membership) will catch your eye as you drive by. On the outside it is a replica of a European castle with a moat, and inside is

THE WINE LINE

For a relaxed wine-tasting experience with a designated driver, take a ride on the Wine Line (805/610-8267, www.hoponthewine-line.com, $60) to savor the flavors of this unique region. This hop-on, hop-off shuttle service goes to San Simeon, Cambria, and Paso Robles. Service is door-to-door, with pickup times 10:30-11:30 A.M.; the end-of-day drop-off at your lodging is around 4-5 P.M. There are 19 wineries that waive the tasting fee if you are part of the Wine Line tour, and there are more than 60 wineries along the route. Lunch can be arranged ($15), or you can pack your own picnic store it in a cooler on the shuttle. The Wine Line makes the wine-tasting experience comfortable and worry-free, and allows you to sample and savor at your own pace.

a 17,500-square-foot gravity-flow wine-production facility. Eagle is celebrated for producing many award-winning reds, whites, and dessert wines, including petite sirah, barbera, cabernet sauvignon, zinfandel, chardonnay, viognier, and brands Royal Red, Trinity, and King's Zin Port.

Located alongside Highway 46 is **Grey Wolf** (2174 W. Hwy. 46, Paso Robles, 805/237-0771, www.greywolfcellars.com, spring-fall daily 11 A.M.-5:30 P.M., winter daily 11 A.M.-5 P.M., tasting $5), a family-owned and operated winery and tasting room on 12 acres of pastures, rolling hillsides, and wide meadows. Bring lunch along as the grounds provide a nice place for a picnic. But first, step into the 60-year-old converted farmhouse that serves as the tasting room to sample the specialty reds, which include the Barton Family Reserve Zinfandel, Alpha Cabernet, and Meritage.

Known for producing distinctive wines exclusively from the vineyards among the rugged limestone hills of West Paso Robles is **Lone Madrone** (2485 Hwy. 46 W., Paso Robles, 805/238-0845, www.lonemadrone.com, daily

10:30 A.M.-5 P.M., tasting $10 includes glass, waived with 3-bottle purchase). Winemaker Neil Collins focuses on grapes from dry-farmed vineyards that are and head-trained to produce remarkable wines. The majority of the wines are blends, with some rare single-varietal wines.

Come and taste the Kruse family's dream come true at **Jack Creek Cellars** (5265 Jack Creek Rd., Templeton, 805/226-8283, www.jackcreekcellars.com, Mon. 11 A.M.-3 P.M., Tues. by appointment, Thurs. 11 A.M.-4 P.M., Fri.-Sun. 11 A.M.-4:30 P.M., tasting $10). For them, it begins with growing remarkable fruit and ends with a labor of love in the winery. Try their chardonnay, pinot noir, pinot noir reserve, and syrah.

There are several tasting rooms in the village of Cambria, including the west-village **Moonstone Cellars** (801 Main St., 805/927-9466, www.moonstonecellars.com, daily 11 A.M.-5 P.M., tasting $5 for 6 flights), with good wines, and a friendly host. They craft an array of whites, reds, and dessert wines; varietals include albariño, viognier, chardonnay, syrah, tempranillo, cabernet sauvignon, merlot, zinfandel, and adularia. Throw down an extra $7 to take the tasting glass home with you to remember your Central Coast adventure.

Enjoy the Roaring '20s-themed tasting room of **Black Hands Cellars** (766 Main St., 805/927-9463, www.blackhandcellars.com, winter Thurs.-Mon. 11 A.M.-5 P.M., summer daily 11 A.M.-5 P.M.). The name has two origins: The first is the owner's great-grandmother and the Mafia's preference for her husband's wine. The second recognizes the stained hands of the workers who harvested the grapes during the 1920s. Enjoy red wines with clever names like Hit and Run, Alibi, and The Deal Maker.

In the east village, **Fermentations** (4056 Burton Dr., 805/927-7141, www.fermentations.com, winter Mon.-Thurs. 11 A.M.-7 P.M., Fri.-Sun. 10 A.M.-10 P.M., summer daily 10 A.M.-10 P.M., tasting $5 includes glass) also carries everything you can think of that goes with wine, from local gourmet food items to wine accessories.

HISTORY OF THE CENTRAL COAST VINEYARDS

The first vineyard on the southern reaches of the Central Coast was at the Mission San Miguel Archangel in 1797. It nearly took 100 years for the word spread, and it wasn't until 1882, when Indiana settler Andrew York began planting vineyards, that wine was produced for the commercial market. It became a steady business, and new vineyards popped up in the area over time.

In the late 1960s and early 1970s, the wine market exploded, and many urban dwellers left their 9-to-5 jobs to grow wine on the Central Coast. The soil and climate of the region is known to produce fruit with unique qualities, and more than 25 grape varietals are grown. Today, the wine business is booming, with a focus on producing premium vintages.

Take a short drive to visit **J. Lohr Vineyards & Wines** (6169 Airport Rd., Paso Robles, 805/239-8900, www.jlohr.com, daily 10 A.M.-5 P.M., tasting free except limited editions and J. Lohr Cuvée Series), where you can enjoy tasting, views of the immense vineyard, and the patio and picnic area. The tasting room is also a shop with apparel, small gifts, and plenty of wine for purchase.

SPORTS AND RECREATION
Beaches

Surfing, hiking, and camping are possible at **Hearst San Simeon State Park** (Van Gordon Creek Rd. and San Simeon Creek Rd., 805/927-2020, www.parks.ca.gov, $10), a large park along 20 miles of the coast that includes five diverse habitats to explore. One of the oldest in the California State Park system, it is somewhat off the radar. There is a visitors center and a discovery center. Beach activity includes kite flying, exploring tide pools, and strolling along the beach. You can launch a kayak here, and the moderate surf is sometimes challenging for surfers and body boarders.

There are two parking lots at the **Washburn Day-use Area** along with picnicking sites and trailheads for walks to the beach and inland on the 3.3-mile San Simeon Trail, which has scenic overlooks of the coastal bluffs.

Just south of Highway 1 is **Moonstone State Beach** (Moonstone Beach Dr., 805/927-2020, free), known for the moonstones that wash up on shore now and then. This long shoreline is ideal for a stroll in the surf or along the boardwalk, which runs from Leffingwell Landing and Day Use area to just north of Weymouth Street. Much of the boardwalk is wheelchair-accessible. The beach stretches a bit farther than the boardwalk and includes the **Santa Rosa Day-use Area** to the south, where you can find additional parking.

Leffingwell Landing at Moonstone Beach offers tide pools to explore, a launch ramp, and a parking lot; you can do some shore fishing from the rocks. Dogs are welcome on the boardwalk and on the beach.

Fiscalini Ranch Preserve

At the center of Cambria is the 364-acre Fiscalini Ranch Preserve (4500 Windsor Blvd., www.ffrpcambria.org, daily sunrise-sunset, free), where you can access 11 trails, some of which run along the bluffs above the ocean. You may see sea otters basking in the sun in Otter Cove, an abundance of seabirds such as egrets and herons, elephant seals, and migrating whales. The Friends of Fiscalini Ranch (www.cambriaranchwalks.com) host docent-led nature walks one Saturday each month 10 A.M.-noon.

ENTERTAINMENT

Live performance in Cambria is at **The Pewter Plough Playhouse** (824 Main St., 805/927-3877, www.pewterploughplayhouse.org), since

Moonstone State Beach

1976 the stage for productions of musicals, dramas, and comedies. The interior has a piano bar and a theater that seem to date from sometime between the gold rush and the Roaring '20s. You can usually catch a show Friday-Saturday at 7:30 P.M., with matinees Sunday at 3 P.M. and the occasional Thursday performance. Check the website for schedules as the theater is not always open.

FESTIVALS AND EVENTS
Spring
In April at the **Chili Cook-off and Car Show** (Veterans Memorial Hall and Pinedorado Grounds, Main St. and Cambria Rd., www.cambriachamber. org), the aroma of chili will draw you in as fancy cars make their way into town. This annual event has plenty of distractions for children as well as music, prizes, entertainment, and frothy beer.

Summer
July 4 sees a 12-hour **Old Fashioned Fourth of July Celebration and Fireworks** (5455 Windsor Blvd., www.cambriachamber.org), held at Shamel Park 10 A.M.-10 P.M. There are children's games, races, live music and performances, and a spectacular fireworks show starting at dusk that lights up the coast for miles.

Fall
Oktoberfest (Veterans Hall, 1000 Main St., www.cambriaoktoberfest.com, $10) in Cambria is October is wunderbar with lots of German beer, food, music, and dancing. Local children perform German folk dances, and there are Mexican folk dances, belly dancing, and choir performances as well as a few traditional contests to participate in. If you're up for it, there are shapeliest-leg contests for men and women as well as chicken dancing.

Winter
Get tickets early for Cambria's three-day **Art and Wine Festival** (www.seecambria.com/

artwine) in January. Be dazzled for two days and nights by local food, wine from 30 local wineries, live entertainment, an art show, a silent auction, and a raffle. There is a barbecue lunch on the last day.

SHOPPING

Cambria has enough distinctive gift and specialty shops to fill an afternoon. At **Old Cambria Market Place and Carwash** (589 Main St., 805/927-8877, daily 7 A.M.-midnight), find all kinds of touristy souvenirs along with small local artworks and a selection of dozens of local wines, often discounted.

One hundred years ago it was a hotel, but today the bright yellow shop in the west village is **Caren's Corner** (755 Main St., 805/927-1161, Mon.-Tues. and Sat.-Sun. 11 A.M.-5 P.M., Wed.-Thurs. 11 A.M.-7 P.M.), with all kinds of trinkets such as seashells, wind chimes, garden flags, and postcards, as well as old-fashioned ice cream parlor.

Exotic Nature (783 Main St., 805/927-2517, www.exoticnature.com, daily 10 A.M.-5 P.M.) has all kinds of luscious spa and body products along with a selection of jewelry, clothing, and unusual gifts.

Just about everything you might need for your kitchen can be found at **A Matter of Taste in Cambria** (4120 Burton Dr., 805/927-0286, www.amatteroftastecambria.com, daily 10 A.M.-5 P.M.), with linens, bakeware, serving dishes, kitchen gadgets, and gourmet food. They also carry the works of local artist Barbara Katz Bierman, who specializes in creating colorful trays, tote bags, floor mats, and original paintings. If you are planning to be in Cambria for a while, check out the cooking classes.

Yarn, yarn, and more yarn can be found at the **Ball & Skein & More** (4070 Burton Dr., 805/927-3280, www.cambriayarn.com, daily 10 A.M.-5 P.M.) along with patterns, hooks, and needles. There are also handcrafted clothing and accessories made of yarn, including hats, shoulder bags, scarfs, and shawls.

GOWA Creative Arts (4009 West St., 805/927-1005, www.g-o-w-a.com, Mon.-Fri. 11 A.M.-5 P.M., Sat.-Sun. 10 A.M.-5 P.M.) are colorful cottages with mannequins along the sidewalk that will most definitely catch your eye. The cottages serve as art studios and an apparel store. Each piece of clothing is one of a kind, modern, fashionable, and wearable art fashioned and airbrushed by Christopher and Dinah Lee.

ACCOMMODATIONS

You wouldn't necessarily guess that there are well over 40 lodging sites in little Cambria. Options range from the seaside to the fragrant forest and from camping to luxury digs.

Camping

Get rugged at one of the two campgrounds at **Hearst San Simeon State Park** (Van Gordon Creek Rd. and San Simeon Creek Rd., www.parks.ca.gov, reservations 800/444-7275, www.reserveamerica.com, Mar.-Sept. 30, $20). Adjacent to the seasonal wetlands and the creek, the 115 San Simeon Creek campsites, for tents and RVs, have picnic tables and fire rings, running water, restrooms, and coin-operated showers. Fresh water is available at the RV dump station and throughout the campground from spigots. Firewood is for sale from the camp host.

For a quieter camping experience, travel farther east into the park to the Washburn Campground, about one mile from the beach, with 68 primitive sites on a plateau overlooking the Pacific and the rolling Santa Lucia Range. Sites are equipped with fire rings, water spigots, and picnic tables. Chemical toilets are available. If you camp here, you still have full access to the facilities in the park, so you can easily drive to San Simeon Creek Campground for a shower.

Under $150

A favorite is the **Olallieberry Inn** (2476 Main St., 805/927-3222 or 888/927-3222, www.olallieberry.com, $135-225), in a charming

19th-century Greek Revival home and adjacent cottage. Each of the nine guest rooms features its own quaint Victorian-inspired decor with comfortable beds and attractive appointments. A full daily breakfast, complete with olallieberry jam, rounds out the experience.

Her Castle Homestay Bed and Breakfast Inn (1978 Londonderry Lane, 805/924-1719, www.hercastle.cc, $120-160) is a bit different from an average B&B, with only two guest rooms and lots of personal attention from the owners. When you make reservations, ask about a half-day wine tour, dinner reservations, or even lunch and dinner provided by the inn. The Her Castle can be a perfect lodging for two couples traveling together.

Watching the dolphins or migrating whales from you own patio or ocean-view room is possible year-round at **Cambria Landing** (6530 Moonstone Beach Dr., 805/927-1619, www.cambrialanding.com, $100-275). There is included Wi-Fi access, continental breakfast, fireplaces, balconies or patios, and a bottle of wine at check-in. Some suites have spacious jetted tubs and roaring fireplaces. Standard rooms have partial ocean views.

Little Sur Inn (6190 Moonstone Beach Dr., 805/927-1329 or 866/478-7466, www.littlesurinn.com, $99-295) is a beachfront property with 17 modern units that have a beach bungalow vibe. Guest rooms are tastefully decorated and have adequate space to spread out. A daily continental breakfast and lunchtime hors d'oeuvres are included in the room rates.

Moonstone Beach Drive is Cambria's hotel row, where you will find **Moonstone Landing** (6240 Moonstone Beach Dr., 805/927-0012 or 800/830-4540, www.moonstonelanding.com, $100-295), with partial-view guest rooms that have the decor and amenities of a mid-tier chain motel as well as oceanfront luxury guest rooms that have travertine marble baths.

The Burton Inn (4022 Burton Dr., 805/927-5125, www.burtoninn.com, $100 till 300)

offers modernity in an attractive setting. Even the standard rooms offer tons of space, and the family suites have multiple bedrooms.

For a great selection from economical standard rooms up to sizable cabins, the **Cambria Pines Lodge** (2905 Burton Dr., 800/445-6868, www.cambriapineslodge.com, $69-389) has guest rooms with TVs, private baths, kitchenettes, and in some rooms, fireplaces.

$150-250

A charming log cabin structure houses the eight guest rooms of **J. Patrick House Bed and Breakfast** (2990 Burton Dr., 805/927-3812, www.jpatrickhouse.com, $165-215). Each room has modern-country kitschy decor, private bath, and plenty of amenities. J. Patrick is dedicated to feeding you, with a big breakfast in the morning, hors d'oeuvres in the afternoon, and chocolate-chip cookies at bedtime.

One of the cuter and more interesting lodgings on hotel row, **Moonstone Cottages** (6580 Moonstone Beach Dr., 805/927-1366, http://moonstonecottages.com, $175-349) offers peace and luxury along with proximity to the sea. Expect your cottage to include a fireplace, a marble bath with a jetted tub, a flat-screen TV with a DVD player, Internet access, and breakfast delivered daily to your door. The views are stellar and the rooms are cozy.

Just across the street from the beach is the **Cambria Shores Inn** (6276 Moonstone Beach Dr., 805/927-8644 or 800/433-9179, www.cambriashores.com, $180-310). Guest rooms are high-end after a recent $3 million renovation, and breakfast, included in the room rates, is served at your door in a basket. You can book a spa treatment on-site, and dogs are welcome.

Indulge yourself at **El Colibri Boutique Hotel & Spa** (5620 Moonstone Beach Dr., 805/924 till 3003, www.elcolibrihotel.com, $150-289), with a spa, luxurious oversize guest rooms, pillow-top mattresses, deep jetted soaking tubs, large windows, Keurig coffeemakers, and included Wi-Fi access. Make sure to check for seasonal packages.

Families and couples will appreciate the comforts of the **Sand Pebbles Inn** (6252 Moonstone Beach Dr., 805/927-5600 or 800/222-9157, www.cambriainns.com/sandpebblesinn, $154-299). You can enjoy many local attractions right outside your door with Moonstone Beach and the boardwalk just steps away. The front desk has games and a DVD collection. Guest rooms have a least partial ocean views, and the full ocean-view rooms are the most expensive.

FOOD
Breakfast
Midway between the east and west villages of Cambria is a little taste of Italy at **Allocco's Italian Bakery** (1602 Main St., 805/927-1501, www.alloccos.com, 7 A.M.-5 P.M., $2-8). Along with imported items are freshly baked breads and pastries, Taralli Italian Gourmet Pretzels, Italian coffee ($1), Italian sodas, and freshly made sandwiches.

For a caffeine fix any time of day, head to **Cambria Coffee Roasting Company** (761 Main St., 805/927-0670, www.cambriacoffee.com, daily 7 A.M.-5:30 P.M., $2-6), for over 10 years serving carefully roasted coffee from around the world. Seating is limited to a few tables upstairs and outside alongside the street, but it's a great grab-and-go stop; Wi-Fi is free.

Casual Dining
One of the best food bargains in town is ◖ **Wild Ginger** (2380 Main St., 805/927-1001, www.wildgingercambria.com, Fri.-Wed. 11 A.M.-2:30 P.M. and 5-9 P.M., $15-18), a tiny pan-Asian café with delicious fresh food at a few tables as well as take-out fare displayed in a glass case. Come early for the best selection.

Spice things up at **Las Cambritas** (2336 Main St., Suite B, 805/927-0175, daily 11:30 A.M.-9 P.M., $8-28) with Mexican food and

friendly service. The burritos are enormous, and the guacamole is delicious. On a nice day, get a table on the patio and enjoy a cold margarita.

Cheap Eats
Caren's Corner (755 Main St., 805/927-1161, Mon.-Tues. and Sat.-Sun. 11 A.M.-5 P.M., Wed.-Thurs. 11 A.M.-7 P.M., $5-10) is a must-stop for the ice cream. Stand at the case to pick your flavor. They also make a good sandwich to take to the beach or on a hike, the fudge is delicious, and there is a full espresso bar.

Fuel up at **Old Cambria Market Place and Carwash** (589 Main St., 805/927-8877, daily 7 A.M.-midnight) and try one of the famous hot dogs, pick up a sandwich made to order, and get your car washed.

Part of a large local family business, **Linn's Restaurant** (2277 Main St., 805/927-0371, www.linnsfruitbin.com/restaurant, daily 8 A.M.-9 P.M., $10) serves tasty, unpretentious American favorites in a casual family-friendly atmosphere. The menu features meatloaf, rack of lamb, homemade soups, fresh salads, and all kinds of sandwiches. You can purchase a ready-to-bake homemade olallieberry, various jams, and homemade vinegar at this café or the original farm stand (6275 Santa Rosa Creek Rd.).

Fine Dining
Locals love ◖ **Robin's Restaurant** (4095 Burton Dr., 805/927-5007, www.robinsrestaurant.com, daily 11 A.M.-9 P.M., brunch Sun. 11 A.M.-3 P.M., $11-26). Flowering vines, wooden birdhouses, and small lanterns decorate the walls, and huge windows bring the outdoors inside, making it a pleasant country garden-style dining experience. The food is homemade, and the menu features seasonal items such as wild king salmon with cranberry almond rice, Malaysian chicken, and tofu with lemongrass and ginger as the cooks combine creativity with local fresh ingredients. Dishes are beautifully presented, and gluten-free and vegan options are available.

The Sow's Ear (2248 Main St., 805/927-4865, www.thesowsear.com, daily 5-9 P.M., $15-38) does its best to create the proverbial "silk purse" dining experience with upscale comfort food and romantic dim atmosphere. Prices for items such as lobster pot pie and chicken and dumplings can run a bit high, but it is definitely a taste of old-fashioned Americana.

Head for the **Sea Chest Oyster Bar** (6216 Moonstone Beach Dr., 805/927-4514, daily 5:30-9 P.M., $25-40, cash only) for seafood. Reservations are not accepted, so expect a long line out the door at opening time, and get here early (or prepare to wait a while) for one of the window-side tables. The seafood tends to be fresh, with a good selection of raw oysters.

Perhaps the most talked-about restaurant in Cambria is the **Black Cat Bistro** (1602 Main St., 805/927-1600, www.blackcatbistro.com, Thurs.-Mon. 5 P.M.-close, $25-45). The interesting California-French menu offers both small and large portions, each with a suggested wine pairing. Despite the upscale food, the Black Cat prides itself on its casual resort-town atmosphere. The menu features many unique dishes with a focus on seafood such as grilled ahi, Idaho rainbow trout, and sea scallops, along with vegetarian plates like three-cheese baked polenta.

Farmers Markets

You can find all sorts of vendors at **Cambria Farmers' Market** (Veteran's Memorial Hall Park, Cambria Dr. and Main St., 805/924-1260, www.cambriachamber.org, Fri. 2:30-5 P.M.). The bounty on offer includes fruits, vegetables, pies, barbecue, and flowers. Local bakeries and restaurants make a weekly appearance as well, and you can find many flavorsome gourmet items to go.

INFORMATION AND SERVICES

The town of Cambria does not have a brick-and-mortar visitors center, but ahead of your

visit check out www.cambriavisitorsbureau.com or www.cambriachamber.org.

The nearest hospital to Cambria is the **Twin Cities Hospital** (1100 Las Tablas Rd., Templeton, 805/434-3500), 24 miles inland near U.S. 101 just south of Highway 46.

Mail service is at Cambria's **U.S. Post Office** (Main St. and Bridge St.).

GETTING THERE AND AROUND

Most visitors to Cambria drive. The Pacific Coast Highway (Hwy. 1) is the prettiest but not the fastest way to get here. A quicker route is U.S. 101 to the Paso Robles area, then west on Highway 46.

By rail, **Amtrak** (www.amtrak.com, 800/872-7245) runs the Seattle-Los Angeles *Coast Starlight* via the Paso Robles station (800 Pine St., Paso Robles) and the San Luis Obispo station (1011 Railroad Ave., San Luis Obispo) once daily in each direction, and 12 *Pacific Surfliner* trains end and originate in San Luis Obispo each day with runs to Los Angeles and San Diego. To subsequently reach the coast, it's easiest to rent a car at the San Luis Obispo station.

The regional bus system **San Luis Obispo RTA** (805/781-4427, bus info 805/541-2228, www.slorta.org, $1.30-3, day pass $5) will get you around the southern part of Central California; Route 12/15 accesses Hearst Castle from Morro Bay via Cambia on three daily round-trips.

The most efficient way to explore Cambria is by car, as the attractions, accommodations, and food are too far apart to walk. A local transportation option is the **Cambria Village Trolley** (805/541-2228, www.cambriacsd.org, June 1-Sept. 4 Thurs.-Mon. 9 A.M.-6 P.M., Sept. 5-May 31 Fri.-Mon. 9 A.M.-6 P.M.), also known as the Otter Bus. There are 24 stops along the loop that starts and ends at San Simeon Pines Resort (7200 Moonstone Dr., Cambria).

Cayucos

Cayucos is a true California beach town that appeals to every kind of beachgoer. Cattle graze on the serene grasslands as the surf crashes on the sandy shore.

SIGHTS
Cass Landing

New England ship's captain James Cass sailed around the Horn in 1867 in search of fertile land. He received a land grant of 320 acres of the original 8,845-acre Rancho Moro y Cayucos Spanish Land Grant. The area was growing in agriculture and trade, and partnering with fellow settler Captain Ingals, they built a pier, a store, and a warehouse to establish the shipping port known as Cass Landing (Cayucos State Beach, end of Cayucos Dr., www.cayucosbythesea.com). Travelers could load up on cheese, hides, beef, fresh water, fish, abalone, and other valuable goods.

Today, the original pier still stands and is a popular spot for fishing or a walk. Views extend across Estero Bay and into the grassy hills of the Santa Lucia Mountains. Morro Rock is visible to the south.

SPORTS AND RECREATION
Harmony Headlands State Park

Harmony Headlands State Park (4500 Hwy. 1, 805/772-7434, www.parks.ca.gov, daily 6 A.M.-sunset, free) has coastal hiking just five minutes' drive north of the center of Cayucos. The park covers 784 acres with a 1.5-mile trail toward the ocean.

About 0.5 miles into the peaceful grasslands are the old Bunk House and some pit toilets, the only restrooms in the park. Farther along is a pond and eventually the seashore. You may see California ground squirrels, rabbits, skunks, a shy coyote, mule deer, possibly a badger, sea mammals, and all sorts of birds. Near the pond, watch for southwestern pond turtles and the endangered California red-legged frog.

Estero Bluffs State Park

Enter 355-acre Estero Bluffs State Park (Hwy. 1, 1 mile north of Cayucos, 805/772-7434, www.parks.ca.gov, 30 minutes before sunrise till 30 minutes after sunset, free) just north of Cayucos. The park comprises seashore, sea stacks, intertidal areas, wetlands, low bluffs and terraces, perennial and intermittent streams, a sandy beach, and a pocket cove.

Within the park are several miles of generally nonstrenuous coastal hiking trails. This is a primitive park, so bring the necessities with you, such as drinking water and a picnic blanket.

Cayucos State Beach

Surf and sun are consistent at Cayucos State Beach (end of Cayucos Dr., 805/781-5930, www.parks.ca.gov, free), with picnic tables, tide pools, and a fishing pier. The beach is long and flat, giving surfers a long ride in. The waves tend to be mostly mild to moderate curls, making it a good spot for beginning surfers or body boarders. Water temperatures in the winter are cool, necessitating a full wetsuit; in summer full wetsuits aren't necessary. Lifeguards are on duty through the peak summer months.

Fishing from the pier doesn't require a fishing license. You can even fish at night, as the pier lights are on. Near the surf, anglers typically pull in large surfperch; halfway out are small boccacio and more surfperch, and at the far end, large halibut are hauled out.

Surf Shops

Find what you need to hit the surf at **Cayucos Surf Co.** (95 Cayucos Dr., 805/995-1000, www.surfcompany.com, daily 10 A.M.-5 P.M.), with surf gear, apparel, and rentals for all ages. You can also take a surfing lesson from one of the instructors.

Good Clean Fun (136 Ocean Front Ave.,

© KRISTIN LEAL

Estero Bluffs State Park

805/995-1993, www.gcfsurf.com, Mon.-Fri. 10 A.M.-6 P.M., Sat.-Sun. 9 A.M.-6 P.M.) has sales, rentals, and repairs of surf gear, skateboards, body boards, kayak equipment, and clothing. You can also get a surfing lesson or a kayak tour for a look at the Cayucos shoreline.

ENTERTAINMENT AND EVENTS
Nightlife

The **Old Cayucos Tavern** (130 N. Ocean Ave., 805/995-3209, daily 10 A.M.-2 A.M.) has an authentic Wild West atmosphere. Come in through the swinging saloon doors to play cards, shoot pool, have a drink or two, and hear some local bands. The building and the decor doesn't seem to have changed much since the 19th century, and you almost expect a cowboy to stumble in.

Spring

Calling all sea glass enthusiasts: The annual **Cayucos Sea Glass Festival** (Vet's Hall, 1661 Mill St., cayucosseaglass@gmail.com, www.

cayucoschamber.org) is a full weekend event held at the beach in March, with handcrafted sea glass treasures that include jewelry, pieces of art, and more. Enjoy local food and wine from many area vendors.

Surf's up and the women are in the water at the **Annual Women's Surf Contest** (south side of Cayucos pier, 805/995-1993, www.cayucoschamber.com) in March, a full-day surf event with a barbecue, goodie bags, prizes, T-shirts, and plenty of chances to get wet.

Step back into the past at the biannual **Antique Street Fair** (Ocean Ave. downtown, www.cayucoschamber.com) in May and October, when Ocean Avenue is blocked off to become a pedestrian-only zone. Hunt for treasure from local and visiting vendors.

The hottest local event is the **Peddler's Faire** (Cayucos Creek Lot, between Hardie Park and Ocean Ave., www.cayucoschamber. com) in May, July, and September. Come hungry and bring cash. Vendors and artists from all

© KRISTIN LEAL

No need for a fishing license along the Cayucos pier.

SAN SIMEON

over gather for this one-day event to share their goods and works of art. The lot is crammed with countless vendors selling jewelry, clothing, antiques, handicrafts, photographs, paintings, multimedia works of art, and hot food.

Summer

Cayucos's **Fourth of July Celebration** (Cayucos State Beach, end of Cayucos Dr., www.cayucoschamber.com) is when everyone gathers on the beach to create sand sculptures in a friendly competition that goes way beyond the usual sand castles: Life-size creatures and monstrous structures built by children, professional sculptors, and others take over the sand. Stay for the barbecue, bingo, and evening fireworks extravaganza at the end of the pier.

Fall

For over 20 years, the **Annual Cayucos Car Show** (Ocean Ave. downtown, 805/995-3809, www.cayucoschamber.com) has been making its way to downtown Cayucos in November. This one-day event is an all-around good old time with shiny cars, local music, lip-smacking barbecue, and, of course, a beer garden. Get tickets early as this event always sells out.

As fall arrives in November, the **Annual Cayucos Wine & Food Festival** (Vet's Hall, foot of the pier, 805/441-5406, www.cayucoschamber.com) delights the taste buds with local treats and handcrafted wines.

Winter

Kick off the new year in January with the annual **Carlin Soulé Memorial Polar Bear Dip** (Cayucos Pier, www.cayucoschamber.com). It all started when Carlin Soulé just couldn't stand the quiet of New Year's Day in Cayucos any longer. He started the first annual Polar Bear Dip three decades ago with about seven other brave souls. Today it attracts people by the hundreds. The festivities begin New Year's Day at 9:30 A.M., and the bone-chilling dip is at noon.

The Old Cayucos Tavern is located on North Ocean Avenue.

© KRISTIN LEAL

SHOPPING
◖ Antiques Shopping

Cayucos has three overflowing antiques shops along the main street. **Remember When Antiques** (152 N. Ocean Ave., 805/995-1232, www.rememberwhencayucos.com, daily 10 A.M.-5 P.M.) is just across the street from the beach, with several vendors selling jewelry, paintings, photos, dishware, Western memorabilia, military attire, outdoor garden pieces, furniture large and small, pop-culture memorabilia, handcrafted birdhouses, and many other treasures.

Just a few doors down is **Rich Man Poor Man Antiques** (146 N. Ocean Ave., 805/995-3631, www.richmanpoormancayucos.com, daily 10 A.M.-5 P.M.), with three stories of unique antiques from 80 different dealers. You can always count on estate jewelry, glassware, furniture, handcrafted items, china, mission-inspired pieces, Victorian tokens, and kitschy collectables.

At the far end of Ocean Avenue in a barnlike building is **Remember When Too Antiques** (36 N. Ocean Ave., 805/995-2074, www.rememberwhencayucos.com, daily 10 A.M.-5 P.M.), where you are likely to stumble on antique and vintage furnishings, jewelry, dishware, rugs, cloths, garden art, record albums, used books, and lamps. Make sure you leave time to explore the shop thoroughly.

Gift Shops

Lady Spencer Galleria and Fine Gifts (148 N. Ocean Ave., www.ladyspencer.com) is not a typical gift shop, and you won't see the usual T-shirts and shot glasses; instead you'll find an assortment of handmade items and unique pieces of art crafted by emerging American artisans. They carry Fire & Light hand-poured glass tableware, soy and specialty candles, handmade jewelry, handbags, sea-glass jewelry, natural soaps, original paintings, woodcarvings, handmade Christmas ornaments, garden items, ceramics, mirrors, and other home accents.

SAN SIMEON

SURFING SPOTS

© KRISTIN LEAL

Surfing is possible all year long in Central California.

All along the northern shoreline of San Luis Obispo County are sections of beach that beckon for all skill levels of surfing, kite surfing, windsurfing, body boarding, kayak surfing, and skim boarding. The beaches are wide with a long flat push into the sea, providing ideal board conditions. Sheltered coves foster beginners, and exposed beaches lure kite surfers.

Toward the north in San Simeon, the winds are pretty constant and attract the kite surfers and windsurfers by the dozen. Hot spots are near **Elephant Seal Vista** (Hwy. 1, 7 miles north of San Simeon) and south to San Simeon. There are many pullouts along Highway 1. When the tide is high or flat, this beach is great for skim boarding.

William Randolph Hearst Memorial State Beach (750 Hearst Castle Rd., 805/927-2020, www.parks.ca.gov, daily dawn-dusk, $10) has a sheltered cove with mellow to moderate swells ideal for children or beginners. The breakers aren't huge and are easy enough to get through; many break a good distance off shore, making for a long ride in.

Farther south, on the border of San Simeon and Cambria, is **Hearst San Simeon State Park** (Van Gordon Creek Rd. and San Simeon Creek Rd., 805/927-2020, www.parks.ca.gov, $10), where you can find nice surf year-round. The parking lot is close to the beach, and there are showers to rinse off. The waves don't get too huge, but there is a steady influx of powerful surf as the beach is more exposed to the open ocean; expect waves of intermediate skill level. The winds pick up here as well for windsurfers and kite surfers.

At Cambria the whole shoreline is one giant beach. **Moonstone Beach** (Moonstone Beach Dr., 805/927-2020, free) is somewhat secluded, but local surfers know this spot well. The surf is constant but crowds are small, even during summer. The beach is flat, and you will cross a few sets of breakers to get to the deeper waters and the big surf. This beach is appropriate for every skill level, but rocks present an obstacle near the shore.

Cayucos State Beach (foot of Cayucos Dr., 805/781-5930, www.parks.ca.gov, free) provides a nice log ride, especially valuable for first-timers and beginning surfers or body boarders. The waves tend to be mild to moderate. The beach is at the northern end of Estero Bay, slightly more sheltered from heavy surf and wind.

Morro Strand State Beach (Hwy. 1 Yerba Buena exit, just north of Morro Bay, 805/772-2560, www.parks.ca.gov, $10) has surf-in, surf-out accommodations, with a day-use parking lot and campsites practically right on the beach. The waves are good for surfers, body boarders, kite surfers, windsurfers, and kayak surfers, as the location in the center of the bay makes for moderate surf with good winds.

One of the most popular spots is **Morro Bay State Park** (Morro Bay State Park Rd., 805/772-2560, www.parks.ca.gov, daily, free) at the Rock. The winds tend to come in strongly at times.

ACCOMMODATIONS
RV Camping
One of the best-kept secrets in Cayucos is the **Bella Vista Travel Trailer Lodge** (350 N. Ocean Ave., 805/995-3644), an RV park just across the street from the beach. There are electric outlets and water at each site, and laundry and restrooms are available. Note that tents are not permitted.

Bed-and-Breakfasts
If beachfront is what you're looking for, **On the Beach Bed and Breakfast** (181 N. Ocean Ave., 805/995-3200 or 877/995-0800, www.californiaonthebeach.com, $149-349) has guest rooms on two floors, many with unobstructed view of the beach and ocean. Guest rooms are spacious, with an antique decor in mild tones and wide windows to showcase the view. Enjoy the comfort of an oversize jetted tub, mini fridge, gas fireplace, double sinks, upstairs balconies, microwaves, and free Wi-Fi.

The **Cayucos Sunset Inn Bed and Breakfast** (95 S. Ocean Ave., 805/995-2500 or 877/805-1076, www.cayucossunsetinn.com, $159-349) is just the place for a romantic getaway, with an in-house spa, five two-room suites with balconies and private ocean views, two-person jetted tubs, fireplaces, fridges, and DVD players. Guest rooms are elegantly decorated with handmade furnishings, and the beds are lavishly done in luxurious linens with down comforters.

Built in 1876 by Cayucos's founding father Captain James Cass, the **Cass House Inn & Restaurant** (222 N. Ocean Ave., 805/995-3696, www.casshouseinn.com, $163-325) is a living, breathing piece of history. The house was lovingly restored as a bed-and-breakfast in 2007 with five guest rooms and a one-bedroom suite. Each guest room is equipped with a large soaking tub, a fireplace, and a terrace. Breakfast is served, as is local wine and cheese in the early evening.

Over $250
If money is no object and you are looking for an exclusive private place, **Cottontail Creek Ranch** (2005 Cottontail Creek Rd., 805/995-1787, www.cottontailcreekranch.com, $1,295, 2-night minimum fall-spring, 3-night minimum summer) has a 4,200-square-foot ranch house on an 850-acre plot nestled among the rolling hills of the Santa Lucia Range. Hike to the property's seasonal creeks, ponds, and fruit orchards.

The ranch house is decorated with handcrafted furniture, local art, and antiques. There are five roomy bedrooms, six baths, two lofts, and a detached multipurpose room. The guest suites feature king and queen beds with phenomenal views of the property's valley. You can start swim in the lap pool, spend the afternoon at the spa, and end the day by the outdoor fire pit. Kick back in the living room next to the stone fireplace, cook your favorite meals in the gourmet kitchen, and gather in the den for an after-dinner drink at the bar.

FOOD
Casual Dining
A casual atmosphere and a variety of local wines are at **Full Moon Wine Bar and Bistro** (10 N. Ocean Ave., Suite 212, 805/995-0095, www.fullmoontastingroom.com, Sun.-Mon. 1-6 P.M., Thurs.-Sat. 4-10 P.M., $5 till 30). Sample local wines by the taste, flight, glass, and bottle with an ocean view. Pair some tempting appetizers and desserts or nibble on a tasty organic green salad, freshly made soups that change daily, or a nice selection of gourmet spreads and dips.

Cheap Eats
The aroma of fresh-baked goodies at **Brown Butter Cookie Co.** (250 N. Ocean Ave., 805/995-2076, www.brownbuttercookies.com, Tues.-Sun. 10 A.M.-3 P.M.) is enough to pull you in from the street. Brown-butter sea salt, the signature ingredient, gives the cookies a unique savory flavor. Try a free sample of the hand-rolled cookies. Make an order ahead of time to

bring some home for family and friends. They also ship all over the country.

Satisfy your sweet tooth at the **Cayucos Candy Counter** (75 Cayucos Dr., 805/995-1197, www.cayucoscandycounter.com, Mon.-Sat. 10 A.M.-9 P.M., Sun. 10 A.M.-6 P.M., $0.25-10), where you'll find old-time favorites as well as a few gourmet goodies. Specializing in old-fashioned candy, the Candy Counter also has an ice cream parlor with scoops and malted milk shakes.

For local wine tasting, the Selkirk family at **Cayucos Cellars** (131 N. Ocean Ave., 805/995 till 3036, Wed.-Mon. 11 A.M.-5:30 P.M.) welcomes you to their tasting room to sample some of their fine creations. Stuart is the official winemaker and can answer questions about the wines and the production process. Featured varietals are chardonnay, pinot noir, cabernet sauvignon, zinfandel, and syrah.

Fine Dining

Enjoy fresh flavors of the region at the **Cass House Restaurant** (222 N. Ocean Ave., 805/995-3696, www.casshouseinn.com, Thurs.-Mon. 5-9 P.M., 4 courses $64, add $28 for wine pairing). Chef Jensen Lorenzen makes it his mission to stock his kitchen with only the finest local ingredients to ensure a memorable meal. The menu changes daily and includes fresh fish, meats, and vegetables. The atmosphere is romantic, with low lighting downstairs in the historic house; servers are well versed in local wines and the changing menu. And if Lorenzen has any of his cured meats on the menu, you are in for a treat.

Farmers Market

Count on the **Cayucos Summer Farmers Market** (Vet's Hall parking lot, 10 Cayucos Dr., 805/296-2056, www.cayucoschamber.com, June 1-Aug. 31 Fri. 10 A.M.-12:30 P.M.) for a sense of the mercantile roots of Cass Landing. Enjoy farm-fresh selections of local produce, plants, flowers, and meats.

INFORMATION AND SERVICES

The nearest hospital to Cayucos is the **Twin Cities Hospital** (1100 Las Tablas Rd., Templeton, 805/434-3500), 20 miles inland near U.S. 101, just south of the Highway 46.

The town of Cayucos does not have an official visitors center, but check out www.cayucoschamber.com or www.cayucosbythesea.com. There is a local **U.S. Post Office** (97 Ash Ave., 805/995-3497).

GETTING THERE AND AROUND

Most visitors to Cayucos drive. The Pacific Coast Highway (Hwy. 1) is the prettiest but not the fastest way to get here. A quicker route is U.S. 101 to the Paso Robles area, then west on Highway 46, and south on Old Creek Road.

By rail, **Amtrak** (800/872-7245, www.amtrak.com) runs the Seattle-Los Angeles *Coast Starlight* via the Paso Robles station (800 Pine St., Paso Robles) and the San Luis Obispo station (1011 Railroad Ave., San Luis Obispo) once daily in each direction, and 12 *Pacific Surfliner* trains end and originate in San Luis Obispo each day with runs to Los Angeles and San Diego. To subsequently reach the coast, it's easiest to rent a car at the San Luis Obispo station.

The regional bus system **San Luis Obispo RTA** (805/781-4427, bus info 805/541-2228, www.slorta.org, $1.30-3, day pass $5) will get you around the southern part of Central California; Route 12/15 accesses Hearst Castle from Morro Bay via Cayucos on three daily round-trips.

SAN SIMEON

Morro Bay

One of California's last true fishing towns, Morro Bay is a fantastic hideaway just south of Monterey County known for the iconic Morro Rock. Locals call it "The Rock," and it is the last in a chain of volcanic peaks called the Nine Sisters. The town has a harbor, a wharf, and large state parks in the vicinity.

SIGHTS
The Wharf
Morro Bay's street-side wharf (Embarcadero Rd., www.morrobay.org) runs the length of Embarcadero Street and offers many attractions for visitors. One side of the buildings here faces the street and the town, while the other side faces the harbor and Morro Rock. Along the Wharf are dining, touristy shops, accommodations, whale-watching charters, fishing charters, kayak rentals, and the semi-submersible boat tours.

◖ Morro Rock
Originating beneath the sea a million years ago, Morro Rock is one of a string of small volcanic peaks that stretch inland to San Luis Obispo. A registered California Historical Landmark, it was described in the journals of Miguel Costanso and Father Juan Crespí in 1769. Today, Morro Bay is a nature preserve.

◖ Morro Bay Estuary
Morro Bay Estuary (Morro Bay-Los Osos, www.slostateparks.com) in Morro Bay is home to dozens of endangered species. On the wide wetlands you will encounter dozens of birds, but the blue herons, snowy egrets, and great egrets seem to be the favorites. Much like the estuary in Moss Landing, these wetlands reach deep into the landscape and open to the ocean at the mouth of the harbor. See this beautiful terrain from several access points from Morro Bay to Los Osos, each offering unique perspectives.

◖ El Moro Elfin Forest
Adjacent to Morro Bay Estuary and south of Morro Bay State Park is the El Moro Elfin Forest Natural Area (end of 11th St. to 17 St., Los Osos, www.elfin-forest.org, daily 30 minutes before sunrise till 30 minutes after sunset, free), with a nice boardwalk that meanders above the wetlands overlooking the quiet bay. There are 19 marked scenic points that make up a self-guided tour that highlights many of the natural inhabitants, including pygmy oak trees. The boardwalk trail is mostly flat and is about one mile long.

SPORTS AND RECREATION
Beaches
The sandy oceanfront of **Morro Strand State Beach** (Hwy. 1 Yerba Buena exit, just north of Morro Bay, 805/772-2560, www.parks.ca.gov) has good surfing with mellow rollers as well as excellent fishing from the shore. At low tide the three-mile-long beach is wide with a hard pack ideal for strolling.

Morro Bay State Park (Morro Bay State Park Rd., 805/772-2560, www.parks.ca.gov, daily, free) has several beach access points from the northern end of Morro Bay to Los Osos. For surfing, head to locally popular Morro Rock; the surf breaks on the north side of the rock, and the long breakers present a moderate challenge. There is a wide parking lot, restrooms, and showers at this location.

Surfing and Stand-Up Paddling
Reasonably priced and brand name-heavy **TDK Surf Shop** (911 Main St. and 571 Embarcadero Rd., 805/772-2431, daily 10 A.M.-6:30 P.M.) has two locations in Morro Bay, both with a

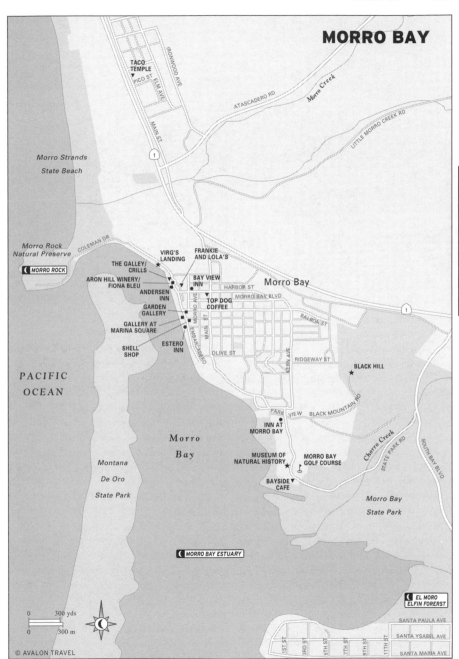

Morro Rock

complete line of surfing and body board gear, accessories, clothing, and equipment.

For apparel and surfing equipment, **Wavelength Surf Shop** (998 Embarcadero Rd., 805/772-3904, daily 9 A.M.-6 P.M.) carries top quality brands and products.

If you want to try the newer sport of stand-up paddling, **Central Coast Stand Up Paddling** (501 Embarcadero Rd., 805/395-0410, reservations 888/837-5610, www.centralcoastsup.com, winter Fri.-Sun. 9 A.M.-5 P.M., Tues.-Thurs. by appointment, summer Fri.-Sun. 9 A.M.-5 P.M., Tues.-Thurs. 8 A.M.-noon) sells and rents stand up equipment, or you can sign up for a mesmerizing guided tour. Stand-up paddling feels like walking on water, and here allows access to the deepest reaches of the Morro Bay Estuary or an open-water tour of the harbor. Half-day tours (daily 9 A.M.) depart from the State Park Marina; reservations are required via the website or by phone.

Whale Watching and Fishing Charters

Morro Bay is a harbor town with a handful of options to get out on the sea. Fishing trips seek out rock cod, king salmon, albacore, and halibut. Whales migrate through the cool waters of Morro Bay year-round, and there is nothing quite as magical as drifting alongside a whale or seeing them breach. The only way to get close to these creatures is a whale-watching trip.

Virg's Landing Morro Bay (1215 Embarcadero Rd., 805/772-1222 or 800/726-5263, www.virgs.com) has family-friendly 2.5-hour whale-watching or deep-sea fishing tours. If you can wake up before dawn, hitch a ride on one of their fishing boats, which go out year-round, and hook yourself some dinner. Rock cod are the easiest to catch, while more avid anglers will relish an albacore or salmon trip. Virg's has a full-service tackle store that rents poles and reels.

Central Coast Sportfishing (801

EGRETS AND HERONS

In the estuaries of California's Central Coast you are likely to encounter the majesty of great blue herons, great egrets, and snowy egrets. They are typically seen in hunting position, standing in shallow water waiting for a fish, frog, or crayfish to come on by. Their speed and accuracy are dramatic. They also like the tall grassy areas near the wetlands where ground squirrels make a good lunch.

Both the egrets and herons nest in colonies called rookeries. You can spot their large nests in the treetops above the ground. Herons start to nest in mid-February, and egrets follow about a month later in March. They generally lay 3-4 eggs every spring.

Look for them throughout the Morro Bay Estuary, El Moro Elfin Forest, and Morro Bay State Park, where there is a rookery just north of the museum in the cluster of dead trees. You can also see them in the large meadows along Highway 1 in San Simeon.

Embarcadero Rd., 805/704-2084, www.centralcoastsportfishing.com) runs day-long rock cod, albacore, and salmon fishing trips (4-12 hours, $46-86 pp) just outside Morro Bay. Midweek, children under age 15 get half off the tour cost. Whale-watching tours in winter typically run Thursday-Friday afternoon and daily in summer and fall, when humpback whales feed on local krill. If you are lucky you might see one breaching.

You can take a 3- to 4-hour whale-watching tour with **Sub Sea Tours** (699 Embarcadero Rd., Suite 9, 805/772-9463, www.subseatours.com, June-Sept. daily, $40 adults, $35 seniors, $30 children). Tours run year-round, and you may see a whale breach, come across a sea otter and pup, or see a fast pod of dolphins. If you are not willing to commit to hours out at sea but still want to see some marine life, take a tour on the semi-submersible *Sea View,* which has a wide window in the hull so you can experience what is below the surface of the ocean. Watch as the captain attracts a feeding frenzy of small fish.

Kayaking

The best way to get close to local marine life is by kayak, and Morro Bay has a variety of launches points, rentals, and tours. **Morro Strand State Beach** (Hwy. 1 Yerba Buena exit,

just north of Morro Bay, 805/772-2560, www.parks.ca.gov) has parking close to the beach, decent breakers for kayak surfing, and quick access to the open sea.

Within the harbor, at the end of Embarcadero Road are the city launch ramps. There is plentiful paid parking and a wide ramp that allows you to drive right up to the water.

At the base of Morro Rock in **Morro Bay State Park** (State Park Rd., 805/772-7434, www.parks.ca.gov, free) on the right is a beach launch point with bigger waves than Morro Strand. On the left is a drop-in point that puts you at the mouth of the harbor, near the open sea or the estuary.

Near the main entrance to **Morro Bay State Park** (Morro Bay State Park Rd., 805/772-2560, www.parks.ca.gov, daily, free), on the right side just before the museum, is another small beach perfect for launching kayaks. Parking spots face the water. But if you don't want to get muddy, head to the marina and use the launch ramps.

All around **Montaña de Oro State Park** (end of Percho Rd., Los Osos, 805/528-0513, www.parks.ca.gov, free) are beach access points to launch a kayak. The parking lots are nearly on the sand, and many of the beaches are in sheltered coves. Take off for the open sea or follow the jagged shoreline for miles in either direction.

KAYAK RENTALS AND TOURS

If you don't have your own equipment, find single-kayak, double-kayak, and 12-pack canoe rentals at **Sub Sea Tours** (699 Embarcadero Rd., Suite 9, 805/772-9463, www.subseatours. com, daily 9 A.M.-6 P.M., 1 hour $15-75, additional hours $5-25). The location allows you to just hop in the boats and go without launching. You can also sign up for a kayak tour to learn more about Morro Bay.

For a personal tour of the lush National Morro Bay Estuary with an expert nature guide, **Central Coast Outdoors** (805/528-1080 or 888/873-5610, www.centralcoastoutdoors. com, Mon.-Fri. 8 A.M.-5 P.M., Sat. 9 A.M.-noon, reservations required, $65-100) takes you near sea lions, seals, sea otters, and countless seabirds. Half-day tours, popular with beginners, have an optional lunch on the dunes; other options are sunset, full-moon, and dinner paddles, and all the required kayaking equipment is included.

Kayaks are always ready to go at Morro Bay State Park Marina, where **The Kayak Shack** (10 State Park Rd., 805/772-8796, www.morrobaykayakshack.com, daily, call for hours, 1 hour $12-16, additional hours $6-8) is just across from the campground and café. Taking off from the back end of the bay allows a fast, easy paddle to the great blue heron rookery, the sand spit, Morro Rock, and the estuary.

Hiking

Morro Bay State Park (State Park Rd., 805/772-7434, www.parks.ca.gov, free) has 15 trails through 2,700 acres with access to vistas and many different habitats. There are trails all around the Morro Rock Natural Preserve and Heron Rookery Natural Preserve for egret and sea otter sightings as well as views of the estuary and Morro Rock. Throughout the Cerro Cabrillo section of the park are chaparral hillsides with groves of coastal live oak trees. In the large eucalyptus trees northeast of the park's

museum are nesting sites of great blue herons, great egrets, and double-crested cormorants.

On the southern shores of Morro Bay is the largest state park in California, **Montaña de Oro** (end of Percho Rd., Los Osos, 805/528-0513, www.parks.ca.gov, free), with hiking trails through 8,000 acres of coastal landscape. Tromp through sandy dunes, fields of wildflowers, seven miles of shoreline, coastal bluffs, tide pools, beaches, streams, 1,347-foot Valencia Peak, and picnic sites with tables and barbecues. The park is expansive enough to provide some solitude.

Walk among the 800-year-old dwarf coastal live oaks at the inland **Los Osos Oaks State Natural Reserve** (Los Osos Valley Rd., Los Osos, 805/772-7434 or 805/772-2694, www. parks.ca.gov, daily 30 minutes before sunrise till 30 minutes after sunset, free). The 90-acre grove has three flat unpaved trails that run about 1.5 miles. You may encounter residents that include California pocket mice, gray foxes, bobcats, coyotes, striped skunks, dusky-footed wood rats, and possibly opossums.

Golf

Play a round at **Morro Bay Golf Course** (Morro Bay State Park, 201 State Park Rd., 805/782-8060, www.slocountyparks.com, $39-48 plus cart fee). You can't beat the views, seclusion, and price of this mostly hilly 18-hole course overlooking Morro Bay and the estuary.

Biking

During low tide, head to the base of **Morro Rock** and ride on the beach north toward Cayucos. Bike along **Embarcadero Road** or throughout **Morro Bay State Park** (State Park Rd., 805/772-7434, www.parks.ca.gov, free). On the southern end of the bay, **Montaña de Oro State Park** (end of Percho Rd., Los Osos, 805/528-0513, www.parks.ca.gov, free) has a variety of paved and dirt biking trails in the dunes and through the forest.

© KRISTIN LEAL

SAN SIMEON

Marvel at the slanting stone at Montaña do Oro State Park.

BIKE RENTALS

Farmer's Kites, Surreys, and More (1108 Front St., 805/772-0113, www.morrobaykites. com, daily 10 A.M.-5 P.M., $10 till 30 per hour) has a variety of bike rentals, including a four-seater surrey, or take a mountain bike to Montaña de Oro for the day. The shops is near Morro Rock, and you can start you ride just outside the front door. Head left along the Embarcadero, or follow the trail to the right to Morro Rock and the beach.

For a full-day experience with knowledgeable guides, **Central Coast Outdoors** (805/528-1080 or 888/873-5610, www.centralcoastoutdoors.com, Mon.-Fri. 8 A.M.-5 P.M., Sat. 9 A.M.-noon, reservations required, $129) offers four different trips that take riders along the Pacific Coast Highway or the wine country of Paso Robles and Edna Valley. If you take the wine tour, look forward to sampling fine local vintages. Reservations are required, and don't forget to ask about youth and group discounts.

ENTERTAINMENT AND EVENTS
Cinema

The only movie theater in town is the **Bay Theater** (464 Morro Bay Blvd., 805/772-2444), built during World War II and revamped during the 1970s. The retro vibe is fitting for the small town. Ticket prices are under $10, and the popcorn is served with real butter. Two showings daily screen the latest wide releases. Make sure to bring cash. Credit cards are not accepted.

Events
SPRING

As the wildflowers start to bloom in March, hot chili and cold beer appear at the **Beer Fest and Chili Cook Off** (1001 Kennedy Way, 818/887-1467, www.chilicookoff.com), an official International Chili Society Event with a first prize of $500 and a *verde* chili and salsa competition along with plenty of beer.

If you can't pass a garage sale without

stopping, Morro Bay has a two-day all-out treasure hunt in March-April called **City Wide Yard Sale** (throughout town, 805/772-4467, www.morrobay.org). You will find just about everything, including antiques, clothing, appliances, yard tools, sports equipment, and fishing gear. You may even find a boat or two for sale.

Up and away as kites take flight at the Rock. The sky fills with color and crowds gather at the family-friendly **Morro Bay Kite Festival** (Morro Rock, 805/772-4467, www.morrobay. org) in April. If you need your own kite, stop at **Farmer's Kites Surreys and More** (1108 Front St., 805/772-0113, daily 10 A.M.-5 P.M.), with every type of kite imaginable.

A true beach-town event is the four-day **Cruisin' Morro Bay Car Show** (Morro Bay Blvd., 805/772-4467, www.morrobaycarshow. org) in May. Old woodies and classic cars from around the country fill the Morro Bay Boulevard. The street is closed to regular traffic and fills with people admiring the shiny vehicles.

Ahoy mates! The **Mermaid and Pirate Parade** (from Dockside Restaurant to Morro Rock, 885/772-4467, www.morrobay.org) is a swashbuckling May event in which children lead the parade and march along the boardwalk to the base of the Rock dressed in full pirate regalia. Adults dress up too as the whole town gets into the spirit. The parade lasts an hour, and the rest of the day is full of celebrations.

Art in the Park (Morro Bay Park, Morro Bay Blvd., 805/772-2504, www.morrobayartassociation.org) is held three times a year in May, June, and September. Local artists and visiting craftspeople display their wares. You will find paintings, photos, handblown glass, birdhouses, jewelry, bags and purses, wind chimes, and other handmade treasures. You can also enjoy local musicians and purchase their CDs.

SUMMER

In June Morro Bay's waterfront hosts the **Morro**

Bay Music Festival (Embarcadero Rd., empty lot across from Boat Yard, 805/772-1155, www. mbmusicfest.com, free). Hear local bands and national rising stars, watch dance troupes, and catch demonstrations by community groups. There is plenty of food as well as microbrews and margaritas.

Celebrate the beginning of summer with **Morro Bay 4th of July** (Tidelands Park, 300 Embarcadero Rd., 800/396-6910, www.morrobay4th.org), a full-day event with family activities and fireworks on the bay. Head to Tidelands Park, the Embarcadero waterfront, or the Rock, or make reservations at one of the ocean-view restaurants for a special evening. Fireworks are launched from a barge on the southern end of the bay about 0.5 miles south of Tidelands Park.

The Morro Bay Garden Club holds the annual **Dahlia Daze and Cypress Nightz** (Morro Bay Community Center, 1000 Kennedy Way, 805/772-3737, www.morrobay.org), a two-day event in August filled with local wines, fine cheeses, and delightful dahlias. Listen to one of the featured guest speakers and see what's for sale among the art, floral arrangements, and dahlias.

FALL

Fill up at the **Avocado and Margarita Festival** (Embarcadero Rd., across from Roses, 805/772-4467, www.morrobayavocadomargaritafestivalevent.com) in September, a full day of vendors gathered on the Embarcadero to celebrate the avocado harvest. Sample California's finest avocados washed down with a margarita.

For over 30 years the **Harbor Festival** (pier and Embarcadero waterfront, 805/772-1155, www. mbhf.com) has been heating up an October weekend with wine tasting, beer chugging, and rock music. Twenty bands take to three different stages, including the Rocktoberfest Beer Garden. Watch the sailboat races, join the Hawaiian shirt contest, and marvel at the live ocean-rescue demonstrations.

© KRISTIN LEAL

The wharf in Morro Bay offers shopping, dining, fishing, and accommodations.

WINTER

See how a fishing town celebrates the holidays at the **Lighted Boat Parade** (Morro Bay Harbor, 805/772-4467, www.morrobay.org) in December. Local boat owners go all out and light up big boats, small boats, and sailboats floating around the bay. You may be dazzled and amused by all the different illuminated interpretations.

An estimated 450 birders from all over the country flock to Morro Bay in January for the annual **Winter Bird Festival** (Morro Bay Estuary, 805/257-4143, www.morrobaybirdfestival.org). Morro Bay is the ideal stage for this four-day celebration as it is in the middle of the Pacific Flyway, and you can expect to see thousands of birds of over 200 species. There are lectures, guided hikes, kayak tours, and photo tours.

SHOPPING

The town of Morro Bay has two major shopping areas. The Embarcadero waterfront caters to visitors and the fishing industry with countless souvenir shops, art galleries, wine-tasting rooms, specialty stores, and clothing shops. The Morro Bay Boulevard area has a different flavor, with antiques shops, secondhand stores, tattoo and piercing parlors, clothing shops, and fashion boutiques.

The Embarcadero

Two stories of touristy shopping at **Marina Square** (601 Embarcadero Rd., www.morrobay.com/shopping) include a bookstore, fine art galleries, jewelry, clothing, and a Christmas store. You can even stop in for wine tasting on the bottom floor. In the mall, **Somewhere in Time** (601 Embarcadero, Suite 14, 805/772-8513, www.morrobay.com/SomewhereinTime/, daily 10 A.M.-6 P.M.) has unique collectables such as teacups, porcelain dolls, Dezine fairies, and Lefton's lighthouses.

The birthplace of pillow pets is **Anita's Pillow Pets** (699 Embarcadero Rd., Suite 4, 805/772-1900, www.anitaspillowpets.com, daily 10 A.M.-5 P.M.). The soft snuggly stuffed animal transforms into a soft pillow. Anita's carries the full line of My Pillow Pets.

Since 1955 the Thomas family has been buying quality shells from around the world and selling them at **The Shell Shop** (590 Embarcadero Rd., 805/772-4137, www.theshellshop.net, daily 9 A.M.-6 P.M.), full of tables and walls lined with glass cases filled with shells. There are shell plant holders, Christmas ornaments, mirrors, and other items adorned in shells.

Find Morro Bay-logoed items at **Outer Bay Gifts** (875 Embarcadero Rd., 805/772-1568, daily 10 A.M.-6 P.M.). Get pirate double shot glass, a Rock coffee cup, T-shirts, hats, sunglasses, key chains, and other kitsch. Kids will love the stuffed sea animals, and there are also scented candles, special soaps, and floral arrangements.

Morro Bay Boulevard and Old Town

A unique shop is **Lina G's All the Trimmings** (468 Morro Bay Blvd., 805/772-7759, daily 10 A.M.-5 P.M.), with ribbon, barrels yarn, and lots lace. The colors are bright, and you can find vintage ribbons, lace, plenty of new pieces, velvets, yards of yarn, and fantastic feathers.

Just across the street is **Treasures Antique Mall** (475 Morro Bay Blvd., 805/772-3300, daily 10 A.M.-5 P.M.), with over 70 vendors carrying everything from sparkling rhinestone jewelry to large pieces of antique furniture. Find vintage greeting cards, used books, teacups, yards of fabric, comic books, nautical items, lamps, and clothing.

Next door is a tiny shop called **Mikkelson's Antiques** (455 Morro Bay Blvd., 805/772-4000, Mon.-Sat. 10 A.M.-5 P.M.). As you walk in you can't help but notice the large metal safe behind the register, along with silverware, jewelry, china, and teacups. Owner Denise also buys antiques.

ACCOMMODATIONS
Camping

Located just outside Morro Bay is the **Bay Pines RV Park** (1501 Quintana Rd., www.baypines.com, $34 daily), with 112 full-hookup sites. You have access to hot showers, coin-operated laundry, and clean restrooms. There is also a heated pool and a spa.

For beach-side camping, the **Morro Strand RV Park and State Beach** (Hwy. 1 Yerba Buena exit, just north of Morro Bay, 805/772-2560, www.parks.ca.gov, $35) has sites behind small dunes just steps from the beach. There are restrooms but no showers or hookups. The closest RV dumping station is at Morro Bay State Beach.

Morro Bay State Park (Morro Bay State Park Rd., 805/772-7434, www.parks.ca.gov, hookups $50, without hookups $35) has semi-secluded sites for RVs, and tent sites are nestled in the shade of the forest. There is also plenty of hiking trails through the park with views of Morro Rock and the bay.

Montaña de Oro State Park (end of Percho Rd., Los Osos, 805/528-0513, www.parks. ca.gov, $25) has 50 primitive sites in a sharp canyon behind the historic Spooner Ranch House for tents or RVs up to 27 feet. There are also walk-in tent sites for more seclusion. There are restrooms here but no showers or dump stations; the nearest are at Morro Bay State Park.

Camp close to the Rock at **Morro Dunes** (1790 Embarcadero Rd., 805/772-2722, www. morrodunes.com, RVs $44, tents $27.50), just inland of Morro Rock and protected by dunes. Sites have partial or full hookups. The place feels something like a parking lot, but there are dividers between many of the sites.

Under $150

Just above the Embarcadero Waterfront is the **Sea Air Inn** (845 Morro Ave., 805/772-4495, www.seaairinn.com, $33-235), with guest rooms that have a king, queen, or two double beds as well as included Wi-Fi, cable TV with HBO, coffeemakers, and free local calling. Some rooms have fridges, there is a microwave in the lobby, and breakfast is included in the room rates.

For simple beach-style guest rooms that

won't drain your wallet, **Morro Shore Inn & Suites** (290 Atascadero Rd., 805/772-0222 or 800/575-4095, www.morroshores.com, $62-159) has modest basic guest rooms with a little extra sitting space, and suites with separate living room and bedroom areas. All guest rooms have 32-inch flat-screen TVs, microwaves, fridges, coffeemakers, irons, ironing boards, and hair dryers.

Bayfront Inn (1150 Embarcadero Rd., 805/772-5607, www.bayfront-inn.com, $59-159) is a European-style hotel that offers unobstructed views of Morro Rock, Estero Bay, and abundant sealife. Guest rooms have fridges, coffee, included Wi-Fi, and HBO on TV. To fully unwind, ask about the California King room, with a full-size spa tub.

Marina Street Inn (305 Marina St., 805/772-4016 or 888/683-9389, www.mainstreetinn.com, $120-160) is a quaint bed-and-breakfast the fills up fast. The four themed suites are spacious and have small sitting areas. Savor gourmet home cooking for breakfast and wine in the late afternoon. You also have access to the kitchen if you want to cook your own lunch and dinner.

Views of Morro Rock are outstanding from guest rooms on the water side of the **Blue Sail Inn** (851 Market Ave., 805/772-2766 or 800/971-6910, www.bluesailinn.com, $89-235). The airy guest rooms have a down-to-earth nautical atmosphere as well as fridges, microwaves, and included Wi-Fi access; many have private balconies and cozy fireplaces. Continental breakfast is included in the room rates.

The suites at **Ascot Suites** (260 Morro Bay Blvd., 805/772-4437 or 800/887-6454, www. ascotsuites.com, $89-279) have European elegance for a romantic getaway. Suites have fireplaces, video players, jetted tubs, coffeemakers, and fridges; some have balconies. The roof garden is delightful for a stroll.

The modern accommodations and contemporary decor of the **Beach Bungalow Inn & Suites** (1050 Morro Ave., 805/772-9700, www.morrobaybeachbungalow.com, $109-269) include an array of room choices, from standard single kings through king suites with full kitchens. Guest rooms include Wi-Fi access, a full breakfast, flat-screen TVs, fridges, coffee and tea service, daily newspapers, chenille robes and slippers, hair dryers, and umbrellas. Pets are welcome.

Grays Inn & Gallery (561 Embarcadero Rd., 805/772-3911, www.graysinnandgallery.com, $120-187) has one-bedroom apartments with wide harbor views, patio decks, and full kitchens. These digs are just the thing for family vacations or an extended visit.

Every guest room at the **Embarcadero Inn** (456 Embarcadero Rd., 888/223-5777, www. embarcaderoinn.com, $120-220) faces the bay. Room options include standard rooms, doubles, and suites, and guest rooms have outdoor patios.

Just inland from Morro Bay, **Apple Farm Inn** (2015 Monterey St., 800/374-3705, www.applefarm. com, $139-249) has large grounds and charming gardens in the countryside. There is a restaurant on-site as well as a spa and massage service, a gift shop, and late-afternoon wine service, and the rooms are country elegant. Rooms are cozy and have fireplaces.

Just steps away from golf and hiking at Morro Bay State Park is the **Inn at Morro Bay** (60 State Park Rd., 805/772-5651 or 800/321-9566, www.innatmorrobay.com, $125-279). Guest rooms range from standards to suites and have a French country style and views of Morro Bay. Indulge yourself at the on-site spa.

$150-250

Make reservations early for **Front Street Inn and Spa** (1140 Front St., Suite C, 805/772-5038, www.frontstreetinn.net, $199), with just two deluxe private guest rooms, both with an elegant modern feel. Every window has stunning views.

Every guest room at **Estero Inn** (501 Embarcadero Rd., 805/772-1500, www.esteroinn.com, $150-329) has views of Morro Bay

Relax in the country comforts of the Apple Farm Inn.

and is equipped with a flat-screen TV, coffee-maker, microwave, fireplace, included Wi-Fi and LAN Internet access; continental breakfast is included in the room rates. The Embarcadero waterfront location is just steps from great recreation, boat charters, shopping, and dining.

Over $250

Positioned on the waterfront overlooking the bay and Morro Rock is the **Anderson Inn** (897 Embarcadero Rd., 805/772-3434 or 866/905-3434, www.andersoninnmorrobay.com, $239-349). The premium guest rooms sit over the water, and the deluxe guest rooms have a full view of the Rock and the northern end of the bay. Both have queen beds, flat-screen HD TVs, balconies with harbor views, fridges, fireplaces, soaking tubs, and safes.

FOOD
Beach Eats

Go to **Roca's Surf Shack** (945 Embarcadero Rd., 805/225-1200, fall-spring daily 11 A.M.-8 P.M., summer daily 11:30 A.M.-9 P.M., $5-13) for the ultimate beach-eats experience. The vibe is about surfing, with chairs covered in beach towels, surfboards hanging from the ceiling, and shark kites flying overhead. Roca's serves burgers, tacos, soups, salads, steamed seafood, fish-and-chips, calamari, a fried rock cod sandwich, clams, and mussels, and there is a children's menu. On a warm day, the outside picnic tables or benches have harbor and Rock views.

There is nothing quite like a cheeseburger and milk shake from **Fosters Freeze** (801 Pine Way, 805/772-8373, www.fostersfreeze.com, daily 10 A.M.-9 P.M., $5-8), which also serves burger shack fare such as corn dogs, chili, hot dogs, burgers, chicken sandwiches, chicken strips, twisters, freezes, and chocolate-dipped cones. Get it to take with you or hang out by the fish tank.

Not only do they sell a wide variety of fresh seafood from the waters of Morro Bay, **Giovanni's Fish Market** (1001 Front St.,

805/772-1276, www.giovanniafishmarket.com, daily 9 A.M.-6 P.M., $4-8) is a fine place to dine, with foot-long fish-on-a-stick, fish tacos, clam chowder, oysters on the half shell, salads, sandwiches, and Mexican fare.

Breakfast

For one of the best home-cooked breakfasts in town, **Carla's Country Kitchen** (213 Beach St., 805/772-9051, www.countrykitchenrestaurants.com, daily 7 A.M.-2 P.M., $8-17) is a great family place with kid-friendly items like PB&J pancakes or turtle pancakes. Menu items include biscuits and gravy, french toast done several creative ways, steak and eggs, chicken-fried steak, and omelets.

A tasty place to start the day is the **Coffee Pot Restaurant** (1001 Front St., 805/772-3176, daily 7 A.M.-2 P.M., $5-10). Get a table inside or a seat at the counter. American breakfasts are served with a seafood twist. On weekends, expect a wait.

Stop in **La Parisienne French Bakery** (1140 Front St., 805/772-8530, daily 6 A.M.-2:30 P.M., $2-8) for espresso drinks, fresh pastries, delicious breakfast sandwiches, and croissants with fruity fillings. Sit inside or out to enjoy the views of the ocean and Morro Rock.

For cinnamon rolls and hot coffee, try **Sun-N-Buns Bakery and Espresso Bar** (830 Embarcadero Rd., 805/772-4117, www.sun-n-buns.com, Sun.-Thurs. 8:30 A.M.-8:30 P.M., Fri.-Sat. 8:30 A.M.-9:30 P.M., $2-8). It also has all sorts of freshly baked goods such as cookies, tarts, and a variety of pastries as well as ice cream.

Casual Dining

Overlooking the south end of the harbor is **Orchid** (Inn at Morro Bay, 60 State Park Rd., 805/772-5651, www.innatmorrobay.com, daily 7-10 A.M. and 4-9 P.M., brunch Sun. 11 A.M.-2 P.M., $14-25), specializing in regional sustainable American cuisine with a focus on local seafood, meat, and produce. The

wine list pairs nicely with many of the menu items. Don't miss live music year-round Friday-Saturday nights, featuring local jazz, blues, and classic rock bands.

Arrive early for a window seat with views of the harbor and Morro Rock at **Embarcadero Grill** (801 Embarcadero Rd., 805/772-0700, www.embarcaderogrill.com, Mon.-Thurs. 8 A.M.-9 P.M., Fri.-Sat. 8-10 P.M., $12-25). Tables fill up fast for breakfast, lunch, or dinner. The menu is built around the wood-fired grill, but you will also find seafood dishes and Mexican staples.

For over 40 years, **Hofbrau** (901 Embarcadero Rd., 805/772-2411, www.hofbraumorrobay.com, daily 11 A.M.-8:30 P.M., $7.50-15) has been making hand-cut roast-beef sandwiches with slow-cooked beef. There is also a children's menu, a fresh salad bar, homemade soups, fish-and-chips, hamburgers, and other hot sandwiches such as pastrami and corned beef.

With a view of Morro Rock, **Distasio's on the Bay** (781 Market St., 805/771-8760, www.distasios.com, daily 11:30 A.M.-2 P.M. and 4-9 P.M., $10-20) serves southern Italian seafood, steak, chicken, veal, pasta, and pizza dishes Dogs are welcome on the enclosed heated patio.

If you are catching a movie at the Bay Theater or doing some afternoon shopping on Morro Bay Boulevard, **Jasmine Thai Cuisine** (355 Morro Bay Blvd., 805/772-5988, Mon.-Thurs. 11 A.M.-8:30 P.M., Fri. 11 A.M.-9 P.M., Sat. noon-9 P.M., Sun. noon-8:30 P.M., $8-15) is a great option for dining with a full menu of soups, appetizers, salads, noodles, rice, curries, and, of course, Thai iced tea. Every dish is made fresh and can be spiced to your taste.

Fine Dining

Overlooking Morro Bay, **Galley Seafood Grill & Bar** (899 Embarcadero Rd., 805/772-7777, www.galleymorrobay.com, 11 A.M.-2:30 P.M. and 5 P.M.-close, $15-46) uses hand-selected ingredients from its own farm, Hearst Ranch,

© KRISTIN LEAL

The bento lunch boxes at Harada are always filling.

local fishing boats, and other local growers; You will also find an impressive wine list.

For an organic gourmet dinner and gorgeous bay views, dine at **Windows on the Water** (699 Embarcadero Rd., 805/772-0677, www.windowsonthewater.net, Sun.-Thurs. 5-8:30 P.M., Fri.-Sat. 5-9 P.M., $30-45). Executive chef Neil Smith creates dishes from locally farmed produce, meats, and seafood, and the plating is stunning.

Locally caught fish is served at **Harada Japanese Restaurant** (630 Embarcadero Rd., 805/772-1410, daily 11 A.M.-2 P.M. and 4:30 P.M.-close, $15-38) in an authentic Asian atmosphere with samurai armor adorning the dining area. Cooked and raw items include *udon* soup, teriyaki beef and chicken, hand rolls made to order, and grilled salmon, tuna, and freshwater eel. You can't go wrong with the lunch specials, always filling and a bit cheaper than dinner.

Farmers Markets

The **Community Farmers' Market** (www.slocountyfarmers.org) kicks off twice a week in the old town (Main St. and Harbor St., Sat. 3-6 P.M.) and in north Morro Bay (2650 Main St., Thurs. 3-5 P.M.).

INFORMATION AND SERVICES

The nearest hospital to Morro Bay is the **Twin Cities Hospital** (1100 Las Tablas Rd., Templeton, 805/434-3500), 24 miles inland near U.S. 101 just south of Highway 46.

It is easy to find the **Morro Bay Visitors Center** (845 Embarcadero Rd., Suite D, 800/231-0592), located where the waterfront action is. You can also check the local Chamber of Commerce website (www.morrobay.org). Morro Bay has a **U.S. Post Office** (898 Napa Ave., 805/772-0839).

GETTING THERE AND AROUND

Most visitors to Morro Bay drive. The Pacific Coast Highway (Hwy. 1) is the prettiest but not the fastest way to get here. A quicker route is U.S. 101 to Atascadero, south of Paso

Robles, then west on Highway 41 to Morro Bay. Another option is to take the U.S. 101 the Madonna exit in San Luis Obispo to Los Osos Valley Road and South Bay Boulevard, which leads to Morro Bay.

By rail, **Amtrak** (800/872-7245, www.amtrak.com) runs the Seattle-Los Angeles *Coast Starlight* via the Paso Robles station (800 Pine St., Paso Robles) and the San Luis Obispo station (1011 Railroad Ave., San Luis Obispo) once daily in each direction, and 12 *Pacific Surfliner* trains end and originate in San Luis Obispo each day with runs to Los Angeles and San Diego. To subsequently reach the coast, it's easiest to rent a car at the San Luis Obispo station.

The regional bus system **San Luis Obispo RTA** (805/781-4427, bus info 805/541-2228, www.slorta.org, $1.30-3, day pass $5) will get you around the southern part of Central California. Routes 11 and 13 connect Morro Bay to San Luis Obispo and Los Osos; Route 12/15 accesses Hearst Castle from Morro Bay on three daily round-trips.

BACKGROUND

The Land

GEOGRAPHY

Monterey Bay and Monterey Peninsula are located 120 miles south of San Francisco, 60 miles southwest of San Jose, and 345 miles north of Los Angeles. A multitude of environments and climates makes up this fascinating stretch of coastline from the Santa Cruz Mountains down to Morro Bay.

The rural inland region of Monterey County has fertile farmland and rows of vineyards. Redwood forests tower in both Monterey and Santa Cruz Counties. Big Sur and Santa Cruz are known for backcountry hiking and biking, and all along the incredibly scenic coast, the surf is up year-round.

CLIMATE

The climate of the Monterey area varies from season to season and from place to place. On a daily basis, inland microclimate areas differ dramatically from the peninsula's seaside climate. On the coast, you can count on cool dry summers, wet winters, and warm falls. More often than not, summer weather is foggy and a bit chilly, especially in the morning and late afternoon. Temperatures tend to be in

© KRISTIN LEAL

SAN ANDREAS FAULT

The San Andreas Fault, the most accessible fault line in the world, is a vivid example of active plate tectonics. It is a sliding boundary or transform fault between the North American Plate and the Pacific Plate that slices California in two from Cape Mendocino in the north through the Mexican border. The plates are slowly moving past each other in opposite directions—a couple of inches per year—to create complex landforms all along its mighty rift.

When these plates shift lock against each other, the pressure becomes too great, and they break free with movement of a few feet at a time. This seismic action sends massive vibration waves in every direction, causing an earthquake. Along with many other fault lines, this is why California is prone to so many quakes; the state is slowly being dragged apart, and sometimes you can feel the rip.

The fault is thought to be about 28 million years old and has moved rocks from great distances. Geologists have found evidence of this movement at places like the Pinnacles National Monument in Monterey County. The Pinnacles themselves are only half of a massive volcanic complex; the other half is known as the Neenach Volcano and sits about 200 miles southeast, in Los Angeles County.

the mid-60s. The best weather on the coast is in September-October. As the children return to school, the heavily visited spots quiet down, and daytime temperatures warm up to low 70s. Winter is the rainy season and lasts November-April, with average temperatures in the low 50s. Heavy storms on the Pacific Ocean throw down substantial amounts of water in a short time, and Santa Cruz usually gets hit the hardest. The yearly average temperature in Monterey County is 57°F with 19 inches of precipitation annually. The coastal climate is usually a bit windy, moist, and foggy. The southern reaches of the Central Coast are normally warmer than farther north, both in the air and in the water. The inland region around Salinas is noticeably hotter and drier, with coastal winds rolling over the neighboring coastal mountains.

ENVIRONMENTAL ISSUES

Several environmental issues are important in the Monterey area, but the hot topics have to do with sustainability, protection of the marine sanctuary, land usage, and a general focus on everyday green practices. Monterey Bay is in a **National Marine Sanctuary** (www.montereybay.noaa.gov) that reaches from Marin County in the north down to Cambria. The federal government and the local population are focused on protecting this treasured environment. The **Monterey Bay Aquarium** (www.montereybayaquarium.org) is also a major environmental advocate in Monterey County, promoting seafood sustainability, the marine sanctuary, and other things we can do to preserve the environment. **Land Watch Monterey County** (www.landwatch.org) is a local nonprofit organization focused on land management. California State University, Monterey Bay, has created a website known as **Environmental Issues and Groups** (www.agriculturaleducationandtraining.org/environmentalissuesandgroups) with a broad range of resources on industry and trade, educational originations, community groups, and companies.

Flora and Fauna

TREES

Throughout Monterey County, Santa Cruz County, and the northern part of San Luis Obispo County, the variety of flora reflects the diverse ecosystems that exist in this region. Found exclusively on the Monterey Peninsula is the **Monterey cypress.** There are only two natural groves of Monterey cypress today, one in Monterey and the other near Carmel in Point Lobos State Natural Reserve. These groves were once part of a large cypress forest that stretched all along the Central Coast 2,000 years ago. The Monterey cypress is a rugged tree that lives in the harsh ocean-side climate. The trees conform to the pressure of the wind and tend to grow with flat tops and twisting limbs.

Monterey pines are native to the area and grow in groves on the rolling hills and slopes of Monterey, Santa Cruz, Año Nuevo, Cambria, Cayucos, and Morro Bay. Today, Monterey pines are among the most popular ornamental trees in the world, grown for both landscaping and commercial cultivation. Monterey pines are hearty with fissured brown bark and limbs covered with sappy pine needles. They are likely a cousin to the Jeffrey pines of the Sierra Nevada Mountains.

The **bishop pine,** also known as the prickle-cone pine, is commonly found throughout Pacific Grove's Huckleberry Hill, along the Santa Lucia Range, and into San Luis Obispo County. Bishop pines look like a smaller sibling of the Monterey pine.

The **knobcone pine** is another local pine species named after its knobbed pinecones. These trees like to root in dry rocky mountain soil, and you will most likely encounter them in the steep terrain of Big Sur and the northern part of San Luis Obispo.

Groves of nonnative **eucalyptus trees** grow along the shores of Santa Cruz and Capitola,

and inland along Highway 156 near Hollister, Pacific Grove, Palo Colorado Canyon, and south throughout Morro Bay. These tall trees, with curling bark and feather-like leaves, are not difficult to pick out; their refreshing scent and unique appearance instantly give them away.

There are several different species of oaks in this area, including the **California live oak, black oak,** and the **tanbark oak.** Oak trees are mostly seen in the inland regions and near the coast on wide grassy hillsides. You can find them on the chaparral hills of Carmel Valley and Salinas Valley, on the meadows and open hills of Big Sur, throughout the Santa Lucia Mountain Range, and down to Morro Bay.

One of the rarest oaks growing along California's Central Coast is the **pygmy oak,** unusual and tiny trees seen along the southern stretch of the Morro Bay Estuary in the El Morro Elfin Forest. They resemble common oak trees in miniature size, 4-20 feet tall, and grow only along the California and Oregon coast.

You can't talk about trees on California's Central Coast without talking about the **coastal redwoods.** There are two large redwood forests in this area, one in the Santa Cruz Mountains and the other in Big Sur. Both are part of the same chain of redwoods and are all continuously connected through their root systems. You can wander among the big trees of Santa Cruz in Big Basin State Park and Henry Cowell State Park. The redwoods of Big Sur grow throughout the region in the Los Padres National Forest's Ventana Wilderness, Andrew Molera State Park, Big Sur State Park, Bottchers Gap, and several other federal and state parks along the coast.

FLOWERS

The diversity of flowering plants in California's Central Coast is magnificent. During spring,

THE CYPRESS TREES OF MONTEREY

The Monterey cypress tree is native to the Monterey Peninsula and grows nowhere else in the world. The iconic Lone Cypress of Pebble Beach has become a recognizable symbol of the region. The tree sits atop an ocean-side cliff along 17-Mile Drive in Pebble Beach and is believed to be about 250 years old.

Monterey cypresses can also be seen at the Point Lobos State Natural Reserve. The cypress grove is accessible along the mile-long Cypress Grove Trail. The loop trail is an easy walk with a few sections of rocks to scramble through. A leisurely walk around the loop takes about 30 minutes.

Pacific Grove's shoreline ignites in brilliant magentas as the **ice plants** bloom, clinging to the sides of steep cliffs. Saffron-colored **California poppies** bloom in clusters along the inland reaches of Carmel Valley, down Highway 1 into Big Sur, and north of Santa Cruz along the curving coast. You will sometimes come across whole fields or hillsides full of brilliant poppies, but most of the time tiny groupings are found here and there. Huge **yellow lupine** bushes can be found all through Big Sur and in the meadows of Andrew Molera State Park. **Purple lupine** lines Highway 68 toward Salinas every year.

The Monterey Chapter of the **California Native Plant Society** (http://montereybay. cnps.org) provides a nearly complete list of local plantlife and where to find specific species.

MAMMALS

Throughout the Central Coast is an abundance of mammals near the ocean's surface and on the land. The Monterey area is famous for whales, dolphins, sea otters, sea lions, and seals that migrate through or make the bays their full-time home.

As many as 7,000 gray whales migrate through the waters of the Monterey Bay December-March. Killer whales, humpbacks, and the colossal blue whale also migrate through. Local whale-watching companies depart daily from Santa Cruz, Monterey, Moss Landing, and Morro Bay to encounter these massive ocean mammals. Elephant seals are found both in Año Nuevo State Reserve and north of San Simeon at the Piedras Blancas rookery year-round. A variety of sea lions and harbor seals are found along the coast.

On the land are black-tailed deer, ground squirrels, wild turkeys, bobcats, mountain lions, coyotes, foxes, raccoons, opossums, bats, wild boars, and many other warm-blooded landlubbers. Wild boars are typically found from Carmel to San Simeon in the Los Padres National Forest. Deer are just about everywhere, especially on the greens of Pebble Beach and the forests of Point Lobos State Natural Reserve.

SEALIFE

One of the special features of Monterey Bay that attracts such a variety of sealife are two submarine canyons deep beneath the surface. The Monterey Submarine Canyon is massive, more than 10 times the size of the Grand Canyon, starting just offshore of Moss Landing and extending 95 miles. It has a maximum rim-to-floor height of 5,577 feet, comparable to the Grand Canyon. The Carmel Submarine Canyon is much smaller, perfect for diving, and full of mature sealife. The canyons are rich with nutrients that attract everything from tiny krill to blue whales. Thick kelp forests and protruding pinnacles are found all around Monterey and Carmel.

The submarine canyons are home to rock cod, leopard sharks, wolf eels, corals, sponges, giant sea anemones, sun fish, strawberry anemones, lingcod, giant sunstars, starfish, abalone, sea urchins, sea cucumbers, squid, jellyfish, and crabs. Great white sharks are also known

© KRISTIN LEAL

Otters frequent the waters of Monterey Bay.

to frequent the cool waters of Monterey Bay. Attacks are rare but do happen occasionally. Most of the time it is a case of mistaken identity, when a great white bites a surfer, thinking it was an elephant seal, which great whites hunt at the Año Nuevo elephant seal rookery. Great whites come north to breed late August-mid-winter.

Along the shoreline, more sealife finds a home in tide pools, which can be found throughout the region. Scenic Drive in Pacific Grove, Pebble Beach, Natural Bridges State Beach, Morro Strands State Beach, and Montaña de Oro State Park have tide pools where you can touch small anemones, starfish, tiny crabs, kelp, sea grasses, and hermit crabs.

BIRDS

The fertile submarine canyons of Monterey Bay attract a plethora of sea, shore, and land birds to the Peninsula. At Moss Landing's Elkhorn Slough, there are more than 200 different bird species. Many choose to make Monterey their home, and others visit on the way through to feed. Some of the more popular residents are the pelicans, egrets, blue herons, sandpipers, peregrine falcons, owls, condors, and cormorants. Popular places for bird-watching include Moss Landing, the Ventana Wilderness, Morro Bay Estuary and blue heron rookery, Wilder Ranch State Park, Point Lobos State Reserve, and Natural Bridges State Beach.

REPTILES

The most common snakes in the area are the gopher snake, Western rattlesnake, Monterey ring-necked snake, long-nosed snake, and California red-sided garter snake. Monterey ring-necked snakes are mildly venomous, but the ones be wary of are the highly venomous rattlesnakes, although it's rare for people to die from snakebite in California. Throughout the wetlands of the region are lizards, frogs, toads, and the endangered Santa Cruz Long-toed salamander.

MONARCH BUTTERFLIES

You can't talk about insects and Monterey without mentioning the world-famous monarch butterfly migration. Escaping winter's chill, the fluttering monarchs begin to make their appearance in Pacific Grove and Santa Cruz in early November and stay until late February. In fact, all along the California coastline to northern Baja California, you can witness the monarch winter migration. They cluster in the foliage in certain locations along the coast, creating a coat of brilliant orange. There are monarch sanctuaries in Pacific Grove, a.k.a. "Butterfly Town USA," and at Natural Bridges State Beach in Santa Cruz.

ARACHNIDS AND OTHER INSECTS

You probably won't come across any, but California's Central Coast is home to tarantulas, black widows, brown recluse spiders, scorpions, and ticks. If you are in the woods, tall grass, or brushy areas, watch for ticks and check your skin and your dog after hiking, especially in spring-summer. Ticks are known to carry Lyme disease, and you should be sure to remove every bit of their body from the skin to avoid infection. Be on the lookout for scorpions in the sandy dunes of Old Fort Ord, Seaside, and Marina. Within the Ventana Wilderness, Santa Cruz Mountains, northern San Luis Obispo County, and the inland reaches of the Central Coast, be wary of tarantulas,

© KRISTIN LEAL

Look closely and walk lightly through the tide pools to catch a glimpse of a quick-moving crab.

black widows, and brown recluse spiders. If you think you have been bitten or stung by one of these creatures, get to a hospital as soon as possible. If you can, try to capture the venomous creature dead or alive (and be careful not to get bitten again) and bring it with you. Apply an ice pack to the site of the bite. If a hospital is not within reach, a local ranger station or fire station should be your next choice.

WHALE MIGRATION

Whale-watching is pretty much a year-round event in Monterey Bay. You can often catch a glimpse of these magnificent creatures with binoculars. The whales travel in pods far offshore and can be seen from scenic Highway 1, Año Nuevo State Park, Wilder Ranch State Park, Point Lobos State Natural Reserve, Carmel Highlands, Pacific Grove, 17-Mile Drive in Pebble Beach, and Morro Rock. For an up-close encounter, join a whale-watching tour with one of the many operators in Santa Cruz, Moss Landing, Monterey, or Morro Bay.

During the winter, California gray whales make their way through Monterey Bay and stop to eat on their long journey from Alaska to Baja California. The massive mammals' journey to Baja is for mating and birthing calves before they make their way home to Alaska by spring. Throughout the migration season, you can see these animals in action, but prime viewing is January-mid-February, and your chance of seeing a mother and calf increases during late February-April.

Throughout the summer and fall, Monterey Bay's marine sanctuary is visited by majestic humpback whales, blue whales, orcas, and a variety of dolphin and porpoise species. The waters off the Monterey coast are rich with nutrients, thick with clusters of krill, and crawling with seal pups for the orcas to eat.

History

EARLY HISTORY

The Native American people of California's Central Coast were well established millennia before the Spanish explorers came in the late 1760s. The major groups living in what is now the Monterey area were the Ohlone, Esselen, and Salinan. The Ohlone people also lived in the area around Santa Cruz, with more than 50 villages in the county. In what is now the San Luis Obispo area, the Salinan and Chumash peoples were the original inhabitants.

COLONIALISM

The first major colonization effort by Europeans began in the late 1760s and lasted until the first part of the 1800s. The Spanish began to occupy the Central Coast and developed the mission system, a series of military outposts and religious compounds built by Spanish Franciscans to convert the indigenous people to Roman Catholicism. In the 1830s the Mexican government shut down the missions. The Spanish and Mexican governments continued to issue land grants and establish rancheros throughout central California until the mid-1800s. Today, the missions are among California's oldest buildings and are visited by thousands of people every year.

STATEHOOD

California officially became a state in 1850 during the gold rush. The first California Constitution was drafted within the walls of Monterey's Colton Hall.

During the U.S. Civil War, California sent funds east to fight the secession but did not send troops.

THE 20TH CENTURY

During World War II, Monterey became known as the "Sardine Capital of the World." Sardine canning had become a booming industry by the 1920s, with Monterey's Cannery Row the hub of the industry. Over the next two decades, an estimated 250,000 tons of sardines per year were processed by the reduction plant and canneries in the Monterey area. This era was short-lived, but the nickname would last. From 1940 the sardine population declined and collapsed, which some blame on changing currents or water pollution but is most likely attributable to overfishing. By the mid-1950s once-bustling Cannery Row had become a ghostly collection of empty and abandoned warehouses. It was during this time that John Steinbeck wrote his famed 1945 novel *Cannery Row*.

THE CENTRAL COAST TODAY

Today, the local economy of the Monterey area is based on tourism, agriculture, and fishing, which often overlap: For example, local fisheries are used both recreationally and commercially, local farms invite visitors to the fields to pick their own berries and pumpkins, and Central Coast vineyards open their doors and offer countless tasting rooms. Many local residents find jobs in the military, the hospitality industry, education, health care, tourism, agriculture, and fishing.

ESSENTIALS

Getting There and Around

AIR

There are two major airports in the Monterey area, one in Monterey and the other in San Jose. The **Monterey Peninsula Airport** (MRY, 200 Fred Kane Dr., 831/648-7000, www.montereyairport.com) has service from United, Allegiant, American Eagle, and America West. Car-rental companies are located inside the airport. Taxi service is available through **Central Coast Taxi** (831/626-3333), or travel in style with a limo through **Arrow Luxury Transportation** (831/646-3175).

The **San Jose International Airport** (SJC, 2077 Airport Blvd., 408/277-4859, www.sjc. org) is about 90 minutes from Monterey, on U.S. 101 in Silicon Valley. The major domestic airlines serve this airport, and there are flights to Mexico. The **Monterey-Salinas Air Bus** (831/373-7777, www.montereyairbus.com, $30-40) takes passengers directly to Monterey, and there are car-rental companies at the airport.

TRAIN

Amtrak's Seattle-Los Angeles *Coast Starlight* train travels through Salinas (Station Place and Railroad Ave., Salinas, daily 8 A.M.-10 P.M.) daily

© MONTEREY COUNTY VISITORS CENTER

CENTRAL COAST TOUR COMPANIES

Throughout the Monterey Peninsula and Santa Cruz County are tour companies that specialize in a variety of sightseeing adventures and guided tours If you are interested in wine tasting, agriculture, guided walking tours, movie tours, wildlife safaris, a helicopter ride, or a food tour, operators in the area have it covered.

Monterey Movie Tours (831/372-6278, www.monereymovietours.com, daily 1-4 P.M., by reservation, $55) will show you the Monterey Peninsula through the tinted shades of Hollywood. Visiting sites where movies were filmed while watching the actual scene on overhead monitors. Visit their website for a $10 discount.

Ag Venture Tours (831/384-7686, www.agventuretours.com, by reservation, full-day and half-day tours $70-130 pp) is known for agricultural, wine-tasting, sightseeing, and customized educational tours. They can take you all around Santa Cruz and Monterey Counties; visit the website for full listings.

Carmel Walks (831/642-2700, www.carmelwalks.com, Tues.-Fri. 10 A.M., Sat. 10 A.M. and 2 P.M., $25 pp) takes you behind the scenes of the fairy-tale village of Carmel-by-the-Sea. Walk the winding streets and hidden pathways, secret courtyards, and stunning gardens. You will also learn about Carmel's rich legacy of artists, writers, and movie stars as you walk by their homes.

Monterey Walking Tours (1 Portola Plaza, Monterey, 831/521-4884, www.walkmonterey.com, Fri.-Sun. 10 A.M., call for availability, $10) visits Cannery Row and historic downtown Monterey. Take a walk with knowledgeable guides that show you the hot spots and explain the local lore and rich history.

Elkhorn Slough Safari and Guided Nature Boat Tour (831/633-5555, www.elkhornslough.com, tours daily by reservation,

$35 adults, $26 children, $32 seniors) takes you through one of California's largest wetlands. Tours are typically two hours, and specialty seasonal tours include photo trips and a springtime baby tour. On board, you will learn about various aspects of the slough's ecology, fascinating history, and birding in the company of a naturalist guide and knowledgeable captain.

Specialized Helicopters (831/763-2244, www.specializedheli.com, daily by reservation, from $99 for 3 people) reveals Monterey Bay from a bird's-eye view. Sign up for a short tour over the fields of Watsonville and New Brighton State Beach, or take an extended trip to Big Sur's infinite coastline.

Santa Cruz Bike Tours (831/722-2453, www.santacruzbiketours.com, daily by reservation, $95 pp) is the place for every kind of bike rider. Guided tours are designed to fit all skill levels and individual group needs. Enjoy getting a little dirty on a mountain biking adventure, or take the family on a sightseeing tour along the Santa Cruz coast. All gear is provided, including water and snacks.

The Santa Cruz Experience (831/421-9883, www.thesantacruzexperience.com, by reservation, $75 pp) will guide you to the finest local wineries and vineyards of the Santa Cruz Mountains. Take in the flavors of the area as a guest of local winemakers. Tours last a full day, and you get to visit many locations that are not generally open to the public.

Santa Cruz Food Tour (800/838-3006, www.santacruzfoodtours.com, Fri.-Sun. 2 P.M., by reservation, $52.50) is the hot foodie ticket in town. You will spend about 3.5 hours exploring the culinary sensations of downtown Santa Cruz along with tales of history and captivating architecture in off-the-beaten-path neighborhoods.

in both directions. It also stops in the region at Oxnard, Santa Barbara, San Luis Obispo, and Oakland. For Amtrak travelers, there is free bus service (30 minutes) to downtown Monterey.

You can get to and from the region's rail lines by bus. Take the Highway 17 Express, run by **Santa Cruz Metro** (831/425-8600, www.

scmtd.com, day pass $4-8), to connect with the San Jose Train Station (65 Cahill St., San Jose), where you can take Bay Area commuter-rail **Caltrain** (www.caltrain.com) to San Francisco.

To get to San Jose from Monterey, **Monterey-Salinas Transit** (831/899-2555, www.mst.org) serves Monterey and Santa Cruz

Counties. Route 55, the **Monterey-San Jose Express** (one-way $5, round-trip $10), takes about 2 hours and 15 minutes each way.

BUS

You can take **Greyhound** (19 W. Gabilan St., Salinas, 831/424-4418, www.greyhound.com, daily 5 A.M.-11:30 P.M.) from just about anywhere in the country to the transit stations in Salinas or Santa Cruz and then make your way to the Monterey area.

From San Jose or Salinas, take **Monterey-Salinas Transit** (831/899-2555, www.mst.org), which serves both Monterey and Santa Cruz Counties. Route 55, the **San Jose-Monterey Express** (one-way $5, round-trip $10), takes about 2 hours and 15 minutes each way. If you're coming into Monterey from Salinas, take Route 20 for (50 minutes, $1-2).

The **Transit Plaza** (end of Alvarado St.) in downtown Monterey is the central place to catch buses (exact change required, $1.50-2). Check on full schedules, routes, fares, and times at the plaza or online at www.mst.org. Once in Monterey, take advantage of the free **WAVE Trolley** (Memorial Day-Labor Day daily 9 A.M.-7:30 P.M.) that loops between downtown and the aquarium.

In San Luis Obispo County, the **San Luis Obispo RTA** (805/781-4427, bus info 805/541-2228, www. slorta.org, $1.30-3, day pass $5) is an easy way to get around. Route 12/15 runs three round-trips daily between Hearst Castle and Morro Bay.

If you are interested in wine tasting, hop aboard **The Wine Line** (805/610-8267, www.hoponthewineline.com, $60) to savor the flavor of the region from San Simeon and Cambria east to Paso Robles. It is a hop-on, hop-off shuttle service that makes the wine-tasting experience comfortable, worry free, and at your own pace.

RV RENTALS

The RV rentals closest to Monterey are in Santa Cruz at **Cruise America** (1186 San Andreas Rd., Watsonville, 800/671-8042, www.cruiseamerica.com). They offer large and standard vehicles perfect for the road trip along the coast. Rental quotes are based on the type of RV and approximate mileage. Between Monterey and Santa Cruz are many RV-friendly camping locations, some nearly right on the beach.

CAR

You can drive directly to the Monterey Peninsula from either San Francisco or San Jose on U.S. 101 south to Highway 156 west, then Highway 1 south. From Los Angles, take U.S. 101 north to Highway 156 west, or take the scenic route by exiting onto Highway 1 north at San Luis Obispo. You can easily get to Santa Cruz from San Jose via U.S. 101 to Highway 17. Monterey is connected to Santa Cruz by Highway 1 north; Big Sur and San Luis Obispo County are south of Monterey along Highway 1.

Tips for Travelers

TRAVELERS WITH DISABILITIES

Access for travelers with disabilities is quite extensive throughout the region. All the primary towns are fully wheelchair-accessible, with sidewalks and crosswalks, and local businesses generally comply with federal Americans with Disabilities Act regulations. In more secluded parts of this region, accessibility lessens, but at places like Big Sur's Nepenthe Restaurant you can drive your vehicle all the way to the top.

Accessible outdoor activities include Elkhorn Slough Safari, access to coastal trails along boardwalks, the Monterey Bay Aquarium, and even Año Nuevo State Park. State parks in particular make efforts to include wheelchair users. Call the park offices if you are in need of special assistance. Park employees are always eager to help out and help you access this beautiful landscape.

TRAVELING WITH CHILDREN

California's Central Coast is an ideal destination for families, with action in every direction year-round at places like Roaring Camp Railroads, the Santa Cruz Beach Boardwalk, and the Monterey Bay Aquarium. Big Sur summons the young adventurer in all of us, and the street-side wharf in Morro Bay is amusing for the whole family. There are countless beaches, state parks, amusement parks, tourist attractions, city and county parks, and federal wilderness areas. The only problem will be determining where to start and how long to stay.

SAFETY

California's Central Coast is a pretty tame place for women traveling alone, but there are some high-crime areas. Salinas has a reputation for being a hotbed of gang-related crime. Some parts of Castroville and Seaside have a reputation for crime. Downtown Santa Cruz and the area near the Boardwalk are known for a variety of illegal mischief.

In general, always use common sense and be aware of your surroundings. Stick to well-lighted areas at night. Halloween in Santa Cruz tends to get a little crazy, and there have been violent incidents every year.

SENIOR TRAVELERS

The Monterey Peninsula is an ideal retreat for retired folks any time of year, but the fall, winter, and spring months tend to be nicest. Camping is peaceful, the towns are practically empty of visitors, and all the best spots are still open. You can get senior discounts at many local attractions, and many restaurants have a seniors menu.

GAY AND LESBIAN TRAVELERS

The entire Monterey area welcomes gay and lesbian travelers with open arms. A local gay, lesbian, bisexual, and transgender outreach office is the **Diversity Center of Santa Cruz** (1117 Soquel Ave., Santa Cruz, 831/425-5422, www.diversitycenter.org), which offers access to local and regional rainbow events, literature, and other services.

For bars in the region, head to Santa Cruz. The main hangout is the **Mad House Bar** (529 Seabright Ave., Santa Cruz, 831/425-2900, Tues.-Sat. 5 P.M.-2 A.M., Sun. 5 P.M.-midnight). **The Crepe Place** (1134 Soquel Ave., Santa Cruz, 831/429-6994, www.thecrepeplace.com, Mon.-Thurs. 11 A.M.-midnight, Fri. 11 A.M.-1 A.M., Sat. 9 A.M.-1 A.M., Sun. 9 A.M.-midnight) is another small gay and lesbian hangout with live music. If you are into the club scene, you'll find more options in San Jose (about 1 hour from Monterey) or San Francisco (2 hours from Monterey).

OPPORTUNITIES FOR STUDY AND EMPLOYMENT

Higher-education opportunities are available at 12 different community colleges and universities in Monterey and Santa Cruz Counties. Monterey County has California State University, Monterey Bay; CET Salinas; Golden Gate University-Monterey; Hartnell College; Heald College-Salinas; the Monterey Institute of International Studies; and Monterey Peninsula College. In Santa Cruz County are Cabrillo College; Bethany University; CET Watsonville; Five Branches University; and the University of California, Santa Cruz. For more information on these colleges and direct links to their websites, visit www.californiacolleges.com.

Employment opportunities are in the wine industry, hospitality, the military, tourism, retail, education, medical positions, agriculture, commercial fishing, and government jobs. Most people living on the peninsula work at least a full-time job; rent is high, and jobs are limited. But it is worth the effort to live in this majestic place.

A good proportion of the peninsula is filled with second and third homes. Many are owned by wealthy businesspeople, developers, tycoons, and movie stars. These homes are primarily around Pebble Beach, Carmel Highlands, Big Sur, Monterra Ranch, and other high-profile housing communities.

Information and Services

Local visitors centers and Chambers of Commerce are good resources throughout the region. Local state parks and the U.S. Forest Service are also valuable sources for information. The rangers and employees are knowledgeable about the area and local activities. You can also learn about the local habitats, geology, and wildlife.

EMERGENCIES AND MEDICAL SERVICES

In cases of emergency, dial 911. The **Monterey Police Department** (3151 Madison St., Monterey, 831/646-3914) is open daily 24 hours.

For medical needs, the **Community Hospital of the Monterey Peninsula** (CHOMP, 23625 Hwy. 68/Holman Hwy., Monterey, 831/624-5311) provides emergency services in the area. In Santa Cruz, get medical treatment and care at **Dominican Hospital** (1555 Soquel Ave., Santa Cruz, 831/426-7700, www.dominicanhospital.org).

The nearest hospital to the towns of northern San Luis Obispo County is **Twin Cities Hospital** (1100 Las Tablas Rd., Templeton,

805/434-3500). It is near U.S. 101 south of Highway 46. The **Big Sur Health Center** (46896 Hwy. 1, Big Sur, 831/667-2580, Mon.-Fri. 10 A.M.-5 P.M.) can take care of minor medical needs and provides an ambulance service and limited emergency care.

If you venture off into the backcountry, make sure to register for all the required permits. They are for your own safety and let the local rangers know you are out there and for how long you plan to be. When people don't come back as scheduled, they are considered missing, and search parties are sent out. It is important to map out your adventure before entering the backcountry.

MONEY

Most local businesses accept all major credit cards. ATMs are located throughout heavily visited areas, downtown areas, and at banks. All major towns have regional and national bank branches. The most common are Wells Fargo, Bank of America, Bank of the West, Rabobank, and the Monterey Credit Union.

COMMUNICATIONS AND MEDIA

The local newspaper is the *Monterey County Herald* (www.montereyherald.com), a daily paper covering the county. It includes a weekly Go section that features current happenings. The *Monterey County Weekly* (www.montereycountyweekly.com) is the alternative weekly with listings of events, including the Club Grind section and a daily events calendar. Both papers also feature local news, sports, arts, and entertainment.

Santa Cruz has its own daily newspaper, the *Santa Cruz Sentinel* (www.santacruzsentinel.com), with a daily dose of national wire-service news and current events, local news, plus some good stuff for visitors. The *Sentinel* has a Food section, a Sunday Travel section, and plenty of up-to-date entertainment information.

VISITOR INFORMATION

In Monterey, the **El Estero Visitors Center** (401 Camino El Estero, Monterey, www. montereyinfo.org) is the local outlet of the Monterey Country Convention and Visitors Bureau. They put out a comprehensive annual guide to Monterey County; you can download the guide from the website or call the office to have one mailed. They also have loads of local flyers promoting many local business and activities.

While it can be fun to explore Santa Cruz following your instincts and sense of the bizarre, those who want a bit more structure can visit the **Santa Cruz Visitors Center** (1211 Ocean Ave., Santa Cruz, 800/833-3494, www.santacruzca.org) for maps, advice, and information.

RESOURCES

Suggested Reading

Below is a basic reading list to further your knowledge about the Monterey area. Topics included are related to literature, recreation, and history. You can also find the **Monterey Visitors Center** (765 Wave St., 831/657-6400, www.seemonterey.com), local museum gift shops, and the various state park visitors centers great places to pick up local literature.

California Coastal Commission. *Beaches and Parks from San Francisco to Monterey: Marin, San Francisco, San Mateo, Santa Cruz, Monterey.* Berkeley, CA: University of California Press, 2012. This is a comprehensive guidebook that focuses on the main attractions related to parks and beaches. Popular and unknown beaches are both covered, along with hiking, surfing, camping, and sightseeing stops.

Chiang, Connie. *Shaping the Shoreline: Fisheries and Tourism on the on the Monterey Coast.* Seattle: University of Washington Press, 2011. Chiang explores the history of Monterey Bay with a focus on the fishing industry and tourism. Learn how the canneries were developed, find out why they all closed, and learn about today's Monterey.

Clifford, Mary, and Candace Clifford. *Woman Who Kept the Lights: An Illustrated History of Female Lighthouse Keepers.* Alexandria, VA: Cypress Communications, 2001. Hundreds of American women have tended the maritime lights. Read the stories of 25 brave and resourceful women who kept the lights along the rugged coast, and learn all about local socialite Emily Fish of Point Piños Light Station in Pacific Grove.

Conway, J.D. *Monterey: Presidio, Pueblo, and Port California.* Monterey, CA: City of Monterey, 2003. This book contains the story of the conflicts between Native Americans and colonizers through images. Learn about the growth of the city of Monterey, the diverse nationalities that make up the population, and the rugged Western landscape of California.

Frost, John. *Monterey Peninsula's Sporting Heritage.* Mount Pleasant, SC: Arcadia Publishing, 2007. This text takes a look at the Monterey Peninsula's sports stars at the beginning of the 20th century. Many were local heroes, and others would go on to gain wider recognition. Learn about these stars' roots and the Del Monte Properties empire, once the ruler of local recreation, with historic photos.

Jeffers, Robinson. *An Anthology of Robinson Jeffers: The Wild God of the World.* Stanford, CA: Stanford University Press, 2003. This anthology is a collection of Jeffers's greatest works. Embark on a journey along California's Central coast through themes of science, history, and God with the "Dark Prince of Poetry."

Kerouac, Jack. *Big Sur.* New York: Penguin USA, reprint 1992. Through the eyes of Kerouac's alter ego, Jack Dulouz, see the darker and desolate side of the man and Big Sur's wilderness. Read about paranoiac confusion and alcohol delirium, and be pulled into the inner most depths of Kerouac's mind.

Miller, Henry. *Big Sur and the Oranges of Hieronymus Bosch.* New York: W. W. Norton, 1978. This is the tale of Miller's life in Big Sur, in which he shares his utopian ideals saturated with an extraordinary landscape, mystics, free spirits, geniuses, adult innocents, and writers that don't write. He lived at his Big Sur sanctuary for 15 years.

Rigsby, Michael. *A Natural History of Monterey Bay National Marine Sanctuary.* Monterey, CA: Monterey Bay Aquarium, 1997. You can always depend on the Monterey Bay Aquarium to put out thoughtfully researched texts. Learn about the natural world both above and below the ocean's surface. Venture into

the shallows and the darkest depths of the Monterey Bay Submarine Canyon.

Steinbeck, John. *Cannery Row.* New York: Penguin USA, reprint 2002. In a time where sardines ruled Monterey Bay, mingle with Doc Ricketts and be consumed by the stench of sardines, the noise about the harbor, and life on Cannery Row.

Steinbeck, John. *East of Eden.* New York: Penguin USA, reprint 1992. This epic tale of the Salinas Valley, a twist on the biblical book of Genesis, was originally published in 1952. Told as the tale of a family living and working in the fertile Salinas Valley, you will feel their hardships and triumphs through Steinbeck's poetic prose.

Stevenson, Robert Louis. *Treasure Island.* Fayetteville, AR: Gambit Publications, reprint 1971. Originally published in 1883, this ultimate pirate tale is said to be inspired by the shores of Point Lobos. It is a treacherous story of swashbucklers, good and evil, treasure, romance, and adventure. Meet Long John Silver, Jim Hawkins, Israel Hands, and many other rogue buccaneers on a quest for gold.

Internet Resources

Access Visitors Guide
www.slovisitorsguide.com
General information on northern San Luis Obispo County, including San Simeon, Cambria, Cayucos, Morro Bay, and surrounding towns.

Big Sur Chamber of Commerce
www.bigsurcalifornia.org
General information on Big Sur and the coastal region.

California State Parks
www.parks.ca.gov
An extensive resource for the area's state parks.

Cambria Chamber of Commerce
www.cambriachamber.org
General information on Cambria.

Carmel Chamber of Commerce
www.carmelcalifornia.org
General information of Carmel, Carmel-by-the-Sea, and Carmel Valley.

Cayucos Chamber of Commerce
www.cayucoschamber.com
General information on Cayucos.

City of Monterey
www.monterey.org
Information on Monterey's upcoming events, local businesses, attractions, employment, and visitor information.

Monterey Bay Aquarium
www.montereybayaquarium.org
General information about the Monterey Bay Aquarium and the Monterey Bay marine sanctuary.

Monterey County Convention and Visitors Center
www.seemonterey.com
General information on Monterey and surrounding towns, including Pebble Beach, Pacific Grove, Moss Landing, Carmel, and Salinas.

Morro Bay Chamber of Commerce
www.morrobay.org
General information on Morro Bay.

Salinas Chamber of Commerce
www.salinaschamber.com
General information on Salinas and the Salinas Valley.

Santa Cruz Chamber of Commerce
www.santacruzchamber.org
Information on Santa Cruz, Capitola, Watsonville, and the Santa Cruz Mountains.

SantaCruz.com
www.santacruz.com
A guide to local attractions, art, entertainment, hotels, and more in Santa Cruz.

Santa Cruz County
www.santacruzca.org
An online travel guide to Santa Cruz County.

San Luis Obispo County: California's Natural Escapes
www.sanluisobispocounty.com
For history buffs, a suggested weekend escape to San Simeon, Cambria, and Cayucos.

San Simeon Chamber of Commerce
www.sansimeonchamber.org
General information on San Simeon.

Index

A

Adventures by the Sea: 66, 67
agriculture: Earthbound Farms 109; Gilroy garlic 133; Rabobank Agricultural Museum 120
Ahlgren Vineyard: 146
air travel: 256
Alfaro Family Vineyards: 145
Alvarado, Juan Bautista: 185
Alvarado Street: 14, 31
American Le Mans Series: 123
Anderson Inn: 22, 244
Andrew Molera State Park: 9, 21, 180, 191, 197
animals: 251-253
Annual Cayucos Car Show: 229
Annual Cayucos Wine & Food Festival: 229
Annual Women's Surf Contest: 228
Año Nuevo State Reserve: 19, 20, 174
antiques: 8; general discussion 8; Antique Street Fair 228; Boulder Creek 173; Carmel-by-the-Sea 98; Carmel Valley 114; Cayucos 210, 230; Moss Landing 81; Pacific Grove 68; Salinas 14; San Juan Bautista 127; Santa Cruz 160-161; Santa Cruz Mountains 175
Antique Street Fair: 228
Aquarium, Monterey Bay: 29-31
Aquarium Adventures: 31
aquariums: 29-31, 142
Aquarius: 19, 167
arachnids: 253
Arroyo Seco: 112
Arroyo Seco River: 112
Art and Wine Celebration: 113
Art and Wine Festival: 222
art/art galleries: 9; Art in the Park 240; Cabrillo Music, Art & Wine Festival 158; Cambria 22, 210, 218; Carmel 15, 95; Carmel Art and Film Festival 98; Carmel Art Association 92; Carmel Art Festival 97; Monterey 34, 49; Monterey Museum of Art 39; Nitt Witt Ridge 218; Pacific Grove 67
Art of America Moonstones Gallery: 219
Asilomar State Beach: 11, 13, 64, 66
AT&T Pebble Beach National Pro Am: 77
At Calera Wine Company: 132
Attic Angels: 14, 127
auto racing: 118, 121-122, 123
auto shows: 123, 159, 229, 240
Aviary: 30
Avocado and Margarita Festival: 240

B

Bach, J.S.: 98
Baja Cantina: 15, 116
Balconies Caves: 132
Barnyard Shopping Village: 15, 100
Beach Bar and Grill: 22, 217
Beach Boardwalk, Santa Cruz: 9, 17, 135, 137-138, 141, 161
beaches: Asilomar State Beach 64; Big Sur 203; Carmel Beach 93-94; Carmel River State Beach 94; Cayucos State Beach 227; Elkhorn Slough National Estaurine Research Reserve 79; Fort Ord Dunes State Park 83; Hearst San Simeon State Park 221; Marina State Beach 82; Monterey 40; Morro Bay 234; Moss Landing State Beach 80; Pfeiffer Beach 189; Point Joe 76; Santa Cruz 9, 147-149; Seal Rock 76; Seaside 85; William Randolph Hearst Memorial State Beach 213, 214
Bear Gulch Cave: 132
beer: 50
Beer Fest and Chili Cook Off: 239
Behind the Scenes Tour: 31
Ben Lomond: 17, 178
Bernardus Winery: 16, 23, 109
Big Basin Redwoods State Park: 19, 135, 174, 175
Bigfoot Discovery Museum: 172
Big Sur: 9, 179-208; accommodations 199-201; beaches 203; camping 197-198, 205-206; food 201-202, 206; highlights 180; itinerary 21-22; maps 181; planning tips 182; recreation 190-196; services 207; transportation 208
Big Sur Bakery: 21, 202
Big Sur Coast Highway: 180, 182
Big Sur Food and Wine: 196
Big Sur International Marathon: 196
Big Sur Jade Festival: 196
Big Sur River: 21
Big Sur Spirit Garden: 187
Big Sur State Park: 21, 191
Big Sur Station: 184, 198
Big Sur Station No. 1: 194
bike shops: 47
biking: Butterfly Criterium 68; Henry Cowell Redwoods State Park 173; Monterey 46-47; Morro Bay 238; Pacific Grove 66; Pebble Beach 76; Point Lobos State Reserve 93;

Santa Cruz 153–155; Sea Otter Classic 122; Toro Regional Park 121
Bird Rock: 13, 75
birds: 252
bird-watching: Big Sur 196; egrets and herons 237; Elkhorn Slough National Estaurine Research Reserve 79; Fiscalini Ranch Preserve 221; Harmony Headlands State Park 227; Morro Bay Estuary 234; Wilder Ranch State Park 154; Winter Bird Festival 241
Bixby Bridge: 21, 180, 183
Black Hand Cellars: 24, 220
Bluebird Antiques and Collectibles: 13–14, 127
boat charters: 152
Bobcat Trail: 191
Bonny Doon Vineyard's Cellar Door: 23, 146
Bottchers Gap: 180, 183, 198
Boulder Creek: 17, 135, 173
Boulder Creek Brewing Company: 19, 176
Bruno's Market and Delicatessen: 16, 107
bus travel: 258
butterflies, monarch: 10, 64, 135, 253
Butterfly Criterium: 68

C
Cabrillo Music, Art & Wine Festival: 158
California International Airshow: 123
California Rodeo Salinas: 123
California's First Theatre: 37
California State University Monterey Bay: 82
Callaway Pebble Beach Invitational: 77
Cambria: 9, 22, 24, 218–226
Cambria Cemetery: 218
Camouflage: 17, 160
camping reservations: 10
Candy Cane Lane: 68
Cannery Row: 8, 12, 14, 28, 31, 35, 44, 52
Cannery Row (Steinbeck): 14
Cannery Row Tree Lighting Ceremony: 51
Capitola Historical Museum: 144
Capitola Mall: 162
Carlin Soulé Memorial Polar Bear Dip: 229
Carmel: 88–116; accommodations 102–104, 114; Carmel-by-the-Sea 91–108; Carmel Valley 109–116; dog-friendly sites 101; food 104–106, 115–116; highlights 89; house numbers 94; itinerary 15–16; maps 90; planning tips 8; recreation 92–94, 112–113; transportation 106–108; wine tasting 23, 109–112
Carmel Art and Film Festival: 98
Carmel Art Association: 92
Carmel Art Festival: 97
Carmel Authors and Ideas Festival: 98
Carmel Bach Festival: 98
Carmel Beach: 15, 16, 89, 93–94
Carmel Belle: 107
Carmel-by-the-Sea: 8, 16, 91–108
Carmel Fourth of July Celebration: 97
Carmel Mission: 8, 15, 89, 91
Carmel Plaza: 15, 98
Carmel River State Beach: 13, 94
Carmel Roasting Company: 15
Carmel's Holiday Tree Lighting: 98
Carmel Valley: 8, 109–116
Carmel Valley Community Park: 112
Carmel Valley Fiesta: 114
Carmel Valley Grapevine Express: 112
Carmel Valley Road: 15, 116
Carmel Valley Village: 109
car racing: 118, 121–122, 123
car travel: 258
Casa del Oro: 37
Casa Soberanes: 37
Cass Landing: 227
Castle Rock State Park: 174, 176
Castro-Breen Adobe: 126
caves: 132
Cayucos: 22, 210, 227–233
Cayucos Cellars: 22, 233
Cayucos Sea Glass Festival: 228
Cayucos State Beach: 22, 227, 231
Chaminade spa: 155
charters, diving: 43
Château Julien: 16, 23, 109
Cherry's Jubilee Motorsports Festival: 123
children, traveling with: 259
children's activities: Beach Boardwalk, Santa Cruz 137–138; Cannery Row Tree Lighting Ceremony 51; El Estero 46; First Night in Monterey 52; Monterey Bay Aquarium 29–31; Mount Hermon Zip-Line Tour 172; My Museum 39; Pacific Grove wintertime 68; San Carlos Beach 40; Santa Cruz Museum of Natural History 139
Chili Cook-off and Car Show: 222
China Cove: 15, 89, 93
Chinese Americans: 35
Chris's Fishing and Whale Watching Trips: 41
Christmas at the Inns: 68
Christmas in the Adobes: 51
City Wide Yard Sale: 240
cliff jumping: 112
cliffs, Big Sur: 9, 179
climate: 248
Coast Guard Wharf: 12, 18

colonialism: 254
Colton Hall: 12, 37
communications: 261
Concours d'Elegance: 77
Concours d'LeMons: 123
condor, California: 196
Cooking for Solutions: 50
Cooper, Captain John Rogers: 185
Cooper-Garrod Estate Vineyards: 23, 146
Cooper Molera Adobe: 37
cowboy poetry: 51
Cowell Beach: 9, 148, 149
C Restaurant: 12, 58
Crossroads Shopping Village: 16, 101
Cruisin' Morro Bay Car Show: 240
Custom House: 33
Custom House Plaza: 12, 32
cypress trees: 251

D

Dahlia Daze and Cypress Nightz: 240
Davenport, Captain John P.: 35
Davenport Landing: 19, 149, 152
day trips: 11
deep reef: 29
Del Monte Center: 52
Del Monte Golf Course: 47
DeRose Vineyard: 131
Dickensen, Duncan: 37
dining: see food
disabilities, travelers with: 259
dive shops: 43
diving: Big Sur 195; Monastery Beach 94;
    Monterey 42–43; Point Lobos State Reserve
    92, 93
Dixieland Monterey: 50
dog-friendly sites: 101, 112, 121
Downtown Monterey: 12, 31–39, 52, 55, 59
Downtown Santa Cruz Holiday Parade: 159

E

Eagle Castle: 24, 219
Earthbound Farms: 15, 109
Earth Day Santa Cruz: 157
Edgemere Cottages: 24, 102
egrets: 237
elephant seals: 19, 21, 174, 210, 213
Elephant Seal Vista: 231
El Estero: 46
Elkhorn Slough National Estaurine Research
    Reserve: 8, 12, 18, 28, 79
Elkhorn Slough Safari: 79

El Moro Elfin Forest: 210, 234
El Sur Ranch: 185
Embarcadero Road: 22, 241
emergencies: 260
Emily's Good Things To Eat: 19, 168
employment: 260
environmental issues: 249
Environmental Issues and Groups: 249
Ernest Ewoldsen Memorial Nature Center: 192
Esalen Institute: 9, 189
Estero Bluffs State Park: 227
events: Big Sur 187, 196 Cambria 222; Carmel-
    by-the-Sea 97–98; Carmel Valley 113–114;
    Cayucos 228–229; Monterey 50 52; Morro
    Bay 239–241; Pacific Grove 67–68; Pebble
    Beach 77; Salinas 122–124; Santa Cruz 157–
    159; surf competitions 151
Ewoldsen Trail: 194

F

Fairy Tale Homes of Carmel: 91
fall: 10
Fall Creek: 173
Farmer's Kites Surreys and More: 240
farmers markets: Big Sur 202; Cambria 226;
    Cayucos 233; Morro Bay 246; Santa Cruz
    Mountains 177
farmers markets/produce stands: Carmel-by-
    the-Sea 106; Gizdich Ranch 144; Monterey
    61; Moss Landing 82; Pacific Grove 72;
    Salinas 124; Santa Cruz 169
fauna: 251–253
Feast of Lanterns: 68
Felton: 17, 177
Fermentations: 24, 220
Fernwood Resort: 197, 199
festivals: see events
5th Avenue Deli & Catering: 107
film festivals: 98, 158
First Awakenings: 11, 70
First Brick House: 37
First Night in Monterey: 52
First Tee Open at Pebble Beach: 77
Fiscalini Ranch Preserve: 221
Fisherman's Wharf: 44
fishing: Arroyo Seco 112; Big Sur 195, 205;
    Cannery Row 31; Cayucos State Beach 227;
    Davenport Landing 149; Garland Ranch
    Regional Park 112; historic Monterey Bay
    35; Loch Lomond Recreation Area 173;
    Monterey 41–42; Morro Bay 236; Moss
    Landing 80; Pinto Lake 155; Santa Cruz 152;
    Santa Cruz Wharf 138; Sunset State Beach

149; William Randolph Hearst Memorial
  State Beach 215
flora: 250-251
flowers: 250
Flying Fish Grill: 15, 106
folk art: 218
food: Avocado and Margarita Festival 240; Beer
  Fest and Chili Cook Off 239; Big Sur Food
  and Wine 196; Chili Cook-off and Car Show
  222; Cooking for Solutions 50; Harvest to
  Table Festival 114; Pebble Beach Food & Wine
  77; picnics 107; sustainable seafood 30, 32;
  Taste of Carmel 98; Watsonville Strawberry
  Festival at Monterey Bay 158; see also farmers
  markets/produce stands; specific place
Forest of Nisene Marks State Park: 154
Forge in the Forest: 107
Fort Ord Dunes State Park: 46, 83, 85
Fourth of July Celebration: 229
Fourth of July Lawn Party: 50
Fremont Peak State Park and Observatory: 9,
  14, 118, 128-129
From Scratch: 15, 101, 105

G

Galley Seafood Grill & Bar: 22, 245
gardens: Big Sur Spirit Garden 187; Casa
  Soberanes 37; Cooper Molera Adobe 37;
  Earthbound Farms 109; Hearst Castle 212,
  213; Larkin House 37-38; Museum of Natural
  History 64; UC Santa Cruz Arboretum 143
Garland Ranch Regional Park 15, 89, 112
garlic: 133
Garrapata State Park: 190, 195
gay travelers: 259
geography: 248
geology: 131
ghosts: 38, 188
Giant Dipper: 17
giant octopus: 29
Gilroy: 132-133
Gilroy Premium Outlets: 132
Gizdich Ranch: 144
Glen Oaks: 21, 201
golf: AT&T Pebble Beach National Pro Am 77;
  Boulder Creek 173; Callaway Pebble Beach
  Invitational 77; Carmel Valley 113; First Tee
  Open at Pebble Beach 77; Monterey 47;
  Morro Bay 238; Pacific Grove Municipal Golf
  Links 67; Pebble Beach 74-76; Ridgemark
  Golf and Country Club 129; Santa Cruz
  Amateur Golf Championship 158; Seaside
  85; Spanish Bay 75-76

Graffix Pleasure: 17, 160
Grapevine Express: 16, 108, 112
Great Wine Escape: 51
Greenfield Certified Farmers Market: 125
Grey Wolf: 24, 220

H

Hahn Winery: 24, 120
Hallcrest Vineyards: 23, 146
Halloween Ball Masque: 196
Hammond Vineyards: 120
Harbor Festival: 240
Harmony Headlands State Park: 227
Harvest to Table Festival: 114
Headlands Trail: 191
Hearst Castle: 9, 21, 210, 212
Hearst San Simeon State Park: 221, 231
helicoptor tours: 144
Heller Estate Organic Vineyards: 16, 23, 111
Henflings Tavern: 19, 176
Henry Cowell Redwoods State Park: 17, 173, 175
Henry Miller Memorial Library: 180, 184
Heritage Center Museum: 39
Heron Rookery Natural Preserve: 22
herons: 237
Highway 1: 11
Highway 46: 24, 219
hiking: Arroyo Seco 112; backcountry 194; Big
  Basin Redwoods State Park 174; Big Sur
  190-195; Bottchers Gap 184; Castle Rock
  State Park 174; Elkhorn Slough National
  Estaurine Research Reserve 79; Estero
  Bluffs State Park 227; Fort Ord Dunes
  State Park 83; Fremont Peak State Park
  and Observatory 128-129; Garland Ranch
  Regional Park 112; Henry Cowell Redwoods
  State Park 173; Jacks Peak County Park 46;
  Los Padres Reservoir 112; McWay Falls 187;
  Morro Bay 238; Palo Corona Regional Park
  93; Pinnacles National Monument 132; Point
  Lobos State Reserve 92; Santa Cruz 153-155;
  Toro Regional Park 121; William Randolph
  Hearst Memorial State Beach 215
historic sites: 31-32; Carmel Mission 91; Casa
  del Oro 37; Custom House 33; Monterey
  homes 37-39; see also missions
history: 254-255
Hollister: 129-130
Hollister Hills State Vehicular Recreation Area:
  129
Holman Ranch: 16
Homestead Cabin: 192
horseback riding: Big Sur 195; Carmel Valley

113; Castle Rock State Park 174; Henry Cowell Redwoods State Park 173; Jacks Peak County Park 46; Pebble Beach 76; Toro Regional Park 121; Wilder Ranch State Park 154
Hot Pink Flamingos: 30
Hot Rods at the Beach: 159
hot springs: 194

IJ

Il Fornaio Café: 107
inland Monterey: day trip to 13; highlights 118; maps 119; planning tips 8; wine tasting 24
insects: 253
Intercontinental Clement Monterey: 12, 55
itineraries: 8, 11-24
Jack Creek Cellars: 24, 220
Jacks: 13, 56
Jacks Peak County Park: 20, 46
jade: 196, 203
Jade Beach Reserve: 203
Jade Cove: 196
Jardines de San Juan: 14, 128
jazz: 50
Jeffers, Robertson: 8, 92
jellyfish: 30
Jingle Bell Run: 68
J. Lohr Vineyards: 221
John Steinbeck's Exhibition Hall: 120
Joyce Vineyards: 16, 112
Julia Pfeiffer Burns State Park: 21, 188, 193, 195

KL

kayaking: general discussion 18; Davenport Landing 149; Elkhorn Slough National Estaurine Research Reserve 80; Hearst San Simeon State Park 221; Monterey Bay 43-46; Morro Bay 237; Pacific Grove 66; Pinto Lake 155; Santa Cruz 151-152; Santa Cruz Kayak and Surf Festival 151; Santa Cruz Wharf 139; Whalers Cove 92
kelp forest: 29
Kirk Creek Campground: 205
kite surfing: 149, 151, 215
kite flying: 83, 93, 221, 240
Land Watch Monterey County: 249
Larkin House: 37-38
Léal Vineyards: 131
Leffingwell Landing: 221
lesbian travelers: 259
LGBT parade: 158
Lighted Boat Parade: 241

Lighthouse Avenue: 53
lighthouses: Pigeon Point Lighthouse 143; Point Piños Lighthouse 63; Point Sur Light Station 186; Santa Cruz 9; Santa Cruz Surfing Museum and Lighthouse 135, 139
Limekiln State Park: 9, 204, 205
Links at Spanish Bay: 75
literature: Carmel Authors and Ideas Festival 98; Henry Miller Memorial Library 180, 184; National Steinbeck Center 120; Robinson Jeffers Fall Festival 98
Loch Lomond Recreation Area: 173
Lodge at Pebble Beach: 76
lodging: 10
Lone Cypress: 13, 75
Lone Madrone: 24, 220
Long Marine Laboratory: 142
Los Padres National Forest: 183, 198
Los Padres Reservoir: 112
Lovers Point: 11, 44, 66
Lovers Point Park: 13, 28, 63
Lower Presidio Historic Park: 39

M

mammals: 251
Manresa State Beach: 148, 149
Marina: 82-85
Marina State Beach: 40, 82
Mazda Laguna Seca Raceway: 118, 121-122
McAbee Beach: 40
McWay Falls: 180, 187
media, the: 261
medical services: 260
Mermaid and Pirate Parade: 240
military sites: 39
Mill Creek: 203
Miller, Henry: 184
Mission Ranch: 8, 94
missions: Carmel Mission 91; Mission San Juan Bautista 118, 126; Mission Santa Cruz 135, 142; Native Americans and 92
Mission San Juan Bautista: 8-9, 13, 118, 126
Mission Santa Cruz: 135, 142
Molera Horseback Tours: 21, 195
Molera Ranch House Museum: 191
monarch butterflies: 10, 253
Monarch Sanctuary: 13, 19, 64
Monastery Beach: 94
money: 260
Monster Truck Jam: 123
Monterey: accommodations 54-56; entertainment 47-49; events 50-52; food 56-61; highlights 28; itinerary 11-14; maps

26-27, 36; northern Monterey County
79-87; Pacific Grove 63-72; Pebble Beach
72-79; planning tips 8; recreation 40-47;
services 61; shopping 52-53; transportation
62
Monterey Bay Aquarium: 8, 11, 18, 28, 29-31, 249
Monterey Bay Aquarium Seafood Watch: 32
Monterey Bay Blues Festival: 50
Monterey Bay Coastal Bike Trail: 46, 66
Monterey Bay Reggaefest: 51
Monterey Bay Whale Watch Center: 42
Monterey Beer Festival: 50
Monterey County Fair: 51
Monterey Cowboy Poetry & Music Festival: 51
Monterey History and Art Association and
    Museum of Monterey: 34
Monterey HistoryFest: 51
Monterey Jazz Festival: 51
Monterey Museum of Art: 12, 39
Monterey Pines Golf Course: 47
Monterey Plaza: 40
Monterey Rock & Rod Festival: 50
Monterey State Beach: 28, 40, 85
Monterey State Historic Park Path of History:
    12, 28, 31
Monterey Wine Festival: 50
Montrio Bistro: 13, 59
Moonstone Beach: 22, 231
Moonstone Cellars: 24, 220
Moonstone State Beach: 221
Morro Bay: 9, 21-22, 22, 24, 234-247
Morro Bay 4th of July: 240
Morro Bay Boulevard: 22, 242
Morro Bay Estuary: 18, 210, 234
Morro Bay Kite Festival: 240
Morro Bay Music Festival: 240
Morro Bay State Park: 22, 231, 234
Morro Rock: 22
Morro Rock Natural Preserve: 22, 210, 234
Morro Strand State Beach: 231, 234
Moses Spring-Rim Trail Loop: 132
Moss Landing: 44, 79-82
Moss Landing State Beach: 80
motorcycles: 113
motorsports: 123
mountain biking: 112
mountains, Santa Cruz: 9, 172-178
Mount Hermon Zip-Line Tour: 17, 172
Mount Manuel Trail: 193
Museum of Natural History: 63
music festivals: Big Sur 196; Monterey 50-51;
    Morro Bay 240; Santa Cruz 158
My Museum: 39

N

Nacimiento-Fergusson Road: 204
National Marine Sanctuary: 249
National Steinbeck Center: 8, 14, 118, 120, 122
Native Americans: 92, 254
Natural Bridges State Beach: 135, 147
Natural Bridges State Park: 9, 18, 19
Nature Center: 173
Nature Trail: 193
Neenach Volcano: 131
Nepenthe: 21, 202
New Brighton State Beach: 147
Next Generation Jazz Festival: 50
Nielsen Bros. Market: 107
Nitt Witt Ridge: 218
Northern Elephant Seal Rookery: 213
northern Monterey County: 79-87
North Fork Trail: 190

O

Ocean Avenue: 15, 89, 98
octopus, giant: 29
off-road vehicles: 113, 129, 204
Ohlone people: 153
Oktoberfest: 222
Old Cayucos Tavern: 22, 228
Old Coast Road: 182
Old Fashioned Fourth of July Celebration and
    Fireworks: 222
Old-fashioned Independence Day: 158
Old Fisherman's Grotto: 12, 58
Old Fisherman's Wharf: 8, 12, 28, 31, 52
Old Pinnacles Trail to Balconies Caves: 132
Old Town Morro Bay: 242
Old Whaling Station: 34
Open Sea: 30
organic vineyards: 145
Organic Wine Trail of the Santa Cruz
    Mountains: 23, 145
Osio Theater: 13, 49
otters: 30, 45, 192
Overlook Trail: 193

P

Pacific Avenue: 135, 160
Pacific Coast Highway (1): 11
Pacific Grove: 8, 11, 13, 63-72
Pacific Grove City Fourth of July BBQ: 68
Pacific Grove Good Old Days: 67
Pacific Grove Historic Homes Tour: 68
Pacific Grove Municipal Golf Links: 67
Pacific Grove Museum of Natural History: 13, 64

Pacific House: 34
Pacific Street: 17, 117
Palo Corona Regional Park: 93
Parade of Lights: 68
Parsonage Village Vineyard: 16, 23, 111
Pátisserie Boissiere: 107
Patricia Griffin Studio & Gallery: 219
Peak Trail: 190
Pebble Beach: 8, 13, 72-79
Pebble Beach Food & Wine: 77
Pebble Beach Golf Links: 75
Peddler's Faire: 228
penguins: 31
performing arts: 96-97, 157
Perry, Manuel: 34
Perry House: 34
Pessagno Winery: 120
Peter Hay Golf Course: 75
Pfeiffer Beach: 21, 180, 189
Pfeiffer Big Sur State Park: 9, 180, 191, 195, 198
Pfeiffer Falls Trail: 193
picnics: 107
Piedras Blancas: 21, 210, 213
Piedras Blancas Lighthouse: 214
Pietra Santa Winery: 132
Pigeon Point Lighthouse: 143
Pinnacles National Monument: 9, 20, 118, 131, 132
Pinto Lake: 155
plane travel: 256
planning tips: 8-10
plants: 250-251
Plaskett Creek Campground: 205
Plaskett Ridge Road: 204
Plaza Hall-Zanetta House: 126
Plaza Hotel: 126
Plaza Stables and Blacksmith Shop: 126
Pleasure Point: 149
Point Joe: 13, 75, 76
Point Lobos State Reserve: 8, 15, 18, 20, 43, 89, 92
Point Piños Lighthouse: 13, 63
Point Sur Light Station: 180, 186, 188
Polar Bear Dip: 229
Poppy Hills Golf Course: 76
Portola Restaurant: 31
Presidio of Monterey: 39-40
Presidio of Monterey Museum: 40
Pride Santa Cruz LGBT Parade: 158
Princess Monterey Whale Watching: 42

QR
Quail Motorcycle Gathering: 113

Rabobank Agricultural Museum: 120
Race Nights on the Row: 50-51
rafting: 112
Ragged Point Resort: 22, 205
Randy's Whale Watching and Fishing Trips: 41
Real Coast Café: 30
Red Bull U.S. Grand Prix: 123
Red House Café: 13, 70
redwoods: Big Basin Redwoods State Park 135, 174; Big Sur 9; Henry Cowell Redwoods State Park 17, 173; Santa Cruz 9; Sykes Hot Springs 194
reptiles: 252
reservations, lodging: 10
Retro Paradise: 17, 160
Ridge Bluff Loop: 191
Ridgemark Golf and Country Club: 129
River Inn: 21, 201
River Road Wine Trail: 24, 118, 120
River Road Wine Trail Valentine's Passport: 124
River Run Vintners: 146
road trip: 11, 23-24
Roaring Camp Railroads: 17, 135, 172
Robert Talbott Vineyards: 16, 23, 111, 120
Robinson Jeffers Fall Festival: 98
Robinson Jeffers's Tor House Garden Party: 97
rock climbing: 132, 174
Rocky Ridge Trail: 190
Rocky's Café: 17, 177
rodeos: 123
Rolex Monterey Motorsports Reunion: 123
Rosie McCann's: 17, 156
Running Iron Saloon: 16, 116
RV travel: 258

S
safety: 259
sailing: 42, 153
Salinas: 8, 120-126; day trip to 13; highlights 118; maps 119; old town 14; planning tips 8; wine tasting 24
Salinas Holiday Parade of Lights: 124
Salinas Valley Fair: 123
San Andreas Fault: 249
San Carlos Beach: 40
San Carlos Cathedral: 39
Sand Dollar State Beach: 21, 203
sand dunes: Fort Ord Dunes State Park 46, 83; Marina State Beach 82-83
Sandy Shore: 30
San Juan Bautista: 126-128
San Juan Bautista Old Town: 9, 118, 126
San Juan Bautista State Historic Park: 13, 126

San Simeon: 9, 24, 212–218
San Simeon Bay Trail: 215
San Simeon Creek Campground: 22, 223
San Simeon village: 213
Santa Cruz: 134–178; accommodations 162–166;
     entertainment 156–157; food 166–170;
     highlights 135; itinerary 17–20; maps 136,
     140; planning tips 9, 137; recreation 147–156;
     services 170; shopping 160–162; sights 137–
     144; transportation 170–172; wine tasting 23
Santa Cruz Amateur Golf Championship: 158
Santa Cruz Beach Boardwalk: 9, 17, 135, 137–
     138, 141, 161
Santa Cruz Blues Festival: 158
Santa Cruz County Fair: 158
Santa Cruz County Symphony: 159
Santa Cruz Experience: 145
Santa Cruz Film Festival: 158
Santa Cruz Harbor: 152
Santa Cruz Kayak and Surf Festival: 151
Santa Cruz Longboard Club Invitational: 151
Santa Cruz Main Beach: 9, 135, 148, 151
Santa Cruz Mountains: 172–178
Santa Cruz Mountain Vineyard: 146
Santa Cruz Mountain Wine Growers
     Association: 145
Santa Cruz Municipal Wharf: 17
Santa Cruz Museum of Natural History: 139
Santa Cruz Mystery Spot: 144
Santa Cruz Surfing Museum and Lighthouse:
     9, 135
Santa Cruz Wharf: 135, 138
Santa Cruz Wine Tours: 145
Santa Rosa Day-use Area: 221
Sardine Factory: 13, 58
scenic drives: Big Sur Coast Highway 182; Los
     Padres Reservoir 112; Old Coast Road 182;
     Pigeon Point Lighthouse 143; 17-Mile Drive
     74–75
scenic views: Bixby Bridge 183; Garrapata State
     Park 191; Lovers Point Park 63
Scott Creek Beach: 150
Scottish Games: 123
scuba diving: 42–43, 92
Seabright Beach: 147
Seacliff State Beach: 148
Seafood Watch: 32
sea kayaking: 18, 43–46
sealife: 251
Seal Rock: 75, 76
Sea Otter Classic: 122
sea otters: 30, 45, 192
Seaside: 85–87

seasons, best travel 10
Sebastian's Café: 22, 217
Secret Lives of the Seahorses: 30
senior travelers: 259
17-Mile Drive: 13, 28, 74–75
Seymour Marine Discovery Center: 142
Sherman Quarters: 38
Silver Mountain Vineyards: 145
Simeon Point: 215
Sloat, John Drake: 33
Soberanes Canyon Trail: 191
Soberanes Point Trail: 190
Soledad Farmers Market: 125
South Coast Road: 205
Spa at Pebble Beach: 77
Spanish Bay: 13, 75–76
spas: 155
Splash Zone: 30
spring: 10
spring break: 158
Spyglass Hill: 75
Stagnaro Bros. Restaurant: 17, 169
stand-up paddling: 234
stargazing: 129
statehood: 254
Steamers Lane: 150
Steelhead and Trout Fishing Hotline: 195
Steinbeck, John: 14, 120, 122
Steinbeck Festival: 122, 123
Steinbeck House: 14, 122
Steinbeck Plaza: 14, 51
Steinbeck's Birthday Celebration: 124
Steinbeck's Spirit of Monterey Wax Museum:
     14, 31
Stevenson, Robert Louis: 38–39
Stevenson House: 38
Stillwell's Fun in the Park: 68
Stokes Adobe: 38
Streetlight Records: 17, 160
study: 260
summer: 10
Summerayne Vineyard: 132
Summer Sleepovers: 31
Sunset State Beach: 149
Surf City Classic: Woodies on the Wharf: 158
surf competitions: 151
surfing: general discussion 231; Annual Women's
     Surf Contest 228; Carmel Beach 93; Carmel
     Surf Lessons 94; Cayucos State Beach 227;
     Marina State Beach 82–83; Monterey 40–41;
     Morro Bay 234; Moss Landing State Beach 80;
     Natural Bridges State Beach 135; Pacific Grove
     66; Pebble Beach 76; Sand Dollar State Beach

203; Santa Cruz 149-151; Santa Cruz Surfing Museum 139; Santa Cruz Wharf 138; Surf City Classic: Woodies on the Wharf 158; Surfing Santa 159; William Randolph Hearst Memorial State Beach 215
Surfing Santa: 159
surf schools: 150
surf shops: 40-41, 150, 227
sustainable seafood: 32
Sweet Pea Antiques: 14, 127
swimming holes: 113
Sykes Hot Springs: 194

T
Tanbark Trail: 194
Taste of Carmel: 98
Thrift Center Thrift Store: 17, 160
Tin Cannery: 11, 14, 53
Tor House: 8, 92
Toro Regional Park: 121
tour companies: 257
tourist information: 261
tours, wine: 145
Trail Camp Beach Trail: 191
Trailside Café: 12, 56
train travel: 256
transportation: 256-258
trees: 250
Triathlon at Pacific Grove: 68
Tyrolean Inn: 19, 177

UV
UC Santa Cruz Arboretum: 143
Underwater Explorers: 31
University of California, Santa Cruz: 143
Vault Gallery: 218
vegetation: 250-251
Ventana Vineyards: 121
Ventana Wilderness: 9, 20, 184, 194
Ventana Wilderness Society: 196
Vine Hill Winery: 23, 145
visitor information: 261

WXYZ
Waddell State Beach: 149

Wagon Wheel: 15, 115
waterfalls: 187, 194
Watsonville Strawberry Festival at Monterey Bay: 158
weather: 10
weekends, long: 11
West Cliff Drive: 153
Whalers Cove: 92
whale watching: general discussion 254; Monterey 41-42; Monterey Bay 12; Morro Bay 236; Moss Landing 80; Pigeon Point Lighthouse 143; Santa Cruz 153
whaling: 34, 35
Wharf, Morro Bay: 234
White Hat Limo: 145
white-water rafting: 112
Wilder Ranch State Park: 19, 153
Wildflower Show: 68
wildlife: 251-253
wildlife viewing: Elkhorn Slough National Estaurine Research Reserve 79; Fiscalini Ranch Preserve 221; Harmony Headlands State Park 227; Piedras Blancas 213; Pigeon Point Lighthouse 143; winter 10
William Randolph Hearst Memorial State Beach: 22, 213, 214, 231
Willow Creek: 21, 203
Willow Creek Road: 205
windsurfing: 151, 215
Wine Line: 220
Winemaker's Celebration: 51
wineries/wine tasting: Art and Wine Celebration 113; Boulder Creek 173; Carmel 16, 89; Carmel Valley 8, 109-112; Central Coast vineyard history 221; Great Wine Escape 51; Highway 46 9, 24, 210, 219; itinerary 23-24; Monterey Wine Festival 50; Pebble Beach Food & Wine 77; River Road Wine Trail 118, 120; Salinas Valley 8; San Benito 131-132; Santa Cruz 145-146; Wine Line 220; Winemaker's Celebration 51
Wine Trolley: 112
winter: 10
Winter Bird Festival: 241
zip lines: 172

List of Maps

Front color map
Monterey & Carmel: 2-3

Discover Monterey & Carmel
chapter divisions map: 9

Monterey
Monterey: 26-27
Cannery Row: 33
Downtown Monterey: 36
Pacific Grove: 65
Pebble Beach: 73
Northern Monterey County: 80

Carmel
Carmel: 90
Around Ocean Avenue: 99
Carmel Valley: 110

Salinas and Inland Monterey
Salinas and Inland Monterey: 119

Santa Cruz
Santa Cruz and Vicinity: 136
Santa Cruz: 138-139
Downtown Santa Cruz: 140

Big Sur
Big Sur: 181

San Simeon, Cambria, and Morro Bay
San Simeon, Cambria, and Morro Bay: 211
Cambria: 219
Morro Bay: 235

www.moon.com

DESTINATIONS | ACTIVITIES | BLOGS | MAPS | BOOKS

MOON.COM is ready to help plan your next trip! Filled with fresh trip ideas and strategies, author interviews, informative travel blogs, a detailed map library, and descriptions of all the Moon guidebooks, Moon.com is all you need to get out and explore the world—or even places in your own backyard. While at Moon.com, sign up for our monthly e-newsletter for updates on new releases, travel tips, and expert advice from our on-the-go Moon authors. As always, when you travel with Moon, expect an experience that is uncommon and truly unique.

KEEP UP WITH MOON ON FACEBOOK AND TWITTER
JOIN THE MOON PHOTO GROUP ON FLICKR